Intersectional Counseling Skills

The Journey to Becoming a Culturally Inclusive Counselor

S. Kent Butler & M. Ann Shillingford, Editors

University of Central Florida

SAN DIEGO

Bassim Hamadeh, CEO and Publisher
Amy Smith, Associate Editorial Manager
Abbey Hastings, Senior Production Editor
Emely Villavicencio, Senior Graphic Designer
Kara Tatum, Licensing Coordinator
Stephanie Adams, Senior Marketing Program Manager
Natalie Piccotti, Director of Marketing
Kassie Graves, Senior Vice President, Editorial
Alia Bales, Director of Project Editorial & Production

Copyright © 2025 by Cognella, Inc. All rights reserved. No part of this publication may be reprinted, reproduced, transmitted, or utilized in any form or by any electronic, mechanical, or other means, now known or hereafter invented, including photocopying, microfilming, and recording, or in any information retrieval system without the written permission of Cognella, Inc. For inquiries regarding permissions, translations, foreign rights, audio rights, and any other forms of reproduction, please contact the Cognella Licensing Department at rights@cognella.com.

Trademark Notice: Product or corporate names may be trademarks or registered trademarks and are used only for identification and explanation without intent to infringe.

Cover image: Copyright © 2021 iStockphoto LP/kastanka.

Printed in the United States of America.

Brief Contents

Preface   xv

Chapter 1 Intersectionality as a Foundation for Counseling Techniques   1
Sravya Gummaluri, LAC, NCC; DeJaunté Marquel Reynolds-Villarreal; and Dr. S. Kent Butler, Jr., NCC, NCSC

Chapter 2 Integrating Ethics into Skill Building   13
Dr. Barbara Herlihy and Madelyn Duffey

Chapter 3 Humanistic Aspects of Counseling   25
Dr. Jung (June) H. Hyun, LMHC, NCC; Dr. Ashlei R. Petion, LPC, NCC; and Marshaya Rountree

Chapter 4 The Therapeutic Relationship   37
Dr. Carla Adkison-Johnson, Dr. Olivia Ngadjui, and Dr. Gemarco Peterson

Chapter 5 Professional Roles   55
Dr. Kristy Christopher-Holloway, Dr. A'tasha M. Christian, and Erin Coleman

Chapter 6 The Use of Clinical Techniques/Culturally Relevant Approaches   65
Dr. Seneka Gainer, Dr. Aishwarya Joshi, and Dr. Amirah Nelson

Chapter 7 Invitational Skills as a Precursor to Counselors' Efforts to Broach Racial, Ethnic, and Cultural Factors With Clients   83
Robtrice Brawner and Dr. Norma Day-Vines

Chapter 8 Paraphrasing and Summarizing   103
Dr. Ann Shillingford, Dr. LoriAnn Stretch, Timothy Eng, MS, and Dr. Mary Hinson

Chapter 9 Reflecting Feelings from a Multicultural and Social Justice Perspective   117
Dr. Anna Locke, Dr. Azilde Sanchez, Ana Barend, Daniel Kimonyi, Bosede Balogun, Samantha Perez, and Andrew Erway

Chapter 10	Reflection of Meaning 139	

Dr. Amanda DiLorenzo-Garcia, Dr. Jessica Tinstman Jones, Dr. Gelawdiyos Haile, Dr. Everette Coffman, Dr. Amber S. Haley, and Brooke Alker

Chapter 11   Challenging Skills   155
Dr. Tristen Hyatt and Dr. Clay Rowell

Chapter 12   Goal Setting   169
Dr. Letitia Browne-James, Shannon Kratky, and Dr. Karla Sapp

Chapter 13   Reframing Termination Through a Culture-Centered Lens   189
Dr. Ebony E. White, Dr. Selma d. Yznaga, Dr. Deryl F. Bailey, Ashley D. Holmes Cosby, and Tabitha Rodriguez

Chapter 14   Assessment and Diagnosis in Counseling   203
Jessi Budyka, LPC, NCC, and Dr. Marty Jencius, NCC

Chapter 15   Creativity   229
Dr. Nivischi N. Edwards, Dr. Lynn Bohecker, Keyona Harper, and Monique Barber

Chapter 16   Sports Counseling Techniques   243
Dr. Taunya Marie Tinsley and Dr. Michelle D. Ellis

Appendix   Wellness as a Critical Clinical Technique   261
Dr. Kellie N. Kirksey, LPCC-S, CRC

Index   267
About the Editors   271
About the Contributors   273

Detailed Contents

Preface   xv

Chapter 1   Intersectionality as a Foundation for Counseling Techniques   1
Sravya Gummaluri, LAC, NCC; DeJaunté Marquel Reynolds-Villarreal; and Dr. S. Kent Butler, Jr., NCC, NCSC
   Learning Objectives   1
   Learning Outcomes   1
   The Sociocultural and Sociopolitical Climate of the United States   2
   A Brief Overview of Intersectionality   2
   What Does Intersectionality Have to Do With the Counseling Fieldwork Courses I Am Taking?   3
      Ethics and Behavior   4
      Humanistic Aspects of Counseling   4
      The Therapeutic Relationship   4
      Professional Roles   5
      Clinical Techniques/Culturally Relevant Approaches   5
      Invitational Skills   6
      Paraphrasing and Summarizing   6
      Reflecting Feelings   6
      Reflecting Meaning   7
      Challenging Skills   7
      Goal Setting   7
      Termination   8
      Assessment and Diagnosis   8
      Creativity   8
      Sports Counseling Techniques   9
      Wellness   9
   Chapter Summary   9
   Chapter Reflection and Discussion Questions   10
   References   10

Chapter 2   Integrating Ethics into Skill Building   13
Dr. Barbara Herlihy and Madelyn Duffey
   Learning Objectives   13
   Learning Outcomes   13

Chapter Highlights   13
What Is Ethics?   15
Two Perspectives on Ethical Reasoning   16
Infusing Ethics into Skills   18
    Invitation Skills   18
    Nonverbal Communication   18
    Reflecting Feelings   18
    Goal Setting   19
    Assessment and Diagnosis   19
    Challenging   19
    Conveying Empathy   20
Chapter Summary   21
Chapter Reflection and Discussion Questions   22
Additional Resources   22
References   22

Chapter 3   Humanistic Aspects of Counseling   25
Dr. Jung (June) H. Hyun, LMHC, NCC; Dr. Ashlei R. Petion, LPC, NCC; and Marshaya Rountree
Learning Objectives   25
Learning Outcomes   25
Setting the Groundwork: What Is Counseling?   26
    Counseling as a Cultural Interaction and Relationship   27
Role of Counselor   28
    Relationship Builder: Building Therapeutic Relationship   28
    Facilitator: Facilitating the Process   29
    Work Through Space: Self-Awareness   30
Building Community   32
    Considering Client Community   32
    Considering Counselor Community   33
Chapter Summary   34
Chapter Reflection and Discussion Questions   34
Additional Resources   34
    Self Care   34
    Professional communities   34
References   35

Chapter 4   The Therapeutic Relationship   37
Dr. Carla Adkison-Johnson, Dr. Olivia Ngadjui, and Dr. Gemarco Peterson
Learning Objectives   37
Learning Outcomes   37
Background Information   38
Critical Race Theory Framework   40
The Therapeutic Relationship Concept   41

Chapter Summary   48
Chapter Reflection and Discussion Questions   49
References   49

Chapter 5 Professional Roles   55
Dr. Kristy Christopher-Holloway, Dr. A'tasha M. Christian, and Erin Coleman
Learning Objectives   55
Learning Outcomes   55
Chapter Overview   55
The Role of the Group Counselor   56
    Group Leadership   56
    Group Dynamics   56
    Diversity in Group   57
The Role of the Addictions Counselor   57
The Role of the Rehabilitation Counselor   58
The Role of the Career Counselor   59
The Role of a Marriage and Family Counselor   59
    Culture in Marriage and Family Counseling   60
Chapter Summary   62
Chapter Reflection and Discussion Questions   63
Additional Resources   63
References   64

Chapter 6 The Use of Clinical Techniques/Culturally Relevant Approaches   65
Dr. Seneka Gainer, Dr. Aishwarya Joshi, and Dr. Amirah Nelson
Learning Objectives   65
Learning Outcomes   65
    Revolutionizing Culturally Oriented Techniques: A New Paradigm   66
    Cultivating Mindfulness for Cultural Competence: Building Connections   67
Introduction to Concept   67
    Bridging the Gap: Integrating Cultural Competence   67
    Understanding Intersectionality: Contextual Power Dynamics   67
Nurturing Therapeutic Relationships: Collaborative Cultural Techniques in Action   68
    Counselor's Worldview: Cultivating Critical Consciousness   68
    Client's Worldview: Bridging Power Dynamics   69
    Contextual Environment: Lived Experiences   69
Counseling Techniques: Applying Techniques
  With a Cultural Perspective   70
    Linguistics and Multilingual Abilities   71
    African American Vernacular   71
    Embracing Cultural Humility and Responsiveness   72
    Exploring Real-Life Stories: Navigating Cultural Contexts   73

Chapter Summary 76
Chapter Reflection and Discussion Questions 77
Examples of Counseling and Advocacy Interventions Relevant to This Topic 77
Additional Resources 78
   Readings and Books 78
    Websites and Organizations 79
References 79

Chapter 7   Invitational Skills as a Precursor to Counselors' Efforts to Broach Racial, Ethnic, and Cultural Factors With Clients 83
Robtrice Brawner and Dr. Norma Day-Vines
Learning Objectives 83
Learning Outcomes 83
Invitational Skills 85
Nonverbal Invitational Skills 85
Second Layer of Nonverbal Invitational Skills 87
Verbal Invitational Skills 91
Continuum of Broaching Behavior 92
Multidimensional Model of Broaching Behavior 95
Chapter Summary 97
Chapter Reflection and Discussion Questions 98
Additional Resources 98
References 99

Chapter 8   Paraphrasing and Summarizing 103
Dr. Ann Shillingford, Dr. LoriAnn Stretch, Timothy Eng, MS, and Dr. Mary Hinson
Learning Objectives 103
Learning Outcomes 103
Chapter Introduction 103
   Paraphrasing 104
   Summarizing 104
Therapeutic Reasons for Paraphrase and Summarize 106
   Paraphrasing 106
   Summarizing 107
   How to Paraphrase and Summarize 107
   When to Paraphrase 110
   When to Summarize 110
   Counseling and Culture: MSJCC (Paraphrasing) 111
   Counseling and Culture: MSJCC (Summarizing) 111
   Client Worldview 112
   Counseling Relationship 112
Chapter Summary 114

Chapter Reflection and Discussion Questions 114
Additional Resource 114
References 115

Chapter 9   Reflecting Feelings from a Multicultural and Social Justice Perspective   117

Dr. Anna Locke, Dr. Azilde Sanchez, Ana Barend, Daniel Kimonyi, Bosede Balogun, Samantha Perez, and Andrew Erway

Meet the Authors 117
Learning Objectives 117
Learning Outcomes 117
Multicultural and Social Justice Counseling Competencies 118
    Reflecting Feelings from a Multicultural and Social Justice Perspective 119
    Emotions vs. Feelings: The Distinction 121
Counselor Self-Awareness 123
    Cultural Auditing Explained 123
Client Worldview 124
    Acculturation 126
    Considerations to the Counselor When Reflecting Feelings to Multiculturally Diverse Clients With Different Levels of Acculturation 126
    Language and Reflecting Feelings 128
Language and Emotional Expression 128
    Language and Gestures With Nonnative Speakers 129
Final Thoughts on the Case of Olga and the Reflection of Feelings 132
Chapter Summary 132
Chapter Reflection and Discussion Questions 133
Additional Resources 133
References 134

Chapter 10   Reflection of Meaning   139

Dr. Amanda DiLorenzo-Garcia, Dr. Jessica Tinstman Jones, Dr. Gelawdiyos Haile, Dr. Everette Coffman, Dr. Amber S. Haley, and Brooke Alker

Learning Objectives 139
Learning Outcomes 139
Understanding Reflection of Meaning 140
Worldview Implications of Reflection of Meaning 141
    Reflection of Meaning in Societal Context 141
Meaning Making Through Attachment 144
Applying Reflection of Meaning in a Counseling Context 145
    When to Use Reflection of Meaning 145
    Strategies for ROM 146
    Challenges With Reflection of Meaning 148
Chapter Summary 152

Chapter Reflection and Discussion Questions   152
Additional Resources   152
References   152

Chapter 11   Challenging Skills   155
Dr. Tristen Hyatt and Dr. Clay Rowell
Learning Objectives   155
Learning Outcomes   155
Challenging   155
   Challenging: A Microskill   156
   MSJCC and Challenging Clients   157
Types of Challenges   157
   The Gentle Nudge   157
   Pointing Out Discrepancies   157
   Wondering Out Loud   158
   Direct Confrontation   158
Barriers to Challenging Clients   159
   Intrapersonal   159
   Systemic   160
Chapter Summary   166
Chapter Reflection and Discussion Questions   166
Additional Resources   167
References   167

Chapter 12   Goal Setting   169
Dr. Letitia Browne-James, Shannon Kratky, and Dr. Karla Sapp
Learning Objectives   169
Learning Outcomes   169
Goal Setting   170
Treatment Planning and Goal-Setting Considerations   171
   Impact of Stigma   171
   Shifting from Treatment Planning to Goal Setting   172
Goal Setting and the Counseling Process   172
   Familiarize Clients with the Goal Setting Process   173
   Empowering Clients With Voice and Choice   174
   Identifying Client Strengths and (Lack of) Access to Resources   175
Stop Calling Clients "Resistant": It's Oppressive!   177
Individualized Goals on the Treatment Plan   178
Case Examples   178
Chapter Summary   183
Chapter Reflection and Discussion Questions   184
Additional Resources   184
References   186

Chapter 13   Reframing Termination Through a Culture-Centered Lens   189

Dr. Ebony E. White, Dr. Selma d. Yznaga, Dr. Deryl F. Bailey, Ashley D. Holmes Cosby, and Tabitha Rodriguez

Learning Objectives   189
Learning Outcomes   189
Chapter Highlights   189
Introduction   190
Historical Considerations   190
Conventional Termination   191
Reasons for Termination   191
Counselor Self-Awareness   192
Termination Continuum   193
Termination as Cyclical   194
Case Studies   196
Chapter Summary   198
Chapter Reflection and Discussion Questions   199
Additional Resources   199
References   200

Chapter 14   Assessment and Diagnosis in Counseling   203

Jessi Budyka, LPC, NCC, and Dr. Marty Jencius, NCC

Learning Objectives   203
Learning Outcomes   203
2024 CACREP Standards Informing this Chapter   205
What Is Assessment?   205
What Is a Diagnosis?   206
Historical Context of Testing and Culture   207
Dove's Counterbalance Intelligence Test   208
Geert Hofstede's Dimensions   208
The Cultural Formation Interview   209
The AARC Standards for Multicultural Assessments   210
ACA Code of Ethics and Multicultural and Social Justice Counseling Competencies   211
Skills of Assessing and Diagnosing   212
    Steps to Assessing and Diagnosing   213
    A Culturally Integrative Framework for Crafting Comprehensive Treatment Plans   216
Chapter Summary   219
Case Example   219
Chapter Reflection and Discussion Questions   223
Additional Resources   224
    YouTube   224
    Podcasts (available on most platforms)   224
    Counseling Organizations   224
References   224

Chapter 15   Creativity   229
Dr. Nivischi N. Edwards, Dr. Lynn Bohecker, Keyona Harper, and Monique Barber
Learning Objectives   229
Learning Outcomes   229
Multicultural and Social Justice Counseling Competencies   230
MSJCC Conceptual Framework   231
Experiential Learning   231
Expressive Arts in Counseling   232
Intervention   233
     Intervention: Broaching With Case Studies   233
Chapter Summary   236
Addendum   236
     Intervention: Multicultural View Through Expressive Poetry Activity   236
     Adapting to a Therapeutic Session   238
Chapter Reflection and Discussion Questions   238
Additional Resources   238
References   239

Chapter 16   Sports Counseling Techniques   243
Dr. Taunya Marie Tinsley and Dr. Michelle D. Ellis
Learning Objectives   243
Learning Outcomes   243
Introduction   244
Literature Review   244
     Multicultural and Social Justice Counseling Competencies (MSJCC) and Sports Counseling   244
     Multicultural Sports Counseling Competencies   246
     Multicultural Techniques in Counseling   247
SMART Goal Example   248
     SMART Goal   248
Conclusion   251
     Implications for Professional Development   251
     Future Directions of Sports Counseling and Sports Counseling Techniques   253
     Recommendations for Counselors and Other Helping Professionals   253
Chapter Summary   254
Chapter Reflection and Discussion Questions   254
Additional Resources   255
     Books   255
     Journals   255
     Professional Organizations and Websites   255
     Online Media   256
References   256

Appendix   Wellness as a Critical Clinical Technique   261
Dr. Kellie N. Kirksey, LPCC-S, CRC

Index   267
About the Editors   271
About the Contributors   273

Preface

Intersectionality as a Foundation for Counseling Techniques

The time has come to do what is right! *Intersectional Counseling Skills: The Journey to Becoming a Culturally Inclusive Counselor* is everything that is right. The right time! The right message! The right approaches to counseling with cultural humility and a realization that if we truly are to meet people where they are we need to really meet them where they are. This textbook is a restatement of existing knowledge but separates itself from the rest because it provides innovative narratives of historically oppressed voices. This publication diverges from conventional norms, as opposed to the prevalent trend where other texts are typically composed from ethnocentric viewpoints; our book, in contrast, cultivates through a multicultural lens.

Intersectional Counseling Skills: The Journey to Becoming a Culturally Inclusive Counselor is practical, innovative, and focused on the relationship between a helping professional and client. The core counseling principles offered throughout the book are infused with aspects of the Multicultural and Social Justice Counseling Competencies (MSJCC). Having been endorsed by the American Counseling Association (ACA); Association for Multicultural Counseling and Development (AMCD); and Association for Spiritual, Ethical and Religious Values in Counseling (ASERVIC), this textbook's choice to use the MSJCC as its guide is considered a relevant and reputable one within the field of counseling.

The book is intended for graduate counseling students, practitioners, counselor educators, and supervisors seeking to elevate their professional practice. Revolutionary in scope, this skill-based counseling textbook aims to seamlessly combine foundational counseling principles with evidence-based techniques and practices rooted in multicultural and social justice competencies. Its aim is to empower novice helpers to evolve into culturally attuned, responsive, and introspective practitioners. By offering innovative perspectives, the book equips counselor educators, supervisors, and practitioners with tools to enrich teaching and prepare students for effectively engaging with diverse clients in their work.

The approach we are taking with this text is unique, in that we have paired seasoned experts and rising stars within the counseling community, who will set the stage for the next generation of helping professionals. The MSJCCs are infused into each chapter focusing solely on developing awareness, knowledge, skills, and actions necessary to be a culturally responsive counselor in today's world. Due to the strong authorship aligned to produce this text, counselors-in-training (CITs) will be able to draw from a wealth of life experiences. Our experiential pedagogical approach will deliberately stem from a culturally focused paradigm designed to enlighten, challenge, and inspire students to understand themselves, others, and the world around them.

The Journey to Cultural Competence Is Yours for the Taking

Intersectional Counseling Skills: The Journey to Becoming a Culturally Inclusive Counselor helps CITs "get it right," from being intentional, to broaching, to showing up as a culturally competent counselor for their clients. This book's approach is quite unique—it is one of the few counseling textbooks that takes a social justice focus to have been published. Though it was deliberately written to stand out from the field, this book is relevant to a broad audience, as it showcases best practices for optimizing client–counselor relationships for individuals with a wide variety of intersectional identities.

Some unique and inspired chapters, written by a team of highly regarded authors in the counseling field, await you in the upcoming pages. *Intersectional Counseling Skills* is a labor of love that has been crafted with the purpose of empowering and compelling CITs to systematically examine their multifaceted intersections and comprehend their implications on their personal lives as well as the lives of their clients. Here is the twist! As you journey through your techniques course, you will find inspiration in the candid narratives and the opportunity to incorporate individuals you are working with into the case examples presented throughout the book. We encourage you to purposefully cut and paste, utilizing the rich examples as a springboard to delve deeper into the life of your specific client. This is attainable by empowering your clients, as this allows you, as a counselor or CIT, to consciously insert whoever may be seated across from you into your theoretical framework and "humanistic-*ally*" see them through a cultural lens that unconditionally respects and honors their inner essence, unconditionally.

Intersectional Counseling Skills: The Journey to Becoming a Culturally Inclusive Counselor is designed to provide culturally responsive instructors with an evidenced based teaching tool for graduate students taking technique, practicum, internship counseling courses. The textbook continually emphasizes the importance of acquiring the techniques and skills essential for becoming proficient culturally competent practitioners. Students reading this text will gain access to the rich reservoir of life experiences provided by the book's strongly aligned authorship team. Finally, *Intersectional Counseling Skills* covers basic skill development and succinctly empowers student learners to successfully integrate more advanced therapeutic techniques into their toolbox.

Intersectionality as a Foundation for Counseling Techniques

Sravya Gummaluri, LAC, NCC; DeJaunté Marquel Reynolds-Villarreal; and Dr. S. Kent Butler, Jr., NCC, NCSC

LEARNING OBJECTIVES

1. Students will gain insight into the historical evolution of the counseling profession and its techniques.
2. Students will recognize the significance of intersectionality in the counseling field.
3. Students will develop cultural humility and appreciate the importance of employing the Multicultural Social Justice Counseling Competencies.
4. Students will incorporate culturally responsive skills into their counseling toolkit.

LEARNING OUTCOMES

1. Students will comprehend and articulate the historical and cultural context of counseling techniques as well as the significance of the Multicultural and Social Justice Counseling Competencies.
2. Students will cultivate skills that emphasize cultural understanding, sensitivity, and the application of CACREP standards.
3. Students will gain self-awareness of implicit biases and learn to integrate culturally sensitive practices into client treatment plans, in accordance with ethical and legal standards.
4. Students will adopt a holistic and inclusive approach to mental health care, acknowledging the importance of cultural factors in client well-being and integrating these considerations into comprehensive treatment planning.

The moment has arrived to act in accordance with what is just! *Intersectional Counseling Skills: The Journey to Becoming a Culturally Inclusive Counselor* aims to embody everything that is just. As stated in the preface, it's the right time, and this book earnestly brings forth the right message. It provides best practices for counseling with cultural humility, acknowledging that to truly meet individuals where they are, we must genuinely understand and embrace their unique perspectives and experiences.

The field of counselor education celebrated its centennial as a formal discipline in 2011. The roots of the discipline can be traced back to Boston and the early history of vocational guidance in its schools, spearheaded by Frank Parsons (Savickas, 2011). The inaugural course, Vocational Guidance, specifically addressed techniques and vital skills within the curriculum. Interestingly, one of the first roles of vocational counselors was to "personally study the home, street, and other influences on the vocational direction of one student in their own classroom. The counselors were required to keep records for comparison and systematic study" (2011, p. 500). This was a courageous decision that aptly met the students where they were, fully embracing their distinctive perceptions and individual life encounters.

The Sociocultural and Sociopolitical Climate of the United States

Fast forward to today, the tenuous sociocultural and political climate in the United States has a direct and harmful impact on the counseling profession and the mental health and wellness of clients from diverse and minoritized communities (e.g., immigrant communities; sexual and gender minorities; Black, Indigenous, People of Color (BIPOC); disabled individuals; and women). Counseling professionals and students have a heightened ethical and moral responsibility to respond appropriately to issues presented to us, especially those that are a direct ramification life experiences instigated by this climate. One of the first spaces for learning evidence-based, culturally responsive approaches to respond to social determinants of health and mental health (SDHM) can happen for counselors-in-training (CITs) on an individual level within counselor education classrooms. Learning about SDHM may empower CITs to engage in community-centered and systemic-based advocacy for minoritized and oppressed clients. It is crucial for counselors' skills training to implement a foundational structure of anti-oppressive, culturally responsive, and socially just practices. The counseling techniques course is one of the first courses CITs are exposed to before engaging in counseling fieldwork for practicum and internship courses, all necessary spaces to integrate theories of multiculturalism, social justice, and liberation.

A Brief Overview of Intersectionality

Intersectionality, a theory, and term coined by Crenshaw (1989, 1991), is a crucial framework for counselor educators to provide CIT with a framework that engages them in the anti-oppressive application of counseling skills. Intersectionality is also a core tenet of critical race theory (Delgado & Stefancic, 2017; Haskins & Singh, 2015). Crenshaw (1989) discusses intersectionality within the context of racism and sexism, framed around Black feminist thought and liberation theory. Crenshaw (1991) further discusses intersectionality in the context of racism, sexism, classism, and gender-based violence. Understanding intersectionality is a key element for counselor educators teaching counseling skills, especially during the time when CITs are exploring and understanding social structures and systems that may eventually impact clients with multiple minoritized identities.

Intersectionality theory consists of six core tenets: social context, power, complexity, social inequality, social justice, and relationality. Despite recent shifts and a focus on integrating the fourth and fifth forces of counseling (i.e., multiculturalism and social justice), the counseling field remains largely Westernized (Chan et al., 2018). Counselor skills training heavily relies on heteronormative textbooks, theories, techniques, interventions, and foundations.

The objective of this textbook is to dismantle the predominantly inequitable and Western-centric approach to counselor training. In its place, it seeks to rebuild the training paradigm by incorporating the Multicultural Social Justice Counseling Competencies (MSJCCs) with intersectionality as the foundational framework. The concept of intersectionality is perceived differently across diverse disciplinary contexts, including—but not limited to—counseling, education, sociology, law, and psychology (Chan et al., 2018; Collins & Bilge, 2016). From one standpoint, intersectionality may be understood as recognizing an individual's sundry social locations and identities. Alternatively, intersectionality may raise awareness related to addressing societal inequities that stem from institutional oppression (Chan et al., 2018). This concise overview touches upon the origins and core principles of intersectionality theory. To gain a more in-depth understanding of its history and intricate details, readers are encouraged to explore the provided references. Doing so will facilitate the operationalization of this theoretical framework, ultimately enriching the application of intersectionality in enhancing counselor skills training.

What Does Intersectionality Have to Do With the Counseling Fieldwork Courses I Am Taking?

Before embarking on postgraduation fieldwork, CITs undergo experiential skills training in counseling techniques, practicum, and internship courses. Acquiring culturally responsive techniques as skills, as outlined in the book's chapter summaries, has the potential to establish a robust foundation for effectively applying these skills in clinical work with clients. In pursuit of this goal, CITs are encouraged to engage in culturally responsive work; unfortunately, there is a notable absence of guidance when it comes to implementing evidence-based, culturally responsive interventions in clinical practice. In an effort to fill this void, this textbook intentionally employs a fundamental structure for counselor skills training. It achieves this by integrating a framework that is culturally responsive, socially just, and intersectional, drawing inspiration from the MSJCCs.

Considering the world's ongoing evolution, particularly within the ever-changing social context of the United States and globally, we must incessantly acknowledge that the definitions and practices of multiculturalism and social justice in counseling (considered the fourth and fifth forces of counseling) will continually evolve. Our understanding of these influential concepts is in a perpetual state of development as we continue to refine and progress in our interpretations. With this in mind, we trust that you will permit *Intersectional Counseling Skills: The Journey to Becoming a Culturally Inclusive Counselor* to provide you with a strong set of guidelines that you willingly adapt as the social landscape vicissitudes and you proactively work to enhance the wellness of diverse and minoritized clients and communities.

Ethics and Behavior

Chapter 2, "Integrating Ethics into Skill Building," highlights vital ethical considerations for cultural responsivity and cultural sensitivity in teaching counseling skills and techniques. This scope of practice has not been explored in depth in prior counselor training textbooks. The authors discuss two ethical reasoning perspectives, principle ethics and relational ethics, which can be used as complementary approaches. *Principle ethics* focuses on the individual, or "I," and refers to the six principles listed in the 2014 ACA Code of Ethics preamble: (a) autonomy, (b) nonmaleficence, (c) beneficence, (d) justice, (e) fidelity, and (f) veracity. *Relational ethics* refers to a collective approach and shared ethical decision-making process, focusing on the "we," actor, and therapeutic relationship emerging between the counselor and client.

The authors brilliantly highlight the significance of the intersection of cultural responsivity and ethical concepts, utilizing the metaphor of a triangle. This triangle alludes to three key points instrumental in integrating cultural responsivity into counselor skills training: (a) skills, (b) multicultural and social justice counseling, (c) and ethics. The conceptual triangle underscores the imperative of conjoining ethical reasoning perspectives; ethical decision-making models; and an intersectional approach that meticulously incorporates the interrelated dynamics of multiculturalism, social justice, and ethics. This is key when observing the social contexts in which clients with minoritized identities exist and to minimize the risk of harm in ethical decision-making. Moreover, this chapter illuminates how the aforementioned ethical reasoning perspectives are applied across six domains pertinent to the development of counselor skills. These domains include (a) invitation skills, (b) nonverbal communication, (c) reflective engagement with emotions, (d) formulation of goals, (e) assessment and diagnostic practices, and (f) the expression of empathy.

Humanistic Aspects of Counseling

Chapter 3, "Humanistic Aspects of Counseling," is written from the premise that culture lies at the core of every single relational interaction. The authors examine the nuances of effective counseling relationships and share ways diverse clientele may differ. The chapter defines counseling and showcases the impact of cultural competence on therapeutic outcomes. Students are encouraged to embrace curiosity and humility as they explore and recognize the value of professional communities in their growth and development. As novice counselors beginning their journey, another important aspect provided within the text is an opportunity to design action plans that support their ongoing professional development. Additionally, it is proffered that counselors who are self-aware enhance their skillset, decrease inhibitions, and open the door to successfully exploring client well-being from the perspectives of relationship builder, facilitator, caretaker, and social justice advocate.

The Therapeutic Relationship

Chapter 4, "The Therapeutic Relationship," discusses the concept and importance of the therapeutic relationship. The primary focus centers on cultural differences and their effects on the counseling alliance. Understanding how one's biases and lived experiences affect one's worldview is imperative in ensuring client safety within sessions. With most educators, workforce leaders, and governing bodies in the United States being heterosexual, cisgender, White men, American society has been shaped to recognize and accept their experiences as the norm. Because of this, many individuals from diverse backgrounds may have their cultural values cast aside or overlooked during the formation of the counseling alliance. Several case studies highlight this chapter, each granting insight into the harm that may come from cultural incompetence, especially during the crucial phase of establishing relationships and building rapport. Proper acquisition of this concept will enable counselors to effectively assist clients from various backgrounds, fostering openness, acceptance, and awareness of cultural nuances.

Professional Roles

Chapter 5, "Professional Roles," highlights counseling roles and the incorporation of multicultural competence across diverse specialized areas: group counseling, addiction counseling, rehabilitation counseling, career counseling, and marriage and family counseling. CITs will explore the concepts of bias, privilege, and oppression and examine how they may inadvertently affect the therapeutic alliance and counseling process. Group counseling is examined from the aspects of leadership style, dynamics (interactions, relationships, and processes), and the interconnectedness of social identities. The authors also focus upon the considerations necessary for the effective provision of addictions counseling. Rounding out the chapter, rehabilitation, career, and marriage and family counseling and the importance of working from a cultural context. Each role discussed with this chapter emphasizes that understanding culture is vital, and stresses that emerging practitioners have an ethical obligation to meet the needs of clients with sundry life experiences enhanced by their unique cultural backgrounds.

Clinical Techniques/Culturally Relevant Approaches

Chapter 6, "The Use of Clinical Techniques/Culturally Relevant Approaches," provides fundamental considerations for developing cognizance regarding cultural contexts clients exist within for CIT clinical skill development. It also provides a judicious paradigm that utilizes the MSJCCs as a framework for revolutionizing culturally oriented techniques and closing the access gap. The chapter showcases how counselors may reconceptualize techniques through action-oriented progression, mindfulness, and awareness, while recognizing that multicultural competence is a lifelong ethical journey with high expectations that practitioners continually enhance their development through interpersonal and intrapersonal reflection. The authors discuss culturally relevant clinical techniques in a variety of contexts, including (a) therapeutic relationships, (b) communication, and (c) cultural humility and responsiveness. Within therapeutic relationships, this chapter covers the influence of the counselor's worldview, the client's worldview, individualism, collectivism, and lived experiences (i.e., environment).

Chapter 6 also implores students to understand the nuances of intersectionality by applying techniques collaboratively from a cultural perspective and enhancing their linguistic and multilingual abilities by embracing African American Vernacular English (AAVE) and other languages spoken by minoritized groups. Culturally responsive communication is essential to developing strong therapeutic rapport, and this chapter speaks to intersectionality in communication, such as language and vernacular differences. Intersectional communication is also pertinent for clients with disabilities, such as individuals who are deaf or hard of hearing. Additionally, the chapter highlights the central role of cultural humility and responsiveness as a crucial practice that must permeate all counseling techniques and skills. The use of cultural humility and culturally responsive skills is inclusive of critical consciousness (i.e., knowledge of social conditions as well as sociocultural and sociopolitical stressors experienced by minoritized individuals; Sharma & Hipolito-Delgado, 2021), awareness of one's worldviews, the clients' worldviews and lived experiences shaping these worldviews, and exploration of one's biases in learning and application of counseling techniques with diverse clients. The concept of cultural humility involves being curious and open to learning more, which may lead to better understanding and stronger therapeutic relationships. The case studies provide a rich cultural perspective for students and practitioners that may easily be translated and readily applied to their work with clients who espouse a myriad of worldviews.

Invitational Skills

Chapter 7, "Invitational Skills as a Precursor to Counselors' Efforts to Broach Racial, Ethnic, and Cultural Factors with Clients," focuses on invitational skills and broaching as well as the power they wield to aid in rapport building within the therapeutic alliance. Even gestures as small as opening a door for clients or modifying an automatic greeting to include a personal touch, verbal and nonverbal messages can change the counseling dyad's trajectory. As the alliance strengthens, counselors may utilize broaching to increase credibility, reassuring clients that their racial, ethnic, and cultural (REC) concerns are considered when determining appropriate treatment options. The chapter also introduces the broaching continuum, developed by Day-Vines et al. (2007), which categorizes counselors based on their level of interaction regarding their client's REC concerns. Finally, case examples and reflection questions are utilized throughout the chapter to illustrate various scenarios, granting counselors unique opportunities for introspection and critical thinking.

Paraphrasing and Summarizing

Chapter 8, "Paraphrasing and Summarizing," focuses on—you guessed it—how to effectively paraphrase, or summarize, while integrating cultural responsiveness and multicultural principles in with these counseling skills. Paraphrasing is a significant counseling technique that requires active listening, which, in turn, supports a counselor's ability to formulate a succinct and empathic reflection of client's narrative. Summarizing abridges lengthier exchanges, while reflecting verbal, nonverbal, or observed patterns shared or exhibited by the client. Together, each requires an awareness of self, coupled with an intuitive ability to navigate cultural nuances, communication styles, and an understanding of a client's worldview and culture without imposing judgment and assumptions. Learning and applying these skills demonstrate that intersecting identities, power, privilege, and culture may convey a deeper connection and understanding of the client's life experiences, ultimately enhancing the therapeutic alliance.

Reflecting Feelings

Chapter 9, "Reflecting Feelings from a Multicultural and Social Justice Perspective," deconstructs the concept of reflecting feelings and emphasizes the importance of counselor self-awareness when engaging with clients from a multiculturally and social justice-oriented, bias-free perspective. Reflecting feelings is a core intervention that fosters responsiveness, validation, and evolution. It involves a parallelling of a client's emotions that allows them to feel heard, understood, and validated. Within the chapter, the authors share the distinctions between feelings (a physical reaction that results from an unconscious reaction to emotive provocations) and emotions (which are mindful acknowledgements of reactions). The chapter also provides readers with a practical guide, "12 Steps to Mirroring a Client's Feelings for Effective Counseling," which clearly outlines how practitioners may competently utilize reflection of feelings. To promote effective communication, counselors must be self-aware, multiculturally competent, and able to avoid the dangerous pitfalls associated with misinterpreting clients' cultural differences.

Reflecting Meaning

Chapter 10, "Reflections of Meaning," covers this advanced counseling skill, which encourages clients to find meaning within underlying messages, their belief systems, or the values they champion. From a multicultural perspective, the authors proffer that self-knowledge may help counselors recognize the impact of their biases, values, worldviews, and social statuses on the therapeutic relationship. This deeper understanding and intentional reflection enable counselors to envision and appropriately respond to their clients' presenting concerns from a greater systemic and policy framework. Timing is everything; when delivered inappropriately (i.e., poor timing, inadequate processing time, and using surface-level reflections), counselors may invalidate a client's perspective and negatively impact rapport in the therapeutic alliance. The importance of incorporating the MSJCCs is also examined, challenging counselors to listen with an intentionality to learn and encouraging them to genuinely embrace their client's unique cultural identities and lived experiences.

Challenging Skills

Chapter 11, "Challenging Skills," highlights that challenging skills should be utilized empathically and respectfully with cross-cultural considerations at the forefront. Counselors may directly or discreetly confront a client's beliefs, cognitions, feelings, or worldview in an effort to move the client towards greater self-awareness, development, and insight. The authors stipulate that all encounters be client-based and not based upon a counselor's value imposition. Through self-reflection, counselors should evaluate themselves and intentionally challenge their own thoughts and perceptions. The chapter discusses several ways counselors may challenge their clients, including the gentle nudge, pointing out discrepancies, wondering out loud, and direct confrontation. Intrapersonal, systemic, and cultural communication barriers to challenging are also examined. Ultimately, the chapter explores how challenging clients requires a counselor's earnest effort to foster inner-change and processing.

Goal Setting

Chapter 12, "Goal Setting," stipulates that counseling is an introspective journey that helps clients identify the final destination(s) and the route(s) to arrive there unharmed. Goal setting and treatment planning, while critical to the counseling process, are not universal. Counselors are culturally attuned agents of transformation, who collaborate with their clients and ensure that clarity of the counseling process is provided. The goal-setting authors explore the impact of stigma as a barrier to counseling and champion how to effectively empower clients with voice and choice. Finally, the chapter invites novice counselors to rethink how they define resistance and exposes them to evidenced-based methods that are culturally responsive and enhance client strengths. Together, goal setting and treatment planning necessitate recognizing client apprehensions, deciphering how they impact their actions, thoughts, or feelings, and making appropriate action plans that stimulate change.

Termination

Chapter 13, "Reframing Termination Through a Culture-Centered Lens," discusses termination and posits the process as cyclical rather than an absolute occurrence. Thus, it is proposed that termination be viewed on a five-stage continuum: (a) alliance building, (b) collaborative resolution, (c) rehearsal, (d) evaluation, and (e) termination. This chapter encourages students to reflect and identify their biases and beliefs surrounding termination, recognizing that relational terminations may ensue when working with clients of color. To avoid mislabeling client behavior, students will learn to differentiate between termination of a session versus that of the counseling relationship, subsequently understanding the motivation behind why populations of color terminate or have prolonged absences. Early termination transpires when a client suspends therapy prior to the achievement of their identified goals or before the suggested timeframe. Environmental constraints, such as transportation needs, employment demands, unaffordable rates, and limited access, may hinder the utilization and consistency of counseling. The authors' YEB continuum of termination ponders an alternate perspective that allows clients to feel efficacious about their sessions and frees them to make choices about returning, without feeling that they have abandoned the process.

Assessment and Diagnosis

Chapter 14, "Assessment and Diagnosis in Counseling," explores the concepts of assessment and diagnosis and describes testing and tools in counseling, specifically highlighting their effects on diverse cultures and populations. Assessments have been administered throughout history to determine many possible diagnoses within countless populations. However, unlike many other tools in the counseling profession, assessments have the power to impact an individual's entire identity in just a few simple steps. With some mental health diagnoses holding longstanding stigmas, therapists must remain diligent, knowledgeable, and collaborative during testing. This chapter discusses cultural biases and incompetence in the early days of mental health assessments, reinforcing the importance of proper education in modern society. Counselors have a duty to provide their clients with culturally appropriate assessments and ensure that any utilized will be administered and interpreted safely. This chapter also informs counselors about the different types of assessments and testing tools available to them, reiterates the importance of cultural awareness, and reminds counselors of their legal and ethical obligations to clients during the process.

Creativity

Chapter 15, "Creativity," underscores the importance of expanding training in counseling skills and techniques to encompass approaches beyond predominantly Western methods of instruction. Incorporating innovative methods into the instruction of counseling skills and techniques is essential, as creative approaches offer a holistic and intersectional approach to ensure that counselor training centers on both a diverse group of trainees and a diverse clientele. Learning creative counseling skills may also help with emotion regulation and normalizing feelings (such as anxiety) when learning and practicing new counseling skills. The chapter covers two learning objectives using the framework of the MSJCCs: (a) to equip students with counseling interventions and prompts to develop awareness about worldviews, values, and beliefs for themselves and others supported by the Awareness and Knowledge competencies of the MSJCCs and (b) to help students learn methods for counselor skills development in broaching while also engaging in the use of the multicultural and social justice praxis supported by the Skills and Action competencies of the MSJCCs.

The chapter also recommends experiential creative interventions, such as power, privilege, oppression in motion, an expressive poetry activity, and broaching with case studies. The first activity aims to help students reflect on the concepts of power, privilege, and oppression, using poetry and reflecting an understanding of intersectionality in this context. The next recommended activity involves practicing broaching through the use of culturally relevant case studies. Oftentimes, CITs express an understanding of the importance of broaching as an intersectional and culturally responsive counseling skill; however, they demonstrate ambivalence about the process of engaging in broaching. Creative exercises like those suggested in this chapter may help prepare students to put culturally responsive skills to use.

Sports Counseling Techniques

Chapter 17, "Sports Counseling Techniques," is a timely new specialization within the field of counseling. It posits that when counselors and athletes maintain positive counseling relationships, the benefits are far reaching, especially as they strive to maximize their personal, academic, and athletic potential. The authors identify four stress reactions patterns that may impede an athlete's overall performance: anxiety, depression, anger, and somatic symptoms. To this end, a mental health practitioner may enhance their expertise by embracing developmental and cultural competencies that specifically address the differences and challenges athletes face. To effectively work with athletes, counselors must adhere to the ethical codes endorsed by professional organizations and embrace the MSJCCs as well as the multicultural sports counseling competencies. It is vital that counselors do no harm to athletes. By participating in formalized trainings that build upon their counseling skillset and becoming culturally competent, counselors will begin to understand the developmental demands of athletes, especially as they relate to their respective sports.

Wellness

Located within the appendix, "Wellness as a Critical Clinical Technique," demonstrates the importance of counselor self-care and wellness. Included within this appendix is a comprehensive self-assessment that stems from eight wellness pillars, a critical component of self-awareness. The author implores students and future clinicians to prioritize self-care and well-being during this pivotal stage of their career, emphasizing its integral role in shaping their counseling identity. Wellness is an act of loving oneself (and future self) enough to make wise choices that serve their best interest. Committing to a holistic framework of wellness taps into one's environmental, emotional, financial, mental, occupational, physical, social, and spiritual dimensions and affords us the ability to stay healthy within our counseling careers. This simple approach will enable CITs and practitioners to maintain professional boundaries through the creation of healthy action plans and the cultivating of supportive meaningful relationships within our communities.

CHAPTER SUMMARY

The chapter focused on the historical aspects of the counseling profession, providing a brief overview of the origins of the vocation. The importance of skill development was emphasized in regard to intersectionality and the sociopolitical climate in the lives of our clients. As stated earlier, in accordance with the aim of this textbook, this chapter began the process of deconstructing the predominantly inequitable and Western-centric approaches still outdatedly being utilized in the training of future counselors. Instead, we proffer a new paradigm that endeavors to reconstruct current training practices by integrating the MSJCCs and intersectionality as the foundational framework.

This chapter also offered a concise preview of the subsequent chapters. Think of it as a movie trailer, giving you a glimpse of the fantastic skill development training that awaits you as you strive to refine the art of counseling. While specific cases may be presented, we encourage you to envision yourself and your future clients, reflecting on how your presence and skillset will influence your counseling relationships and outcomes.

CHAPTER REFLECTION AND DISCUSSION QUESTIONS

1. Provide an example of how you will be intentional this semester, as you matriculate through this course.
2. As you consider your future role beyond being a CIT, what are you excited about learning this semester in your techniques class? How might this course prepare you for future counseling sessions.
3. With a colleague, practice each intervention until you have mastered it and feel comfortable presenting it as a novice counselor.
4. Which textbook chapter(s) most resonate with you? Why?
5. How does the terminology "anti-oppressive," "culturally responsive," and "socially just practices" resonate with you? Do you believe they should have a place in counseling? Why, or why not?
6. How might my client's worldview and my worldview impact the counseling relationship, and what steps do I need to take to remain culturally humble?
7. How might you apply intersectionality to analyze and understand various social issues and systems of oppression experienced by clients to engage in the use of culturally responsive counseling skills?
8. Reflect on some of your lived experiences and salient identities. What might help or present as a growth edge in applying an intersectional framework to the various counseling skills and techniques discussed in this text?

REFERENCES

Chan, C. D., Cor, D. N., & Band, M. P. (2018). Privilege and oppression in counselor education: An intersectionality framework. *Journal of Multicultural Counseling and Development*, *46*(1), 58–73. https://doi.org/10.1002/jmcd.12092

Collins, P. H., & Bilge, S. (2016). *Intersectionality*. Polity Press.

Crenshaw, K. W. (1989). Demarginalizing the intersection of race and sex: A Black feminist critique of antidiscrimination doctrine, feminist theory and antiracist politics. *University of Chicago Legal Forum*, *1989*, 138–167. https://doi.org/10.4324/9780429500480

Crenshaw, K. W. (1991). Mapping the margins: Intersectionality, identity politics, and violence against women of color. *Stanford Law Review*, *43*(6), 1241–1299.

Day-Vines, N. L., Wood, S. M., Grothaus, T., Craigen, L., Holman, A., Dotson-Blake, K., & Douglass, M. J. (2007). Broaching the subjects of race, ethnicity, and culture during the counseling process. *Journal of Counseling & Development*, *85*, 401–409.

Delgado, R., & Stefancic, J. (2017). *Critical race theory: An introduction* (3rd ed.). New York University Press.

Haskins, N. H., & Singh, A. (2015). Critical race theory and counselor education pedagogy: Creating equitable training. *Counselor Education and Supervision*, *54*(4), 288–301. https://doi.org/10.1002/ceas.12027

Savickas, M. L. (2011). The centennial of counselor education: Origin and early development of a discipline. *Journal of Counseling and Development*, *89*(4), 500–504. https://doi.org/10.1002/j.1556-6676.2011.tb02848.x

Sharma, J. & Hipolito-Delgado, C. P. (2021). Promoting anti-racism and critical consciousness through a critical counseling theories course. *Teaching and Supervision in Counseling*, *3*(2), 15–25. https://doi.org/10.7290/tsc030203

Integrating Ethics into Skill Building

Dr. Barbara Herlihy and Madelyn Duffey

LEARNING OBJECTIVES

1. Explain how counseling skills, ethics, and cultural competence are related to each other.
2. Describe two major approaches to ethical decision-making, and discuss how they can work together to foster best practices in counseling.
3. Integrate ethical awareness and knowledge of the ethical decision-making process into practice sessions when learning culturally sensitive basic counseling skills.

LEARNING OUTCOMES

1. Students will be able to explain how ethics, skills, and multicultural competencies are interconnected.
2. Students will be able to describe two major approaches to ethical decision-making and discuss how they can work together to foster culturally competent counseling skills.
3. Students will be able to apply knowledge of ethics, skills, and cultural competence to a case study.

Chapter Highlights

- Integration of ethics with skill building and multicultural competence.
- Definition and clarification of related terms: morals, values, ethics, and law.
- Discussion of two different but complementary approaches to ethical decision making.
- Examples of how to integrate ethics and cultural competence into specific counseling skills.
- Application of chapter learnings to a case study.
- Questions to guide self-reflection and personalization.

> A triangle is the strongest shape in nature. No matter how much weight you put on any side, it will not break.

One of the exciting features of this textbook is that it integrates diversity, equity, and inclusion with skill building throughout each chapter, so you adopt a multicultural lens from the beginning of your studies. This text is grounded in the belief that counseling skills cannot be learned properly without attending to the cultural variables clients and counselors bring to their professional relationship. In this chapter, we introduce you to ethics as a third, and equally foundational, part of the process of learning and applying skills with cultural sensitivity. We believe that the strength of a triangle composed of skills, diversity, competence, and ethical awareness provides the most solid platform on which to build further learnings.

Ethical practice and multicultural competence are inseparable. One cannot exist without the other. This interdependence is articulated in the American Counseling Association's (ACA) Code of Ethics (2014), which contains multiple standards related to cultural diversity throughout the document. The Code (2014, preamble) states that "honoring diversity and embracing a multicultural approach in support of the worth, dignity, potential, and uniqueness of people within their social and cultural contexts" is a core professional value of counselors.

As a beginning student, you will be introduced to the ACA and will be expected to join as a student member, if you haven't already done so. Although there are a number of professional organizations for counselors, the ACA is your primary professional home, and its resources will be invaluable to you as you continue to develop your professional identity as a counselor. Among those resources, the ACA Code of Ethics (2014) is the most germane to this chapter. The Code of Ethics, now in its seventh iteration, is a living document, whose history mirrors the evolution of counseling as a profession. Back in the 1960s, when counseling was first emerging as a profession, counselors were essentially a monocultural group (Remley & Herlihy, 2020), and little attention was paid to cultural diversity issues. Likewise, the infusion of multiculturalism into the Code of Ethics is a fairly recent development. Although the Code of Ethics has existed since 1960, early versions of the document made no mention of cultural diversity. It wasn't until 2005 that multiculturalism was first given a prominent place in the Code (Remley & Herlihy, 2020). This attention to diversity was strengthened in the current (2014) version, and since it was adopted, our profession has continued to work to further our commitment. In 2015, the president of the Association for Multicultural Counseling and Development (AMCD), a division of ACA, formed the Multicultural Counseling Revisions Committee and tasked committee members with developing a conceptual framework to help counselors understand and strengthen skills related to multiculturalism, diversity, and social justice. The committee developed the Multicultural and Social Justice Competencies (MSJCC; Ratts et al., 2016) to help counselors understand the intersections of power, privilege, and oppression counselors and clients experience while working with one another. The MSJCC compels counselors to be aware of their biases and belief systems, to actively endeavor to understand their clients' worldviews, and to develop the necessary skills to help clients from various intersectional backgrounds. Taken together, the Code of Ethics (2014) and the MSJCC (2016) provide a basis for the counseling profession's abiding commitment to cultural diversity, attention to various intersections of identities, and social justice as integral to ethical practice.

The question we tackle in this chapter is this: How can ethical awareness and sensitivity as well as social justice and diversity competence be integrated into the teaching of skills? To address this question, we begin by introducing you to some basic concepts, and then we focus on specific skills through a combined ethical and diversity-sensitive lens. We begin by defining "ethics" and explaining how it differs from similar concepts, such as morals, values, and law. We then introduce you to two differing but complementary ways of looking at ethics. Finally, we integrate consideration of ethics and multicultural competence into a discussion of some of the skills presented in later chapters and conclude with a case study.

What Is Ethics?

Even highly experienced counselors can find it difficult to distinguish between morals, values, and ethics or between ethical and legal issues. Morals, values, and ethics are all alike, in that they involve judgments about good and bad as well as right and wrong, yet they take on different meanings when applied to the beliefs and behaviors of counselors. These differences are important for you to consider as you begin to develop your identity as a counselor.

Morals are beliefs about right and wrong behavior that individuals develop as they mature. You have developed a sense of moral selfhood, perhaps without conscious effort, through your life experiences and reflections on those experiences. This internal compass guides how you interact with others and with society at large. Morals differ from individual to individual and culture to culture. If we think of morals as being personal in nature, we can contrast them to values, which for counselors, are both personal and professional in nature.

Values are a bit more complicated than morals because they provide a foundation for your professional behaviors as well as your personal choices and beliefs. As we noted previously, the counseling profession holds certain values articulated in the ACA Code of Ethics (2014) preamble. Thus, it is vital to ascertain whether your personal and professional values are congruent. If you cannot embrace the professional values of the profession, you (and your professors) may have cause to be concerned about whether you are well suited for the profession (Remley & Herlihy, 2020). As you progress through your studies, you will be asked to self-reflect and become increasingly aware of your values; you will be tasked with learning to "bracket" (Kocet & Herlihy, 2014), or set aside, your personal values during your counseling sessions. Keep in mind that you will encounter clients whose values and beliefs are very different from your own, and if you get caught up in feeling angry or upset when they express these beliefs in session, you will find it difficult to be fully present with them. At such times, it can be challenging to remember that it is not your job to impose your values on clients or to try to change their values and beliefs. You are there for the client.

Ethics is a branch of philosophy that focuses on human conduct and professional behavior. Ethical counselors strive at all times for best practice in their work with clients. When counselors, as a professional group, develop consensus about certain behaviors, these behaviors become codified in a code of ethics, to which all counselors (including students) are bound. Although we refer throughout this chapter to the ACA Code of Ethics (2014), which is the primary code for counselors, you will see that ethics involves much more than obeying a code, or even multiple codes.

Laws are created by members of a society to establish basic principles for living together as a group (Remley & Herlihy, 2020). Counselors who base their professional practice on concern about staying out of legal trouble (e.g., being sued for malpractice or brought up on charges before an ethics committee or licensing board) are practicing at a minimally acceptable level, which Corey et al. (2024) have termed "mandatory ethics." These authors use this term to distinguish it from "aspirational ethics," a level of practice that aims to provide the best possible services. "Ethical" refers to the highest standard of practice, whereas "legal" describes the minimum required. Although legal issues can be frightening to counselors, there is good news—very few laws exist that pertain to counseling practice, and those laws tend to support counselors in their work. It is also true that lawsuits against counselors occur infrequently and are often unsuccessful.

Two Perspectives on Ethical Reasoning

In this section of the chapter, we first describe the approach to ethics that guided the development of the ACA Code of Ethics (2014), which is known as "principle ethics." We then discuss a newer, alternative approach, called "relational ethics." These two ways of thinking about ethics are different, but they are often complementary.

The ACA Code of Ethics (2014) originated in and remains grounded in principle ethics; that is, the code was created by applying certain moral principles that were believed to be "universal" for all helping professionals. Six principles are articulated in the ACA Code of Ethics:

- *Autonomy* means to foster self-determination. Counselors honor the rights of clients to make their own choices and control their own lives.
- *Nonmaleficence* means to do no harm. This principle, which originated in the medical profession, recognizes that counselors must avoid taking actions (or failing to take actions) that risk hurting clients, even unintentionally.
- *Beneficence* is the flip side of the coin to maleficence. It means that counselors must go beyond simply avoiding harm and proactively work for the benefit of clients and client systems.
- *Justice* refers to being fair in our interactions with clients and others in our professional world as well as to our profession's commitment to social justice.
- *Fidelity* exhorts counselors to keep the promises they make to clients. This principle undergirds several standards in the code, such as keeping client disclosures confidential.
- *Veracity* means truthfulness. Counselors must be honest in their dealings with clients and others.

So how do these principles work in actual counseling practice? They help you answer the question, "What should I do?" in a counseling situation that raises an ethical challenge. For example, imagine that your client says they are feeling depressed and are "starting to wonder whether it's all worth it." The client quickly adds, "Of course I would never take my own life. I don't want my family to worry. I wouldn't have said anything if I didn't trust your promise that counseling is confidential." As you hear this, you fear for the client's safety. You want to live up to the trust inherent in your pledge to confidentiality (fidelity) and allow the client to make their own decisions (autonomy), but further exploration with the client leads you to believe that the client is at risk, despite their disclaimer. Can you uphold fidelity and autonomy if it appears that the most effective way to avoid harm (nonmaleficence) is to involve someone else in the client's life who cares about them and will help keep them safe when they are not in session with you (beneficence)? In practice, moral principles can conflict with each other. If you rely solely on principle ethics in this scenario, you must now decide which principles are the most important, sacrifice the others, and respond accordingly.

This scenario illustrates the drawbacks of using a single approach to ethical reasoning. Although principle ethics can be useful, they are limited by the question they ask. When you ask yourself, "What should I do?" the important words are "I" and "do." Relational ethics, by contrast, puts the focus on the actor, rather than the action (changing the verb from "do" to "be"), and on the "we" of shared decision-making, rather than the "I" of principle ethics. When you practice relational ethics, you ask yourself, "Who do I want to *be*, in this relationship with the client?" Relational ethicists recognize that ethical moments occur in a relationship in which the client is an equal partner so that ethical decision-making becomes a shared process.

Relational ethicists also look beyond the counselor–client dyad, acknowledging how the context of the counselor's world, the client's world, and their shared experience influence the work done in session. Relational ethicists emphasize the importance of certain characteristics such as self-awareness, integrity, discernment, and interdependence with the community (Meara et al., 1996). You will be encouraged throughout your studies to strengthen your *self-awareness* so that you avoid imposing your assumptions, biases, values, and beliefs on your clients. *Integrity* involves being motivated to do what is right because it is right, not out of fear of negative consequences (much the same as the difference between mandatory and aspirational ethics). *Discernment* involves the ability to perceive potential and existing ethical issues in a counseling relationship and a tolerance for the ambiguity inherent in those issues. To practice ethically, you certainly will need to develop a tolerance for ambiguity—in the ethics arena, there are very few "right" answers to ethical dilemmas, and the answer to almost every question is "it depends." Finally, *connectedness to the community* draws in the diversity and social justice component of the triangle. Counselors need to understand the values and expectations of the communities in which they work, keeping in mind that every counseling session occurs in a context.

Principle ethics and relational ethics can be complementary. Principle ethics can help you consider whether your decisions are helpful, harmless, fair, honest, and respectful of clients' right to make their own choices. Relational ethics can guide you in prioritizing the relationship first and foremost and ensuring the client is an equal partner. Clients, by virtue of being in the help-seeker role, enter the counseling relationship in a "power-down" position, and although you may be uncomfortable acknowledging it, you are in the "power-up" position. Because the shared decision-making process in relational ethics empowers the client, it seems essential to include it in any counseling practice that incorporates cultural sensitivity and social justice. Relational ethicists recognize that many clients experience systemic disempowerment in their daily lives, so they strive to avoid replicating that disempowerment in the counseling relationship.

After you practice new skills during mock sessions throughout this course, we encourage you to reflect on your sessions by asking yourself these questions:

- What ethical principles were germane to the session and how did I uphold or fail to uphold them? How did I prioritize the principles and what was the outcome for the client?
- How do I feel about the session and about myself in the session? Did my responses help to empower the client and strengthen our relationship?

Asking these questions might help you develop the habit of being the reflective practitioner we hope you will become.

Infusing Ethics into Skills

We have described how having a strong ethical foundation allows counselors and counseling students to support and empower clients to reach their goals in a manner that maximizes good while avoiding harm. Developing strong counseling skills and techniques, rooted in cultural competence and social justice, gives counselors the tools they need. So how are counseling skills tied to ethics and multicultural competence? Let's consider the connection by examining a few common skills that you will learn later in this book.

Invitation Skills

Both CITs and clients often feel myriad emotions, including excitement, anxiety, anticipation, and self-consciousness, during their first sessions. For CITs, this anxiety diminishes as they learn invaluable counseling skills to help build rapport and establish a solid therapeutic relationship. Counselors utilize a variety of skills when getting to know their clients, from where to sit to how and when to ask questions. While some clients might enter a first session enthusiastically, others might be skeptical, nervous, or unsure. Inviting the client into a safe space is a vital first step in building a counseling relationship. Including questions about the client's culture in the intake session and asking open-ended questions about a client's family and background can give counselors valuable information about the client and indicate a willingness to engage in cultural conversations.

Nonverbal Communication

You might have noticed in your daily interactions that people often communicate even when they are not speaking. A person's eye contact, facial gestures, and body language can convey many emotions, such as empathy, openness, and attentiveness. Although nonverbal communication is universal, the messages sent and received are nuanced and influenced by culture and context. For example, researchers found that direct eye contact is less prevalent in Japanese culture than in Western European and American cultures (Akechi, 2013). In the spirit of beneficence, as a culturally competent counselor, you will assess the client's comfort with eye contact and use it accordingly. As a relational ethicist, you will work to discern alternative ways to enhance the relationship if the client seems uncomfortable with sustained eye contact.

Reflecting Feelings

Has anyone ever said something that made you feel truly *seen* and *heard*? Listening to a client and verbally reflecting what they are feeling back to them is a common and powerful counseling skill. It can strengthen the therapeutic relationship, make the client feel connected and understood, and give the client an opportunity to clarify their feelings. One principle-ethics based consideration that might arise when utilizing this skill is nonmaleficence. Culture, which can include race, ethnicity, gender, nationality, religious orientation, and other variables, can influence a person's comfort level with verbalizing feelings and emotions. For example, a client might be less likely to overtly express strong feelings due to gender or ethnic socialization (Sue et al., 2019). Consequently, to provide ethical care, you will need to understand your client's cultural background, norms, values, and comfort with discussing feelings and tailor your responses in a culturally informed manner. From a relational ethics perspective, your connectedness to the shared community in which you and the client are working will help you make these assessments.

Goal Setting

Goal setting is an integral component of the therapeutic process. Creating and accomplishing goals can increase clients' hope, confidence, and wellness (Young, 2020). While it may be tempting for counselors to set goals for their clients, it is imperative for clients and counselors to identify and agree on goals collaboratively (Sue et al., 2019). Goal consensus promotes client buy-in, engagement, and progress as well as honors the ethical principle of autonomy and empowers the client through shared decision-making. Therapeutic interventions are often geared toward what counselors and clients can do to meet clients' individual goals. Counselors must also understand clients live within, and are impacted by, complex social systems and structures. Again, from a relational ethics perspective, ethical practice requires counselors to consider sociocultural, sociopolitical, and environmental factors when working with clients to set goals and select interventions (Gallardo et al., 2011).

Assessment and Diagnosis

Let's consider for a moment how someone might feel when receiving a mental health diagnosis. Relieved? Ashamed? Confused? Hopeful? A proper diagnosis can provide clients with clarity, resources, and an actionable path forward toward wellness. However, counselors and other mental health professionals have a history of misdiagnosing and pathologizing clients from marginalized populations (ACA Code of Ethics, 2014; Ault et al., 2023). Counselors' biases can influence diagnoses. For example, research results indicate that clinicians are more likely to diagnose Black children with oppositional defiant disorder (ODD) than their White peers, even when the children exhibit similar behavior (Ballentine, 2019). Striving to remain aware of your biases will help you avoid this kind of harmful practice, thus promoting beneficence and nonmaleficence. Taking a relational approach, you can involve the client in the process by sharing information about and explaining the purpose of a possible diagnosis, exploring with the client what diagnosis might be most accurate, and emphasizing that a diagnosis does not define a person. Later in this book, you will learn more about what we as counselors do to prevent misdiagnosing or overdiagnosing clients from diverse backgrounds.

Challenging

While validating clients' experiences is a critical component of counseling, there are also times when counselors need to ask clients to reevaluate inconsistent and unhelpful thoughts, feelings, or stories. Let's say an adult client's parents consistently told him he was lazy during his childhood. Even as a successful, industrious, high-achieving adult, he might lament not working hard enough or accomplishing more. A counselor could challenge these negative thoughts and help the client develop a fuller and more truthful self-image. As counselors, we are individuals with rich, intersectional cultural backgrounds, and our age, gender, race, ethnicity, and religion all interact to influence how we challenge a client. We need to remain aware of these influences as we work to determine the most effective way to apply this skill with a particular client. Some clients prefer directness, while others, including many Native American, Asian American, and African American clients might respond to gentle challenges, metaphors, and less-direct methods (Young, 2020).

Conveying Empathy

One of the first terms you will learn as you embark on your journey to becoming a counselor is "empathy." Empathy refers to having the ability to enter the client's world and experience it from their perspective. All the skills you will learn are aimed at increasing your empathic understanding. From an ethical standpoint, when you are fully with a client, empathizing with their struggles, you are helping to ensure that you are putting the client's welfare first. Client welfare is, perhaps, the most basic of all the ethical mandates found in the ACA Code of Ethics (2014). In fact, the very first standard in the code states, "The primary responsibility of counselors is to respect the dignity and promote the welfare of clients" (standard A.1.a.). By promoting client welfare, you will be upholding the ethical principles of beneficence and nonmaleficence, and by respecting the client's dignity, you will be honoring their cultural context.

It may be difficult, at first, to give your full attention to your client in a way that conveys empathic understanding. It may take time to silence your internal "chatter" that keeps nagging at you with questions like, "Am I saying the right thing? Did I just demonstrate the correct skill? How do I get out of my own head?" We hope you will give yourself grace to be a learner. It is natural to worry about saying or doing the wrong thing; in fact, we'd be worried if you weren't a bit worried. But remember that human beings are remarkably resilient and that saying or doing "the wrong thing" can be tolerated within a strong, empathic relationship.

We also want to emphasize the importance of "empathy balance" (Skovholt & Trotter-Mathison, 2016). You will need to learn how to enter the client's world without getting lost in that world. As Corey et al. (2024) aptly stated, too little empathy results in the absence of caring but too much empathy may result in counselors losing themselves in their clients' stories. What a task you are being asked to master—to be fully present with the client while remaining separate so that you don't lose yourself in the process! To be honest, counseling is hard work. A long time ago, Squyres (1986) commented that counselors make a *loan of the self* to the therapeutic relationship, and they receive less in return. We believe it is vital that you learn to keep your balance as you undertake this challenging endeavor. Practice self-care by being kind to yourself, trusting your guides, and acknowledging that, for all its altruism, choosing a career as a counselor is a selfish decision because the work is infinitely rewarding.

CASE STUDY

Mei, a 24-year-old, cisgender, Chinese American practicum student recently began seeing her first client, Marisol. Marisol, the 17-year-old daughter of Mexican American immigrants, grew up in a close-knit family with clearly defined gender roles. Two years ago, when Marisol did not menstruate during puberty, her parents disclosed to her that she was born intersex and that they had allowed doctors to perform a surgical procedure so that her genitals matched her sex assigned at birth (female). Marisol reacted with a mix of emotions, feeling distressed, ashamed, angry, and confused. When she questioned her parents about their choice, her father argued that as the head of the family, he knew what was best and wanted to make life easier for her. Since that time, Marisol has retreated into silence. She interacts only as necessary with her parents and has withdrawn from her friends. In addition to grappling with her gender identity, Marisol does not know what to make of her parent's decision and, although she loves them, is unsure whether she feels comfortable living in their household.

Hearing Marisol's story, Mei feels uncertain and overwhelmed. Although Mei recognizes that both she and Marisol are children of immigrants, Mei worries about understanding Marisol's culture, gaining her trust, developing a therapeutic relationship, and helping Marisol navigate her gender identity. With so much at stake, where should she begin?

Discussion

How do ethics, skills, and culture intersect in this case study? Taking an intersectional perspective, Mei will consider both Marisol's and her own cultural identities. She and Marisol are both children of immigrant parents, and they both belong to racial and ethnic minority groups in the United States. There may be additional similarities between their cultures, such as a deep respect for elder family members. Mei's empathy for Marisol may be enhanced as she reflects on these commonalities, and she can convey that empathy through her nonverbal attentiveness and by reflecting the feelings that Marisol is expressing. However, to ensure ethical practice, it is also important for Mei to listen and learn about Marisol's culture and experiences and avoid making assumptions about Marisol's experience as a Mexican American youth or imposing her own worldview. Finally, because the ACA Code of Ethics (2014) requires counselors practice within their realm of competence, it would be prudent for Marisol to talk to her supervisor about her developmental stage and competency surrounding intersex individuals and ensure that she has the necessary skills, knowledge, and training to support Marisol.

These are just a few ethical considerations that appear in Mei and Marisol's case. What other ethical considerations can you identify?

CHAPTER SUMMARY

As you begin to learn and practice the skills described in the remainder of this text, what are some ideas you can take with you from this chapter? We hope you will make use of what you have learned here about the alignment and interconnection of ethics, cultural diversity and social justice, and skills. Going forward, you will have the opportunity and the ethical responsibility to learn about your clients' cultural backgrounds and life experiences and to infuse this knowledge into your skills.

In this chapter, we have introduced you to a triangle (skills, cultural diversity and social justice, and ethics) that will provide a strong foundation for your studies. As you progress, keep in mind the strength of the triangle—it can hold the weight as you progress through your training program and continue to learn more about the work of the counselor.

CHAPTER REFLECTION AND DISCUSSION QUESTIONS

1. In what ways and to what extent and are your personal and professional values congruent with each other? Are there any areas of incompatibility between your personal and professional values, and if so, how might these impact your work as a counselor?
2. Do you find yourself drawn more toward principle ethics or relational ethics as you contemplate the ethical dilemmas you anticipate encountering in your work? How can you integrate both approaches?
3. If you were the practicum student working with Marisol, the client in the case study presented, how do you think you would approach your work with her?
4. What do you see as your greatest strengths as you begin to learn to integrate ethical awareness and cultural sensitivity into your skill building? What are your greatest areas of challenge?
5. In what ways do you think your growing knowledge and understanding of ethics, cultural diversity and social justice, and counseling skills will contribute to your developing professional identity as a counselor?

ADDITIONAL RESOURCES

Birrell, P., & Bruns, C. (2016). Ethics and relationship: From risk management to relational engagement. *Journal of Counseling & Development*, 94, 391–397.

Herlihy, B., James, A. E, & Taheri, K. S. (2018). Social justice and counseling ethics. In C. C. Lee (Ed.), *Counseling for social justice* (3rd ed.; pp. 334–360). American Counseling Association.

Herlihy, B., & Painter, E. (2019). Ethical issues in multicultural counseling. In C.C. Lee (Ed.), *Multicultural issues in counseling: New approaches to diversity* (5th ed.; pp. 255–271). American Counseling Association.

Herlihy, B., & Watson, Z. E. (2002.) Ethical issues and competence in multicultural counseling. In F. D. Harper & J. McFadden (Eds.), *Culture & counseling: New approaches* (pp. 363–378). Allyn & Bacon.

Kocet, M., & Herlihy, B. (2014). Addressing values-based conflicts within the counseling relationship: A decision-making model. *Journal of Counseling & Development*, 92, 180–186.

Remley, T. P., Jr., and Herlihy, B. (2025). *Ethical, legal, & professional issues in counseling* (7th ed.). Pearson.

REFERENCES

Akechi, Senju, A., Uibo, H., Kikuchi, Y., Hasegawa, T., & Hietanen, J. K. (2013). Attention to eye contact in the West and East: Autonomic responses and evaluative ratings. *PloS One, 8*(3), e59312–e59312. https://doi.org/10.1371/journal.pone.0059312

American Counseling Association. (2014). *ACA code of ethics.* https://www.counseling.org/resources/aca-code-of-ethics.pdf

Ault, H., Gantt, H., & Barrio Minton, C. (2023). Anti-racist considerations for teaching CACREP assessment and diagnosis courses. *Teaching and Supervision in Counseling, 5*(1), 53–64. https://doi.org/10.7290/tsc05dxpf

Ballentine, K. L. (2019). Understanding racial differences in diagnosing ODD versus ADHD using critical race theory. *Families in Society, 100*(3), 282–292. https://doi.org/10.1177/1044389419842765

Corey, G., Corey, M. H., & Corey, C. (2024). *Issues and ethics in the helping professions* (11th ed.). Cengage.

Gallardo, M. E., Yeh, C. J., Trimble, J. E., & Parham, T. A. (2011). *Culturally Adaptive Counseling Skills: Demonstrations of Evidence-Based Practices.* SAGE. https://doi.org/10.4135/9781483349329

Kocet, M. M., & Herlihy, B. (2014). Addressing value-based conflicts wit6hin the counseling relationship: A decision-making model. *Journal of Counseling & Development, 92*, 180–186.

Meara, N. M., Schmidt, L. D., & Day, J. D. (1996). Principles and virtues: A foundation for ethical decisions, policies, and character. *Counseling Psychologist, 24*, 4–77.

Ratts, M. J., Singh, A. A., Butler, S. K., Nassar-McMillan, S., & McCullough, J. R. (2016). Multicultural and social justice competencies: Practical applications in counseling, *Counseling Today, 58*(8), 40–45.

Remley, T. P., & Herlihy, B. (2020). *Ethical, legal, and professional issues in counseling* (6th ed.). Pearson.

Skovholt, T. M., & Trotter-Mathison, M. (2016). *The resilient practitioner: Burnout and compassion fatigue prevention and self-care for the helping professions* (3rd ed.). Routledge.

Squyres, E. (1986). An alternative view of the spouse of the therapist. *Journal of Contemporary Psychology, 16*, 978–106.

Sue, D. W., Sue, D., Neville, H. A., & Smith, L. (2019). *Counseling the culturally diverse: Theory and practice* (8th ed.). John Wiley & Sons, Inc.

Young, M. E. (2020). *Learning the art of helping: Building blocks and techniques.* Pearson.

Humanistic Aspects of Counseling

Dr. Jung (June) H. Hyun, LMHC, NCC; Dr. Ashlei R. Petion, LPC, NCC; and Marshaya Rountree

LEARNING OBJECTIVES

1. Define counseling and the components of counseling.
2. Explore counseling from culturally diverse perspectives.
3. Explore the roles of counselors in the multifaceted counseling process.
4. Explore the importance of professional communities for counselors and therapists, particularly in the context of providing support, sharing knowledge, and addressing issues related to diversity and cultural competence.

LEARNING OUTCOMES

1. Students will be able to articulate a comprehensive definition of counseling.
2. Students will demonstrate an understanding of how counseling practices vary across different cultures and the impact of cultural competence on therapeutic outcomes.
3. Students will identify and explain the various roles counselors play in different settings and the multifaceted nature of the counseling process.
4. Students will evaluate the role of professional communities in supporting counselors and therapists.
5. Students will design an action plan for ongoing professional development in the context of a diverse society, highlighting how they will engage with professional communities.

> **OPENING SCENARIO**
>
> Adu was a 35-year-old male, who recently decided to change his career from a financial advisor. He was born and raised in an immigrant family. As a financial advisor, he was financially successful but felt empty and experienced depressive symptoms. While it's frowned upon to see a counselor or therapist in his culture, he sought out a counselor on his friend's recommendation. He shared that he wanted to feel fulfilled and have something meaningful in his life. He started volunteering at a local elementary school through the Big Brothers Big Sisters program after receiving his counselor's recommendation. One day, he talked to a school counselor in the school and learned about school counseling. After consideration, he applied to a counseling program and recently got accepted to a school counseling program. He does not know anything about counseling except for his experience of a few sessions with his counselor.
>
> Like Adu, you may have very limited knowledge about counseling, or you may have extensive knowledge through experience and exposure. The chapter will explore what counseling is and what is involved in the counseling process.

Setting the Groundwork: What Is Counseling?

By this point in your graduate program, you've probably already taken an Introduction to Counseling course or discussed your professional orientation in many of your courses. However, we introduce a consensus definition of counseling from the American Counseling Association (ACA) to promote a common definition and unity among all professional counselors: "Counseling is a professional relationship that empowers diverse individuals, families, and groups to accomplish mental health, wellness, education, and career goals" (ACA, 2010).[1]

The professional relationship encompassed by the preceding definition can vary from setting to setting and depending on the client population. For example, in your upcoming practicum and internship, you may be placed at a site that provides inpatient counseling services (i.e., a hospital setting in which patients are admitted overnight). In inpatient settings, there tends to be less one-on-one, traditional talk therapy and more around-the-clock care by multiple different healthcare providers (e.g., professional counselors, psychiatrists, social workers and case managers, and behavior technicians). While talk therapy may be part of the services provided, group counseling is also the norm within inpatient settings. One of the focuses of group counseling in inpatient settings is on immediate stabilization with the goal of connecting clients to outpatient services upon their discharge.

On the other hand, outpatient counseling can involve the traditional one-on-one talk therapy, in which there is one counselor and one or more clients (e.g., an individual, couple, family, or group) sitting across from each other to discuss diagnosis and treatment planning, psychoeducation, client progress, and eventual termination. While inpatient counseling involves stabilizing clients

---

[1] We use the terms "counselor," "counseling," "therapist," and "therapy" interchangeably and may gravitate toward the use of more counseling-focused language for the purpose of fostering a professional counseling identity.

in crisis, outpatient counseling involves clients being more in control of their goals or their reason for seeking counseling.

While counseling can be categorized into inpatient and outpatient settings, we can also categorize counseling services by specialization or even the population served. For example, school counselors are mental health professionals who work within K–12 school settings to promote access and equity for all students through academic achievement strategies, emotional and interpersonal learning, and planning for postsecondary success (American School Counselor Association [ASCA], 2023). While school counselors are typically employed by school systems and manage an ideal caseload of about 250 students per counselor, mental health counselors can also work alongside the school system as school-based mental health counselors to provide one-on-one counseling and group counseling to children in need, during their school day. Other examples of counselor specialties include play therapy, couples counseling, group counseling, and eye movement desensitization and reprocessing (EMDR) therapy.

Despite the various settings and modalities in which counselors work and the diversity of the types of clients to be served, counselors are all grounded by the consensus definition of counseling and the expectation of using basic counseling skills to connect with clients. Clients seek out counseling with a presenting concern, whether relevant to "mental health, wellness, education, and career goals" (ACA, 2010). It is up to us, the helpers, to gather sufficient information, empathize with the client, help the client feel seen and heard, and set therapeutic goals toward resolving the presenting concern and promoting their wellness.

Counseling as a Cultural Interaction and Relationship

It is important to know that every interaction counselors have with a client is a cultural interaction. Even if a counselor and their client share multiple social identities, they are two different individuals with different upbringings, backgrounds, lived experiences, personalities, and expectations, which are all shaped by the cultural groups we belong to. Thus, it is important to approach each interaction a counselor will have with their clients with an attitude of curiosity and humility. Techniques and strategies to build a culturally humble and curious stance as a counselor will be discussed and demonstrated throughout this book.

It is also important to acknowledge the global context of counseling and the counseling profession. Generally speaking, counseling is a Western concept that has not always adapted itself effectively to different cultural groups. Think about it: The idea that an educated, professionally dressed stranger will help people work through their greatest emotional challenges on a weekly basis inside of a dimly lit room with a couch and a chair is very situationally focused. Further, even the concept of suicide intervention can be considered a Western concept; not every country mandates mental health professionals (if they even exist as a profession) to intervene when individuals share thoughts of hurting themselves. The counseling concepts that are considered norms in our society may be much different, or even nonexistent, in others. Instead, healing practices may look unique in various cultures, including having different types of helpers, concepts of illness and wellness, and methods for helping individuals heal.

Additionally, counseling and other helping professions (e.g., psychiatry and social work) have not always had positive relationships with marginalized groups. In fact, some marginalized groups have been historically harmed by helping professions. As a result, there may be a general distrust between marginalized communities and mental health service providers, due to ongoing cultural and interpersonal stigmas against counseling. For example, some LGBTQ+ clients may associate professional counseling services with what used to be called "conversion therapy", an unfounded, unethical practice used by helpers in an effort to "convert" queer clients to heterosexuality and cisgender, heterosexual norms (American Medical Association [AMA], 2019). The lasting, harmful effects of this treatment have caused deep harm to queer communities, rightfully forming a wedge that may discourage queer individuals from seeking professional mental healthcare (Substance Abuse and Mental Health Services Administration [SAMHSA], 2015). Although these practices are no longer commonplace, the counseling profession still aims to acknowledge the harm that has been caused and make significant strides toward repairing our relationships with marginalized communities as well as the reputation of the profession. This acknowledgment and repair can take place at different levels, including the interpersonal (e.g., a conversation you may have with a new client who is initially skeptical of the counseling process) and community (e.g., engaging in professional and social advocacy that helps to dispel myths about counseling) levels.

All in all, culture is at the heart of every interpersonal interaction, and the counseling relationship is not exempt. Given the global context of helping and healing, as well as the historical perspectives of counseling in various communities, counselors continue to explore their role in utilizing helping techniques to facilitate positive change in clients' lives. The following section will delve deeper into counselors' role in navigating some practical techniques to facilitate a therapeutic relationship with culture in mind.

Role of Counselor

Counseling begins when individuals seek out help for their mental health concerns or specific objectives (e.g., improving their relationship with a spouse or feeling more content at work) or through referrals (e.g., a recommendation from a teacher or a court order). The process unfolds as the client and the counselor meet. What transfers during these sessions, and when does counseling conclude? Counseling embodies a collaborative process, wherein a counselor and client convene to jointly establish and pursue agreed-upon goals. Throughout this process, the counselor assumes multifaceted roles, paralleled by the client's active participation. Each session is a step toward the client's personal growth and fulfillment of their aspirations, guided by the counselor's expertise.

Relationship Builder: Building Therapeutic Relationship

Scholars, including Wampold (2015), have underscored the significance of the therapeutic relationship as a core element contributing to positive treatment outcomes (Lambert & Barley, 2011; Norcross & Lambert, 2011). A primary responsibility of a counselor is to develop a therapeutic rapport, also known as trust, with the client. This trust is not automatically granted to counselors; clients do not divulge their innermost thoughts simply because someone is claimed to be a professional counselor. Therefore, counselors initially strive to establish a setting in which clients feel comfortable revealing their inner world. This paves the way for clients to assist counselors in grasping their experiences, thereby facilitating effective collaboration.

When clients share their stories, they communicate with the counselor both nonverbally and verbally. Counselors respond authentically, without judgment, and with unconditional positive regard, actively listening to the client in both nonverbal and verbal forms. By embracing clients' experiences without judgment and while understanding their worldviews, counselors can validate their clients' complex emotions, deep pains, and lived experiences. Chapters 4 and 7, "The Therapeutic Relationship" and "Invitational Skills," respectively, will provide comprehensive guidance for counselors-in-training (CITs), like Adu. These chapters focus on mastering skills essential for building therapeutic relationships and developing invitation skills, which are crucial for establishing and deepening a trust-filled bond with clients.

Facilitator: Facilitating the Process

Sometimes, clients seek counseling urgently to help de-escalate their situations or regulate intense emotions. In the school setting, students often visit the counseling office due to externalizing behaviors or uncontrolled emotional responses. A key consideration for school counselors at the end of a session is assisting students in reaching an emotionally functional level, enabling them to return to the classroom ready to learn. In other cases, clients may require more extended support. For instance, in outpatient agencies, clients might need regular check-ins with their counselor for addiction issues. In counseling agencies or community mental health centers, clients may continue therapy until their symptoms lessen or until they achieve specific life goals for which they seek assistance. These scenarios highlight a common aspect: Counseling is an ongoing process.

MAGNIFIER

Once a trusting relationship is established between the client and the counselor, the counselor assists in expanding the client's understanding of their experiences, identifying their strengths to cope, and implementing strategies to promote their well-being. For instance, counselors can help clients recognize systemic oppression that may have caused generational trauma, enabling them to avoid self-blame and, instead, work toward liberating themselves from this legacy. In cases like a student exhibiting somatic symptoms only on testing days, school counselors can deduce that the student might be easily stressed and have a low tolerance for pressure, lacking healthy coping strategies. The counselor can then assist the student in understanding their behavioral and thought patterns and develop more effective coping skills.

STRENGTHS FINDER

Counselors focus on a client's strengths and successful strategies rather than on flaws or weaknesses. This approach is based on the fundamental goal of counseling, which is to empower clients to initiate changes in their lives independently. It is not the counselor's role to fix an issue or symptom; instead, they help the client recognize and understand their problems and find ways to address them. For clients to do the work for themselves later, they need to understand they have power and strengths in them. Counselors believe clients innately have an ability to cope with the problems. Additionally, counselors support clients in becoming self-advocates and agents of change. For example, school counselors might work with a student struggling to adjust after moving from one state to another. They would assist the student in finding ways to acclimate and, perhaps, develop an advocacy plan for newcomers in the school.

REFLECTING MIRRORS

In the facilitating process, counselors act as mirrors, reflecting the client's contributions to the session, including feelings, thoughts, and behaviors. They paraphrase the clients' words and actions, echo their feelings, and mirror their thoughts. Counselors also summarize the discussion, asking clarifying questions and prompting clients to delve deeper into their issues or broaden their perspectives. When clients gain clear insights into their lives, counselors encourage them to exercise their autonomy in deciding how they wish to effect change. They assist clients in setting goals and provide both challenge and support when progress toward these goals stalls. These microskills, including paraphrasing, asking questions, reflecting feelings, interpreting meaning, goal setting, and challenging, will be explored in greater detail in subsequent chapters.

Work Through Space: Self-Awareness

As the counseling space works like a mirror, psychoanalytic scholars pay attention to phenomena happening in the counseling space: transference and countertransference. *Transference* involves the client unconsciously projecting onto the therapist's emotions, attitudes, and imaginings that stem from important relationships in the client's history (Corey, 2017). Transference can occur especially when the client's childhood experience emerges to the surface as the counseling progresses from the unfinished business of the client. On the other hand, *countertransference* can occur at any time during therapy, as it encompasses the therapist's subconscious emotional reactions to a client, which are influenced by the therapist's own background and experiences. With transference, the client may view you as being similar to important people in their life, whereas with countertransference, the client or the counseling context with a specific client may influence the therapist's affect irrationally and objectively negatively. It is important to acknowledge and explore when as well as why this comes up. If not explored, the counselor will work from a place that is harmful to the client. As stated earlier about clients possessing complex emotions, so do counselors.

In addition to fostering a therapeutic alliance and facilitating a healing process, counselors create a space where clients are encouraged to become change agents in their own lives. This involves acknowledging that clients bring their own baggage, stigmas, and biases into the therapeutic setting. Counselors, especially those of color, who, as Sue and Sue (2023) highlighted, face unique challenges when working with clients, often confront these stigmas and biases. These challenges include being questioned about their credibility, feeling pressured to demonstrate their competency, unintentionally transferring feelings of racial hostility onto White clients, being seen as the exemplary counselor of color, and dealing with racist comments or behaviors from clients. Moreover, it is crucial for counselors to recognize that clients may come to therapy with experiences of oppression from governmental or medical systems. These histories significantly impact the therapeutic process. *Broaching*, or the act of initiating and navigating discussions about race and culture, becomes vital in this context (Day-Vines et al., 2007). It allows for the open exploration of how race and cultural dynamics impact the client's experiences and the therapeutic relationship. This exploration includes acknowledging and discussing the client's potential biases toward the counselor and their expectations from the counseling process.

It is also important for counselors to reflect on and explore their own stigmas and biases, as outlined in the Multicultural and Social Justice Counseling Competencies (MJSCC; Ratts et al.,

2016). This self-awareness is critical to ensuring that these biases do not negatively impact the therapeutic relationship and process. Broaching enables both the counselor and the client to address these complex dynamics, fostering a more understanding and effective therapeutic environment.

CARETAKER: CARING FOR THE SELF

Counselors often emphasize the importance of self-care to clients, but they might overlook their own need for it. Virginia Satir, in her work on the *self-of-the-therapist*, highlighted the crucial role of self-care for counselors, particularly the need to resolve unresolved family-of-origin issues to achieve therapeutic congruence (Satir et al., 1991). Similarly, Harry Aponte in his work, *person-of-the-therapist*, emphasized that counselors must engage in introspection on personal issues that could affect the therapy process (Aponte, 1994).

As CITs begin their work with clients, they often navigate a variety of emotions before, during, and after sessions with clients. Research by Roach and Young (2007) and Smith et al. (2007) indicates that CITs frequently experience heightened psychological stress. Skovholt and Trotter-Mathison (2016) have identified this stress as compassion fatigue when repeatedly being exposed to clients' distressing narratives, often due to their limited experience, skills, or support systems. The failure to address this issue in the helping professions can lead to burnout and a reduced ability to effectively assist clients (Litam et al., 2021). School counselors are also susceptible to burnout, as reported by Wilkerson and Bellini (2011). Self-care, therefore, is not merely a choice but a requirement. The ACA's *Code of Ethics* (ACA, 2014) and the *Ethical Standards for School Counselors* (ASCA, 2022) mandate self-care as a professional responsibility to uphold ethical standards and deliver high-quality service to clients. For activities to increase the resilience and wellness of CIT as well as practicing mental health counselors, see the Appendix, "Wellness."

> ### 3.1 Self-Care Activity
>
> As an activity, partner with another classmate and list other ways you can engage in self-care while becoming a counselor and how you plan to implement these activities.

SOCIAL JUSTICE ADVOCATE

Counseling aims to enhance clients' well-being, and a counselor's role often extends beyond individual sessions, particularly in school settings. School counselors, for example, may collaborate with community agencies to raise awareness about the mental health of children and adolescents and its impact on their academic and career success. They might also provide resources and information to parents and caregivers. Similarly, mental health counselors, when working with a client considering gender transition surgery, might compile a resource list for future clients facing similar decisions. These actions can be viewed as forms of social justice advocacy, recognizing that clients' issues and challenges are deeply intertwined with societal factors. Therefore, to effectively promote clients' well-being, it is essential for counselors to endeavor to change systemic structures in addition to working with individual clients.

Building Community

Where does counseling happen? Maybe in a room with a big window with sunlight coming in, a huge bookcase filled with books, or a comfortable sofa where clients sit and talk? Yes, counselors meet clients in a physical space. At the same time, beyond a mere physical room, often portrayed in media with two chairs and a desk or coffee table, counseling occurs in the communities. Counseling happens within a shared realm, where multiple systems meet. Counseling, and the healing potential it brings, transcends the boundaries of concrete walls. It is a place of transcendence, where clients' intricate worlds, encompassing micro, meso, exo, macro, and chrono systems, meet the counselor's systems. Therefore, counselors should consider those systems in understanding the client and the interactions of multiple systems in the therapeutic relationship in taking actions to support the client's healing journey.

Considering Client Community

Culturally competent counselors must acknowledge that the location where counseling unfolds varies, depending on the diverse backgrounds of the clients. A counselor and a client from different walks of life position the healing space within distinct quadrants of the MSJCC model (Ratts et al., 2016). With these multifaceted considerations in mind, the moment a client extends an invitation to the counselor, encompassing their world through the act of counseling, the counselor becomes a part of a transcendent community. Regardless of whether counselors are part of the client's community physically, they should put concerted efforts into learning about and understanding the client's community, not only their cultural values and worldviews but also changes in laws and policies that impact the client's community that may influence the client's mental health. As telehealth becomes more prevalent, it seems that counselors are less likely to live within the client's community. That means counselors' responsibility to be aware of clients' values and worldviews is extended to the world, wherever our clients are.

The MSJCC model (Ratts et al., 2016) encourages counselors to continue to broach the systems a client belongs to. Especially with the understanding that mental health agencies may be considered oppressive systems to a client, counselors reach out to the community outside of the agency first rather than waiting for a client to seek out mental health support. Further, counselors may want to be intentional even when choosing a place to meet for counseling. For instance, mental health agencies are likely to encounter the enduring effects of generational trauma, resulting from historical oppression within the counseling space in the agency. For example, when working with Native American clients, counselors can consider holding a session in nature, where many Native Americans feel a sense of belonging and deep connection, to promote the therapeutic relationship (Gallardo et al., 2012).

Counselors must discern the changes that occur and the healing that emerges through these communal transformations. Culturally competent counselors will discuss the impact of changes a client brings due to their own healing on the client's community, which the client will, in turn, experience and interact with. For example, consider a situation in which a counselor is working with an Asian immigrant adolescent, who has been struggling with their sexual identity. The counselor should discuss with their client how their community (family, friends, school, etc.) may respond when the client decides to come out to their family and assist the client in navigating challenges that may be caused by their own healing process.

Considering the client's community does not stop when changes happen in the client's behaviors, thoughts, and feelings. Multicultural and social justice counselors take action to support the wellness of clients and the community (Ratts et al., 2016), and it is one of the core values to promote social justice (ACA, 2014). Beyond the therapy room, counselors can work with their clients to find a community where they feel they belong. In the example of the Asian immigrant adolescent, the counselor can help the client use their strengths to speak up for their voice in and outside the community. Further, counselors can work with the school board to change policies and regulations that have discriminated against or oppressed sexual minorities to create a safer learning environment and help bring social justice to the community.

Considering Counselor Community

CITs enter the professional community when they are accepted to the counselor preparation program. During the program, the professional community can include course instructors, program staff, classmates, and practicum/internship sites. CITs learn and develop attitudes, knowledge, and skills from their course instructors in the program. They continue to hone their skills during practicum and internship. During practicum and internships, counselors in training can apply their knowledge and improve their skills by sharing their experiences, giving and receiving feedback, and reflecting on their experiences with their peers and supervisors (who may be their internship course instructors).

After graduating from a counselor preparation program, candidates are usually required to obtain a certain number of hours under supervision to get certified and licensed in a particular state. For school counselors, they may not need more supervised hours to get certified or licensed. (Please check your state licensing board for the requirements.) Although the title is different state by state (e.g., registered interns in Florida versus mental health counselor associates in Washington), graduates will continue to engage in a professional community that extends to colleagues (when you work in an agency or a school), a supervisor(s), and the professional organizations. Counselors involve individual or group supervision with supervisors, peer supervision, and/or consultation and continue to learn via professional development opportunities, such as attending webinars, lectures, and conferences.

After graduating and obtaining full certification and licensure, counselors benefit greatly from engaging with their professional community. There are three key reasons this connection is essential: professional development, professional advocacy, and self-care. First, counselors continuously refine their counseling skills and strategies for the ever-evolving needs of diverse clients. Additionally, staying informed about policy and legislative changes that impact their profession and clients enables counselors to effectively advocate for the profession's welfare and the well-being of their clients. Furthermore, counselors require a supportive professional community to prioritize self-care. It is crucial for counselors to maintain physical and mental well-being, as they cannot provide optimal care to their clients if their own health is compromised. Becoming a member of a professional organization is an excellent way to address these three needs. In most of the states, fully certified and licensed counselors are required to accumulate a certain number of professional development hours. By joining professional organizations (e.g., the American Counseling Association), counselors gain access to leading journals, such as the *Journal of Counseling & Development*. Moreover, they can participate in conferences and workshops with reduced rates, exclusively available to members. Books, podcasts, and other professional materials are available to members as well.

While post-licensure supervision may not be obligatory, counselors often desire to establish a professional network in which they can connect with colleagues and other helping professionals in their community. These connections enable peer supervision and consultation, fostering a supportive environment to discuss challenging cases and maintain ethical practices that ensure the delivery of high-quality care.

In summary, active involvement in professional communities offers numerous advantages for fully certified and licensed counselors. It supports their ongoing professional development, empowers them to advocate for their profession and clients, and promotes their personal well-being.

CHAPTER SUMMARY

This chapter introduces the foundational definitions of counseling, incorporating culturally diverse perspectives and delineating the various roles counselors play in assisting clients with a range of issues. It emphasizes the importance of counselors recognizing the communities that they engage with intentionally to support not only their clients but also themselves and their profession. Prior to delving into the specific counseling micro-skills employed by counselors, the chapter establishes an overarching framework. It is hoped that readers will revisit this chapter as a touchstone when they encounter challenges in mastering micro-skills, realigning with the guiding principles presented here.

CHAPTER REFLECTION AND DISCUSSION QUESTIONS

1. How has your understanding of counseling evolved before and after engaging with the chapter?
2. Which counselor role(s) do you feel most connected to, and why?
3. How is counseling viewed within your cultural context?
4. What strategies will you implement to expand your professional network? Please provide a detailed action plan outlining how you intend to continually develop culturally inclusive skills and integrate this knowledge into your counseling practice.

ADDITIONAL RESOURCES

Self Care

- https://www.counseling.org/resources/topics/professional-counseling/workplace-wellness-self-care#

Professional communities

- ACA divisions, regions, and branches: https://www.counseling.org/about/divisions-regions-branches
- ACA connect: https://community.counseling.org/home
- National Board for Certified Counselors: https://www.nbcc.org/
- American Mental Health Counselors Association: https://www.amhca.org/home
- American School Counselor Association: https://www.schoolcounselor.org/

REFERENCES

Aponte, H. J. (1994). How personal can training get? *Journal of Marital and Family Therapy, 20,* 3–15. https://doi.org/10.1111/j.1752-0606.1994tb01007.x

American Counseling Association. (2010, March). *20/20: Consensus definition of counseling.* https://www.counseling.org/about-us/about-aca/20-20-a-vision-for-the-future-of-counseling/consensus-definition-of-counseling

American Counseling Association. (2014). *ACA code of ethics.*

American Medical Association. (2019). *LGBTQ change efforts (so-called "conversion therapy").* https://www.ama-assn.org/system/files/2019-12/conversion-therapy-issue-brief.pdf

American School Counselor Association. (2023). *Who are school counselors?* https://schoolcounselor.org/getmedia/ee8b2e1b-d021-4575-982c-c84402cb2cd2/Role-Statement.pdf

Corey, G. (2017). *Theory and practice of counseling and psychotherapy.* Cengage.

Day-Vines, N. L., Wood, S. M., Grothaus, T., Craigen, L., Holman, A., Dotson-Blake, K., & Douglass, M. J. (2007). Broaching the subjects of race, ethnicity, and culture during the counseling process. *Journal of Counseling & Development, 85*(4), 401–409. https://doi.org/10.1002/j.1556-6678.2007.tb00608.x

Douglass, M. J. (2007). Broaching the subjects of race, ethnicity, and culture during the counseling process. *Journal of Counseling & Development, 85,* 401–409.

Gallardo, M. E., Yeh, C. J., Trimble, J. E., & Parham, T. A. (2012). *Culturally adaptive counseling skills: Demonstrations of evidence-based practices.* SAGE.

Lambert, M. J., & Barley, D. E. (2001). Research summary on the therapeutic relationship and psychotherapy outcome. *Psychotherapy: Theory, Research, Practice, Training, 38*(4), 357–361. https://doi.org/10.1037/0033-3204.38.4.357

Litam, S. D. A., Ausloos, C. D., & Harrichand, J. J. S. (2021). Stress and resilience among professional counselors during the COVID-19 pandemic. *Journal of Counseling & Development, 99*(4), 384–395. https://doi.org/10.1002/jcad.12391

Norcross, J. C., & Lambert, M. J. (2011). Psychotherapy relationships that work II. *Psychotherapy, 48*(1), 4–8. https://doi.org/10.1037/a0022180

Ratts, M., Singh, A., Nassar-McMillan, S., Butler, S. K., McCullough, J. R. (2016). Multicultural and social justice counseling competencies: Guidelines for the counseling profession. *Journal of Multicultural Counseling & Development, 44*(1), 28–48. https://doi.org/10.1002/jmcd.12035

Roach, L. F., & Young, M. E. (2007). Do counselor education programs promote wellness in their students? *Counselor Education and Supervision, 47,* 29–45. https://doi.org/10.1002/j.1556-6978.2007.tb00036.x

Satir, V. & Bitter, J. (1991). The therapist and family therapy: Satir's human validation process model. In A. M. Horne & J. L. Passmore (Eds.), *Family therapy and counseling* (pp. 13–45). F. E. Peacock.

Skovholt, T. M., & Trotter-Mathison, M. (2016). *The resilient practitioner: Burnout and compassion fatigue prevention and self-care strategies for the helping professions* (3rd ed.). Routledge.

Smith, H. L., Robinson, E. H., & Young, M. E. (2007). The relationship among wellness, psychological distress, and social desirability of entering master's-level counselor trainees. *Counselor Education and Supervision, 47,* 96–103. https://doi.org/10.1002/j.1556-6978.2007.tb00041.x

Sue, D. W., & Sue, D., Neville, H. A., & Smith, L. (2023). Multicultural counseling competence and cultural humility for people of color counselors and therapists. In D. W. Sue, D. Sue, H. A. Neville., & L. Smith (Eds.), *Counseling the culturally diverse: Theory and practice* (pp. 149–168). Wiley.

Substance Abuse and Mental Health Services Administration. (2015). *Ending conversion therapy: Supporting and affirming LGBTQ youth.* https://store.samhsa.gov/sites/default/files/d7/priv/sma15-4928.pdf

Wampold, B. E. (2015). How important are the common factors in psychotherapy? An update. *World Psychiatry, 14*(3), 270–277. https://doi.org/10.1002/wps.20238

Wilkerson, K., & Bellini, J. (2006). Intrapersonal and organizational factors associated with burnout among school counselors. *Journal of Counseling & Development, 84*(4), 440–450. https://doi.org/10.1002/j.1556-6678.2006.tb00428.x

The Therapeutic Relationship

Dr. Carla Adkison-Johnson, Dr. Olivia Ngadjui, and Dr. Gemarco Peterson

LEARNING OBJECTIVES

1. To understand that a culturally responsive counselor–client of color (especially related to Black clients) relationship is required for meaningful and curious engagement and to encourage progressive social and behavioral change.
2. To recognize how historical and contemporary factors have negatively influenced the therapeutic environment and have oppressed racially minoritized (especially Black) clients.
3. To apply reflective and critical thinking skills to gain insight into the assumptions, worldviews, values, beliefs, biases, and privileged and minoritized statuses that influence the therapeutic relationship in counseling.

LEARNING OUTCOMES

1. Students will be able to understand how their identities and experiences impact their ability to create and maintain a therapeutic relationship that respects the diversity of the client.
2. Students will be able to maintain curiosity toward and ensure they are fully understanding of their client's perspective and cultural background.
3. Students will be able to utilize case studies crafted to increase the student's knowledge of how to work with clients with intersectional identities and gain the ability to recognize the dynamics of power, privilege, and oppression that influence the counseling relationship.
4. Students will be able to implement culturally appropriate approaches to meeting the clients' diverse needs presented in the case studies. Students will gain insight into the unique supervision, consultation, and interdisciplinary approaches often needed to meet the needs of various clients.

This chapter will address the following Multicultural and Social Justice Counseling Competencies (MSJCCs):

- **Awareness:** This chapter challenges students' previously held beliefs that may contradict the importance of respecting and valuing differences within the counseling relationship. Assumptions and stereotypes will be addressed as students review the contextual factors of the therapeutic relationship. Students will recognize the influence of other personal dimensions of identity and their role in cultural self-awareness. Presented case studies examine the counseling and advocacy interventions that promote culturally responsive action steps on behalf of the counselor.
- **Knowledge:** Effective communication is essential in developing and sustaining a sound counselor–client relationship. This chapter illustrates how previous counselor training programs may not adequately prepare students for real life situations with clients. Critical detail is provided in relation to the behavioral impact of and reaction to the communication styles of White American counselors on members of the African American population. Case studies in this chapter explore and correct counselor behaviors that disrupt the ability to meaningfully engage with minoritized populations.
- **Skills:** The ability to understand and navigate the contextual dimensions of the counseling relationship requires relevant educational experience and clinical engagement with real clients. This chapter illustrates the importance of acquiring reflective and critical thinking skills to gain insight into the assumptions, worldviews, values, beliefs, biases, and privileged and minoritized statuses that influence the counseling relationship.
- **Actions:** This chapter motivates counseling students to engage in social action to alter the local, state, and federal laws and policies that benefit privileged clients at the expense of minoritized clients. It is the responsibility of students, counselor educators, and clinical supervisors to employ social advocacy to ensure that local, state, and federal laws and policies are equitable for all clients.

Background Information

Establishing a sound therapeutic relationship is essential for culturally responsive counseling. This chapter examines the importance of building a counseling alliance grounded in the reality that the client and counselor live in an increasingly diverse society. Race has been acknowledged as an organizing principle in the therapeutic relationship, while cultural and racial bias can impede the formation of a supportive therapeutic environment (Jamal et al., 2020; Johnson & Caldwell, 2011; Hardy & Laszloffy, 2012). Historical as well as modern researchers and clinicians in the counselor education, social work, psychology, and marriage and family therapy professions have indicated that the therapeutic relationship is related directly to client change, even more significantly than counseling techniques (DeAngelis, 2019; Devore & Schesinger, 1981; Hardy & Bobes, 2016; Hill et al., 2018; White & Parham, 1990). The therapeutic relationship is the building block that unites therapists and clients in solving problems and relieving symptoms derived from emotional stress and pressures (Allen-Meares & Burman, 1999; Hill et al., 2018).

Yet the Council for Accreditation and Counseling and Related Programs (CACREP), which accredits over 900 counselor education programs, does not require specific curricular experiences (classroom or clinical) that focus on racial minoritized populations. In fact, the 2016 CACREP

Standards (which impacts the training of current graduates) mentions the term, "race" or "racism" rarely, if at all. Although the 2024 CACREP Standards includes curricular experiences regarding racism, power, oppression, privilege, marginalization, microaggressions, violence or counselors and clients, there are still no specific or direct service requirements in working with racial minoritized clients and other marginalized groups. This is particularly important and concerning, given the historical and current racial unrest in the United States.

It is important to note that over 50 years ago, the founding members of the Association of Non-White Concerns, known today as the Association for Multicultural Counseling and Development (AMCD) and the Association of Black Psychologists (ABPSI) voiced their concerns about the fact that clinicians were not being trained to work with Black clients and other racial minoritized populations (e.g., Gunnings, 1971; Franklin, 1971; Williams, 1971). For instance, Gunnings (1971) stated that counseling students, particularly Black students, had to contend with a curriculum that was racist and inadequate to prepare students to work with clients of color. He argued that counseling students were taught to interpret and diagnose material from a White-centering perspective and the practicum and internship experiences and supervision did not meet the needs of a diverse society. Likewise, Franklin (1971) stated,

> Preparing the White counselor for work in the Black community is difficult. Not only must he acquire skills as a counselor, but he must also become knowledgeable and sensitive to the plight of Black people. The likelihood of his acquiring this from current counseling programs is negligible. (p. 111)

Even today, several studies and scholars have affirmed that graduate students in the mental health fields from all racial backgrounds are not trained adequately to work with clients of color (Abrams & Moio, 2009; Carter & Pieterse, 2020; Goode-Cross & Grim, 2016; Holcomb-McCoy, 2022; Williams et al., 2016). For example, while reflecting on his own clinical training and the present situation for therapists, Dr. Kenneth Hardy (2022), an African American marriage and family national scholar, argued that clinical programs prepare students to work with White clients and become good White therapists. He stated,

> How could someone like me, who was completely educated and trained by Whites, who was fully indoctrinated in Eurocentric ideology, whose clinical exposure was primarily to White clients, and who was consistently and systematically discouraged from paying too much attention to race throughout his training, be anything but a good White therapist? (p. 460)

Hardy's statement highlights the current context of clinical training in counselor education that informs the way counselors in training perceive the therapeutic environment. For example, the Council for Accreditation of Counseling and Related Educational Programs' (CACREP) 2021 Vital Statistics include 3,260 full-time faculty in counselor education identifying as White (65.82% White, 17% Black, 5.6% Hispanic) and note that White faculty are largely comprised of White women, with 40.98% women and 24.26% men (CACREP, 2021). With respect to the 63,510 counselor education students enrolled in CACREP accredited master's programs, 55.94% identify as White, 16.57% as Black, and 10.17% as Hispanic, and many counseling students who identify as White are women (45.87% women and 9.73% men). These findings indicate that although our client population is becoming increasingly diverse, counselor education students are being trained through a White cultural lens and more likely in the future, a White, female professional counselor will see a greater amount of racially minoritized clients. This discovery is particularly troubling, given the current and historical policing of Black Americans by White women (Height et al., 2022). These circumstances in contemporary society are a direct reflection of potential harm or similar policing occurring in the counselor–client relationship.

Moreover, Helms (2017) confirmed that Whiteness is the frame for educational and scientific practices, which includes counseling professionals' teaching, research, and practice. Hence, this chapter is focused on the relationship between the professional counselor and client. We believe that addressing racial context is an important tool in building and sustaining the therapeutic relationship. You will notice that we do not provide a "how-to" or "step-by-step" approach to encountering people of color in the therapeutic process. We recognize that each racial minoritized or any other culturally oppressed group deserves its own discussion, which is beyond the scope of this chapter. All of the chapter authors are counselor educators and clinicians who identify as Black and/or African American and have experience with and train counselors in establishing and sustaining therapeutic relationships with Black clients. We focus on the dynamics between African American clients and White American counselors to illustrate the way racial context is foundational in the therapeutic relationship (Williams et al., 2022).

Critical Race Theory Framework

Over the last decade, counselor educators have been adopting critical race theory (CRT) as a lens to deconstruct power, privilege, structural barriers, colonization, and racism in counselor education and the therapeutic environment (Branco, 2019; Cokley, 2021; Odegard & Vereen, 2010; Singh et al., 2021; Tripp & Adams, 2022). In the early 1970s, Bell drafted the blueprints that laid the foundation for CRT (Bell, 1970, 1976). In deconstructing White supremacy within the judicial system, Bell (1980) argued "the phenomenon that is racism in American law cannot be understood by reading statutes and legal decisions removed from the context of the events and concerns that motivated and influenced them" (p. 2). Earlier, Bell (1970) identified discernable components that operate in the court system that included the following:

1. An abiding, albeit seldom expressed and often unconscious, belief that Blacks as a group are inferior to Whites.
2. A predisposition to resolve conflicts involving Black injustices and the needs of the White majority in a manner that protects and promotes the latter, even if it perpetuates the former. (p. 270)

In this chapter, we will use the original blueprints of critical race theory as an explanatory tool with which to understand race's influence on the therapeutic relationship. Since the birth of the field of psychology, Black Americans have been placed outside the human family and have been subjected to inferior clinical treatment from mental health clinicians (Johnson, 2016). Although a therapist's self-reflection and critique, curiosity, and openness to a client's varied cultural experiences (Tervalon & Murray-Garcia, 1998; Zhu et al., 2022) are necessary for client engagement, these are not sufficient to alleviate the hurt, pain, and other clinical symptoms associated with, or exacerbated by, daily assaults on African Americans' humanity (Goode-Cross & Grim, 2016; Hardy & Laszloffy, 2005; Johnson, 2016). What is clear is that counselor education students are expected to know basic therapeutic skills and demonstrate a level of competency to work with clients, primarily White Americans. It is equally important that the focus of clinical training be on teaching students to demonstrate specific skills in establishing a culturally responsive therapeutic relationship conducive for underrepresented groups.

The Therapeutic Relationship Concept

A critical component in counselor education training is establishing the therapeutic relationship. If there is no meaningful engagement between the counselor and client, it will be difficult or even impossible to provide culturally responsive insight or to encourage behavioral change (if needed). Because counselor competence has a direct influence on the quality of counselor–client interactions, much effort has been made to identify specific skills used in the counseling process (Carkhuff, 1969; Roffers et al., 1988). Carkhuffs's human relations training and Ivey's microcounseling operationalized levels of counselor functioning and behavior. These behaviors include listening skills, conveying an open invitation to talk, and reflective responding.

However, historically, writers have argued that such skill-based training models may not be sufficient to help students establish a relationship with "real clients." For example, Haase et al. (1972) conducted a 1-year follow-up study of students who completed microskills training and reported a general decline in attending skills, to levels like pretraining. Similarly, Roffers et al. (1988) conducted a two-semester follow-up evaluation of students who had completed Carkhuffs's skill-based training program. The authors found that although beginning trainees maintained skill levels significantly above pretraining levels, they were unable to transfer their newly acquired skills to actual client interviews.

In dealing with actual clients and the counseling relationship, Rogers (1957) identified such factors as trust, being genuinely engaged, and the therapist conveying unconditional positive regard as essential elements in building a sound therapeutic relationship. Desirable client characteristics, such as being able to pay (with cash, credit card, or private insurance only), intelligent, motivated, verbal (English speaking), attractive, articulate, personable, trusting, and disclosive have also been associated with client qualities needed for a productive counseling relationship (Parham et al., 2011). Several multicultural counseling scholars (e.g., Arredondo et al., 1992; Helms, 2017; White & Parham, 2002) have asserted that stereotypes of typical White clients match those characteristics valued most highly in ideal client populations. Conversely, stereotypical attitudes of racial minoritized clients often conflict with the ideal client characteristics. For instance, African American and Latinx populations continue to be characterized in the counseling literature as being resistant in counseling, unable to pay for services, less verbal, reactionary, violent, and traumatized (Adkison-Johnson & Johnson, 2019; Eghaneyan & Murphy, 2019; Johnson, 2016; Parham et al., 2011; Ward, 2005; White & Parham, 1990).

It is important to note that the way African American clients perceive the therapeutic relationship determines the way they will respond to the counselor. Much of what we know in the counseling literature on clinician–client relationships with African Americans is focused on racial differences, same-race experiences in the client–counselor dyad, or the application of specific theoretical frameworks or counseling techniques. However, some qualitative investigations have explored African American clients' perception of the therapeutic relationship specifically. For example, Ward (2005) examined the perspectives of 13 adult African American clients from a clinical mental health center in the Midwest. Nearly all of the participants had a White American counselor and 62% had a White American, female counselor. Findings from the study indicated that the participants performed an assessing process. Specifically, they assessed the client–therapist match, safety in therapy, and the counselor's effectiveness. The assessment of the match helped clients determine whether the counselor could relate to their race and ethnicity, gender, age, or beliefs about parenting (e.g., the way the counselor was raised). The participants defined safety as the sense of trust and emotional comfort they felt when working with the counselor. One 39-year-old female participant stated, "[I] like walking into your house, I feel safe walking into my house" (p. 476). The participants related counselor effectiveness to the counselor's experience and effectiveness. Clients monitored their self-disclosure deliberately as they assessed their counselor's effectiveness and their own level of safety.

Safety in the therapeutic relationship is of special concern for African American clients, particularly when the clinician is a White American. Historically, White American, female counseling professionals in particular have raised safety concerns when interacting with African American clients, knowing that state-controlled agencies (e.g., Child Protective Services or Courts, Schools) will hear of, and act upon, their criminalization and pathologizing of African American men, women, and children's behaviors immediately (Adkison-Johnson, 2022; Blow, 2020; Roberts, 2022). This sense of White American counselors "not feeling safe" during the therapeutic encounter also serves as a silencing tool. Silencing is a form of oppression and interpersonal violence that prevents oppressed groups from engaging in self-assertion and expression (Jemal et al., 2020). In a more recent study of the clinical experiences of African American women in substance abuse treatment, the findings indicated that the participants experienced emotional and psychological injury from being treated as inferior persons (Jemal et al., 2020). They were often perceived as "angry" and "intimidating," and the women had to "speak in a certain manner" and were told to "hold their gut" (no emotional outbursts). The participants' authentic voice, presence, and feelings were always perceived as problematic in comparison to their White counterparts, which complicated or extended their recovery.

Thus, the therapeutic relationship needs to be viewed within a historical and cultural context. A 2020 study of Latinx immigrants (Adame et al., 2020) reminds us that lengthening residence in the United States is associated with self-depression. Latinx women in particular are also subjected to heightened stress in the form of ethnic and sexist discrimination (Mata-Greive et al., 2020). Even the counselor's interpersonal practices and communication styles can affect or create an oppressive, threatening, and violent therapeutic environment for their clients. As a result, understanding and appreciating clients from marginalized groups' lived experiences may not be sufficient to grasp the depth and breadth of the therapeutic encounter with actual clients.

Building an appreciation for the values, traditions, and culture of marginalized populations is only the beginning in establishing an effective therapeutic relationship with clients. Direct experiences (clinical and nonclinical) need to be included to provide real meaning of the content and research that has been presented in the classroom. It has often been desirable for counselors to engage in self-assessments, self-reflection, and cultural genograms to explore their issues concerning implicit bias and equity. However, you can't genuinely engage in or reflect on a culture or with an individual whose lived experience you don't know anything about. To maximize effectiveness during the therapeutic encounter, counselor education programs may include a pre-techniques experience or course focused on culturally interpersonal engagement. This strategy was recommended by African American scholars during the racial unrest in the 1970s in preparing clinicians to address real-life experiences of racial minoritized clients (e.g., Franklin, 1971; Gunnings, 1971). This preclinical experience centers on interacting with underrepresented groups, by attending cultural events, volunteering, and participating in encounter groups or workshops with marginalized populations that have or have had negative experiences with the mental health system or other groups (e.g., White American men; White American, middle-class women; or heterosexual populations). This will help students gain cultural awareness and understand the impact of their clinical behavior on the populations they will serve.

To promote further understanding of this chapter's cultural considerations of the formation of the therapeutic relationship when working with clients from underrepresented clients, we will present three case studies that illustrate the way counselors and counselors' trainees today are navigating the therapeutic relationship process. These counselors and clients are a compilation of the therapeutic encounters that all three of the authors have supervised or addressed while teaching or providing clinical consultation this past year. Informed consent was obtained, and limits to confidentiality instruction were provided to the participants before they engaged in therapy.

THE CASE OF LEE, JONATHAN, AND MAURICE

Richard, a White, LGBTQ+-identifying, cisgender man with pronouns of they, them, and theirs works with Black and African American individuals in a confinement setting that mandates group counseling. They have been working in the confinement setting for 15 years and have facilitated several counseling groups. One group includes three individuals who identify as Black and African American, range in age from 18–25, and come from varied regions of the United States. The group has varying ethnicities, socioeconomic statuses, educational backgrounds, and familial circumstances. Richard has been facilitating this group for several months and recalls that today's session is their eighth session together. They facilitate a session on strategies for healthy interpersonal dynamics and decision-making. Richard discusses the fact that choices are based upon an individual's decision-making and that unhealthy choices are symptomatic of a person's irrational behavior. They note further that anyone can make a healthy choice when interacting with those around them and encourage the group to be more conscious of their decision-making when interacting with people in society, while reminding them they do not want to return to the confinement setting.

Lee, a group member, is a 22-year-old Black, heterosexual, and cisgender man, who was a college athlete involved in a minor team circumstance. He notes that choices are not something he has when interacting cross-culturally and indicates that he feels afraid to say more, for fear that his sentence will be extended, because he is supposed to be released soon. His peers were able to afford legal representation without repercussions, while he could not because of his socioeconomic and generational status as a first-generation college student and full scholarship recipient.

Lee mentions his reason for being in the setting and explains that he never felt that he could truly express himself as a college athlete. He describes experiencing pressure to perform while smiling and being unable to express anger during interactions with his non-Black teammates. Lee states further that if he demonstrated emotions other than happiness, his non-Black teammates would not be emotionally present after intense tennis matches. He notes also that he learned to agree with his non-Black teammates because he experienced greater tension if he did not go along with their requirements, which contrasted greatly with his upbringing with his two parents while at home. The other two group members, Johnathan and Maurice, agreed and mentioned a similar feeling of discomfort with the restriction of not being able to express their emotions fully with their peers and colleagues in varied settings (e.g., private schools and corporate organizations).

Case Analysis

A reality in working in an agency setting or other public institutions is counseling clients whom the court has ordered to undergo individual or group counseling. This is an important consideration, given the power of the court (based upon the counselor's evaluation), to incarcerate individuals. Black and African American men are severely overrepresented in the penal system (Gramlich, 2021), and it is highly likely that Black Americans in mandated group counseling will have a White facilitator. Lee's disclosures primarily bolster the intersecting variation in his cultural background and the way his Black identity influences his decisions (Collins & Bilge, 2016; Crenshaw, 1989). His disclosures also acknowledge the disparity in his socioeconomic status compared to that of his non-Black peers when considering his legal status.

To provide greater cultural sensitivity while facilitating group counseling for Black American individuals, Richard must participate in introspection and reflexivity to understand their own privileged and minoritized identities in relation to race, ethnicity, sexual orientation, gender, gender expression, gender identity, socioeconomic status, and region, among many other cultural elements (Ratts et al., 2016). After continued introspection, Richard must remain curious, sensitive, and open to the Black and African American group members' varied experiences without overidentifying with their minoritized status or assuming population omniscience to invalidate Black clients' experiences (Frye, 2014). Specifically, Richard must combat the assumption of knowing the way it feels to be a Black person because of their minoritized proximity or assuming full awareness of the individual because he recalls literature about the individual's population without verifying whether the literature is consistent with the Black individual (Crenshaw, 1989).

Further, Richard must integrate an understanding of varying circumstances (e.g., immigration, individual, organizational, and structural discrimination) that limit the choices for Black individuals in the United States and engage in further introspection about the way their proximity may differ, depending on their own privileged and minoritized identities (McIntosh, 2014; Ngai, 2014; U.S. Commission of Civil Rights, 2014). Richard's adherence to these recommendations would make it less likely that microaggressive behavior would be perpetuated when working with Black and African American individuals (Sue, 2008).

CASE STUDY OF JOSHUA

Rebecca, a White, cisgender woman, finds herself in need of a new clinical site to complete her clinical hours for licensure. The clinical site where she is currently is situated in the upper-class area of the city, where many of her clients are wealthy and private insurance holders. Because Rebecca grew up in a similar area, she expressed how simple it is to work with clients at this site. Much of Rebecca's clinical experience in working with adults is in individual therapy and treatment planning. A month ago, Rebecca learned that her current site would be making cutbacks and would no longer employ clinicians who are not licensed fully. Thus, Rebecca began to search frantically for a new site to complete the remainder of her clinical hours.

She secured a new position at an inner-city community mental health agency, whose client population is primarily low income. The agency largely serves youth whom the local school district refers who may be experiencing homelessness, substance use, and behavior issue problems. Rebecca and her supervisor met to discuss the caseload and the way Rebecca could successfully complete her clinical hours. During the meeting, Rebecca indicated that she is excited to work with a different age group (12–18) and does not anticipate any issues in providing individualized therapy services. Rebecca stated that it had always been easy for her to establish a therapeutic relationship with previous clients because of their similar backgrounds and identities.

Joshua is an 18-year-old, cisgender, Black male with visual impairments, who is currently a senior in the local inner-city school and is struggling to decide what to do after he graduates in 6 months. Joshua is a Beta Club and Spelling Club member, who serves as a student manager of the basketball team. Joshua is the oldest of his three siblings, the youngest of whom is six years old and resides at home with his mother. Joshua's mother works two jobs and often cannot attend any of Joshua's after-school activities. While she works, the neighbor usually provides childcare services for the younger siblings. Joshua has not told Rebecca that the neighbor relocated and can no longer watch his siblings while his mother is at work. Joshua also has not shared that his mother lost one of her jobs and is struggling to make ends meet; therefore, Joshua has a part-time night shift job. Joshua also does not indicate that he must ensure now that his siblings get home and that they do their homework and eat before his mother gets home from work.

Over the last month, Joshua's behaviors in school have changed, resulting in his referral from the school to the mental health agency. Joshua's behaviors were "aggressive, violent, lacked self-control, and impulsive." During the intake, Rebecca did learn that Joshua has been staying out late, missing curfew, arriving at school late, and leaving early. Joshua disclosed that he does not understand why people who are not from his community come into his community to help Black people. Joshua said that he does not trust people who do not look like him. He said that he does not know Rebecca, and Rebecca does not know him or the things he deals with daily. Rebecca believes the changes are due to the client being suspected of engaging in gang activity and substance use.

After months of feeling like the sessions needed to be progressing, Rebecca and her supervisor met to discuss the client. Rebecca revealed that Joshua is always at least 10 minutes late to a session, and when he attends sessions, he appears to be distracted and mumbles whenever he responds to a question. Rebecca has attempted to address the behaviors and experiences that are disrupting his life, but Joshua responds with, "I am fine" or "You would not understand." Rebecca is frustrated and becomes tearful because she feels Joshua is a difficult client. After Joshua leaves their last session early, Rebecca feels she cannot get him to change his behaviors. Rebecca expressed that it is usually easy to establish a relationship with clients, and she is using the rapport-building skills she used with previous clients at her previous site.

Case Analysis

The issues related to White therapists treating Black clients are not new and are complicated because African Americans experience inequities on all levels. Historically, African Americans experience economic, political, educational, and social oppression by Whites (Frazier, 1965; Jones & Seagull, 1977; Kardiner & Ovesey, 1951). In the case of Rebecca and Joshua, there is a disconnect between the two. Rebecca struggles to recognize the external and internal factors that cause disturbances in Joshua's life. Rebecca's inexperience working with the age group and with inner-city youth suggests that she needs cultural awareness. There is baseline information that Rebecca must obtain to begin understanding the external factors that may be affecting Joshua. Conditions in inner cities are often direct results of systems of oppression (economic, political, educational, and social). These systems may contribute to the distrust Joshua has of White individuals.

Rebecca has opportunities to self-reflect and practice cultural sensitivity. She appears to be unaware of the effect of her assumptions. Assuming Joshua's behavior changes are attributable to gang activity and substance use is a stereotype of inner-city youth and is culturally insensitive. Rebecca's statement about gang activity and substance use reveals biases, assumptions, and cultural insensitivity potentially rooted in racism. Rebecca must confront these thoughts to prevent microaggressive behaviors.

Rebecca also struggles to acknowledge the changes in Joshua's home, demonstrating a need for greater awareness. Because of the family's financial challenges and lack of resources, there is a chance that Joshua's role and responsibilities in the family have changed. The two have not explored Joshua's home life and the modifications that could contribute to his behavioral changes. Rebecca's previous experience with clients from upper-class families prevents her from recognizing the challenges many culturally diverse families experience. It is common for communities of color to rely on their family for childcare. In fact, birth order (being the eldest child) often indicates who will assist in the childcare of younger siblings.

Finally, Rebecca should consider the interpersonal and internal conflicts Joshua is experiencing. With his added responsibility and roles and a lack of resources in the community, it may be challenging for Joshua to engage in career discovery or career planning. Rebecca must consider the client's vocational goals, career aspirations, and transition from childhood to adulthood. It is not uncommon for transition-aged youth (16–24) to experience anxiety and demonstrate inappropriate behaviors because of the fear of the transition.

To establish the therapeutic relationship, Rebecca must increase her cultural awareness and reflexivity and eliminate her assumptions about the client. Rebecca must remain curious about African Americans' experiences, specifically those living in the inner city. In recognizing the cultural differences, Rebecca must work to achieve a basic understanding of the client's community, challenges, and resources (even if limited) to begin to forge a relationship.

THE CASE OF RANDY AND CATHY JAMES

Randy and Cathy James were referred to counseling by their church outreach coordinator, who noticed the couple arguing on several occasions in the church parking lot. The couple has been anxious about finding affordable housing, so they moved in with friends who had children the same age as their two children, Shawn (age 9) and Quinn (age 5). During the first session in their telehealth appointment, the couple and their children were huddled up in front of the camera on the cell phone in the basement of their friend's house. When she logged on, the couple told the counselor they were using a friend's cell phone while the couple's phone was out of service until the following week (when they would pay the bill). The counseling intern, Carol, a White, heterosexual, 48-year-old woman, became concerned about confidentiality immediately and told the couple that in future sessions, they would have to use their own phone.

Carol noticed in the background that snow was coming through a hole in a window. She remembered (from review of the intake form) then that the couple lived in a "less than desirable" neighborhood in the city. She asked Cathy whether she and the children feel safe in the house. Randy answered quickly, "Of course they're safe, they're with me." Still feeling concerned, the intern asked the couple what brought them to counseling. While listening to them, she texted her supervisor and warned him that she had a "potentially hostile situation" and did not feel safe with the family.

Although the couple shared their housing situation with the counselor, they also indicated concerns that the school was not working with their 9-year-old, whom they described as having special needs. Carol advised the couple that they should prioritize their concerns and choose the one that is the most pressing for them at this time. However, Cathy responded that "all of them are important—that's why we're here." At that point, Cathy told Carol, "Hold up," and she turned and told her 5-year-old, who had walked away from the phone camera, "Get back over here until I tell you to move, this session is important for our family." Carol interrupted nervously, "I am glad to hear that you think counseling will be beneficial for you as a family. I do as well." Before Carol concluded the session, she administered the ACE survey to see whether Cathy or Randy had experienced childhood trauma, as she was concerned that the children might be abused. Although the couple agreed to schedule a counseling session for the following week, they never returned. Carol thought she handled the session bravely and assumed the couple did not come back because they could not afford it. She was also relieved that she did not have to face them again.

Case Analysis

Unfortunately, this case study reflects the lived experience of many African American families who interact with mental health professionals. It also illustrates the missed opportunity on the part of the counselor–trainee and the lack of corrective action that the clinical supervisor should have taken.

It is important to acknowledge that the COVID-19 pandemic has exposed further the vulnerabilities of many underrepresented populations as well the multicultural shortcomings in counselor preparation programs. Ethical issues, such as the right to privacy and being free from judgment of your personal safe space, have created additional inequities and disparities for clients and families, who were struggling already before the pandemic. Often, counselor–client relationships were formed by clients in locations such as a closet in the home, a car, at a park bench, or anywhere else the client felt sufficiently safe to talk.

The therapeutic relationship between the counselor and the family could have been established properly if Carol had recognized and appreciated the family's determination to address their problems, despite all that life had presented them in the past weeks. Acknowledging each family member individually while affirming the parents' role would have conveyed the counselor's positive regard to the family and demonstrated her competence concerning child rearing in African American families. Additionally, Carol's perception of Randy informed the way she responded to him. African American fathers are the most misunderstood members of African American families. Both scholarly and popular discourses have consistently depicted African American fathers as unwilling to provide or take responsibility for their families and as potentially violent (Adkison-Johnson, 2021; Hamer, 2001; Johnson, 2016). As in many instances discussed in this chapter, a counselor determined Randy was a threat, and she used a form of therapeutic violence to silence him. To be clear, whenever a counselor is in real danger, they should ask for help. However, in this case study, the counselor was not at risk of being harmed, and neither was Cathy nor their children. The anger Randy expressed was an appropriate response to being profiled and dehumanized.

Cathy's experience with this counselor was similar in nature. Society maintains many stereotypical images of and beliefs about African American mothers. Their depiction as feeble-minded, incompetent, lazy, reckless, and in need of supervision while attending to their children is embedded in many Americans' minds. In fact, many African American parents are monitored by child welfare professionals and officers of the court, who often subscribe to the automatic assumption that "parenting while Black" means children are at risk of harm (Roberts, 2022; Adkison-Johnson et al., 2016).

It is equally important to assume that like all competent parents, African American mothers and fathers are trying their best to rear their children properly. This affirming perspective can facilitate an atmosphere of trust and respect for them that encourages them to engage in the counseling process. It is unfortunate that the counselor did not discuss some of the concerns the couple raised. She would have realized that the issue with respect to the couple's son receiving services in school was related to the fact that the school psychologists had identified him as gifted. The parents used the term "special needs" to describe the services gifted children receive at the school, but they experienced resistance from the school staff.

In essence, the counselor needed to be open to allow the relationship to unfold. In that case, the parents would have eventually settled on one topic once they "assessed" that the counselor could address their presenting situation.

CHAPTER SUMMARY

This chapter examined the importance of building a therapeutic relationship grounded in the reality that the client and counselor live in an increasingly diverse society. Infusing multicultural content into a counseling techniques, practicum, or internship course is merely a beginning step in preparing students to establish culturally responsive therapeutic relationships with their clients—there is need for greater and more intentional effort to embody a lifelong commitment. According to the 2016 AMCD Multicultural Counseling Competencies, acquiring multicultural awareness, knowledge, skills, and action is not a static process but requires counselors, counselor–educators, and clinical supervisors to engage in a lifelong process of experiential and scholarly learning. However, experiential and scholarly learning with direct, real-life counseling experiences with clients from minoritized populations are required to further promote genuine application. Without this direct exposure, theoretical assumptions regarding the counselor's self-awareness, knowledge, and skills and the client's expectations regarding the counseling relationship are devoid of real meaning, with a detrimental disconnect that might continue to perpetuate an inequitable environment. Thus, the therapeutic relationship is an ongoing empathic relationship among the counselor and client. To develop empathy while working with African American clients, counselors must remain sensitive, curious, and open to being challenged, due to working with clients who may not have had the opportunity to have their needs met in society but rightfully deserve the affirming experience of being heard in their sessions.

CHAPTER REFLECTION AND DISCUSSION QUESTIONS

1. With consideration of the Multicultural and Social Justice Counseling Competencies (MSJCC) Conceptual Framework, which quadrant(s) would each of the counselor or therapist's client relationships relate to, and why?
2. What identities outlined in the case vignettes might need more cultural sensitivity when interacting, and why?
3. Rebecca is struggling to build a therapeutic relationship with Joshua. Considering the MSJCC's developmental domain of counselor's self-awareness, what steps can Rebecca take to help the client feel safe in the therapeutic environment?
4. How do historical and cultural context impact building the therapeutic relationship with clients from minoritized populations?
5. What might Richard need to consider when interacting with Lee, Jonathan, and Maurice together versus individually?

REFERENCES

Abrams, L. S., & Moio, J. A. (2009). Critical race theory and the cultural competence dilemma in social work. *Journal of Social Work Education, 45*(2), 245–261. https://doi.org/10.5175/JSWE.2009.200700109

Adame, J. L., Lo, C. C., & Cheng, T. C. (2022). Ethnicity and self-reported depression among Hispanic immigrants in the U.S. *Community mental health journal, 58*(1), 121–135. https://doi.org/10.1007/s10597-021-00801-0

Adkison-Johnson, C., & Johnson, P. (2019). Counseling people of the African Diaspora in the United States. In C. Lee (Ed.), *Multicultural issues in counseling: New approaches to diversity* (pp. 47–60). The American Counseling Association.

Allen-Meares, P., & Burman. S. (1999). Cross-cultural therapeutic relationships: entering the world of African Americans. *Journal of Social Work Practice, 13*(1), 49–57.

Arredondo, P. (1999). Multicultural counseling competencies as tools to address oppression and racism. *Journal of Counseling & Development, 77*(1), 102–108. https://doi.org/10.1002/j.1556-6676.1999.tb02427.x

Arredondo, P., Toporek, R., Brown, S. P., Jones, J., Locke, D. C., Sanchez, J., & Stadler, H. (1996). Operationalization of the multicultural counseling competencies. *Journal of Multicultural Counseling and Development, 24*(1), 42–78. https://doi.org/10.1002/j.2161-1912.1996.tb00288.x

Bell Jr., D. A. (1970). Black students in White law schools: The ordeal and the opportunity. *University of Toledo Law Review, 2*, 539.

Bell, D. A. (1973). Racism in American courts: Cause for Black disruption or despair? *California Law Review, 61*(1), 165–203. https://doi.org/10.2307/3479879

Bell, D. A. (1976). Serving two masters: Integration ideals and client interests in school desegregation litigation. *The Yale Law Journal, 85*(4), 470–516. https://doi.org/10.2307/795339

Bell, D. A. (1980). *Brown v. Board of Education* and the interest-convergence dilemma. *Harvard Law Review, 93*(3), 518–533. https://doi.org/10.2307/1340546

Bell, D. A. (1980). *Race, racism, and American law*. Little, Brown and Company.

Bell, D. A. (1995). Who's afraid of critical race theory? *University of Illinois Law Review, 4*, 893–910.

Bradley, C., & Fiorini, J. (1999). Evaluation of counseling practicum: National study of programs accredited by CACREP. *Counselor Education and Supervision, 39*(2), 110–119. https://doi.org/10.1002/j.1556-6978.1999.tb01222.x

Branco, S., & Jones, C. T. (2021). Supporting Black, Indigenous, and People of Color counselors: Considerations for counselor skills training and practice. *Journal of Mental Health Counseling, 43*(4), 281–300. https://doi.org/10.17744/mehc.43.4.01

Carter, R. T., & Pieterse, A. L. (2020). *Measuring the effects of racism*. Columbia University Press.

Carkhuff, R. (1969). *Helping and human relations*. Holt.

Chang, D. F., & Berk, A. (2009). Making cross-racial therapy work: A phenomenological study of clients' experiences of cross-racial therapy. *Journal of Counseling Psychology, 56*(4), 521–536.

Chang, D. F., & Yoon, P. (2011). Ethnic minority clients' perceptions of the significance of race in cross-racial therapy relationships. *Psychotherapy Research, 21*(5), 567–582. https://doi.org/10.1080/10503307.2011.592549

Cokley, K. (2021). Black psychology's relationship with critical race theory. *Psychology Today*. https://www.psychologytoday.com/us/blog/black-psychology-matters/202109/black-psychology-s-relationship-critical-race-theory

Collins, P. H., & Bilge, S. (2016). *Intersectionality*. Polity Press.

Constantine, M. (2007). Racial microaggressions against African American clients in cross-racial counseling relationships. *Journal of Counseling Psychology, 54*(1), 1–16. https://doi.org/10.1037/0022-0167.54.1.1

Council for Accreditation of Counseling & Related Educational Programs. (2016). *CACREP standards*. http://www.cacrep.org.

Council for Accreditation of Counseling and Related Educational Programs. (2022). *CACREP vital statistics 2019: Results from a national survey of accredited programs*.

Crenshaw, K. (1989). Demarginalizing the intersection of race and sex: A Black feminist critique of antidiscrimination doctrine, feminist theory and antiracist politics. *University of Chicago Legal Forum*, 139–167.

Day-Vines, N. L., Wood, S. M., Grothaus, T., Craigen, L., Holman, A., Dotson-Blake, K., & Douglass, M. J. (2007). Broaching the subjects of race, ethnicity, and culture during the counseling process.

Journal of Counseling & Development, 85(4), 401–409. https://doi.org/10.1002/j.1556-6678.2007.tb00608.x

Day-Vines, N. L., Booker Ammah, B., Steen, S., & Arnold, K. M. (2018). Getting comfortable with discomfort: Preparing counselor trainees to broach racial, ethnic, and cultural factors with clients during counseling. *International Journal for the Advancement of Counselling, 40*, 89–104.

DeAngelis, T. (2019). Better relationships with patients lead to better outcomes. *Monitor on Psychology, 50*(10). https://www.apa.org/monitor/2019/11/ce-corner-relationships

Devore, W., & Schlesinger, E. G. (1981). *Ethnic-sensitive social work practice.* Allen & Bacon.

Drustrup. (2020). White therapists addressing racism in psychotherapy: An ethical and clinical model for practice. *Ethics & Behavior, 30*(3), 181–196. https://doi.org/10.1080/10508422.2019.1588732

Eghaneyan, B. H., & Murphy, E. R. (2019). Mental health help-seeking experiences of Hispanic women in the United States: Results from a qualitative interpretive meta-synthesis. *Social Work in Public Health, 34*(6), 505–518. https://doi.org/10.1080/19371918.2019.1629559

Franklin, A. J. (1971). To be young, gifted and Black with inappropriate professional training: A critique of counseling programs. *The Counseling Psychologist, 2*(4), 107–112. https://doi-org.libproxy.library.wmich.edu/10.1177/001100007100200411

Fripp, J. A., & Adams, J. J. (2022). Enhancing the therapeutic alliance with African American clients: Using a critical race theoretical approach to navigate conversations about racism. *Journal of Multicultural Counseling and Development, 50*(3), 108–117. https://doi.org/10.1002/jmcd.12251

Frye, M. (2014). Oppression. In P. S. Rothenberg & K. S. Mayhew (Eds.), *Race, class and gender in the United States: An integrated study* (9th ed., pp. 149–152). Worth. (Original work published 1983)

Goode-Cross, D. T., & Grim, K. A. (2016). "An unspoken level of comfort": Black therapists' experiences working with Black clients. *Journal of Black Psychology, 42*(1), 29–53. https://doi-org.libproxy.library.wmich.edu/10.1177/0095798414552103

Gramlich, J. (2021, August 18). *America's incarceration rate falls to lowest level since 1995.* Pew Research Center. https://www.pewresearch.org/fact-tank/2021/08/16/americas-incarceration-rate-lowest-since-1995/

Gunnings, T. S. (1971). Preparing the new counselor. *The Counseling Psychologist, 2*(4), 100–101. https://doi-org.libproxy.library.wmich.edu/10.1177/001100007100200408

Haase, R. F., DiMattia, D. J., & Guttman, M. A. (1972). Training of support personnel in three human relation skills: A systematic one-year follow-up. *Counselor Education and Supervision, 11*, 194–199.

Hamer, J. F. (2001). *What it means to be Daddy: Fatherhood for Black men living away from their children.* Columbia University Press.

Hardy, K. V. (2022). *The enduring invisible and ubiquitous centrality of whiteness.* Norton Professional Company.

Hardy, K. V., & Bobes, T. (2016). *Culturally sensitive supervision and training: Diverse perspectives and practical applications.* Routledge.

Haskins, N., & Singh, A. (2015). Critical race theory and counselor education pedagogy: Creating equitable training. *Counselor Education and Supervision, 54*(4), 288–301. https://doi.org/10.1002/ceas.12027

Height, T., Ngadjui, O. T., Hoover, F.-A., & Dillon, J. A. (2022). The 2020 social and environmental apocalypse: Reimagining Black America. *American Studies, 60*(3/4). https://journals.ku.edu/amsj/article/view/16385

Helms, J. E. (2017). The challenge of making Whiteness visible: Reactions to four Whiteness articles. *The Counseling Psychologist, 45*(5), 717–726. https://doi.org/10.1177/0011000017718943

Hill, C. E., Knox, S., & Pinto-Coelho, K. G. (2018). Therapist self-disclosure and immediacy: A qualitative meta-analysis. *Psychotherapy, 55*(4), 445–460. https://doi.org/10.1037/pst0000182

Holcomb-McCoy, C. (2022). *Antiracist counseling in the schools and communities.* American Counseling Association.

Ivey, A. E. (1994). *Intentional interviewing and counseling: Facilitating client development in a multicultural society.* Brooks/Cole.

Jemal, A., Gunn, A., & Inyang, C. (2020). Transforming responses: Exploring the treatment of substance-using African American women. *Journal of Ethnicity in Substance Abuse, 19*(4), 659–687. https://doi.org/10.1080/15332640.2019.1579141

Locke, D. C. (1990). A not so provincial view of multicultural counseling. *Counselor Education and Supervision, 30*, 18–25.

Maharaj, A., Bhatt, N. V., & Gentile, J. P. (2021). Bringing it in the room: Addressing the impact of racism on the therapeutic alliance. *Innovations in Clinical Neuroscience, 18*(7–9), 39–43.

Mata-Greve, F., Torres, L., & Cardemel, S. (2020). Ethnic discrimination, sexism, and depression among Latinx women: The roles of anxiety sensitivity and expressive suppression. *Journal of Latinx Psychology, 8*(4), 317–331. https://doi.org/10.1037/lat0000154

McIntosh, P. (2014). White privilege: Unpacking the invisible knapsack. In P. S. Rothenberg & K. S. Mayhew (Eds.), *Race, class and gender in the United States: An integrated study* (9th ed., pp. 175–179). Worth. (Original work published 1988)

Ngai, M. (2014). Impossible subjects: Illegal aliens and the making of America. In P. S. Rothenberg & K. S. Mayhew (Eds.), *Race, class and gender in the United States: An integrated study* (9th ed., pp. 224–234). Worth. (Original work published 2004)

Parham, T. A., Ajamu, A., & White, J. L. (2011). *The psychology of Blacks: Centering our perspectives in the African consciousness.* Routledge.

Ratts, M. J., Singh, A. A., Nassar-McMillan, S., Butler, S. K., & McCullough, J. R. (2016). Multicultural and social justice counseling competencies: Guidelines for the counseling profession. *Journal of Multicultural Counseling and Development, 44*(1), 28–48. https://doi.org/10.1002/jmcd.12035

Ridley, C. R., Kelly, S. M., & Mollen, D. (2011). Microskills training: Evolution, reexamination, and call for reform. *Counseling Psychologist, 39*(06), 800–824.

Roberts, D. (2022). *Torn apart: How the child welfare system destroys Black families and how abolition can build a safer world.* Basic Books.

Roffers, T., Cooper, B., & Sultanoff, S. M. (1988). Can counselor trainees apply their skills in actual client interviews? *Journal of Counseling & Development, 66*, 385–388.

Rogers, C. (1957). The necessary and sufficient conditions of therapeutic personality change. *Journal of Consulting Psychology, 21*(2), 95–103. https://doi.org/10.1037/h0045357

Snyder, C. M. A., & Anderson, S. A. (2009). An examination of mandated versus voluntary referral as a determinant of clinical outcome. *Journal of Marital and Family Therapy, 35*(3), 278–292. https://doi.org/10.1111/j.1752-0606.2009.00118.x

Sue, D. W., Nadal, K. L., Capodilupo, C. M., Lin, A. I., Torino, G. C., & Rivera, D. P. (2008). Racial microaggressions against Black Americans: Implications for counseling. *Journal of Counseling & Development, 86*(3), 330–338. https://doi.org/10.1002/j.1556-6678.2008.tb00517.x

Sue, D. W., & Sue, D. (2008). *Counseling the culturally diverse: Theory and practice* (5th ed.). John Wiley & Sons.

Tervalon, M., & Murray-Garcia, J. (1998). Cultural humility versus cultural competence: A critical distinction in defining physician training outcomes in multicultural education. *Journal of Health Care for the Poor and Underserved, 9*(2), 117. https://doi.org/10.1353/hpu.2010.0233

United States Commission on Civil Rights. (2014). The problem: Discrimination. In P. S. Rothenberg & K. S. Mayhew (Eds.), *Race, class and gender in the United States: An integrated study* (9th ed., pp. 263–273). Worth. (Original work published 1981)

Ward, E. C. (2005). Keeping it real: A grounded theory study of African American clients engaging in counseling at a community mental health agency. *Journal of Counseling Psychology, 52*(4), 471–481. https://doi.org/10.1037/0022-0167.52.4.471

White, J. L., & Parham, T. A. (1990). *The psychology of Blacks*. Prentice Hall.

Williams, J., Lugo, R. G., & Firth, A. M. (2022). Exploring the therapeutic alliance and race from sports psychologists' and athletes' lived experiences: A pilot study. *Heliyon, 8*(1), e08736–e08736. https://doi.org/10.1016/j.heliyon.2022.e08736

Yeo, E., & Torres-Harding, S. R. (2021). Rupture resolution strategies and the effect of rupture on the working alliance after racial microaggressions in therapy. *Psychotherapy, 58*(4), 460–471. https://doi.org/10.1037/pst0000372

Zhu, P., Isawi, D. T., & Luke, M. M. (2022). A discourse analysis of cultural humility within counseling dyads. *Journal of Counseling & Development*, 1–13. https://doi.org/10.1002/jcad.12457

Professional Roles

Dr. Kristy Christopher-Holloway, Dr. A'tasha M. Christian, and Erin Coleman

LEARNING OBJECTIVES

1. Discuss competencies in application to professional roles.
2. Examine the counselor's role as advocate.
3. Discuss the roles of group, marriage and family, substance abuse, rehabilitation and career counselors from an intersectional approach.
4. Provide clinical vignettes for discussion.

LEARNING OUTCOMES

1. Students will be able to evaluate concepts of race, culture, identity, and diversity with regard to Indigenous education.
2. Students will be able to apply the principles and practices of culturally sensitive treatment approaches to the stated professional identities.
3. Students will be able to participate in conceptualization exercises to examine cultural considerations of clients.

Chapter Overview

This chapter focuses on the various professional roles of counselors. The authors discuss counseling at various levels, including group counseling, addiction counseling, rehabilitation counseling, career counseling, and marriage and family counseling. The authors also provide a case study and an opportunity for the reader to reflect on the content learned.

The Role of the Group Counselor

Group counseling is a form of psychotherapy in which a trained mental health counselor leads a group of individuals who share similar concerns or issues. By using various discussions, activities, and exercises, mental health professionals help group participants address their psychological, emotional, and interpersonal concerns. The professional role of a group counselor, also referred to as a "group therapist" or "group facilitator," is to provide support, guidance, and therapeutic intervention to a group of individuals who are facing similar issues or challenges.

The counselor's role in group counseling is vital for creating a safe, supportive, nonjudgmental, and confidential environment for group members to explore their thoughts, feelings, and experiences. Similar to individual counseling, group counselors assess the needs and goals of potential group members, plan and structure the group sessions, and develop treatment plans tailored to each group member's goals, using group therapy as a means to achieve these goals.

In most groups, the group counselor often acts as the facilitator of the group, responsible for setting the tone of the sessions, maintaining order, and guiding discussions, while helping the group to remain focused on its goals and objectives. Effective group counselors establish a space where group members can openly express themselves, share their experiences, and engage in meaningful discussions. Group counselors are supportive of the group taking on its own style, yet they also help establish ground rules and guidelines for the group, to ensure everyone's opinions are respected and the group functions smoothly.

Group counseling presents a unique opportunity for both the group counselor and group members to develop beyond individual counseling. Often serving as an adjunct to individual treatment, group counseling positions the member for greater insight into various treatment concerns and learning from shared experiences. Because a group consists of several people, group leadership and dynamics will take on a macro-culture of various subcultures. To informatively meet the respective needs of each member, group counselors also attend to not only the development of each member but also to the cultural aspects of the group and its members.

Group Leadership

The Association for Specialists in Group Work (2021) encourages group counselors to attend to the welfare of individual group members as well as the group as a whole. Group counselors offer emotional support to group members as they navigate their challenges. They also empower participants to take an active role in their own healing and personal growth. Focusing on each individual member and the group can, at times, seem daunting; however, the group counselor can be mindful of the individual and collective membership by being aware of their own cultural identity, their leadership style in various group settings, and to give attention to the cultural dynamics present throughout the group. For example, being aware of sociocultural factors allows the group counselor to not only assist group members in gaining insight, but it also allows leaders to address the various multilayered dimensions that contribute to the group member's concern and how to navigate those concerns.

Group Dynamics

Group counselors monitor group dynamics and interactions to identify recurring themes, patterns, and issues within the group. They also offer insights and feedback to help members gain a better understanding of their own and others' experiences. Group counselors are also aware of the need to adjust the group therapy approach and interventions as needed to maximize the effectiveness of the group process goals. Depending on the group topic, group membership may or may not present as homogeneous. Furthermore, the group counselor may represent various cultural identities opposite from the group members. The dynamics of a group may be directly impacted by to the varying identities present. Group counselors must be aware of how culture, in the simplest terms, makes us who we are individually and collectively. Because of this, it is expected for many intersections to be represented in any given group and how this may impact group outcomes. Similar to the individual counseling relationship, group counselors are aware that marginalization and privilege also exists within groups by individual members as well as the leader.

Diversity in Group

Diversity in group counseling is an important aspect of providing effective and culturally competent mental health care. Group counselors are aware of the diversity in group settings and actively implement their skills to address any challenges that may arise. Counselors must be culturally competent and sensitive to the diverse backgrounds, values, and belief systems of group members. This includes, but is not limited to, understanding various cultural norms, communication styles, and potential biases that may affect the group dynamics. Not only do group counselors adapt their leadership style in culturally diverse groups, but they must also be aware of the challenges of culturally diverse groups, the goals of multicultural groups, how to assess cultural diversity in a group, and how to work with different cultural populations in groups. The Multicultural and Social Justice Counseling Competencies (MSJCC) provides counselors with a multilevel framework to help group counselors meet the diverse needs of group members. Applying the MSJCC developmental domains of (a) counselor self-awareness, (b) client worldview, (c) the counseling relationship, and (d) counseling and advocacy interventions, along with the group leader's skills and abilities, allows the group leader to pay careful attention to the various intersections and dynamics that are present in the group that influence the stages of the group (forming, storming, norming, performing, and closing).

The Role of the Addictions Counselor

Culture is a fundamental component of addictions treatment because the people's experiences are intrinsically linked to their specific cultural heritage and influence their clinical experience. The setting for treatment, identification of social supports, and accessibility to care are all affected by a client's culture. Consequently, counselors must understand culture as a broad concept, including an individual's shared beliefs, regardless of how they relate to the counselor's own unique set of beliefs.

The 2019 National Survey on Drug Use and Health provides addiction statistics for various cultural demographics (Substance Abuse and Mental Health Services Administration [SAMHSA], 2020). While these demographics are relevant, it is paramount that emerging counselors remain mindful that addiction is a disease that is no respecter of culture, race, religion, age or socioeconomic status; addiction can impact anyone at any moment. Data from the 2019 survey indicates as many as 10.2% of American Indian and Alaskan Natives meet the diagnostic criteria for a substance use disorder. Black Americans follow this demographic at 7.6%. Approximately 5% of Asians/Native Hawaiians and other Pacific islanders and Hispanics, Latinos, and other groups of Spanish-speaking origin live with a substance use disorder (SAMHSA, 2020).

For counselors to offer culturally aware treatment, we must first examine the professional lens of the counselor. We begin with the identification of bias. Bias is inevitable, but how we manage that bias is fundamental to the counseling relationship. In many counseling classrooms, there is an eternal debate regarding whether addiction is a disorder or a disease. One vital rule of thumb for emerging counselors, and counselor educators as well, is to allow the client and or the classroom to flesh out their thoughts about this debate. Interjecting too quickly might result in heightened bias, which can be damaging.

The role of the addictions counselor is often multifaceted. Some counselors are licensed clinical mental health practitioners who have a focus on addiction, while other clinical mental health counselors are dually licensed in both clinical mental health and addictions treatment. This training influences the lens of the counselor and guides how the counselor will operate. Depending on the clinical setting, the counselor may address the addiction secondary to the mental health diagnosis. When discussing professional roles, we must also examine the identity of the office settings, not just the professional identity of the counselor. For example, it is important for staff to be aware of the client's first language and for the facility to provide, if necessary, an option for treatment services in that language. Agency directors should place heavy emphasis on hiring staff from culturally diverse communities to provide a basis for enhanced culturally sensitive treatment. Because heritage, background, beliefs, and traditions are varied across different demographics, treatment modalities should be tailored to reflect the client's individual, culturally influenced needs, values, and preferences. This will aid in ensuring a supportive environment for treatment. It is also vital for treatment facilities to consider how cultural awareness fits into specific aspects of treatment modalities. For example, traditional detoxification programs and other treatment models may not fit into some cultural belief systems. Some religious or spiritual communities may resist medication management, which will be important information for counselors to gather during the clinical assessment.

One consideration for culturally aware treatment for addictions is to use a village approach. While we often discuss collaborative care as an efficacious treatment strategy for addiction, we should be careful not to exclude this approach in discharge. Consider the following example: Using a village approach (common for many historically disenfranchised communities), the discharge plan for a client leaving an addictions program may include a cultural celebration and words from the elders or treatment team. Incorporating such an approach may serve to close part of the cultural gap, if it exists, between the counselor and the client.

The Role of the Rehabilitation Counselor

Clinical rehabilitation counselors offer comprehensive rehabilitation counseling services, such as vocational rehabilitation counseling for people with disabilities in a variety of practice settings, including public, private, research, hospital or clinical, and community-based settings. Clinical rehabilitation counselors operate with a unique skill set within the scope of clinical mental health counseling, as much of their work, fundamentally, is designed to aid clients with improving their overall quality of life, which is often adversely impacted by environmental and societal barriers. The clinical rehabilitation counselor may often serve as the liaison for all stakeholders in a person's system of care. Because of this, their lens must be one of advocacy and understanding the intersections of one's life.

It is imperative that rehabilitation counselors, just like clinical mental health counselors, develop a broader knowledge base and skill set to work with a diverse clientele. A client's identification and sense of connectedness to their disability is often affected by another cultural identity, including socioeconomic status, gender, ethnicity, and sexual orientation. When there is an intersection of marginalized identities, the counselor must be able to conceptualize the individual through the lens of those intersections. Rehabilitation counselors should seek to understand the context of how disability is viewed within a client's culture. Treatment approaches must consider the multicultural considerations that exist to ensure that a client's lived experiences are given a voice in treatment planning.

The Role of the Career Counselor

Career counseling, while arguably a specialized approach, is a core competency that has a distinct set of theories and approaches. While it may be specialized, it is equally important for cultural consideration to be included in courses and, ultimately, practice. Because career counseling often includes the client's entire lifespan, such as breaking down varying life roles and understanding environmental stress and trauma, career counselors are tasked with ensuring that the career counseling experience is one of meaning and substance, which must begin with conceptualizing culture. For example, incorporating the Multicultural Social Justice Counseling Competencies (MSJCC) creates an opportunity for the career counselor to broach intersections, by using a highly supported and regarded model. Being able to contextualize how the client views the world from either a space of marginalization or privilege can aid with developing a therapeutic relationship between counselor and client.

There are some career counselors who consider taking this approach a step further and developing their own set of multicultural career counseling competencies. In her book, *Gaining Cultural Competence in Career Counseling,* Evans (2008) posits that culturally aware career counselors should select counseling techniques that not only address their clients' challenges but also includes their cultural backgrounds. While this is often assumed, it is not always used in practice. Career counseling has its own set of theories and interventions that may not always be inclusive of culture, so it is important that the career counselor infuses intersectionality throughout one's interventions. It is equally imperative that the role of the career counselor is one of a social justice advocate. Social justice is not limited to multicultural courses; it must be interwoven into one's practice. A career counselor should take effort in understanding how barriers, such as discrimination, racism, poverty and microaggressions, may impact the client's openness and could inhibit the client. The role of the culturally aware career counselor is to be mindful of discriminatory practices in the workforce that may affect the emotional well-being of the client and develop ways to give that client a voice.

The Role of a Marriage and Family Counselor

Marriage and family counseling typically involves two or more clients in a relational dynamic. The terms "marriage" and "family" include, but are not limited to, dating, married, or divorced couples as well as any combination of parents, children, and extended family members. To help understand the many dynamics at play in this form of relational counseling, marriage and family counselors often use a systems perspective to navigate the many influences each person brings to the relationship. A client's system, or their individual experience in the world, produces various interpretations of emotions, behaviors, and thoughts, based on these influences. Simultaneously, the clients' relationship comprises one collective system that houses the presenting problem. The marriage and family counselor highlights the contributions each client brings to the counseling process by examining the individual and collective experiences with the presenting problem.

In this role, the marriage and family counselor helps guide clients through relational issues, such as life transitions, role adjustments, communication breakdowns, intimacy struggles, and more. Often, these presenting problems indicate deeper mental or emotional dynamics within the system that clients need assistance uncovering. The counselor helps relational clients explore these dynamics and implement new ways of interacting that resolve the presenting problem. Therefore, the marriage and family counselor has three goals:

1. Evaluate the couple or family's relationship by listening to the client's feedback.
2. Synthesize the problem's function in the system.
3. Set the system up for change.

Counselors serve as a guide through this process, extracting themes and patterns that perpetuate the presenting problem's existence in the system. Additionally, marriage and family counselors help their clients construct new ways of thinking, feeling, and behaving with each other that create the new desired relationship.

As a part of their professional role, marriage and family counselors should always maintain a curious and unbiased stance. Clients will come to view and understand the presenting problem through the lens of their culture. As a result, counselors cannot help their clients restructure their relationships without being curious and unbiased about the multiple intersectionalities at play. This includes understanding the influences of things like gender roles, faith and spirituality, generational differences, education, and even social media. Marriage and family counselors curious about the impact of these influences widen their worldview to include that of the clients and increase their capacity to facilitate change in the system.

Culture in Marriage and Family Counseling

Culturally responsive marriage and family counselors seek to incorporate cultural interpretations and coping mechanisms into therapy outcomes. For example, an African American family may present in counseling with a parentified child struggling to regulate emotions. A culturally competent counselor should examine how the child's emotional outbursts are interpreted by both the child and the parent. Additionally, the counselor should explore how family, socioeconomic status, and religion have influenced this child being parentified and feeling crushed under the weight of assuming responsibility for their younger siblings. The counselor should consider the cultural rules regarding the parent–child hierarchy, which deems such emotional dysregulation as disrespect and, therefore, not tolerated in the household.

In the end, culture establishes guidelines for how people behave. Marriage and family counselors cannot adequately address a system without addressing the cultural influences that govern it. Attempting to do so would provide shallow fixes to complex problems instead of addressing their underlying causal patterns. When working with couples or families, a culturally competent counselor may encounter several cultural influences that offer competing rules and value systems. Marriage and family counselors guide their clients to finding better alternatives to addressing their problems while also celebrating the wisdom their cultural backgrounds bring. Culturally sensitive counselors work with couples and families to construct a relational culture that respects each client's identity and sets productive rules for the client system's peaceful coexistence.

CASE STUDY

Rena has been receiving pro bono individual counseling for 3 months to provide her with support for the grief of her recent pregnancy loss. Due to her inconsistent and unpredictable work schedule, it is difficult for Rena to consistently attend her sessions. For extra support, Rena's therapist recommended a virtual and open community grief and loss support group. At the first meeting, Rena had difficulty logging in to the virtual platform due to her limited internet access. Once logged in, Rena, a biracial widow, noticed that many of the group members were older than she is, in partnered relationships, had older children, and were navigating the loss of a parent. What multicultural factors must the group leader attend to? How can applying the MJSCC developmental domains assist the group leader in meeting Rena's treatment needs?

Case Discussion

In the case of Rena, several cultural factors are present that the group leader must attend to. First, the group leader should assess whether Rena wishes to remain in the group or be referred to a group specific to pregnancy loss. While this group focuses on loss, it is not homogenous and there are different losses experienced by the members. Rena may not be able to relate, and therefore have her needs met, to the parent loss experiences of most group members. Other important factors include Rena's partnered status in relation to the other group members as well as the parental status of many members. Again, Rena may be further bereaved as members discuss their partners and their grief and memories of their parents as grandparents and the impact of the loss on the group members' own children. Further, as a widow, Rena may further struggle with group belongingness and feeling cohesive with members.

Next, the group leader will need to attend to any deficits in accessing the group due to connectivity concerns. Rena has trouble connecting to a stable internet service, which may impact her ability to attend and engage in group meetings. The group leader will need to discuss other modes to access the group, such as dialing in, should the internet become a barrier to attendance. Finally, while the racial and ethnic identities of the other group leader and members is not mentioned, even if all participants share the same identity membership, the group leader cannot assume that they share the same life experiences. The group leader will still need to understand the importance of intersectionality while being aware of factors of privilege and marginalization and its impact on the group dynamic. The group leader must also be aware of how positionality impacts the members' experiences of grief and loss.

In this case, the counselor's self-awareness will aid the group leader in identifying how their worldview shapes their values, beliefs, and biases. This can assist the group leader in reducing risks of group member harm by unintentionally imparting their worldview on group members. Similarly, the group leader's self-reflection and insight into their worldview, values, beliefs, and biases contributes to their understanding how each group member's worldview shapes their individual values, beliefs, and biases. Having this knowledge assists the group leader in attending to the multicultural factors of the group members as well as the emerging culture of the group. Finally, with the group leader's knowledge and awareness of culture, intersectionality, worldview and experiences, values and beliefs, and privilege and marginalization, they can focus on social justice and advocacy actions in the counseling relationship and developing group interventions, activities, and assignments.

CASE STUDY

Esmerelda, the child of two El Salvadoran immigrants, was raised in Maryland. She is the youngest of five siblings, and due to her stellar academic performance, received a scholarship to a prestigious university. In high school, her school counselors often pushed her to pursue a career in business, a push that was echoed by her college advisors. Yet Esmerelda meets with you for career counseling as she prepares for the postgraduation workforce. To begin, she will need to move four states away from her family, a move which would be out of the family norm, although it would place her on the fast track for career advancement. Esmerelda's college advisors are puzzled at her hesitance—it is an opportunity that, to them, students should jump at, if given the chance. What is being overlooked, however, is Esmerelda's fear, not of success but of how she will be received and how this may potentially disconnect her from her family. Esmerelda is at a crossroads between her worldview and the worldviews of those whom she respects professionally.

Case Discussion

In the case of Esmerelda, the career counselor must acknowledge the internal dilemma she is facing. A life she has always known is in potential conflict with the life she is approaching. The career counselor should use a variety of career counseling interventions and theories, such as trait-factor theory, and other counseling approaches, such as narrative and existential theories. Consider the following:

1. What are Esmerelda's known intersectionalities? How do these intersections impact Esmerelda's worldview as it pertains to career goals?
2. How might your own worldview as a counselor impact your clinical approach?
3. What are some treatment goals you would consider presenting to Esmerelda for discussion?

CHAPTER SUMMARY

Counselors occupy various professional roles, including group counseling, addiction counseling, rehabilitation counseling, career counseling, and marriage and family counseling. Regardless of their role, effective mental health counselors are aware of their sociocultural factors that impact counseling and the counseling relationship. This aids counselors in applying relevant skills that are embedded in honoring the experiences of each client they work with.

As the diversity of Americans continues to grow, the related needs of many of its citizens are yet unmet. Our emerging practitioners will need to develop an understanding of the entire lifespan, incorporating varying life roles, cultural reference points, and racial and ethnic implications. It is attendance to and awareness of these varying personal constructs that inform appropriate and successful multicultural career counseling interventions.

CHAPTER REFLECTION AND DISCUSSION QUESTIONS

1. What professional role do I most align with? How do my worldview, values, beliefs, and biases influence my professional role alignment, and how can I apply the MSJCC in my professional role?
2. Am I aware of how my own socioeconomic status influences my lens on client accessibility?
3. Counselors can possess various professional roles, and they often work in a variety of settings, including mental health clinics, schools, community organizations, and private practices. In what ways can social justice and advocacy be implemented in each of these settings?
4. How can my intersectionality be pivotal in my professional role choice, and how can I increase my self-awareness in my given role?
5. How might my client's worldview and my worldview impact the counseling relationship, and what steps do I need to take to remain culturally humble?

ADDITIONAL RESOURCES

As there is a focus on applicability and practice in this text, in-text resources are often beneficial.

Experiential Activities for Teaching Multicultural Competence in Counseling (American Counseling Association, 2011).

American Counseling Association. (2011). Experiential Activities for Teaching Multicultural Competence in Counseling. Retrieved from Resources: ACA: https://imis.counseling.org/images/large/72904-FM.pdf

SAMHSA: Improving Cultural Competence Quick Guide for Clinicians (SAMHSA, 2016).

Substance Abuse and Mental Health Services Administration. (2016). SAMHSA: Improving Cultural Competence Quick Guide for Clinicians. Retrieved from Resources: SAMHSA: https://store.samhsa.gov/sites/default/files/sma16-4931.pdf

Minimum Competencies for Multicultural Career Counseling and Development (National Career Development Association, 2009).

National Career Development Association. (2009). Minimum competencies for multicultural career counseling and development. Author. https://www.ncda.org/aws/NCDA/asset_manager/get_file/26627?ver=50664

REFERENCES

Association for Specialists in Group Work. (2021). *Guiding principles for group work*. ASGW Professional Standards for Group Work. https://asgw.org/wp-content/uploads/2021/07/ASGW-Guiding-Principles-May-2021.pdf

Evans, K. (2008). *Gaining cultural competence in career counseling*. Lahask Press.

Ratts, M. J., Singh, A. A., Nassar-McMillan, S., Butler, S. K., & McCullough, J. R. (2016). Multicultural and social justice counseling competencies: Guidelines for the counseling profession. *Journal of Multicultural Counseling and Development, 44*(1), 28–48.

Substance Abuse and Mental Health Services Administration. (2020). *Key substance use and mental health indicators in the United States: Results from the 2019 National Survey on Drug Use and Health* (HHS Publication No. PEP20-07-01-001, NSDUH Series H-55).

The Use of Clinical Techniques/Culturally Relevant Approaches

Dr. Seneka Gainer, Dr. Aishwarya Joshi, and Dr. Amirah Nelson

LEARNING OBJECTIVES

1. Foster awareness of the cultural and social justice disparities in mental health care by highlighting real-world examples and case studies, helping readers recognize the importance of culturally relevant approaches to addressing these disparities.
2. Provide readers with a comprehensive understanding of culturally relevant approaches in clinical techniques, offering insights into the theoretical foundations, evidence-based practices, and historical context of multicultural mental health, equipping them with the knowledge needed for culturally sensitive care.
3. Develop practical skills by introducing culturally responsive assessment and intervention techniques, encouraging them to engage in self-reflective exercises, role-plays, and case analyses, enabling them to apply culturally relevant approaches effectively in clinical practice.
4. Inspire readers to take proactive steps in promoting social justice within their clinical work and beyond, encouraging them to advocate for equitable mental health policies, engage in community outreach, and collaborate with diverse populations to address systemic inequalities.

LEARNING OUTCOMES

1. Students will critically assess their own cultural biases and values, enhancing their counselor self-awareness to better recognize how their worldview influences their clinical practice.
2. Students will gain the ability to identify and respect diverse client worldviews, enabling them to create a more culturally sensitive and inclusive counseling environment.
3. Through case studies and practical exercises, students will demonstrate an understanding of how culturally relevant approaches can strengthen the counseling relationship, leading to more positive therapeutic outcomes.
4. Students will develop a toolkit of culturally appropriate counseling and advocacy interventions, empowering them to address the unique needs of clients from diverse backgrounds effectively.

As the United States becomes more diverse in terms of race, ethnicity, gender, identity, sexuality, and socioeconomic status, counselors must also evolve in the techniques and approaches used in therapeutic spaces. As this colorful mix takes shape, counselors need new ways to help people and learn how culture and identity affect someone's mental health and relationship with counseling. In this chapter, we are starting a journey. We will discuss techniques that respect different cultures and backgrounds and then share tips to improve these techniques with people who might not have had a voice before. Moreover, we will ask questions that prompt you to think deeply about how this fits into your idea of being a counselor. At the chapter's end is a toolbox filled with practical case studies. We will present real stories to show you how these techniques can be used. Even though this whole journey is like a complicated dance, the goal is simple: to increase cultural awareness. To do that, we use a unique lens called *multicultural competence*. It is like a pair of glasses that lets counselors see the world through the eyes of their clients.

DeAngelis (2015) describes multicultural competence as "the ability to understand, appreciate, and interact with people from cultures or belief systems different from one's own." The Multicultural and Social Justice Counseling Competencies (2016) also designate awareness, knowledge, skills, and action as key dimensions of multicultural competence. In other words, it means connecting with and appreciating people from all walks of life, even if they differ. However, there is a catch. If counselors only use their ideas and biases, their help might not work well or hurt someone. Consequently, clinical approaches rooted in one's biases yield ineffective and potentially damaging therapeutic services (Busaca, 2002; Ridley et al., 2000). Professional counselors must realize that their worldviews and experiences vary from their clients (Grant, 2006; Mares, 2022). It is like wearing different glasses that show them the world uniquely.

Imagine counselors having a unique tool—a mindful and culturally relevant approach. It is like paying extra close attention to things. And guess what? People who use this tool tend to be better at understanding different cultures. They build bridges between themselves and others, celebrate differences, and use their techniques with purpose.

Revolutionizing Culturally Oriented Techniques: A New Paradigm

The field of mental health is like an evolving story. Research indicates that the mental health profession, thus, needs a reconceptualization of culturally oriented techniques and an innovative approach to provide enhanced professional guidance (Ridley et al., 2021) to counselor trainees. Although the intentions of early pioneers and professional organizations are noteworthy, progress linked to the operationalization of counseling techniques has stalled (Mollen & Ridley, 2021). For example, for over 35 years, the counseling field has been increasingly observant of the significance of developing the therapeutic relationship between counselors and members of oppressed groups and diverse cultures (e.g., Bemak & Hanna, 1998; Hanna & Cardona, 2013; Robinson & Ginter, 1999; Sue, 1981; Sue & Sue, 2012; Ratts et al., 2016). Chiefly absent from the culturally oriented techniques literature is a discussion of actual techniques and approaches designed to decrease the impact of psychological oppression and the isolation often associated with being a member of a seemingly alienated group. A possible approach for developing such techniques might be by increasing the awareness of counselors through mindfulness and a subsequent understanding of the internal and external stressors that impact both counselor and client well-being. Think about it as a puzzle: Some pieces, like how to use these cultural ideas in real-life situations, need to be included. This chapter combines those pieces by identifying how to help people who might feel alone or oppressed.

Cultivating Mindfulness for Cultural Competence: Building Connections

Campbell et al. (2018) identified that individuals who considered themselves more mindful in their daily lives (especially those who reported an ability to monitor and describe their experiences without automatically reacting) tended to think of themselves as more multiculturally competent. This concept definition reflects the goal of authentic connection with others and acknowledging and honoring differences. It also highlights the importance of intentionality when using clinical techniques. To this end, in this chapter, we begin by laying the foundation for using culturally relevant techniques; exploring important concepts, terms, and approaches to enhance efficacy when working with underrepresented populations; and presenting reflection questions to encourage deep thinking about how these methods fit one's counselor identity. We conclude by providing an overview of practical ways to integrate culturally oriented techniques and case studies demonstrating the use of said methods. Although these clinical functions interact dynamically at multiple levels within the counseling process, this chapter aims to attain positive therapeutic outcomes by recognizing cultural competency as a clinical lens through which we see others.

Introduction to Concept

Bridging the Gap: Integrating Cultural Competence

While the interplay of these clinical functions unfolds within counseling, the chapter's central objective is clear: fostering positive therapeutic outcomes through the lens of cultural competence. Multicultural competence is a continuous, lifelong process of improvement and learning (Dieser, 2021). This journey requires interpersonal and intrapersonal reflection and development. For example, the ACA Code of Ethics (2016) calls for counselors to maintain awareness and sensitivity concerning cultural meanings of confidentiality and privacy and respect differing views toward disclosing information (B.1.a). Similarly, the Multicultural and Social Justice Counseling Competencies (MSJCC) conceptual framework describes the significant concepts related to developing a multicultural and social justice lens (Ratts et al., 2016). The essence of the MSJCC is the belief that multiculturalism and social justice should be at the core of counseling. This conceptual framework also encourages counselors and CITs to familiarize themselves with the framework to inform practice. Additionally, the MSJCC provides a structural lens for addressing the intersecting identities that clients and counselors bring to the therapeutic relationship and sets the expectation that counselors address issues of power, privilege, and oppression that impact clients (Ratts et al., 2016).

The MSJCC directs counseling professionals to view client issues from a culturally contextual lens and recommend individual and systemic interventions. A pivotal piece to recognize is that culture and multicultural competencies are a construct on the spectrum of contextual continuity. In other words, the *context* (environment) in which the therapeutic counseling relationship is constructed and established is critical to recognize.

Understanding Intersectionality: Contextual Power Dynamics

The theoretical framework of *intersectionality* expounds on the need to recognize cultural context, and any discussion on the cultural relevance of clinical skills without considering intersectionality is incomplete. Coined by Kimberlé Crenshaw in 1989, the earlier concept of intersectionality recognizes the experience of Black American women, considering the intersection of racial and gender identity. However, since then, the framework of intersectionality has evolved considerably (see Collins & Bilge, 2020; Chan et al., 2018; Gopaldas, 2013, etc.), and the considerations for one's social identities do not suffice. The evolved framework of intersectionality goes beyond social identities. It considers the positionality of one's social identities on the spectrum of power, privilege, and oppression in a specific context (environment; Killian & Floren, 2020; Joshi et al., 2021; Chan et al., 2018; Joshi et al., 2022). For instance, utilizing intersectionality (Crenshaw, 1989), the construct of intersecting social identities constitutes essential aspects in understanding one's lived experiences. The *intersection* of these social identities that comprise an individual may impact their experience in the world (Avent-Harris et al., 2019). Thus, it would be misleading to ask a person to focus solely on their gender when other aspects of their identity, such as race, topographical location, and social class, are interwoven (Crenshaw, 1989).

Throughout this chapter, the authors discuss a variety of contexts (environment) and the intersections of the social positionality of counselor educators, counselors in training (CITs), and clients, which influences the learning and embodying of clinical techniques and clinically relevant approaches. This chapter advocates for an inclusive therapeutic approach through culturally relevant techniques. As counselors and CITs tread the path of cultural competence, the journey spans reflection; awareness; adaptation; and, ultimately, fostering meaningful therapeutic bonds across diverse contexts.

However, remember that this journey never really ends. It is like a treasure hunt for better ways to increase awareness and apply clinical techniques. It is about looking inside ourselves and learning every step of the way. The rules keep changing, like the rules of a game, and we need to keep up. So let us start this adventure into counseling's colorful world, where culture, diversity, and understanding make the magic happen.

Nurturing Therapeutic Relationships: Collaborative Cultural Techniques in Action

In the following sections, we delve deeply into diverse cultural contexts that we encourage counselors to consider as they refine their clinical skills for fostering therapeutic relationships. It is crucial to recognize that these cultural contexts are unique, intricate, and molded by individuals' lived experiences, which shape their personal values and belief systems. Furthermore, we offer illustrative case vignettes to showcase how counseling techniques can be effectively applied within these cultural contexts, guided by the principles of MSJCC and intersectionality. The cornerstone of the counseling profession is the therapeutic relationship, a bedrock for social, emotional, and behavioral transformations. Hersoug et al. (2001) underline the working alliance's consistent role in predicting positive therapy outcomes. This link between a strong therapeutic alliance and positive results was reaffirmed in another study, which found that clients with weaker alliances were more likely to discontinue therapy (Sharf et al., 2010). Within this construct, three key factors wield considerable influence: the counselor's worldview, the client's worldview, and the contextual environment in which the therapeutic relationship unfolds.

Counselor's Worldview: Cultivating Critical Consciousness

Considering the counselor's pivotal role in the relationship and the associated power dynamics, counselor trainees are uniquely positioned to cultivate skills of critical consciousness. In academic settings, counselor trainees should address their implicit and explicit biases as they learn counseling techniques. The Multicultural and Social Justice Counseling Competencies (MSJCC) framework (Ratts et al., 2016) encourages counselors to raise awareness and confront the impact of their oppressed identities. Toton and Nick (2015) stress the significance of embodying counseling techniques for enriching the therapeutic alliance. Recognizing and embodying the techniques align with CITs' evolution toward effective practice.

Client's Worldview: Bridging Power Dynamics

While counselors hold significant power and privilege, recent research highlights the pivotal role of clients' lived experiences and cultural perspectives in shaping the counselor–client relationship (Bayless-Conway et al., 2021; Dari et al., 2019; Harrichand et al., 2021; Steele & Newton, 2022). Understanding and considering the client's worldview is paramount in both the learning of counseling techniques and the cultivation of the therapeutic bond. It is essential to distinguish between how counselor trainees learn a technique and how it is interpreted through a client's worldview. For example, maintaining eye contact may evoke feelings of shame in certain cultures. Mindful of this, counselors can be mindful of how they engage in the skills of SOLER and maintain eye contact while remaining attuned to cultural nuances and focusing on building the therapeutic relationship. SOLER is a communication acronym used in therapeutic settings to promote effective and empathetic communication between the counselor and client. Gerard Egan (2014) introduced the acronym SOLER within his work "The Skilled Helper," outlining its significance as a non-verbal listening technique in counseling. This approach is essential to counselor training, emphasizing practical communication skills. It stands for:

- Sit squarely: Position yourself in a way that conveys openness and attentiveness, such as facing the client directly.
- Open posture: Maintain a relaxed and open body posture, avoiding crossed arms or closed-off gestures that may signal defensiveness.
- Lean towards the other: Lean slightly towards the client to show interest and engagement in the conversation.
- Eye contact: Maintain appropriate eye contact to convey attentiveness and connection while being mindful of cultural and individual differences in eye contact preferences.
- Relax: Stay relaxed and composed to create a calm and supportive atmosphere during the interaction.

Mindfulness encourages counselors to remain reflexive in their thinking and approaches (Kabat-Zinn, 1994; Guiffrida, 2015) to sustain the client–counselor relationship. This culturally oriented approach goes beyond recognizing the role of culture and broaching behavior. It requires counselors to be intentional in not only how they engage in learning these skills but also to be vigilant in how the skill delivery should be individually tailored to fit the client's culture and lived experiences.

Contextual Environment: Lived Experiences

When we consider the context of lived experiences we must discuss individualism and collectivism. *Individualism* entails a positive self-perception, emphasizing personal identity development and pursuing individual goals for enhanced well-being and life satisfaction (Oyserman et al., 2002; Diener & Diener, 1995; Markus & Kitayama, 1991). On the other hand, *collectivism* revolves around group membership as a core component of one's interpersonal identity. Within this framework, life satisfaction is interwoven with nurturing successful interdependent relationships and contributing to the greater good of the community (Markus & Kitayama, 1991; Oyserman, 1993; Triandis, 1995). While the counseling field was initially shaped by individualistic Euro-American ideologies, contemporary sociopolitical shifts, and evolving counseling practices have steered the profession toward a more interdependent nature, emphasizing the significance of therapeutic relationships.

Recognizing that individualistic and collectivistic ideals are diverse and multifaceted across cultures is crucial when implementing culturally relevant counseling techniques. Various cultures embody differing degrees of both individualism and collectivism. For counselor trainees, this calls for an adaptable approach to conceptualizing and utilizing counseling skills. Simultaneously, trainees must be attuned to their clients' contextual frameworks of individualism or collectivism, as this context shapes their engagement in the therapeutic relationship.

For instance, consider a trainee with a client from a collectivist background. In this scenario, the trainee should consider whether an individual-focused counseling approach is optimal or if the client might benefit more from a group or family-centered counseling strategy. CITs can appreciate the intricacies of each cultural lens and tailor their techniques accordingly to foster a more effective and culturally sensitive therapeutic alliance.

Counseling Techniques: Applying Techniques With a Cultural Perspective

Carl Rogers (1961) highlighted that psychotherapy addresses communication failures and that effective psychotherapy is, at its core, good communication. Josef Breuer, an associate of Sigmund Freud, referred to psychotherapeutic treatment as the "talking cure" nearly eighty years earlier (Strachey, 1977, p. 13). Similarly, Thomas Szasz (1979) emphasized that psychotherapy is a unique form of personal influence primarily rooted in communication. Kottler (1991, pp. 149–150) emphasized the significance of language in therapy, stating, "Since therapy is an act of communication, much of what takes place is centered around the content and structure of linguistic processes. As therapists, we must be sensitive to our client's use of language." From its inception to the present, effective communication between client and counselor has always been central to the counseling process (Kottler & Balkin, 2017). Although nonverbal cues and silences play a role, spoken words and contextual understanding dominate the interaction in mental health counseling.

A mental health counselor can grasp the meaning of a client's words and their contextual implications. According to Patterson (1986), empathic understanding is pivotal in a therapeutic setting. Therefore, culturally oriented clinical skills involve listening attentively and comprehending the client's intended meaning (Ratts et al., 2016). Misinterpreting a client's words or their significance in the client's world can lead to reduced counseling effectiveness and potential harm, as misunderstandings hinder connection and may lead to incorrect conclusions. Misinterpretation can also lead to *microaggressions*. An example of a microaggression is making assumptions about a client's background based on their presentation (appearance or communication). This can erode trust and rapport, making it challenging to establish a positive therapeutic relationship.

Linguistics and Multilingual Abilities

In the context of the United States, counseling heavily relies on English oral communication. As the profession strives for diversity, equity, and accessibility, recruiting ethnically diverse counselors introduces linguistic diversity, including multilingualism. This aspect is often overlooked in counseling education, particularly in training counselors in techniques. According to Lerma et al. (2015), bilingual, Spanish-speaking counselor trainees often struggle when supervised by monolingual supervisors. They find themselves translating not just for clients but also for supervisors as nuanced experiences get lost. Joshi et al. (2021) reaffirmed the challenges multilingual counselors and educators face due to not using English as their primary language, urging counselor educators to be aware of potential language-based biases. Counselor trainees can focus on nonverbal communication training and ethical practices to support linguistically diverse clients. For multilingual counselors, self-care is crucial due to the demands of continuous language translation during therapy sessions while building a therapeutic alliance.

African American Vernacular

African American Vernacular English (AAVE) is a way of speaking that reflects cultural differences in how people express themselves. Like any language, AAVE has its own rules and patterns. Linguists tell us that all languages have these variations, and there is no one "right" or "wrong" way to speak (Norbahira & Radzuwan, 2018; Adler, 2021). It is like how different regions have accents or ways of saying things.

Counselors play a unique role in helping people. Understanding AAVE and other languages spoken by minoritized groups can aid in developing the therapeutic alliance and the clinical approach. This understanding helps counselors connect better with people with different cultural backgrounds. Imagine it like counselors learning a new language to talk to someone. When counselors are aware of cultural biases and differences in language, they can provide more effective support to people who are different from them (Cukor-Avila & Balcazar, 2019; Kroll & Townsend, 2022; Thomas, 2018).

Think of it this way—imagine you are talking to someone, but they do not really understand your way of speaking. They might feel disconnected or like you are not getting their point. This disconnect happens to racial minority clients more often than White clients (Sue & Sue, 1990). The client speaks one language, and the counselor speaks another.

Even in schools, differences in language can lead to misunderstandings between students and teachers. Similar things can happen in counseling if the counselor needs to become more familiar with how their client communicates (Orr, 1987; Beaman, 1994). It is like conversing in French with someone who only speaks German. This mismatch can create barriers to understanding (X, 1966).

Experts have noticed this issue, too. They say that when counselors do not understand their clients' language patterns, it can affect how they see the clients and how effective the counseling is (Gladding, 1992; Sperry & Sperry, 2020). It is like wearing glasses that make everything look blurry. The counselor might need to see the client clearly and could make mistakes in helping them.

Differences between clients and counselors can appear in various ways—like the words they use, how they say things, and even their attitudes (Avent & Cashwell, 2015; Kim et al., 2019). For example, slight changes in phrasing can convey different meanings in AAVE. Saying, "He is working when the boss comes in" means something slightly different from, "He be *workin'* when the boss comes in." These nuances matter: If a counselor misses them, they might not fully understand what the client is trying to say. Also, tone of voice and repeating words can be misunderstood in translation, making a client seem aggressive or unclear (Beaman, 1994). Some subtleties in AAVE show the timing and duration of actions more precisely than in standard English. In short, it is vital for counselors to learn and respect different language patterns like AAVE to bridge communication gaps and truly connect with their clients. Understanding these differences is key to effective counseling (Brooks et al., 2019).

Likewise, understanding the situations that shape a client's experiences can significantly improve the relationship between the client and counselor. To illustrate this point, consider the following story, inspired by Beaman (1994) and Orr (1987), which can apply to a mental health counselor:

> Imagine a second-grade teacher who gave the class a problem to solve. She said that four birds were sitting on a tree, and she asked how many would be left if you threw a rock at one of them. A White child answered that three would be left, subtracting one from four. An African American child, however, answered that none would be left because the others would fly away when one is hit.

This story emphasizes how crucial it is for counselors to understand context and personal experiences. The African American child's response reflects a cultural perspective, as Orr (1987) described. From this viewpoint, hitting one bird would cause the others to flee, avoiding the same danger and sparing the community from more trouble and loss. People from collectivistic cultures often voice their concerns for the group, even when discussing individual matters in counseling. Counselor trainees should be aware of these thinking and communication style differences when analyzing clients' issues. Misunderstanding these nuances can lead to ineffective use of therapeutic techniques and impact the counselor's approach. Counselors can benefit from approaches that recognize the significance of AAVE, understanding that it can sometimes be more precise than standard English (Cukor-Avila & Balcazar, 2019; Kroll & Townsend, 2022; Thomas, 2018).

Applying techniques with a cultural perspective can give counselors a deeper insight into the current situation and the underlying attitude (Ratts et al., 2016). It is important to note that in this discussion, AAVE is being used as a tool for learning. Using this dialect in your personal life is not recommended, as it could unintentionally appropriate it. Remember, genuine allyship involves avoiding performative actions and focusing on developing cultural competence and humility.

Embracing Cultural Humility and Responsiveness

It is essential to understand that meeting clients where they are does not mean counselors need to be experts in every aspect of their cultural backgrounds. Counselors can only know so much about various cultures. However, counselors can show clients that they are ready to listen and support them in the ways they need. *Cultural humility* involves recognizing what we do not know and being curious to learn more. Even if it feels uncomfortable, this willingness to learn can lead to better understanding and stronger client connections.

Being intentional about culturally oriented approaches goes beyond simply being aware of different cultures. It is about genuine understanding and creating meaningful connections that delve beneath the surface. Techniques rooted in cultural humility allow counselors and clients to explore diversity, ask questions, and create environments where growth can happen naturally. It is an ongoing process, recognizing that knowledge is built within specific contexts.

Cultural humility, as defined by Davis et al. (2020), follows a continuum that involves the following:

1. recognizing your self-awareness
2. valuing others' perspectives
3. striving for continuous growth

This concept considers how counselors use mindfulness in the context of different cultural backgrounds (Davis et al., 2018). Cultural humility means maintaining a perspective that focuses on the client's cultural identity and what is important to them (Hook et al., 2013). This process encourages self-reflection and understanding how our interpretations and power dynamics shape our interactions (Curtis et al., 2019; Stubbe, 2020). The language of humility adds an essential dimension to the multicultural values integrated into the training of helping professionals (Danso, 2016; Fisher, 2020).

Cultural humility is both a way of interacting with others and understanding ourselves. Interacting with others means putting aside feelings of superiority and focusing on the client's perspective. When looking inward, it involves recognizing our strengths and limitations. Because our group affiliations can sometimes lead to biases, cultural differences can challenge the practice of humility (Davis et al., 2018), which means counselors have an opportunity to exercise cultural humility when using counseling techniques, to enhance their awareness of interactions and build stronger connections with clients from diverse backgrounds.

Exploring Real-Life Stories: Navigating Cultural Contexts

Now, let us venture into actual stories that give life to our explored concepts. These case studies act like windows into the counseling world, where cultural contexts shape the therapeutic journey. Each case study is like a snapshot, capturing a unique moment. They showcase the interplay between counselors and clients, highlighting the impact of cultural nuances. However, remember, these stories are not universal templates—they are examples specific to certain situations. Counselor trainees will discover diverse narratives here, revealing how different cultural backgrounds influence the counselor–client relationship. As you read, remember that no single case study can encompass every cultural scenario that counselors might encounter.

So let us dive into these stories. They offer insights into the art of counseling, where cultural sensitivity and awareness play a pivotal role. Through these real-life encounters, we will unravel how counselors can develop essential clinical skills and culturally relevant approaches to engage clients from diverse backgrounds effectively.

CASE STUDY 1: EMBRACING TRAUMA-INFORMED COUNSELING: A VITAL APPROACH

Imagine a puzzle of life experiences, where more than half of American adults have faced something truly tough. It's like a hidden hurt that stays with them. But here's the thing—even counselors, those who guide us through tough times, carry their own stories too.

Recognizing this, CITs and experienced professionals are joining hands to learn about trauma-informed care. It's like adding special tools to their toolbox, a way to offer extra support to those who need it most. Employing some key strategies from the Substance Abuse and Mental Health Services Administration, (SAMHSA, 2014) for example, counselors can find ways to connect better with clients that strengthens the therapeutic alliance. It's like speaking the same language in moments of crisis. And when they mix in cultural, historical, and gender insights, counselors become even better at understanding how to help—not harm.

In this case scenario, we'll walk through a story that shines a light on how CITs can learn to provide effective support for clients who've faced trauma. It's a journey of empathy and learning, all in the name of making a difference. Moreover, when responsiveness to cultural, historical, and gender nuances is combined (Levenson, 2020), CITs and professional counselors from dominant cultural backgrounds gain insight into unintentional actions that can perpetuate lasting trauma, while also exploring methods to manage crises. The case scenario will highlight this significant developmental piece.

Case Study 1

Tanya was in her mid-thirties and had been working as an executive administrative assistant. While Tanya desired connection, she isolated herself and feared getting close to others. Most evenings after work, she would go home, read a book, or talk on the phone with her parents or close friends from high school.

By the time Tanya came to counseling, she had begun to experience panic attacks, including shortness of breath and heart palpitations. The counselor began exploring Tanya's fear of connection with new people, and they began to discuss why she chose not to date. It was discovered that Tanya had been sexually abused by her stepfather when she was nine years old. The abuse continued over three years. She had never disclosed this to her parents or close friends. It is also revealed that in her late teens, Tanya was sexually abused by her stepbrother.

Reflection Questions

1. What are the cultural implications presented in this scenario?
2. "Trauma" refers to a deeply distressing or disturbing experience that overwhelms a person's ability to cope and leaves a lasting emotional impact. In what ways have you been affected by trauma?
3. While working with this client, you become exposed to vicarious trauma. What are some ways you can mitigate the effects of your own personal trauma to continue working with this client?
4. What self-care practices do you engage in to help you stay engaged from daily exposure to trauma?

CASE STUDY 2: NAVIGATING COUNSELING IN A DIVERSE LANDSCAPE: A LOOK AT IMMIGRATION AND THERAPEUTIC ALLIANCES

As evidenced by the U.S. Census Bureau's 2020 decennial data, there has been a quite notable 16% surge in the influx of immigrants to the United States, marking the highest level since 1965. Simultaneously, the escalating presence of international students and faculty in the field of counseling and counselor education (Interiano & Lim, 2018; Anandavalli, 2021; Attia, 2021; Joshi et al., 2021; 2022) prompts crucial questions:

- Are CITs receiving comprehensive training to effectively build therapeutic alliances with foreign-born individuals in the U.S.?
- Do CITs feel adequately equipped to engage with international clients?

The following vivid case study sheds light on these inquiries and illustrates how a CIT might approach counseling an international client in the United States.

Case Study 2

Upon arrival to the United States, Emiko, an international student from Japan, shared that she was excited about attending an American university. She became acquainted with the culture in her spare time by enjoying American books, trying new foods, and watching American television shows. Over her first semester, however, Emiko began noticing the significant dissimilarities in the actions and behaviors of American students. In addition, she noticed how their beliefs, values, and lifestyle conflicted with hers and contributed to her difficulty in making friends.

In the spring, Emiko decided to meet with a campus counselor. She disclosed that she lived on campus in the residential dormitories and had an American roommate. Although reluctant to speak on her experiences, she shared her challenges in making friends; relating to American students; and, more personally, the access her roommate would give her boyfriend to their room. Emiko disclosed that she strongly valued her privacy and personal space. She shared how discomfited she was when her roommate's boyfriend would walk in unannounced and how openly they would kiss and hug each other.

Emiko shared with the counselor that her adjustment at an American university was hard during her first semester, considering the differences in culture and practices. However, Emiko said that her most considerable growth edge was discovering how to appreciate her values while learning to appreciate American values. While much of the values differed from hers, she was learning to adjust.

Reflection Questions

1. What are the cultural inferences that underpin the clinical techniques and approaches you use in counseling? How can you ensure those inferences are appropriate for the worldviews of your clients?
2. What competencies would help you to increase inclusive cultural approaches for counseling international students?
3. Considering Emiko's experiences, what opportunities do you see for counselors to influence internationalization on campus to help encourage the integration of international students in the educational institution and the local community?
4. How would a CIT support Emiko to preserve her cultural distinctiveness and identity as she learns more about American culture and having the desire to make friends?

CASE STUDY 3: EXPLORING POVERTY'S IMPACT ON MENTAL HEALTH

Picture poverty like a puzzle with pieces like race, gender, and education. It's not just about money—it's about how these pieces fit together. This puzzle can affect mental health in different ways, like a hidden thread weaving through our feelings.

When someone's money situation improves, their feelings of anxiety and sadness might improve too. But poverty isn't the same for everyone. It's like a changing chameleon, adapting to different situations. It can mean not having enough money or facing struggles with jobs or education—it's a complex pattern.

Counselors understand that poverty isn't just numbers—it's people's lives. It's a puzzle of experiences that connect with how we feel inside. Each person's story is unique.

Now, let's dive into a real-life story that shows how CITs can learn to support those facing poverty or homelessness. This case scenario will highlight the skills and techniques they need to make a difference. It's all about listening, connecting, and offering help to those who need it most.

Case Study 3

Joshua is a 34-year-old White man living in Florida. In the past year, Joshua experienced divorce and lost his property due to flooding from a severe hurricane. Joshua has used his savings and does not have family or friend support.

As a result of Joshua's experiences, he resides in a tent community. Joshua desires a home again, but his access to resources is limited. He also needs help maintaining essential documents, as the conditions associated with living outside make it challenging. Joshua panhandles to get bus fare to a community center across town. He can use computers to apply for jobs, take a self-help class in exchange for a bag of food from the pantry, and see a counselor. Unfortunately, Joshua has difficulty keeping up with his appointments because of the financial strain it causes and its distance from the tent community. Joshua communicates to his counselor that lack of transportation is a barrier because he must catch the 3:00 p.m. bus daily to make it home before dark and protect his items.

Reflection Questions

1. What are the cultural implications presented in this scenario?
2. How did culture play a role in the crisis that occurred in this community?
3. Suppose you were employed as Joshua's counselor. You might or might not share several social identities with your client concerning race, gender, or sexual orientation; however, you may not share his identity as a person currently living in poverty. Reflect on how the correspondence of these identities (or the lack thereof) between you and your client would affect the treatment. How would you integrate your knowledge of these issues within your work with Joshua?

CHAPTER SUMMARY

Culturally relevant approaches and techniques often possess the necessary attributes leading to the growth and development of one's counselor identity. According to Ridley et al. (2021), exploring clinical techniques and innovative approaches provides enhanced professional guidance to CITs.

Additionally, it aids in shaping theoretical orientations and foundations. Culturally oriented techniques include exploration of biases, mindfulness of counselor and client worldviews, and awareness of variations in applying foundational counseling skills when working with diverse populations. As a result, counselors may play an integral role in closing the access gap by widening their capacity and approach as multiculturally competent clinicians. Efforts to make sustainable changes require counselors to collaborate. The infusion of the MSJCC (Ratts et al., 2016) and cultural humility must be considered an extension of oneself as a cultural human being.

CHAPTER REFLECTION AND DISCUSSION QUESTIONS

These reflection questions can help readers engage with the material in the chapter and encourage deeper thinking about the topics discussed:

1. How can the integration of various clinical techniques and therapeutic approaches enhance the effectiveness of counseling for diverse client populations?
2. What are the ethical considerations and challenges that counselors may encounter when applying specific clinical techniques, and how can they navigate these ethical dilemmas effectively?
3. In what ways do cultural competence and awareness play a role in selecting and utilizing clinical techniques in counseling, and how can counselors ensure they provide culturally sensitive care?
4. Reflect on a specific case or scenario in which a particular clinical technique or approach was instrumental in achieving positive therapeutic outcomes. What lessons can we draw from this case for future counseling practice?
5. How can counselors stay up to date with the latest research and advancements in clinical techniques and approaches to continually improve their counseling skills and better serve their clients?

EXAMPLES OF COUNSELING AND ADVOCACY INTERVENTIONS RELEVANT TO THIS TOPIC

Counseling and advocacy interventions that incorporate clinical techniques and culturally relevant approaches are essential for addressing the unique needs of diverse client populations. The following are some notable examples:

- **Narrative therapy with a cultural focus:** Narrative therapy allows clients to explore and reframe their life stories. Counselors can integrate cultural elements into these narratives to help clients make sense of their cultural identities and experiences.
- **Culturally tailored cognitive-behavioral therapy (CBT):** Counselors can adapt CBT to align with the client's cultural beliefs and values. This may involve modifying the language, using culturally relevant metaphors, and addressing culturally specific stressors.
- **Family systems therapy with multigenerational perspective:** In family therapy, understanding the impact of cultural factors on family dynamics is crucial. Counselors can explore how cultural values, traditions, and intergenerational conflicts influence family relationships.

- **Mindfulness and meditation practices grounded in cultural traditions:** Integrating mindfulness and meditation practices from a client's cultural background can promote emotional regulation and well-being—for instance, using Buddhist mindfulness techniques for clients who desire this form of treatment from Asian cultures.
- **Advocacy for culturally competent mental health services:** Counselors can engage in advocacy efforts to promote culturally competent mental health services within their communities and organizations. This might include collaborating with local organizations to provide mental health resources in culturally sensitive ways.
- **Group counseling focused on cultural identity:** Group therapy can be centered on exploring and celebrating cultural identity. Counselors can facilitate discussions and activities that allow clients to connect with others who share similar cultural experiences.
- **Art and expressive therapies with cultural symbolism:** Art and expressive therapies can incorporate cultural symbols and themes to help clients express their thoughts and emotions—for instance, using Indigenous art techniques for clients from Native American communities.
- **Trauma-informed care with cultural competency:** Counselors can implement trauma-informed care while being aware of how cultural factors may influence trauma experiences and healing. This approach respects the client's culture while addressing trauma.
- **Dialectical behavior therapy (DBT) with a focus on emotional regulation in cultural context:** DBT can be adapted to help clients from different cultural backgrounds manage emotions and interpersonal challenges, acknowledging how cultural norms influence emotional expression and regulation.
- **Advocacy for inclusive and culturally competent policies:** Beyond individual counseling, counselors can advocate for systemic changes by working with policymakers to develop and implement inclusive and culturally competent mental health policies that reduce disparities in access and care.

These examples demonstrate how counselors can apply clinical techniques while considering cultural relevance to support the mental health and well-being of clients from diverse cultural backgrounds. The key is to tailor interventions to the individual needs of each client, while respecting and honoring their cultural identities and experiences.

ADDITIONAL RESOURCES

The following are some additional readings, resources, and websites related to the use of clinical techniques and culturally relevant approaches in counseling. They can serve as valuable resources for further exploration of clinical techniques and culturally relevant approaches in counseling, and they can help counselors and practitioners stay informed and culturally competent in their work.

Readings and Books

- ***Counseling the Culturally Diverse: Theory and Practice* by Derald Wing Sue and David Sue:** This widely used text provides an in-depth exploration of cultural competence in counseling and offers practical techniques for working with diverse client populations.

- ***Multicultural Issues in Counseling: New Approaches to Diversity* by Courtland C. Lee:** This book covers various multicultural issues in counseling and offers guidance on applying culturally relevant approaches.
- ***Handbook of Multicultural Counseling* edited by Joseph G. Ponterotto, J. Manuel Casas, Lisa A. Suzuki:** This comprehensive handbook offers insights into the most current research, theory, and practice related to multicultural counseling.
- ***The Racial Healing Handbook: Practical Activities to Help You Challenge Privilege, Confront Systemic Racism, and Engage in Collective Healing* by Anneliese A. Singh:** This book provides practical exercises and strategies for personal and collective healing related to racial and cultural issues.
- ***The Transgender and Gender Nonconforming Child: A Developmental Perspective* by Rachel Crandall:** This book focuses on the development and counseling of transgender and gender nonconforming youth, offering insights into culturally relevant approaches for this population.

Websites and Organizations

- **American Counseling Association (ACA):** The ACA provides resources, webinars, and publications on multicultural counseling and culturally relevant approaches. https://www.counseling.org/
- **The National Association for Multicultural Education (NAME):** NAME offers resources and conferences focused on multicultural education and counseling. http://www.nameorg.org/
- **The Association of Black Psychologists (ABPsi):** ABPsi provides resources on culturally competent counseling and psychological services for the Black community. https://www.abpsi.org/
- **The National Latino Psychological Association (NLPA):** NLPA is dedicated to promoting psychological research, practice, and education that reflects the needs of the Latino community. https://www.nationallatinopsych.com/
- **The Asian American Psychological Association (AAPA):** AAPA offers resources and information on mental health issues and counseling within the Asian American community. https://www.aapaonline.org/
- **The National Council on Family Relations (NCFR):** NCFR provides resources on family dynamics and cultural diversity, which can be relevant to family therapy and counseling. https://www.ncfr.org/

REFERENCES

Adler, A. (2021). Language, or dialect, that is the question. How attitudes affect language statistics using the example of Low German. *Languages, 6*(1), 40. https://doi.org/10.3390/languages6010040

American Counseling Association. (2014). *ACA code of ethics.*

Avent, J. R., & Cashwell, C.S. (2015). The Black church: Theology and implications for counseling African Americans. *The Professional Counselor, 5*(1), 81–90. https://www.doi.org/10.15241/jra.5.1.81

Avent-Harris, J. R., Trepal, H., Pardo, A., & Robinson, J. (2019). Women counselor educators' experiences of microaggressions. *The Journal of Counselor Preparation and Supervision, 12*(2).

Bayliss-Conway, C., Price, S., Murphy, D., & Joseph, S. (2021). Client-centered therapeutic relationship conditions and authenticity: A Prospective Study. *British Journal of Guidance & Counselling, 49*(5), 637–647.

Beaman, D. (1994). Black English and the therapeutic relationship. *Journal of Mental Health Counseling, 16*(3), 379.

Brooks, L. A., Manias, E., & Bloomer, M. J. (2019). Culturally sensitive communication in healthcare: A concept analysis. *Collegian, 26*(3), 383–391. https://doi.org/10.1016/j.colegn.2018.09.007

Bullock, H. E. (2019). Psychology's contributions to understanding and alleviating poverty and economic inequality: Introduction to the special section. *American Psychologist, 74*(6), 635–640. https://doi-org.ju.idm.oclc.org/10.1037/amp0000532

Campbell, A., Vance, S. R., & Dong, S. (2018). Examining the relationship between mindfulness and multicultural counseling competencies in counselor trainees. *Mindfulness, 9*, 79–87. https://doi.org/10.1007/s12671-017-0746-6

Clark, M., Ausloos, C., Delaney, C., Waters, L., Salpietro, L., & Tippett, H. (2020). Best practices for counseling clients experiencing poverty: A grounded theory. *Journal of Counseling & Development, 98*(3), 283–294. https://doi-org.ju.idm.oclc.org/10.1002/jcad.12323

Conlin, W. E., & Boness, C. L. (2019). Ethical considerations for addressing distorted beliefs in psychotherapy. *Psychotherapy, 56*(4), 449–458. https://doi.org/10.1037/pst0000252

Crenshaw, K. (1989). Demarginalizing the intersection of race and sex: A Black feminist. Critique of Antidiscrimination Doctrine, Feminist Theory, and Antiracist Politics. University of Chicago Legal Forum, 139–67.

Cukor-Avila, P., & Balcazar, A. (2019). Exploring grammatical variation in the corpus of regional African American language. *American Speech, 94*(1), 36–53. https://doi-org.ju.idm.oclc.org/10.1215/00031283-7321989

Curtis, E., Jones, R., Tipene-Leach, D., Wlaker, C., Loring, B., Paine, S. J., & Reid, P. (2019). Why cultural safety rather than cultural competency is required to achieve health equity: a literature review and recommended definition. *Int J Equity Health, 18*(174). https://doi.org/10.1186/s12939-019-1082-3

Danso, R. (2016). Cultural competence and cultural humility: A critical reflection on key cultural diversity concepts. *Journal of Social Work, 18*(4), 410–430. https://doi.org/10.1177/1468017316654341

Dari, T., Laux, J. M., Liu, Y., & Reynolds, J. (2019). Development of community-based participatory research competencies: A Delphi study identifying best practices in the collaborative process. *The Professional Counselor, 9*(1), 1–19. https://www.doi.org/10.15241/td.9.1.1

DeAngelis, T. (2015). In search of cultural competence. *Monitor on Psychology, 46*(3), 64. https://www.apa.org/monitor/2015/03/cultural-competence

Dieser, R. B. (2021). A call to the profession: Cross-cultural competence and learning from a sister profession. *Therapeutic Recreation Journal, 55*(4), 369–383. https://doi-org.ju.idm.oclc.org/10.18666/TRJ-2021-V55-I4-10995

Dunn, M., Chambers, C., Cho, J., & Cheng, M. (2022). Future counselors' voices: A qualitative investigation of microaggression training. *Journal of Multicultural Counseling & Development, 50*(4), 238–255. https://doi-org.ju.idm.oclc.org/10.1002/jmcd.12260

Egan, G. (2014). *The skilled helper: A problem-management and opportunity-development approach to helping* (10th ed.). Brooks/Cole.

Fisher, E. S. (2020). Cultural humility as a form of social justice: Promising practices for global school psychology training. *School Psychology International*, *41*(1), 53–66. https://doi.org/10.1177/0143034319893097

Goode-Cross, D. T., & Grim, K. A. (2016). "An unspoken level of comfort": Black therapists' experiences working with Black clients. *Journal of Black Psychology*, *42*(1), 29–53. https://doi.org/10.1177/0095798414552103

Guiffrida, D. A. (2015). *Constructive clinical supervision in counseling and psychotherapy*. Routledge.

Hanna, F. J., & Cardona, B. (2013). Multicultural counseling beyond the relationship: Expanding the repertoire with techniques. *Journal of Counseling & Development*, *91*(3), 349–357. https://doi-org.ju.idm.oclc.org/10.1002/j.1556-6676.2013.00104.x

Harrichand, J. J. S., Litam, S. D. A., & Ausloos, C. D. (2021). Infusing self-care and wellness into CACREP curricula: Pedagogical recommendations for counselor educators and counselors during COVID-19. *International Journal for the Advancement of Counseling*, *43*(3), 372–385. https://doi.org/10.1007/s10447-021-09423-3

Heberle, A. E., & Carter, A. S. (2020). Is poverty on young minds? Stereotype endorsement, disadvantage awareness, and social-emotional challenges in socioeconomically disadvantaged children. *Developmental Psychology*, *56*(2), 336–349. https://doi-org.ju.idm.oclc.org/10.1037/dev0000883.supp

Hook, J. N., Davis, D. E., Owen, J., Worthington, E. L., & Utsey, S. O. (2013). Cultural humility: measuring openness to culturally diverse clients. *Journal of Counseling Psychology*, *60*(3), 353–366. https://doi.org/10.1037/a0032595

Hostinar, C. E., & Miller, G. E. (2019). Protective factors for youth confronting economic hardship: Current challenges and future avenues in resilience research. *American Psychologist*, *74*(6), 641–652. https://doi-org.ju.idm.oclc.org/10.1037/amp0000520

Kabat-Zinn, J. (1994). *Wherever you go, there you are: Mindfulness meditation in everyday life*. Hyperion.

Kim, R., Roberson, L., Russo, M., & Briganti, P. (2019). Language diversity, nonnative accents, and their consequences at the workplace: Recommendations for individuals, teams, and organizations. *The Journal of Applied Behavioral Science*, *55*(1), 73–95. https://doi.org/10.1177/0021886318800997

Kottler, J. A. (1991). *The complete therapist*. Jossey-Bass.

Kottler, J. A., & Balkin, R. S. (2017). *Relationships in counseling*. American Counseling Association.

Kroll, T. A., & Townsend, C. (2022). The sociopsychological cost of AAE-to-SAE code-switching: A symbolic interactionist account. *Journal of Interactional Research in Communication Disorders*, *13*(1), 120–144. https://doi-org.ju.idm.oclc.org/10.1558/jircd.21167

Levenson, J. (2020). Translating trauma-informed principles into social work practice. *Social Work*, *65*(3), 288–298. https://doi.org/10.1093/sw/swaa020

Light, Jr., D., & Keller. S. (1979). *Sociology*. Knopf.

Ling, J., Zahry, N. R., & Liu, C.-C. (2021). Stress management interventions among socioeconomically disadvantaged parents: A meta-analysis and moderation analysis. *International Journal of Nursing Studies, 120*. https://doi-org.ju.idm.oclc.org/10.1016/j.ijnurstu.2021.103954

Malcolm X. (1966). *Malcolm X speaks*. Grove Press.

Mares, L. (2022). Unconscious processes in psychoanalysis, CBT, and schema therapy. *Journal of Psychotherapy Integration*, *32*(4), 443–452. https://doi-org.ju.idm.oclc.org/10.1037/int0000276

Meyer, O. L., & Zane, N. (2013). The influence of race and ethnicity in clients' experiences of mental health treatment. *Journal of Community Psychology*, *41*(7), 884–901. https://doi.org/10.1002/jcop.21580

Mollen, D., & Ridley, C. R. (2021). Rethinking multicultural counseling competence: An introduction to the major contribution. *The Counseling Psychologist, 49*(4), 490–503. https://doi.org/10.1177/0011000020986543

Norbahira, M. N., & Radzuwan, A.R. (2018). A review of theoretical perspectives on language learning and acquisition. *Kasetsart Journal of Social Sciences, 39*(1), 161–167. https://doi.org/10.1016/j.kjss.2017.12.012.

Orr, E. W. (1987). *Twice as less.* Norton.

Patterson, C. H. (1986). *Theories of counseling and psychotherapy.* Harper & Row.

Perrigo, J. L., Samek, A., & Hurlburt, M. (2022). Minority and low-SES families' experiences during the early phases of the COVID-19 pandemic crisis: A qualitative study. *Children and Youth Services Review, 140.* https://doi-org.ju.idm.oclc.org/10.1016/j.childyouth.2022.106594

Ratts, M. J., Singh, A. A., Nassar, M. S., Butler, S. K., & McCullough, J. R. (2016). Multicultural and social justice counseling competencies: Guidelines for the counseling profession. *Journal of Multicultural Counseling & Development, 44*(1), 28–48. https://doi.org/10.1002/jmcd.12035

Ridley, C. R., Sahu, A., Console, K., Surya, S., Tran, V., Xie, S., & Yin, C. (2021). The process model of multicultural counseling competence. *The Counseling Psychologist, 49*(4), 534–567. https://doi.org/10.1177/0011000021992339

Rogers, C. R. (1961). *On becoming a person.* Houghton Mifflin.

Siegel, J. M. (1974). A brief review of race in clinical service interactions. *American Journal of Orthopsychiatry, 44*(4), 555–562.

Steele, J. M., & Newton, C. S. (2022). Culturally adapted cognitive behavioral therapy as a model to address internalized racism among African American clients. *Journal of Mental Health Counseling, 44*(2), 98–116. https://doi-org.ju.idm.oclc.org/10.17744/mehc.44.2.01

Strachey, J. (Ed.). (1977). *Five lectures on psychoanalysis.* Norton.

Stubbe, D. E. (2020). Practicing Cultural Competence and Cultural Humility in the Care of Diverse Patients. *Focus (American Psychiatric Publishing), 18*(1), 49–51. https://doi.org/10.1176/appi.focus.20190041

Substance Abuse and Mental Health Services Administration. (2014). *SAMHSA's concept of trauma and guidance for a trauma-informed approach.* https://ncsacw.samhsa.gov/userfiles/files/SAMHSA_Trauma.pdf

Sue, D. W., & Sue, D. (1990). *Counseling the culturally different: Theory and practice* (2nd ed.). Wiley.

Szasz, T. (1979). The *myth of psychotherapy.* Anchor Books.

Thomas, C. (2018). Negotiating words and worlds: An autoethnography of linguistic identity development. *International Journal of Qualitative Studies in Education, 31*(7), 612–625.

Triandis, H. C. (1995). *Individualism and collectivism.* Westview Press.

Van Ausdale, S., & Swank, J. M. (2020). Integration of trauma based education in counselor education. *Journal of Counselor Preparation & Supervision, 13*(2), 105–125. https://doi.org/10.7729/42.1354

Invitational Skills as a Precursor to Counselors' Efforts to Broach Racial, Ethnic, and Cultural Factors With Clients

Robtrice Brawner and Dr. Norma Day-Vines

LEARNING OBJECTIVES

1. Students will become more aware of specific counselor behaviors that can invite and alienate clients in the counseling space.
2. Students will become more knowledgeable about specific counseling behaviors and strategies that can contribute to stronger therapeutic relationships with diverse clients.
3. Students will be able to identify and apply broaching attitudes and behaviors as invitational skills to improve the counseling experience for diverse clients.
4. Students will be introduced to the multidimensional model of broaching behavior as a tool for engaging in invitational broaching skills.

LEARNING OUTCOMES

1. Counselors examine their own attitudes, biases, and assumptions that may promote or inhibit the ability to execute invitational skills.
2. Counselors consider clients' value orientations in the context of creating a set of welcoming conditions for counseling.

3. Counselors broach the extent to which issues of race, ethnicity, and culture are embedded with the client's presenting concerns, in an effort to validate the client's sociocultural and sociopolitical realities, help the client feel heard and understood, alleviate the client's psychological distress, and deepen the therapeutic alliance.
4. Counselors engage in advocacy interventions by broaching at the infusing category of the continuum of broaching behavior, to improve the sociopolitical climate for clients outside the counseling dyad.

Scholars have expended tremendous time and energy documenting the importance of the counselor's broaching behavior. Essentially, *broaching* refers to the counselor's effort to explore the extent to which issues of race, ethnicity, and culture (REC) impact the client's presenting concerns (Day-Vines et al., 2007; Day-Vines et al., 2021; Jones & Welfare, 2017; Zhang & Burkard, 2018). Consideration of clients' REC concerns creates a measure of psychological safety that permits clients to experience personal vulnerability within the safety of the counseling dyad. The client's perceived sense of psychological safety and security can subsequently give way to the sharing of more personal thoughts and feelings about the embeddedness of REC within the client's presenting problems (Fuertes et al., 2002). To illustrate, a client who presents for counseling with work-related challenges may experience the therapeutic encounter more fully if invited to consider how issues of racism, classism, religion, national origin, linguistic diversity, and sexism impact their presenting concerns, as opposed to talking about psychological distress exclusively from a culturally neutral stance. In fact, an emerging body of research suggests clients who withhold information about their cultural concerns have less favorable counseling outcomes (Drinane et al., 2018).

A spate of previous research indicates that the counselor's broaching efforts increase counselor credibility, the depth of client self-disclosure, and a willingness to return for follow-up sessions (Knox et al., 2003; Atkinson et al., 1992; Gim et al., 1991; Pomales et al., 1986; Sue & Sandberg, 1996). In as much as we ascribe the counselor's broaching repertoire to improved counseling outcomes, we contend that broaching behavior is a necessary, albeit insufficient, criteria for establishing psychological safety within the therapeutic dyad. That is, counselors must engage in a set of pre-requisite invitational behaviors that convey respect, openness, and trust before enlisting broaching strategies. In this chapter, we put forward the argument that prior to implementing the broaching framework, counselors must convey that clients' expression of concerns are warranted and integral to the counseling process.

The purpose of this chapter is to make important connections between the counselor's invitational counseling skills and broaching behaviors. We proffer that before the counselor can broach clients' REC concerns, the counselor must first communicate verbally and nonverbally a genuine acceptance and appreciation of the client. We open this chapter with a definition and description of invitational skills counselors can exhibit. We continue by noting that once the therapeutic relationship has unfolded, the counselor can proceed with a set of broaching strategies and techniques that further the invitational process. In this chapter, we place a specific focus on the use of invitational skills with minoritized clients whose distinctive sociocultural and sociopolitical realities warrant special consideration. We also use an interdisciplinary literature base (e.g., sociology and psychiatry) to analyze case examples. Next, we introduce the broaching framework as an invitational skill and close the chapter with implications for counseling.

Invitational Skills

Much of what is shared by clients is very personal in nature and reflects thoughts, feelings, and behaviors that have not been disclosed to anyone else. When first meeting clients, counselors are given a very small window of opportunity to create conditions for forging a strong therapeutic alliance, which includes establishing a relationship, creating realistic goals, and encouraging clients to talk freely. Essentially, counselors exhibit invitational skills or a sequence of actions, behaviors, and words enlisted to encourage clients to develop a sense of comfort and ease within the counseling dyad (Schmidt, 2004).

An integral part of helping a client feel comfortable involves the use of invitational skills, such as verbal and nonverbal behaviors and gestures that communicate respect and acceptance of the client, and a genuine interest in exploring the client's full humanity. The therapeutic relationship exemplifies the interpersonal connection between the counselor and the client; moreover, it denotes the client's willingness to engage in a working relationship with the counselor toward meeting predetermined goals and objectives (Hill, 2020). Invitational theory outlines a means and process of communication that considers a person's total environmental experience to ensure optimal benefit from the therapeutic relationship. Invitational skills include programs and policies to which clients are exposed, intentional and unintentional ways of encouraging or discouraging communication, as well as the choices that both the counselor and client make in communicating effectively and accepting the messages being sent (Schmidt, 2004). These skills "invite" the client to converse freely with the counselor and are demonstrated in both nonverbal and verbal interactions.

Nonverbal Invitational Skills

We surmise that the counselor's demonstration of invitational skills begins prior to the intake process and precedes the client's entrance into the counseling space or therapeutic relationship. This may include the counselor's organizing principles and policies, such as whether the counselor takes insurance, the office location, and even quotations the counselor may use as signatures on their emails and marketing materials (e.g., website and business cards). Invitational theory indicates that the counselor's decisions can promote or inhibit open communication between the counselor and client.

Certain nonverbal indicators can ultimately reflect uninviting messages that alienate clients emotionally from the therapeutic process (Schmidt, 2004). To illustrate, a counselor who is "out of network" for certain types of insurance (e.g., Medicaid vs. Blue Cross/Blue Shield), does not take insurance at all, and does not offer counseling services on a sliding scale may inadvertently project an elitist attitude that suggests clients of low socioeconomic status are not welcome in the practice. Upon seeing this policy, a client may speculate that a counselor who does not take insurance may be less poised to hold space for concerns that are germane to the client, such as discussions that underscore intersections of race, gender, social class positionality, national origin, and others. As an example, Rosario is a Latinx client who after months of deliberation finally decided to seek counseling. As a married mother of two whose husband recently lost his job, Rosario worries that she is being selfish for pursuing counseling given her family's precarious financial predicament and the reality that in her culture seeking mental health treatment is considered taboo.

As Rosario peruses the list of available counselors in her community, she realizes that very few individuals take insurance. At that moment, Rosario begins to feel inadequate and worries that counseling services are designed for affluent people. She worries too that if she does find a counselor that accepts her insurance, the counselor may not be able to relate to her financial struggles. Rosario also harbors concerns that her counselor may judge her negatively on the basis of her intersectional identity domains (e.g., race, gender, and class status). Although the client's construal of the counselor's positionality may be inaccurate, counselors must consider the full range of client interpretations surrounding the metamessages that practice norms convey.

The location of the counseling office may also communicate welcoming or unwelcoming messages to clients. For instance, an unwelcoming message might be an office that is not accessible via public transportation or that is situated far from a city center, requiring clients to own a vehicle, have a valid driver's license, and possibly work painstakingly to travel to the office. *Invitational theory* refers to the consideration of metamessages as a counseling process factor (Schmidt, 2004). The office location may communicate a metamessage that the office location is intentionally designed to exclude people from marginalized groups. Essentially, office policies that are more convenient for people who are materially privileged or that reflect dominant culture worldviews can discourage people who are less materially privileged from engaging in the therapeutic process (Schmidt, 2004).

In addition to office policies, counselors must consider issues such as the office layout, artifacts, and other symbol systems that represent certain social causes that may inadvertently convey invalidating messages to some clients. These seemingly benign acts of counselor identity can imply both positive and negative messages regarding the types of topics that are open for discussion. For instance, Bob is a young adult male, who is questioning his sexual identity. He feels a great sense of reassurance when he enters his counselor's office and immediately sees a Safe Zone sticker displayed in the office. To him, the sticker signaled that LGBTQIA+ concerns are welcome in the counseling space and that he could talk openly about his sexual orientation without fear of reprisal.

Contrariwise, a counselor who displays quotes either in the office or on marketing materials that express xenophobic and racist ideas could convey to clients a lack of sensitivity and communicate that discussions of race and culture may not be welcome or understood. To illustrate, Alfred is an African American male, who sought counseling reluctantly. As he sat in the waiting area of the counseling suite, he noticed wall art that said, "All Lives Matter." The slogan is politically loaded and reflects an oppositional stance to Black Lives Matter statements that began surfacing in 2013 following the shooting death of unarmed teenager Trayvon Martin in Florida by a White, middle-aged male assailant. Alfred internalized the All Lives Matter slogan as offensive and as intended to diminish the racialized violence perpetrated against many African Americans. As he waited to see his counselor, he ruminated about whether the counseling process would exacerbate rather than resolve many of his encounters with racialized stress and his own experience of being accosted by police or vigilante types. For all intents and purposes, the office environment should exude warmth, interest, inclusivity, and understanding (Schmidt, 2004). Counselors should carefully consider the messages and feelings certain office artifacts can evoke in clients because some messages may unintentionally exude hostility and indifference.

Similarly, Ravi is a first-generation South Asian male, who has come to counseling to process concerns about assimilation into American culture. While he is waiting to meet with his counselor, he thumbs through magazines; however, most magazines in the waiting area reflect White, middle-class norms, only show Whites on the cover and leave him feeling a sense of estrangement. Not seeing himself represented in the magazine selections made Ravi wonder whether he would be able to discuss his cultural concerns during treatment. In other words, the absence of representative magazines and artifacts may suggest that at some level, discussions about REC would be off limits or poorly understood by the counselor.

> **Reflection Questions**
> 1. What makes these environments uninviting for Alfred and Ravi?
> 2. How might you create a more inviting experience for clients like Alfred and Ravi?
> 3. How might you determine if your changes were effective?

Second Layer of Nonverbal Invitational Skills

The second layer of nonverbal invitational skills includes the counselor's use of purposeful silence, body language, facial expressions, gestures, posture, and overall physical demeanor—more specifically, the way a counselor reacts to the client and the information they are discussing. *Invitational theory* refers to these behaviors as "styles" and can be inclusive of being either invisibly or visibly appropriate or inappropriate (Schmidt, 2004, pp. 34–35). For example, purposeful silence could be waiting 2–3 seconds before providing a verbal response to the client or asking a question. Thus, allowing the client to reflect on what was just shared and consider what more they would like to add to the expression. In this manner, purposeful silence creates an environment that conveys patience and a willingness to allow clients to set their own pace in counseling. Ming Yue is a Chinese international student matriculating in a U.S. university. She has sought mental health treatment for concerns related to acculturative stress. Ming Yue's counselor recognizes that she speaks English as a second language and may need some additional time to process her feelings and possibly translate from her language of origin to English. In an effort to respect and show deference to the client and her culture, the counselor allows Ming Yue time to organize her thoughts before responding verbally.

Similarly, the manner in which the counselor uses eye contact to demonstrate an effort to listen intently is important. Body language includes gestures such as whether counselors fold their legs or cross their arms while the client is discussing topics that might be particularly embarrassing. Facial expressions include the use of raised or furrowed eyebrows to mirror the client's expression of thoughts and feelings or the use of a strategic smile. These expressions convey personal warmth as well as a welcoming environment for clients and help build rapport.

Posture and overall physical demeanor includes the way the counselor may lean in or out when the client discusses certain topics to show interest, demonstrate empathy, or track the conversation being laid out by the client. Although all of these nonverbal counseling behaviors are meant to encourage the client to speak freely at their own pace and demonstrate that counseling is a safe space to be vulnerable, these gestures can sometimes convey judgment and highlight a power dynamic within the counseling dyad, and as a consequence, they may discourage the client from talking openly and establishing a strong therapeutic relationship alliance with the counselor. A counselor's inability to establish an early connection with the client may impede opportunities for subsequent broaching events.

The ability to join early with the client and foster a healthy therapeutic alliance is critically important when working with minoritized clients due to the frequency with which many have had negative counseling experiences. A spate of previous research has documented high rates of premature termination among minoritized clients. Further, microaggressions perpetrated in session by the counselor can leave clients feeling a sense of alienation and woundedness. More specifically, compared to White clients, minoritized clients have lower participation rates of mental health counseling and higher rates of premature termination that scholars have linked, in large measure to cultural miscommunication, limited access to quality mental health care services, prohibitive costs, concerns about stigma, cultural inhibitions about discussing personal concerns with strangers, the lack of bilingual counselors, and other factors (De Haan et al., 2018; Kearney et al., 2005; Leong & Kalibatseva, 2011; Owen et al., 2014; Owen et al., 2012).

Research findings indicate that many clients from minoritized backgrounds have reported a pattern of cultural mistrust; cultural concealment, or the tendency for clients to withhold cultural concerns from counselors; the ethnocentric monocultural nature of counseling; adequacy of counseling services; as well as historical encounters with mental health abuse (Nabors et al., 2022; Drinane et al., 2018; Leong & Kalibatseva, 2011). Because the counseling environment functions as a microcosm of society, the therapeutic alliance can be hampered by problematic microaggressions or those slights and indignities directed toward people from marginalized groups. That is, interpersonal behaviors that play out within society may also infiltrate the counseling relationship in ways that hinder the therapeutic alliance. In fact, Hook et al. (2016) surveyed more than 2,000 ethnic minority individuals who received counseling services during the prior year. Findings demonstrated that 80% of respondents reported that their counselors engaged in microaggressive behaviors. Incidentally, researchers defined counselors' minimization and avoidance of their clients' REC concerns, denial about having cultural biases, and expression of stereotypes about the client, as specific types of microaggressions. The following case illustrates this point.

Alfredo is a Puerto Rican male, who decided to seek counseling after having lost multiple family members during the COVID-19 pandemic. He harbored reservations about counseling because in his community of origin, seeking mental health support is considered unacceptable. As a consequence of experiencing numerous encounters with racism and discrimination, Alfredo has a hard time trusting and finds himself being hypervigilant around people he doesn't know well. He was hoping to find a Puerto Rican male counselor or, at the very least, a Latinx, male counselor. Much to his chagrin, the practice where he sought counseling services did not have any Latinx male counselors, which led him to wonder whether his counselor would understand how cultural issues shaped his presenting problems. He braced himself for what he worried would be an inevitable microaggression.

During his initial counseling session, Alfredo entered the counseling office prepared to shake his counselor's hand. As Alfredo extended his hand to engage in a customary handshake, his White, male therapist clasped his hands behind his back. Alfredo wondered if the counselor withdrew his hands to avoid touching Alfredo. As the reader might imagine, Alfredo was both confused and put off by this gesture because he witnessed the therapist shake the prior client's hands as she was leaving her session. Alfredo's preoccupation with the counselor's motivation for not shaking his hand detracted from the counseling experience. Instead of focusing on his healing and wellness experience, Alfredo is fixated on the counselor's refusal to shake hands, and he interpreted his counselor's behavior as a symbolic gesture that perpetuated White dominance. Consequently, Alfredo questioned whether he would be able to trust his White, male provider to recognize and respect his humanity.

Although there exist myriad explanations the counselor may have used to justify his decision not to shake Alfredo's hand, it's likely that Alfredo could have interpreted the counselor's behavior through the prism of race, gender, or class. Counselors must examine the optics of their behavior. Although the counselor may have been reasonably intentioned, it is important to recognize the impact that neglecting to shake Alfredo's hand has on Alfredo's anticipation of the therapeutic process. The predominant filter Alfredo may use in this scenario is the lens of race and the White racial frame.

Counselors must monitor their nonverbal actions and anticipate how clients may interpret subtle, seemingly innocuous behaviors (e.g., inconsistent shaking of client hands) that may result in some clients experiencing certain gestures as hurtful and detrimental to the therapeutic process. Given that many clients of color are keenly attuned to racial frames that depict them in derogatory ways, subtle behaviors may shape how the client sees therapy and the therapist. Although Alfredo's counselor may construe Alfredo's concern as a nonissue, it is important to recognize the detrimental impact that refusing to shake Alfredo's hand has on his perception of the therapeutic process. Such unnamed interactions may lead to ruptures that negatively impact counseling.

Many clients of color harbor apprehensions about encounters with racism and discrimination and, as a consequence, exhibit what African American psychiatrists William Grier and Price Cobbs (1992) term "healthy paranoia." Ordinarily, we construe paranoia with unwarranted suspicion and mistrust about people's actions. Grier and Cobbs asserted that all paranoia is not bad. They argue that chronic exposure to racism and discrimination results in an adaptive response that renders one as hypersurveillant because not being guarded may be detrimental to one's social, psychological, and physical safety.

Consider the example of Alfredo. Given Grier and Cobbs' conceptualization of healthy paranoia, Alfredo's circumspection about his White, male therapist may be warranted, yet Alfredo's intrusive thoughts may interfere with his ability to profit from the counseling process.

It's very possible that the counselor may vehemently deny that his conduct was racialized; however, Eduardo Bonilla-Silva (2010) has conducted an extensive body of research on colorblind racism, documenting the fact that many people camouflage racist behavior and intentions in very nuanced ways. Participants in his groundbreaking study used a variety of responses to conceal racist intention. Notably, they vehemently denied that their behavior was biased, without considering even the remote possibility that their behavior emanated from a type of colorblind racism. Bonilla-Silva asserted that the inability to entertain even the slight chance that one's conduct may be biased reflects a kind of colorblind racism. Clients may interpret denial and defensiveness on the part of the counselor as a kind of hypocrisy that undermines trust and contributes to therapeutic ruptures.

In a related theory, sociologist Joe Feagin (2010) described a construct he refers to as the "White racial frame," which reflects a set of conscious and unconscious narratives governing the instantiation of racial ideas, values, stereotypes, narratives, norms, and emotions that rationalize white racial superiority and consign individuals from marginalized backgrounds to subordinate statuses. Feagin argued that this form of systemic racial oppression originated during U.S. colonial history and that creates scripts about treatment of people from dominant and subordinate groups in the modern United States. These negative stereotypes and assumptions often remain unquestioned and are used to dictate how people relate to one another, such that the counselor in this scenario could enact a racial frame that allows him to regard people from minoritized groups as less clean and, therefore, less human, thereby justifying the decision not to shake Alfredo's hand, which Alfredo interpreted as condescending. All too often, these belief systems govern human interactions.

Contemporary examples of the White racial frame in action include former President Bush's visit to Haiti following the major earthquake in 2010. Video footage shows President Bush wiping his hands on former President Clinton's shirt after shaking the hand of a local Haitian citizen (https://www.youtube.com/watch?v=5kvfkcTJyxc). News accounts pounced on former President Bush's behavior, suggesting he was enacting this frame by assuming superiority and seeing the Haitian citizen as dirty or unclean. Although media outlets interpreted President Bush's behavior variously, this illustration implies that clients may interpret the counselor's behavior with suspicion. Although the counselor was oblivious to the impact of not shaking Alfredo's hand, there is a strong possibility that Alfredo's interpretation of the situation may cloud his ability to feel a sense of psychological safety and security in the counseling session. Cultural mistrust may lead to Alfredo's cultural concealment within the treatment environment. Although counselors may be impervious to client interpretations of similar situations, it is important for counselors to remain attuned to their behaviors and innuendos that may impact the counseling relationship.

Feagin (2010) argued that Whites are not the only people who can internalize the White racial frame. He asserted that given the embeddedness of the White racial frame in our worldview, people of all racial and ethnic backgrounds can enact the frame. For instance, a fourth-generation Latinx female counselor working with an undocumented Latinx immigrant may exhibit contempt through body language, through a haughty air, and by exhibiting a cool distance towards the client. Initially, Louisa was relieved she was assigned a Latinx counselor; however, Louisa felt judged by her counselor when she refused to greet her in Spanish and appeared annoyed when Louisa struggled to find English words for her concerns. Despite this opening interaction, Louisa began discussing concerns about the way she was being treated at work, due to her accent and Spanish-speaking abilities. At work, Louisa was frequently asked to translate for other non-Spanish-speaking counselors working with Spanish-speaking clients. As Louisa discussed her feelings of being devalued and unrecognized for skills she brought to the office outside of being Spanish speaking, the counselor focused on the amount of Spanish-speaking clients needing language services. The counselor attempted to empathize by implying that the client would not have these experiences if more Hispanic people spoke English. The counselor also explored opportunities for the client to deemphasize her Spanish accent and suggested this may improve the way she was treated at work. Although the counselor thought she was being helpful, Louisa experienced the counselor's behavior as condescending.

> **Reflection Questions**
> 1. How was the Latinx counselor demonstrating a White frame?
> 2. What are some other areas of concern the counselor could focus on?
> 3. What suggestions might you have for Louisa?

In the next section of this chapter, we discuss verbal behaviors that function as invitational skills. A primary focus of this section centers first on verbal invitation skills and then on the use of broaching behaviors as a tool to engage clients in meaningful and substantive discussions about the extent to which REC impacts clients' presenting concerns. That is, once the counselor and client build the therapeutic alliance, the counselor is better poised to explore the client's REC concerns more directly (Day-Vines et al., 2021).

Verbal Invitational Skills

Verbal invitational skills encourage engagement by the client and can include tone of voice, use of small talk, open and closed questions, minimal encouragers, and broaching behaviors. When counselors first begin to learn the art of counseling, the "counseling voice" is typically encouraged. This tone is generally representative of a calm, relatively modulated style of speaking used to convey warmth and serenity. The use of small talk can help orient clients to the counseling space and enhance the development of the interpersonal relationship. For example, instead of opening the session with *What brings you in today?*, counselors can open with *How was your weekend?*, *What do you think about the weather outside?*, *I love those shoes–where did you get them?*, or a similar inviting question.

Counselors may also consider using open and closed questions. For example, an open question would be *Tell me more about your relationship with your father*, while a closed question would be *Are you looking forward to the holidays?* These are more direct styles of engagement and are especially beneficial for clients who are new to the counseling space or do not yet feel sufficiently comfortable talking freely. It is important to note that some cultures prefer more directive styles of counseling and will look for counselors to employ more of the verbal styles of invitational skills (Sue & Sue, 2019). Likewise, minimal encouragers are words or statements used specifically to encourage clients to keep talking. For example, words like "uh huh," "yes," "yeah," and "OK" are generally combined with a head nod. These behaviors can convey to a client that you are listening; following the conversation; and, quite possibly, understanding what they are discussing.

Broaching is relatively new to the invitational skills repertoire and describes attitudes and behaviors specifically designed to invite clients to discuss issues, concerns, or experiences related to racial, ethnic, and cultural (REC) unease, power, privilege, oppression, and so on (Day-Vines et al., 2007; Day-Vines et al., 2020). We assert that to fully immerse multiculturalism into counseling practice, there must first be a recognition that discussions of REC with clients should be at the forefront of counseling training. To date, a paucity of scholarship refers to broaching as an invitational skill.

We contend that the counselor's broaching efforts are aligned with the Multicultural and Social Justice Counseling Competencies (MSJCC). The MSJCC asserts that cultural responsiveness and social justice are central to the counseling relationship (Ratts et al., 2015). The competencies enumerate the complexity of counselor client relationships. Historically, we have presumed unquestioningly that counselors were privileged and clients were marginalized; however, the demographic composition of both the counseling force and the client population has changed considerably. As such, the complexity of an individual's identity structure indicates that counselors and clients may possess both dominant and marginalized identities (e.g., race, gender, social class, religion, and immigration status). That is, a counselor may experience privilege on the basis of their social class status but marginalization on the basis of their racial designation (e.g., middle-class Latina). Contrariwise, a client may experience privilege on the basis of his sex and race, but marginalization on the basis of his sexual orientation (e.g., gay, White male). As such, pairings may include dominant counselors who treat marginalized clients and marginalized counselors who treat clients with dominant identity structures. To practice in a culturally responsive and just manner, counselors must consider their own attitudes biases and assumptions and the impact of those personal positions on the client, recognize the client's worldview and how it shapes presenting concerns, assess the strength and the quality of the counseling relationship, and engage in counseling and advocacy interventions. The MSJCC indicates that counselors are expected to "acquire culturally responsive cross-cultural communication skills to interact with privileged and marginalized clients" (Ratts et al., 2015, p. 8). We contend that the broaching framework constitutes the counselor's effort to engage in culturally responsive cross-cultural communication skills.

In an effort to reinforce broaching as a skill and strategy in the overall practice of counseling, the latter half of this chapter will focus on a broader definition of broaching, describe broaching attitudes and behaviors as they relate to a case study, as well as describe specific strategies to implement broaching behaviors in session.

> **Case Example**
>
> Judy is a 23-year-old Black, Muslim woman with very limited English proficiency skills. She immigrated to the United States from Somalia in 2012 and has begun attending counseling due to feelings of depression and anxiety. Judy believes that being Black and Muslim may impact her distressing feelings and is hoping she will be assigned to a counselor willing to explore these issues. Recently, Judy has been experiencing some microaggressions at work due to her limited English skills and has been feeling isolated, as she is the only woman of color and Muslim at her job. Today is Judy's first counseling session, and she has been assigned to Margaret, a 45-year-old, White, agnostic woman.

Continuum of Broaching Behavior

Day-Vines et al., (2007, 2022) developed the continuum of broaching behavior to describe the orientations counselors may assume as they determine whether or not to broach clients' REC concerns. The continuum consists of five categories that proceed from the counselor's refusal to address REC content during treatment to more nuanced and stylized efforts to explore clients' culture specific concerns: avoidant, isolating, continuing/incongruent, integrated/congruent, and infusing.

Avoidant counselors exhibit a race-neutral perspective, minimize racial differences, and exude resistance and defensiveness toward broaching behaviors. For example, in considering the opening case study, the avoidant counselor would not feel there was a connection between the client's racial, ethnic, or religious identities with her presenting mental health concerns. The counselor would ignore any references to the client's concerns about being Black and Muslim with limited English proficiency and simply focus on feelings of depression and anxiety. The avoidant counselor might feel it rude to connect the client's presenting identities with her mental health concerns and resist efforts by the client to suggest its importance. Avoidant counselors have difficulty recognizing the significance of REC discussions; moreover, they may remain oblivious to client reactions to not addressing REC concerns and would not ask clarifying questions. In such instances, the client may feel uncomfortable discussing REC concerns, where the counselor appears to have withdrawn emotional support and has seemed disinterested in topics around REC. This approach is similar to the idea of being "unintentionally disinviting" from invitational theory (Schmidt, 2004, p. 29). While it may not be the counselor's intent to send harmful messages about REC and its discussion in counseling, the results can still be damaging and quite possibly irreparable. Because the counselor wields the balance of power within the counseling dyad, it is incumbent upon them to at the very minimum to create conditions that allow the client to explore their concerns around REC.

Isolating counselors make an attempt to broach cultural factors in session, but their broaching style is oversimplified and superficial. In fact, among isolating counselors, broaching behavior occurs out of obligation and not due to a genuine belief in its appropriateness or effectiveness. Likewise, once the counselor initiates a broaching event, no other mention of cultural factors are considered. For example, in the opening case study, the isolating counselor would remember that they need to broach on at least one of the client's presenting identities (e.g., race, gender, and religion) based on previous training and would make a perfunctory attempt to do so. The counselor's minimal attention to the client's REC concerns would not become apparent until the client makes a broaching statement themselves. For example, the client might say, "As a Black Muslim it's been really hard navigating American culture." The counselor might ask, "How do you feel about working with a counselor that is not Black?" Before the client could respond, the counselor would follow up with, "If it ever becomes a problem, feel free to let me know." Once the client explains that it's OK and that they just hope to be able to address concerns related to their identity as they come up, the *isolating* counselor would simply nod their head as a sign of agreement and move on to the next topic, without returning to the client's desire to discuss the relatedness between her presenting concerns and issues around race, gender, religion, and representation. The reader will notice that even though the counselor may have thought they were broaching, they shifted topics. The client talked about the challenges related to race, gender, and religion, and instead of validating the client's concerns, the counselor made it all about themselves. The counselor focused on how the client felt about their cultural differences. Although that discussion is important, it should not preempt the client's discussion about her REC distress.

Being Black and Muslim will never be broached again by the counselor, and the counselor will not likely make the connection that these identities could be related to the client's presenting concerns. Likewise, should the client bring these identities up again or suggest these identities might be related to their presenting concerns, the isolating counselor will nod as a show of understanding but will not delve further into discussions of race or religion and their impact on the client, thus conveying an uninviting message about the discussion of REC-related topics (Day-Vines et al., 2018). It should be noted that although current analysis of the continuum of broaching behavior has found no empirical support for the isolating category along the continuum (Day-Vines et al., 2013). Based on our clinical and supervisory experience, we contend that the absence of empirical support may be related more to measurement error than to nonexistence of the isolating category.

Continuing/incongruent counselors invite clients to discuss the client's sociocultural and sociopolitical concerns and the relationship between the client's presenting problems and ask about these issues throughout the counseling experience. Although continuing/incongruent counselors may be eager to facilitate REC discussions with clients, they may lack the requisite skills to fully explore the client's concerns, thereby making progress but not being effective. Similar to the isolating example, the counselor might ask the client how they feel about working with a counselor who does not identify as Black or Muslim. Once the client explains that it's OK, as long as they are able to discuss the impact of these identities when necessary, the counselor may agree with and begin to share with the client their understanding of Black and Muslim culture and their disagreement with how Muslims were treated after 9/11 and the importance of the Black Lives Matter movement. Likewise, the counselor will try to connect the client's racial and religious identities as frequently as possible but generally out of context and not relevant to the individual needs of the client (Day-Vines et al., 2018). For example, the counselor might encourage the client to discuss specific challenges she is having at her job. In turn, the client might mention language barriers and how those experiences relate to her anxiety. The continuing/incongruent counselor might try to relate these issues to her being Black or Muslim. The counselor might reflect "I hear you saying it's really difficult being Black and Muslim at your job." While this may be true, it may not represent the depth of the client's feelings and concerns underlying her current anxiety state. Similar to the avoidant counselor, this approach would also be similar to being "unintentionally disinviting" (Schmidt, 2004, p. 29). While it is not the intent of the counselor to be harmful, "ill timed, careless, and misguided" attempts to discuss REC concerns with clients can still prove to be "hurtful and counter-productive" (Schmidt, 2004, p. 29).

Integrated/congruent counselors broach subjects of race, ethnicity, and culture effectively and have integrated this behavior into their professional identity. For integrated/congruent counselors, broaching has become not just a technique but represents a routine practice of counseling. They encourage clients to make culture-specific interpretations of their counseling concerns and can distinguish between culture-specific behaviors and unhealthy human functioning. Integrated/congruent counselors can also recognize the complexities of race and the heterogeneity that characterizes culturally diverse clients (Day-Vines et al., 2018). That is, the counselor would recognize that not all Black and Muslim clients have identical experiences or worldviews. An integrated/congruent counselor working with the client in the opening case study would encourage the client to explore how her identities of being Black, Muslim, female, and having limited English proficiency skills have impacted her current emotional state. The counselor might normalize those feelings for the client and encourage her to consider other aspects of her identity that may be contributing to her presenting concerns. The counselor might also ask the client how it feels to discuss these concerns with someone who does not identify as Black or Muslim or who does not have limited English proficiency skills. The counselor might ask if those feelings are consistent with what she typically feels when conversing with others who represent differing identities. The counselor would validate experiences raised and normalize any potential difficulties that might arise due to the cross-cultural dyad. The counselor would encourage an egalitarian approach to interventions and frequently check in with the client to ensure the strategies are respectful of the client's racial, cultural, and religious identities.

Infusing counselors share many similarities with integrated/congruent counselors. The addition is a focus on broaching as a way of being outside of the counseling process. There is a commitment to social justice and an orientation that requires complex comprehension of sociopolitical issues (Day-Vines et al., 2018). They are change agents. For example, the infusing counselor would engage very similarly to the integrated/congruent counselor but would also look for ways to identify and improve the sociopolitical climate for their clients. In this instance, the counselor might help the client identify social service agencies serving those who are Black, Muslim, and speak English as a second language. The counselor might not only encourage their client to volunteer with these organizations but would willingly volunteer themselves. The counselor might assist the client in identifying diversity, equity, and inclusion resources at their place of employment and encourage the client to reach out or become involved, if possible. If there are no resources available at the client's place of employment, the counselor might assist the client in establishing those much-needed resources onsite or in collaboration with community resources. Both the integrated/congruent and infusing counselors' approaches would be most synonymous with being "intentionally inviting" according to invitational theory (Schmidt, 2004, p. 30). These counselors are deliberately creating environments centered on REC concerns that aim to make clients feel heard, seen, and valued.

Multidimensional Model of Broaching Behavior

Along with the continuum of broaching attitudes and behavior, Day-Vines et al. (2020) conceptualized the multidimensional model of broaching behavior. This framework consists of four broaching domains counselors can enlist to facilitate the broaching experience: intra-counseling, intra-individual, intra-REC, and inter-REC. These domains are each designed to create a culturally safe space for the client and represent a few of the ways counselors can initiate conversations about REC with clients.

The *intra-counseling* dimension refers to the counselor's direct attempts to gauge the client's comfort with establishing and maintaining a therapeutic relationship with the counselor. In keeping with the MSJCC, recognizing that within the privileged counselor and marginalized client roles, the client might have some trepidation working and relating in this dyad. This strategy falls directly within the domain of "the counseling relationship" and the category of "action" (Ratts et al., 2015). Therefore, when considering the case example with Judy and Margaret, Margaret might open the session exploring Judy's comfort with working specifically with Margaret. For example, Margaret might ask, "As a Black, Muslim woman, how do you feel about working with a White, non-Muslim woman?" Regardless of the response, Margaret might also follow up with, "If there are any times in our working relationship where you feel I am missing the mark, please feel free to let me know." This exchange recognizes and validates the known differences in the room, extends an invitation to continue to engage in conversations about the impact of REC in the room, and demonstrates that an open and candid discussion of REC is welcome in this space.

The *intra-individual* dimension refers to the counselor's use of cultural knowledge and the sociopolitical experiences of the client to explore the potential impact of those experiences on the presenting concern. As addressed in the MSJCC under the domain of "client worldview" and the category of "knowledge," to utilize this dimension, counselors must have specific knowledge of marginalization, oppression, discrimination, and similar factors as well as understand how those realities might shape the worldview and experiences of clients from marginalized backgrounds (Ratts et al., 2015). For example, in the case of Judy and Margaret, Margaret might explore the realities of being Black and Muslim in America and how those experiences could be contributing to her feelings of depression and anxiety. Of course, Judy is not seeking counseling services because she is Black or Muslim, but being Black and Muslim may engender sources of oppression that contribute to psychological distress.

Margaret could initiate a broaching event by stating, "Judy I'm wondering if being a Black woman in a country that doesn't typically value or demonstrate empathy for that position or being

Muslim in a country that valorizes Christianity contributes to your feelings of depression and anxiety?" This type of exchange could validate the sociopolitical realities of the client and could therefore aid in the building of the therapeutic alliance and identification of culturally appropriate counseling interventions.

The *intra-REC* dimension refers to the counselor's ability to explore within group dynamics centering on REC. Similar to the intra-individual dimension and the MSJCC domain and category of "client worldview" and "knowledge," counselors need to be well versed in within-group dynamics to effectively demonstrate and utilize this dimension. Likewise, the intra-REC dimension falls under the MSJCC domain of "counseling and advocacy interventions" and the "interpersonal" category (Ratts et al., 2015). For example, when considering culturally appropriate counseling interventions for depression and anxiety, Margaret may need to explore with Judy any potential within-group dynamics centering on the intersectionality of religion and race. Margaret may want to explore family and cultural beliefs about depression and help-seeking behavior. If seeking social support from a counselor is considered taboo in her culture, Judy may want to explore feelings of guilt she experiences because she has decided to pursue counseling. Processing related feelings may serve as a cathartic experience for Judy that helps her feel heard and understood.

On a related note, Margaret may want to encourage Judy to get involved with a local Muslim organization to build community and alleviate some of her depressive symptoms. However, without considering the racial makeup of the organization, this intervention may prove to be equally isolating if Judy is not readily accepted based on racial differences. Therefore, Margaret might start a conversation by asking Judy, "Have you been able to establish and maintain a sense of community among other Black women or other Muslim women?" This will give Margaret a sense of what some of the within-group similarities or differences may be, and it continues to demonstrate that this is a safe space to discuss all types of REC concerns and can help build a structure for more culturally appropriate interventions.

Finally, the *inter-REC* dimension refers to the counselor's ability and willingness to engage clients in candid conversations about their overall experiences with racism, discrimination, microaggressions, and so on. Inter-REC differs from intra-individual in that the exploration is not focused on the presenting issue in the inter-REC dimension, as it is in the intra-individual dimension. Inter-REC focuses on sociopolitical experiences in general and lays the foundation for counselors to engage in all aspects of the MSJCC domain of counseling and advocacy interventions. For example, Margaret might explore microaggressions at Judy's workplace and engage in conversations around best strategies to address this workplace challenge. Given that Judy has encountered microaggressive behavior at work, Margaret might say, *Tell me more about the microaggressions you've been experiencing at your job, How have you been impacted by these incidents?, What support systems do you have at work?, What is the policy surrounding microaggressions in the workplace?,* or *What do you think would be the best way to tackle this behavior at your job?* This process validates the client's experience with these encounters and demonstrates a willingness to take it seriously and engage in social change behaviors.

It is important to note that not all REC experiences or concerns will be linked to the client's presenting concerns. Likewise, not all clients will want to explore REC concerns with their counselor. However, for those who do, these strategies are designed to provide a pathway for that exploration. Similarly, as counselors continue to strive for multicultural and social justice competence, counseling spaces must represent a safe space to explore and address social injustices impacting their client community.

CHAPTER SUMMARY

The foregoing discussion implies that invitational skills serve as an important prerequisite to the counselor's broaching behavior. That is, counselors must establish conditions for making a connection by using verbal and nonverbal behaviors that convey empathy and acceptance to help the client establish a sense of increasing comfort. Nonverbal invitational skills include organizing principles and policies that send metamessages to clients signaling an inviting aura within the counseling environment. Whether or not a counselor accepts insurance, has an office location that clients can easily access, has representative magazines in their waiting room, or displays welcoming artwork in the office communicates strong symbol systems to clients that signal whether or not they are welcome and, by extension, whether or not their intersectional identities and sociocultural and sociopolitical realities will be validated and affirmed. The counselor's body language also conveys welcoming or unwelcoming messages.

Given the high rates of premature termination among many minoritized clients that have been linked to microaggressions, cultural mistrust, cultural concealment, historical nature of mental health abuse, and the ethnocentric monocultural nature of counseling, counselors should remain attuned to how their behavior comes across to clients. Because the counseling environment operates as a microcosm of society, many clients may interpret the counselor's behavior through a sociopolitical lens. In fact, Grier and Cobbs described "healthy paranoia" as the lens through which clients may view the client–counselor relationship, given the historical and contemporary nature of racism and discrimination. Joe Feagin's analysis of the White racial frame may be more obvious to minoritized clients than to relatively privileged counselors. Attention to this frame is incredibly important if counselors expect to forge healthy therapeutic alliances with clients.

Verbal Invitational skills reflect the foundational counseling skills (e.g., small talk and active listening skills) that help create the therapeutic conditions that give rise to the client's openness to the counselor's broaching behaviors. The counselor's broaching behaviors operate as a special type of verbal invitation. Essentially, counselors operating along the first three categories of the broaching continuum (avoidant, continuing/incongruent, and integrated congruent) experience difficulty generating facilitative responses that address the contextual dimensions of REC with clients. These challenges can create uninviting messages to clients of all types that can rupture and harm the therapeutic process (Day-Vines, 2018). Ideally, we expect that beginning CITs would enter counseling programs minimally operating at the continuing/incongruent category with a strong willingness and ability to develop into the integrated/congruent and infusing categories. Unless counselors are deliberate and intentional about their broaching efforts, they may discourage clients from examining the relationship between REC and their presenting problems. We suspect that as counselors have more opportunities to practice invitational skills (e.g., verbal, nonverbal, and broaching), they will develop the finesse to help clients remain in treatment until they have fulfilled their therapeutic goals.

CHAPTER REFLECTION AND DISCUSSION QUESTIONS

Have there been times where you felt uninvited in a space? What made you feel that way, and how might the space have been more inviting?

1. Identify a nonverbal invitational skill that was not mentioned in the chapter, and discuss the message(s) that behavior may convey to clients from minoritized groups?
2. Describe the manner in which a counselor may exhibit the White racial frame to develop problematic scripts about clients and discuss how counselors may, in turn, work to eliminate these biases.
3. What stage of the continuum of broaching behavior would you consider yourself to be in? Explain your reasoning.

ADDITIONAL RESOURCES

Ali, W. (2022). *Go back to where you came from: And other helpful recommendations on how to become American.* W.W. Norton.

Anderson, C. (2016). *White rage: The unspoken truth of our racial divide.* Bloomsbury.

Blau, J. R. (2003). *Race in the schools: Perpetuating white dominance.* Lynne Renner.

Bonilla-Silva, E. (2021). *Racism without racists: Color-blind racism and the persistence of racial inequality in America.* Rowman and Littlefield.

Crucet, J. C. (2019). *My time among the Whites: Notes from an unfinished education.* Macmillan.

Feagin, J. R., (2010). *The White racial frame: Centuries of framing and counter-framing.* Routledge.

Gomez, L. E. (2020). *Inventing Latinos: A new story of American racism.* The New Press.

Heumann, J. (2020). *Being Heumann: An unrepentant memoir of a disability rights activist.* Beacon Press.

Hong, C. P. (2020). *Minor feelings: An Asian American reckoning.* One World.

Hook, J. N., Davis, D., Owen, J., & DeBlaere, C. (2017). *Cultural humility: Engaging diverse identities in therapy.* American Psychological Association.

Kendall, M. (2020). *Hood feminism: Notes from the women that a movement forgot.* Penguin Random House.

Ladau, E. (2021). *Demystifying disability: What to know, what to say, and how to be an ally.* Penguin Random House.

Lee, E. (2015). *The making of Asian America: A history.* Simon & Schuster.

Lew, J. (2006). *Asian Americans in class: Charting the achievement gap among Korean American youth.* Teachers College.

Menakem, R. (2017). *My grandmother's hands: Racialized trauma and the pathway to mending our hearts and bodies.* Central Recovery Press.

Metzl, J. (2009). *The protest psychosis: How schizophrenia became a Black disease.* Beacon.

Oluo, I. (2019). *So you want to talk about race.* Seal Press.

Ramos, P. (2020). *Finding Latinx: In search of the voices redefining Latino identity.* Penguin Random House.

Singh, A.A. (2019). *The racial healing handbook: Practical activities to help you challenge privilege, confront systemic racism and engage in collective healing.* New Harbinger.

Sjunneson, E. (2021). *Being seen: One deafblind woman's fight to end ableism.* Simon & Schuster.

Steele, J., & Newton, C. S. (2023). *Black lives are beautiful: 50 tools to heal from trauma and promote positive racial identity.* Routledge.

Talusan, G. (2019). *The body papers: A memoir.* Restless Books.

Villavicencio, K. C. (2020). *The undocumented Americans.* Penguin Random House.

Wang, Q. J. (2021). *Beautiful country.* Penguin Random House.

Wong, A. (2020). *Disability visibility: First-person stories from the twenty-first century.* Penguin Random House.

REFERENCES

Atkinson, D. R., Casas, A., & Abreu, J. (1992). Mexican American acculturation, counselor ethnicity and cultural sensitivity, and perceived counselor competence. *Journal of Counseling Psychology, 39,* 515–520.

Bonilla-Silva, E. (2010). *Racism without racists: Color-blind racism and racial inequality in contemporary America* (3rd ed.). Rowman and Littlefield.

Day-Vines, N. L., Anmah, B. B., Steen, S., & Arnold, K. M. (2018). Getting comfortable with discomfort: Preparing counselor trainees to broach racial, ethnic, and cultural factors with clients during counseling. *International Journal of Advancements in Counselling, 40,* 89–104. https://www.doi.org/10.1007/s10447-017-9308-9

Day-Vines, N. L., Bryan, J., & Griffin, D. (2013). The broaching attitudes and behavior survey (BABS): An exploratory assessment of its dimensionality. *Journal of Multicultural Counseling and Development, 41,* 210–223. https://www.doi.org/10.1002/j.2161-1912.2013.00037.x

Day-Vines, N.L., Bryan, J., Griffin, D., & Brodar, J. (2022). Grappling with race: A national study of the broaching behaviors of school counselors, clinical mental health counselors, and counselor trainees. *Journal of Multicultural Counseling and Development, 50,* 25–34.

Day-Vines, N. L., Cluxton-Keller, F., Agorsor, C., Gubara, S., & Otabil, N. A. (2020). The multidimensional model of broaching behavior. *Journal of Counseling & Development, 98,* 107–118. https://www.doi.org/10.1002/jcad.12304

Day-Vines, N.L., Cluxton-Keller, F., Agorsor, C., & Gubara, S. (2021). Strategies for broaching the subjects of race, ethnicity and culture. *Journal of Counseling & Development, 99,* 348–357.

Day-Vines, N. L., Wood, S. M., Grothaus, T., Craigen, L., Holman, A., Dotson-Blake, K., & Douglass, M. J. (2007). Broaching the subjects of race, ethnicity, and culture during the counseling process. *Journal of Counseling & Development, 85,* 401–409.

De Haan, A. M., Boon, A. E., De Jong, J. T. V. M., & Vermeiren, R. R. J. M. (2018). A review of mental health treatment dropout by ethnic minority youth. *Transcultural Psychiatry, 55,* 3–30. https://www.doi.org/10.1177/1363461517731702

Drinane, J. M., Owen, J., & Tao, K. W. (2018). Cultural concealment and therapy outcomes. *Journal of Counseling Psychology, 65*(2), 239–246. https://doi.org/10.1037/cou0000246

Feagin, J. (2010). *The White racial frame: Centuries of racial framing and counter-framing.* Routledge.

Fuertes, J. N., Potere, J. C., & Ramirez, K. Y. (2002). Effects of speech accents on interpersonal evaluations: implications for counseling practice and research. *Cultural Diversity and Ethnic Minority Psychology, 8*, 346–356.

Gim, R., Atkinson, D., & Kim, S. (1991). Asian American acculturation, counselor ethnicity and cultural sensitive, and ratings of counselors. *Journal of Counseling Psychology, 38*, 57–82.

Grier, W. H., & Cobbs, P. M. (1992). *Black rage: Two Black psychiatrists reveal the full dimensions of the inner conflicts and desperation of Black life in the United States.* Basic Books.

Hill, C. E. (2020). *Helping skills: Facilitating exploration, insight, and action.* (5th ed.). American Psychological Association.

Hook, J. N., Farrell, J. E., Davis, D. E., DeBlaere, C., Van Tongeren, D. R., & Utsey, S. O. (2016). Cultural humility and racial microaggressions in counseling. *Journal of Counseling Psychology, 63*(3), 269. https://doi.org/10.1037/cou0000114

Jones, C. T., & Welfare, L. E. (2017). Broaching behaviors of licensed professional counselors: A qualitative inquiry. *Journal of Addictions & Offender Counseling, 38*(1), 48–64. https://doi.org/10.1002/jaoc.12028

Kearney, L. K., Draper, M., & Baron, A. (2005). Counseling utilization by ethnic minority college students. *Cultural Diversity & Ethnic Minority Psychology, 11*, 272–285. https://www.doi.org/10.1037/1099-9809.11.3.272

Knox, S., Burkard, A. W., Suzuki, L. A., & Ponterotto, J. G. (2003). African American and European American therapists' experiences of addressing race and cross-racial psychotherapy dyads. *Journal of Counseling Psychology, 50*, 466–481.

Leong, F. T. L., & Kalibatseva, Z. (2011). Cross-cultural barriers to mental health services in the United States. *Cerebrum: The Dana forum on brain science, 2011*, 5.

Neighbors, H., Day-Vines, N.L., Jones, A.W. (2022). *The effect of vicarious racism on Black mental health.* Hurdle Health.

Owen, J., Imel, Z. E., Adelson, J., & Rodolfa, E. (2012). No-show: Therapist racial/ethnic disparities in client unilateral termination. *Journal of Counseling Psychology, 59*, 314–320. https://www.doi.org/10.1037/a0027091

Owen, J., Tao, K. W., Imel, Z. E., Wampold, B. E., & Rodolfa, E. (2014). Addressing racial and ethnic microaggressions in therapy. *Professional Psychology: Research and Practice, 45*, 283–290. https://www.doi.org/10.1037/a0037420

Pomales, J., Claiborn, C. D., & LaFromboise, T. D. (1986). Effects of Black students' racial identity on perceptions of White counselors varying in cultural sensitivity. *Journal of Counseling Psychology, 33*, 57–61.

Ratts, M. J., Singh, A. A., Nassar-McMillan, S., Butler, S. K., McCullough, J. R., & Hipolito-Delgado, C. (2015). *Multicultural and social justice counseling competencies.* Association for Multicultural Counseling and Development. https://www.counseling.org/docs/default-source/competencies/multicultural-and-social-justice-counseling-competencies.pdf?sfvrsn=20

Schmidt, J. J. (2004). Diversity and invitational theory and practice. *Journal of Invitational Theory and Practice, 10*, 27–46.

Sue, D. W. & Sue, D. (2019). *Counseling the culturally diverse: Theory and practice.* (8th ed.). John Wiley & Sons.

Sue, D., & Sundberg, N. D. (1996). Research and research hypotheses about effectiveness in intercultural counseling. In P. B. Pedersen, J. G. Draguns, W. J. Lonner, & J. E. Trimble (Eds.), *Counseling across cultures* (4th ed., pp. 323–352). SAGE.

Zhang, N., & Burkard, A. W. (2008). Client and counselor discussions of racial and ethnic differences in counseling: An exploratory investigation. *Journal of Multicultural Counseling and Development*, *36*(2), 77–87. https://doi.org/10.1002/j.2161-1912.2008.tb00072.x

Paraphrasing and Summarizing

Dr. Ann Shillingford, Dr. LoriAnn Stretch, Timothy Eng, MS, and Dr. Mary Hinson

LEARNING OBJECTIVES

1. Develop awareness of how to appropriately use paraphrasing and summarizing with diverse clients.
2. Understand the skills needed to adequately paraphrase and summarize from diverse client perspectives.
3. Understand how to utilize the Multicultural Social Justice Counseling Competencies (MSJCC) to address client needs.
4. Develop awareness of the counselor role in the therapeutic setting from a cultural context.

LEARNING OUTCOMES

1. Students will be able to apply knowledge of paraphrasing and summarizing skill.
2. Students will be able to appropriately demonstrate how to paraphrase and summarize clients narratives.
3. Students will be able to address clients' needs from a multicultural lens, using the MJSCC as a guide. Utilizing the following skills and expertise:
   - Paraphrasing
   - Summarizing
   - Culturally Responsiveness
   - Multicultural Social Justice Counseling Competencies (MSJCC)

Chapter Introduction

Think about a conversation you've had with a friend or family member, one when you had a difficult time following their story or understanding what they were trying to say. What did you do? You may have asked a question, such as, "What do you mean by … ?" You may have encouraged the person to say more in hopes of catching up, "what else happened?" You may have even interjected with a good old, "Wait, back up a little." What many of us would also do is reflect on what we've heard: "So you're saying that the work is hard." In this last instance, we have essentially paraphrased what the person has just said—or what we think we heard the person say. Conversely, the person may have shared a significant amount of information, and you want to let them know that you understand what they have said and that you are prepared to move on with the conversation. In this case, you would summarize what has been said by this individual: "OK, you were worried about your job, but now you feel better since talking with your boss. What are you planning on doing about that hairstyle now?" That may be a stretch, but hopefully, you get the point. In this chapter, we will discuss paraphrasing and summarizing and the benefits of both techniques in the therapeutic setting. Each technique will be discussed from a multiculturally focused lens.

Paraphrasing

Paraphrasing, considered an active listening skill, involves listening to what someone is saying and then repeating in your own words the essence of the person's statements. That is, you are repeating what you think you heard the person say without parroting. *Parroting* means repeating exactly what the person is saying. We don't want to do that. Young (2021) indicates that paraphrasing includes two parts: carefully listening to your client and providing a nonjudgmental, concise reflection of the client's content. When paraphrasing, the best practice is to focus on the most important details of the person's story. Linguistically speaking, paraphrasing involves "reformation of sentences into the author's own words while at the same time, emphasizing the importance of retaining the original idea" (Khrismawan & Widiati, 2013). In counseling sessions, counselors encourage clients to speak up freely and share their experiences. Sometimes, the client may have so much to tell that they don't know where to begin or where to end. They will tell you all the story or none of the story. Paraphrasing helps dig through the story to the most important facts. When the counselor gets it right, the client may often give an indication with a head nod or even a "that's right" statement. The client will likely feel heard and supported.

You will want to paraphrase when the client shares important content that has emphasis or significance to the client. Say, for example, your client is telling you about a family vacation. You are listening to what the client is saying. You are listening for key points that stand out. You then repeat what the client has said without saying the same words. Easy right? Not really. You will want to home in on what is most important to the client and listen carefully to how the client is telling the story. You will want to identify which content is portrayed with more emphasis and to which content the client has a physical response. To accurately paraphrase, you will have to pay as much attention to how the client shares the content as to what content they share. Ultimately, a paraphrase is a succinct reflection of content that captures the most important facts and thoughts of the client's story (Young, 2021). This will include what is spoken and what misunderstood from the client's story.

Summarizing

The goal of a *summary* is to reflect what the client has said (directly or indirectly) over a period of time within a session or across multiple sessions. Summaries should be succinct counselor reflections of the client's verbal content, nonverbal content, or process. Young (2021) shared summaries allow the client to hear their viewpoint in a more organized way. The key is for the counselor to home in on what is most important to the client. What is most important will depend on the client's therapeutic goals, context, and culture. Summarizing direct content is probably the easiest way to summarize. To summarize verbal content, the counselor will identify the most important content the client has stated. The most important information the client needs to have reflected depends on their goals, current needs, and emotional emphasis. However, clients do not always directly state what is most important to them. There can be significant meaning in what the client does not say directly as well. Summarizing the meaning "between the lines" is important to reflect as well. How the client shares their story is known as the process. Counselors can summarize the client's process by observing how the client tells their story through tone, intonation, language, body movements, and eye contact. Understanding the cultural norms of the client will be essential to accurately interpreting how the client tells the story.

Let's look at an exchange between a counselor and a client and identify four different summaries that could be used. In this exchange, the client is an 18-year-old biracial youth, who identifies as nonbinary. The counselor is a 52-year-old, White female. In this therapeutic relationship, the client has been discussing their relationship with their boyfriend with whom they have lived for a year. In the last four sessions, the client has consistently discussed more and more that they are realizing the relationship is not fulfilling, and they have been working on becoming less codependent. Let us analyze the following statement made by the client:

> I *know* I need to break-up with Aaron." (Client's voice gave more emphasis on the word "know.") I made a list of pros and cons about our relationship and while the cons are shorter than the pros, the cons weigh *a lot*. (Client gestured hands down as if holding something heavy and emphasized "a lot.") I just wish I knew how he felt about our relationship and if he has considered other living options. (Client wiped their face with a tissue as some tears rolled down their cheek.)

Now, let's consider three different ways the counselor could summarize the client:

- **Direct content summary:** "You know the cons outweigh the pros, and you want to know what Aaron is thinking."
- **Indirect content summary:** "Despite knowing what you want, you still need assurance that Aaron is on the same page with you."
- **Process summary:** "Trusting what you know is hard and brings up a lot of emotion for you."

In addition to summarizing content and process, there are four primary types of summaries: focusing, signaling, thematic, and planning. A *focusing summary* will identify the primary issues and will clarify the client's connection to what is being shared. In this type of summary, the counselor will clarify what the client is working on in the session or across multiple sessions. Young (2021) states that a focusing summary identifies key themes while encouraging the client's accountability for the issues they are facing. In the previous exchange, the counselor might demonstrate a focusing summary by saying, "In our last four sessions, you have been clarifying your reasons for staying with or breaking up with Aaron." A signaling summary provides the counselor with a way to acknowledge what has been said and helps redirect the client to a previous or new topic. In the previous exchange, the counselor could use a signaling summary by saying, "You want assurance that Aaron is on the same page as you so that you can begin to plan for what is next."

A *thematic summary* is a summary that highlights a theme the client has conveyed. A theme is a value or meaning that underlies a client's narrative either in a few comments or across multiple sessions. A thematic summary requires that the counselor be able to identify connections across content, emotions, and meaning while encouraging the client toward deeper reflection (Young, 2021). The theme might have been stated directly or simply conveyed. For example, imagine that a client has been seeing you for infertility and recently visited their in-laws over the weekend. The client shares how their in-laws pay a lot of attention to the grandchildren and the parents of those grandchildren. The client has provided several situations that happened over the weekend when they felt "it didn't matter if we were there or not." The counselor might provide a thematic summary stating, "You feel invisible because you have been unable to have children." Counselors often have to read between the lines to capture the meaning of what a client is saying. This is why counselors must use a multicultural lens when listening to a client's story. The same client just discussed may be from a culture that assigns value to a woman based on how many children she has. The counselor will want to acknowledge this cultural value and check in with the client about how the cultural value may be exacerbating or alleviating a stressor. For example, the counselor could say, "As you have noted previously, your value as a woman is commensurate with the children you are able to have."

A planning summary helps the client and counselor review progress and agreements made in the therapeutic process (Young, 2021). Counselors need to review a client's progress continuously during the therapeutic relationship. Summaries can be an effective way to reflect what the client has accomplished and what is still left to do. Imagine a client has seen the counselor six times to work on adjusting to a divorce, developing a co-parenting plan, and starting to date again. The client has spent a lot of time working on the first two goals and has not addressed the third. A counselor might reflect, "You have made progress on feeling settled after your divorce and report that you are hitting your stride with the co-parent. Maybe it is time to tackle your third goal of starting to explore dating."

Therapeutic Reasons for Paraphrase and Summarize

Paraphrasing

So why do we paraphrase and summarize? Incorporating paraphrasing skills allows counselors to listen and respond to clients for clarification, which enhances the therapeutic relationship because the client feels heard (Newman et al., 2023; Weger et al., 2014). Ultimately, we are trying to convey four essential therapeutic messages to our clients: *I am here, I hear you, I care, and I understand.* These are messages best conveyed nonverbally, rather than said. When working with clients, we must honor their unique life experiences. Saying, "I am here, I hear you, I care, and I understand" may minimize the uniqueness of the client's experience. Conveying that you are there, hear them, care, and understand, however, will have a powerful effect on establishing therapeutic rapport. Ivey and Daniels (2016) noted helping professionals who effectively use paraphrasing and summarizing become more empathetic and demonstrate enhanced communication skills.

Suppose your client is a storyteller; they'll want to tell you everything in one session. Oftentimes, such clients are difficult to follow, and a counselor can get lost in the process. Paraphrasing may help with conversation management through attentiveness and responding appropriately (Weger et al.,

2014). In the case of storytelling, you want to be able to "keep up" with the client, so you paraphrase (e.g., *Let's pause for a moment. You were living with your parents, and you're saying that now you live in a different state with your best friend!*). We also paraphrase to clarify something the client has said (e.g., *So, before you wanted to go to college, but now, you aren't so sure.*). Thus, paraphrasing demonstrates that you are actively listening to information being offered by the client (Weger et al., 2014). In this paraphrasing example, you may have heard what the client said but want to be sure. Your client is sharing an event that has been quite difficult for them—say, a death in the family or loss of employment. Your client is emotional in session. What do you do then? You paraphrase to empathize with the client (e.g., *You've experienced a significant loss.*). When empathizing with your client, it is important to be mindful of voice tone and body language. Conveying a sense of understanding with the use of paraphrasing is one of the ways counselors can express empathy to our clients (Newman et al., 2023). Additionally, though certainly not the last reason for paraphrasing, you may simply want to connect with the client's story or experiences and build rapport. In all of these paraphrasing opportunities, you are conveying to your client, *I am here, I hear you, I care, I understand.*

Summarizing

In contrast, summarization is used to recap more content than a paraphrase is. Young (2021) notes that summarizing occurs when a counselor captures the meaning of a client's story during a session or across multiple sessions. It allows the larger conversation to be broken down into smaller parts, which enables the counselor to still be verbally active and provide overviews versus specific details, similar to bullet point notes. This skill is often practiced halfway through a session and at the conclusion of the session. However, like paraphrasing, you may want the client to know that we have heard and understood what they have shared (e.g., *You've shared the challenges you've experienced in migrating to America.*). Summarizing allows the client the opportunity to correct any inaccuracies in what they have said or any misunderstandings from the counselor (e.g., *I came to America with my cousin, not my aunt.*). Summarizing also serves as a recap to the content of what has already been said and brings closure to the empathy circle of sharing and actively listening (e.g., *Jay, thanks for correcting me. So far, you've shared about your experiences in America and sadness at leaving your family in Ghana. I would like for us to now talk about how it felt when your parents were finally able to join you in America.*). In this example, the counselor is summarizing by reviewing what was already discussed as well as introducing what is to come in the same session. Young (2021) suggests that a summary brings together the client's content, emotions, meaning, and future intentions. The counselor will also summarize at the end of the session by recapping what was discussed, sharing what the focus of the next session was, and maybe even giving some homework (e.g., *Today, you shared about your experiences in America and the sadness you felt at leaving your family in Ghana. Next week, I would like for us to talk about how it felt when your parents were finally able to join you in America. In preparation for the next session, I would like for you to write down the different emotions that you experienced on that first visit. How does that sound to you?*)

How to Paraphrase and Summarize

Imagine you are watching a movie with someone, and that person leaves the room. When they return, they ask you to retell what they've missed. You would be a millionaire if you were able to repeat what was missed verbatim (parroting). Instead, you would give the highlights using keywords and any emotions that you felt were expressed by the characters. In this instance, what you did was (a) listen to the actors and (b) repeat the facts and emotions you heard and felt from the characters. You paraphrase the important content of what the client has said. It is important to paraphrase without judgment, bias, or reservations. If you are incorrect in your paraphrase, the client will most likely tell you. Young (2021) explains that paraphrasing is more than mimicking the client because it captures the essence of the client's story, maybe even elaborating on what the client has shared using what knowledge the counselor has of the client's perspective on the shared situation.

EXAMPLE ONE: PARAPHRASING

> Client: "Yesterday my boss called me into his office and told me that he was not satisfied with my work. He said I had one month to 'get my act together' or I will be fired. I am so worried that I will lose my job. What will I do then?"
>
> Counselor: "Your boss told you that he is dissatisfied with your performance, and you are concerned that he will fire you."

In this example, what fact or thought was noted by the client? The main idea is that the boss is not happy with the client's performance. Do we need to mention that he was called into the boss's office? No! That is not relevant to the client's experience. Next, were there emotions that you heard or senses from the client? Yes! He is worried. So in your paraphrase, you can repeat the word "worried," or you can choose a similar word in your own "language." In my example, I choose to use "concerned." Next, if you note an emotion, then you need to note the connection. In this case, the client was not just concerned or worried about his boss being dissatisfied with his performance, he was also worried about losing his job. In this one statement made by the client, we are therefore paraphrasing three key things: (a) what happened, (b) how he felt, and (c) why he felt that way. Note that a paraphrase does not always have to include an emotion if one was not expressed or detected.

EXAMPLE TWO: PARAPHRASING

> Counselor: "Hello, Bridget. Nice to see you today. When we last met, you were telling me about the family vacation that you had planned."
>
> Client: "Yes. My partner and I took the kids and our parents to Cabo, Mexico, and we had such a nice time. The kids played on the beach for hours every day with the adults. My partner and I got to spend a lot of time together. We even went skydiving."
>
> Counselor (*paraphrase*): "The entire family got to spend quality time together."

The following are facts derived from this exchange:

- The family went on vacation together.
- The kids played together with the adults.
- The partners spent time with each other.

So what is the general theme here? It is that the family spent time together. Notice I did not mention where they went or what they did. That is because this information is not relevant at this time.

In Bridget's case, the counselor has begun the session with a recap of the last. The client is excited to share their story and the counselor reflects in a very concise manner. Conciseness is important in paraphrasing. Being concise keeps the focus on the client's story instead of shifting too much to the counselor. Sometimes, being too wordy with paraphrasing may take essence out of the client's experience and may even throw the client off. Paraphrasing should be done with just a few words or one or two brief sentences. It is important to note also that unlike summarizing, the intent of paraphrasing is to allow the client to continue sharing without interrupting their trend of thought. If your paraphrasing is too lengthy, the client needs to stop and listen to you, potentially throwing them off. Another point to remember when paraphrasing is to be nonjudgmental. Often, when we listen to someone speak, our natural processing interplays what we have heard with our personal values. When this happens, we begin to set assumptions about the client and their experience and miss important points being shared.

EXAMPLE THREE: SUMMARIZING

Counselor (*focusing summary*): "Hello, Bridget. Nice to see you today. When we last met, you were telling me about the family vacation that you had planned."

Client: "Yes. My partner and I went to Cabo, Mexico and we had such a nice time. We spent our time talking and sharing our thoughts and feelings with each other. We did some cool things too, like skydiving."

Counselor (*paraphrase*): "You and your partner spent quality time together."

Client: "Yes, we did."

Counselor: "As you reflect on your time together in Cabo, what feelings are coming up for you?"

Client: "I am relieved that we got to spend this time together. I am also rejuvenated and ready to fight to make my marriage work and keep my family together."

Counselor: "Fight for your marriage."

Client: "Yes, we deserve to fight hard for our marriage. I realize now that I was getting lazy and in some ways was taking tomorrow for granted. I had also forgotten why I love my partner. We had stopped having fun together and were so caught up in the day-to-day grind of parenting and life in general."

Counselor (*signaling summary*): "This vacation really highlighted what you loved about your marriage and why it's important to invest in your relationship. This seems like an important value for you to continue to explore."

Client: "I think so. I need to reflect more on why I want to be with my partner than the reasons we should be apart. I need to find ways to stay connected and engaged with my partner. The vacation was so eye opening."

Counselor (*thematic and planning summaries*): "You've worked hard in communicating and connecting with your partner by initiating different activities. Now you are feeling hopeful for the future of your marriage. In our next few sessions, I would like to shift the focus to your future career plans, as I recall you mentioning that this is an area of concern for you as well."

In this example, client and counselor spent time essentially "phasing out" this portion of the therapeutic journey. The counselor realizes that the client has really spent time working on that aspect of their goal (e.g., partner relationship/marriage) and gentle processes that growth. The counselor is now ready to shift the focus of upcoming sessions to another theme that was most likely identified as a therapeutic goal.

When to Paraphrase

Now that we have discussed how to paraphrase, we need to know when it is appropriate to paraphrase and summarize. It is appropriate to paraphrase when you need to:

- *Check for accuracy.* The client has shared some information, and although you've heard what was said, you want to ensure that you've heard currently and are on the right track. You want to capture the meat of the client's story in a succinct manner that does not sidetrack the client. So you would pause the client and rephrase what was said. When checking for accuracy, you want to do so as soon as you start to question your understanding. Wait for the client to take a breath, and then go for it. If you wait too long, you will start to lose the essence of the client's story.
- *Clarify a confusing statement.* In this case, you've heard what was said and have some understanding of what is being said, but something just doesn't add up. Maybe, the client is contradicting themselves or has made a mistake in their account of an event. Your paraphrase would be helpful to both clarify things for you as well as make the client aware of the inconsistency. We will talk about the skill of confronting in another chapter.
- *Highlight issues being brought up by the client.* Maybe you detect a theme in what the client is saying, and you want them to see that. You paraphrase the key points. Maybe the client is sharing a traumatic event, and you want the client to go deeper, or you want the client to connect their thoughts being shared, so you paraphrase the more salient content.
- *Convey active listening or build rapport.* You want the client to know that you are listening and are following what they are saying. Paraphrasing helps the client feel heard and subsequently, build connection with the client, as well as build trust in the therapeutic process.

When to Summarize

Summarizing should be intentional and purposeful. Here are a few instances when it is appropriate and necessary to summarize:

- *Highlight a theme.* You want the client to recognize that there is a theme to what they have been sharing. These connections could be within one session or multiple sessions. For example, you might say, "Seems there are several things that have impacted your mood. You've mentioned challenges with your children, racial conflict at work, lack of spiritual connection. All three areas seem to contribute to you feeling discouraged and despondent. I would like for us to talk about each of these three topics and how they affect you." In this example, the counselor has recognized a connection in the client's stories as aims to bring more focused direction to the sessions.

- *Start a follow-up session.* You want to remind the client of what was discussed in the previous session. For example, you might say, "Last session we talked about your spiritual life and the conflicts you are having with your church. Where would you like to start today?"
- *Bring closure to a topic or theme.* The client has shared a lot on a given topic and seemed to have shared all vital information. You, as the counselor, get the picture and think it is time to move on. The goal of summarizing at this point is to bring closure to the topic so you can move forward.

Counseling and Culture: MSJCC (Paraphrasing)

As with any reflecting or counseling approach, paraphrasing should be done in a manner that is culturally appropriate and affirming. Counselors should have an understanding of the client's worldview, cultural values, beliefs, and biases as well as how these factors could potentially impact their behaviors and decision-making. Most likely, the clients' experiences are enmeshed with their unique identities, intersectionalities, and cultural influences. Therefore, it is helpful for counselors to approach the thread of support through these lenses. To do so, counselors need to be aware of their own cultural influences, biases, and worldviews.

Counseling and Culture: MSJCC (Summarizing)

Let us look at the four domains of the Multicultural Social Justice Counseling Competencies (MSJCC).

COUNSELOR SELF-AWARENESS

Your worldview will have a significant impact on your perspective on what a client says or does in session. As a counselor, you will want to take a deep dive into understanding yourself and how what you believe and what you have experienced impacts how you view your clients. The following are some questions to consider:

1. What biases do you hold? Biases can be positive or negative. We all have biases, so it is not a matter of whether you have them; it is a matter of identifying them and becoming aware of your biases so that you can bracket them accordingly and truly meet your client where they are. One way to examine your biases is to take some of the Harvard Project Implicit Association Tests (IAT; https://implicit.harvard.edu/implicit/takeatest.html). There are tools to examine potential biases related to disability, weight, race, gender, religion, and more.
2. What are your cultural values? Often it is hard to "see" one's cultural values until you seek out opportunities to experience other cultures. Getting outside your own culture will help you identify beliefs that you once held as absolute truths. Experiencing other cultures will help you experience alternative ways of living and thinking. If you do not have the ability to live with or visit another culture (beyond being a tourist), then seek out opportunities to engage in films, documentaries, books, podcasts, and other media to learn about cultures beyond your own. Immersion activities are also useful experiences to broaden your worldview.

Our worldview is much like a kaleidoscope. We are born into a culture that contributes the first pieces of glass in our kaleidoscope. As we experience life and develop new beliefs about the world around us, we add more pieces of glass, and with each turn of life, our kaleidoscope moves and the glass in the viewer shifts and makes room for new pieces of glass. Over time, certain pieces of our experience take precedence and others move to the background, but all of our experiences and beliefs make us who we are. We never look at similar situations the same way because our worldview is ever evolving.

Client Worldview

The client's lived experiences impact dialogue used in counseling sessions and, in turn, the method in which clinicians apply skills during sessions. For example, in some languages, there is no vocabulary to identify or translate specific emotions. There are also instances in which the emotion does not translate in the intended way. Take "aenduh," rooted in Persian culture, which conveys "grief" and "regret" in English. The Dargwa people uses "dard" to express "grief" and "anxiety." Persian communicators, it appears, think of grief as more connected to regret, while the Dargwas may connect it more to anxiety (Jackson et al., 2019). As clinicians, we will need to check in more if cultural communication differences exist to ensure we translate client feedback correctly when paraphrasing and summarizing.

Counseling Relationship

Counselors should be proactive in monitoring their internal responses and potential biases related to client communication patterns. In some instances, clinicians may be observed or supervised to receive feedback. However, if clinicians do not seek feedback about their own communication patterns and application of skills, the counseling relationship could adversely be impacted. To decrease the likelihood of this occurring, it is recommended to check in with clients occasionally to ensure clarity in the counseling process:

1. What is working?
2. What is not working?
3. What do they want to see more of?

This check-in provides an opportunity to correct any existing miscommunications and understand which communication patterns are helpful in the counseling process.

CASE STUDY

In some instances, counselors may actually stunt the emotional experience of a client by failing to recognize when to paraphrase versus summarizing. For example, if a summary was used after a client discloses something very intimate or frustrating, there could be a missed opportunity to attach emotional importance.

Counselor: So where would you like us to focus our time today?

Client: There's just so much ... this has been a rough week for me, and I'm definitely struggling.

Counselor: Well, let's start with the part that you feel keeps you most stuck.

Client: Things have not gotten better with my partner; this week they moved out of our bedroom. I am just so frazzled, and it feels like the walls are caving in on me. I don't know what's going to happen.

Counselor (*summarizing*): So your partner moved out of the room, you're frazzled, and you are unsure what's happening.

Client: *Nods.*

Counselor: So, let's talk about your partners moving out. ...

In this example, the counselor did use summary by capturing the three main points; however, paraphrasing could have been more useful here:

Counselor: So where would you like us to focus our time today?

Client: There's just so much ... this has been a rough week for me, and I'm definitely struggling.

Counselor: Well, let's start with the part that you feel keeps you most stuck.

Client: Things have not gotten better with my partner; this week they moved out of our bedroom. I am just so frazzled, and it feels like the walls are caving in on me. I don't know what's going to happen.

Counselor (*paraphrase*): So you're very uncertain about what's happening in your relationship, and it feels like the world is crumbling around you.

Client: *Nods.*

Counselor: That's difficult to go through.

By identifying the emotional doorways with the paraphrase, it is easier to broach the underlying emotions.

Paying attention to what the client is doing while they speak is also an important part of deciding when and how to use the skills. Let's look at the same example with nonverbals noted.

Counselor: So where would you like us to focus our time today?

Client: There's just so much ... this has been a rough week for me, and I'm definitely struggling.

Counselor: Well, let's start with the part that you feel keeps you most stuck.

Client: Things have not gotten better with my partner; this week they moved out of our bedroom. (*The client wipes tears from their face.*) I am just so frazzled (*shoulders sag*), and it feels like the walls are caving in on me. I don't know what's going to happen.

Counselor (*summarizing*): Things are not improving, and you are feeling weighed down by not knowing what is next.

In this example, the counselor notes the physical response the client is having and incorporates that observation into the summary, effectively reflecting the client's verbal content and nonverbal experience. Ultimately, you cannot go wrong with either skill; the choice will hinge upon on determining what will most help the client go deeper and feel heard and supported.

CHAPTER SUMMARY

In this chapter, we discussed key concepts of paraphrasing and summarizing with respect to diverse client populations and the MSJCC. Paraphrasing requires active listening and describes the ability to formulate a concise, empathetic reflection of the client's words. A good paraphrase will impart a sense of validation, which communicates that you really understand your client's thoughts, feelings, and experiences. You may experience challenges composing an accurate paraphrase that does not mimic or parrot what the client is saying. However, it is helpful to focus on the important details and the significance of how their story impacts them.

Summarizing consists of succinct reflections of the client's verbal content, nonverbal content, or patterns you might have picked up within a session or across multiple sessions. Summaries can help you manage the dialogue within the session by focusing on major issues, identify themes or patterns, and signal a transition. Essentially, summaries allow the client to hear what they have been expressing in a more organized way, which may support the client in gaining more insight and clarity into their thoughts and feelings.

Utilizing the MSJCC as a framework is an essential component to ensure that counselors strive to effectively serve the needs of a diverse clientele. As such, a counselor's ability to accurately paraphrase and summarize when working with individuals from different backgrounds requires an awareness of self as well as the ability to navigate cultural nuances, varying communication styles, and the worldviews of our clients. Ultimately, acknowledgment of the roles of the client and counselor's intersecting identities, power, privilege, and culture when paraphrasing and summarizing can convey a deeper sense of understanding behind the client's life experiences and enhance the therapeutic alliance.

CHAPTER REFLECTION AND DISCUSSION QUESTIONS

1. What are the similarities and differences between paraphrasing and summarizing?
2. How may the client's willingness or unwillingness to engage impact how you use any of the skills discussed?
3. How may cultural communications patterns and language impact the counseling process?
4. What are some instances when it is appropriate and necessary to summarize instead of paraphrase, and vice versa?
5. What are cultural factors to consider when paraphrasing or summarizing?

ADDITIONAL RESOURCE

Project Implicit. (1998). *Implicit association tests.* Harvard University. https://implicit.harvard.edu/implicit/takeatest.html

REFERENCES

Khrismawan, B., & Widiati, U. (2013). Student's perceptions about paraphrasing and their cognitive processes in paraphrasing. *TEFLIN Journal: A Publication on the Teaching & Learning of English, 24*(2). https://doi.org/http://dx.doi.org/10.15639/teflinjournal.v24i2/135-157

Ivey A. E., & Daniels, T. (2016). Systematic interviewing microskills and neuroscience: Developing bridges between the fields of communication and counseling psychology. *International Journal of Listening, 30*(3), 99–119, https://www.doi.org/10.1080/10904018.2016.1173815

Ratts, M. J., Singh, A. A., Butler, S. K., Nassar-McMillan, S., & McCullough, J. R. (2016). Multicultural and social justice counseling competencies: Practical applications in counseling. *Journal of Multicultural Counseling and Development*, v44 n1 28–48.

Newman D. S., McIntire, H., Barrett, C. A., Gerrard, M. K., Villarreal, J. N., & Kaiser, L. T. (2023). A qualitative content analysis of novice consultants' responses to a consultee's request for assistance. *Psychology in the Schools*, 1–17. https://doi.org/10.1002/pits.22882

Weger Jr., H., Castle Bell, G., Minei, E. M., & Robinson, M. C. (2014). The relative effectiveness of active listening in initial interactions. *International Journal of Listening, 28*(1), 13–31. https://doi.org/10.1080/10904018.2013.813234

Young, M. E. (2021). *Learning the art of helping: Building blocks and techniques* (7th ed.). Pearson.

Reflecting Feelings from a Multicultural and Social Justice Perspective

Dr. Anna Locke, Dr. Azilde Sanchez, Ana Barend, Daniel Kimonyi, Bosede Balogun, Samantha Perez, and Andrew Erway

MEET THE AUTHORS

This chapter was written from the perspective of five authors, who represent a variety of cultures and experiences. Thus, we will accentuate the importance of expressing our location within the multicultural and social justice paradigms, for this position influences our self-awareness, worldview, counselor relationships, knowledge, and skills, which ultimately guide our actions as counselors and humans (Ratts et al., 2016).

LEARNING OBJECTIVES

1. Students will learn the components of reflecting feelings through a multicultural and social justice perspective.
2. Students will gain awareness of client and counselor aspects that influence reflecting feelings.
3. Students will learn, through a case study, how to apply the microskill of reflecting feelings in a manner that is honorable, respectful, and ethical, using the Multicultural and Social Justice Counseling Competencies.

LEARNING OUTCOMES

1. Students will understand the importance of counselor self-awareness when reflecting feelings.
2. Students will consider the various aspects of client worldview and how to strengthen the counseling relationship by reflecting feelings in a multiculturally and social justice-oriented manner.
3. Students will learn, through a case study, how to use reflection of feelings during counseling and advocacy interventions.

This chapter will teach you, a novice counseling student, to reflect on your clients' feelings through multicultural, social justice, and ethical lenses. Usually, the multicultural and social justice aspects of the counseling profession and practice are implemented into curriculums as an addendum or a separate class. This book was birthed out of a desire to change this paradigm by making multiculturalism preeminent. In this chapter, you will learn what reflecting feelings is, how to apply it from a culturally humble and socially just perspective through a case study and develop a curiosity for the future evolution of this microskill. We will explore how to effectively reflect feelings using a humble and multicultural lens. Specifically, we will apply the Multicultural and Social Justice Counseling Competencies (MSJCC; Ratts et al., 2016) to this microskill to demonstrate how to reflect feelings in a manner consistent with the client's worldview, meaning we must address the beliefs, appraisals, experiences, memories, meanings, and cognitions our clients hold. We will provide a brief introduction to the nature of feelings and emotions. Then, we will introduce you to Olga, our fictitious client. By examining Olga, we will learn how to reflect feelings from a multicultural and social justice perspective. So put on your seat belts, and enter a nonjudgmental zone!

Multicultural and Social Justice Counseling Competencies

There are four domains that will serve as the framework for the cultural application of reflecting feelings with Olga: (a) counselor self-awareness, (b) client worldview, (c) counseling relationship, and (d) counseling and advocacy interventions. Embedded within these domains are attitudes and beliefs, knowledge, skills, and action (Ratts et al., 2016). As you read how to reflect feelings with Olga using this framework, you will see how the aforementioned competencies play a role in applying this skill in a multicultural and social justice manner.

Before we go further, let's meet, Olga. We will use her story to apply the various concepts explained in this chapter. After an explanation of a specific aspect related to our topic, we will provide a case application using Olga to demonstrate how it translates into counseling practice. There will be process questions along the way to guide you in thinking about how to reflect feelings in a culturally appropriate manner.

Meet Olga

Olga is a 34-year-old Latina, who is single and was born in the United States to parents from El Salvador, who never obtained legal citizenship. Her parents were hard workers and provided for her material needs, but she felt neglected emotionally. Olga graduated high school and decided to join the workforce instead of pursuing further education. She got pregnant when she was 22, and the father of her child died in military service when the infant was one year old. She now has a 12-year-old son, Carlos, who lives with her and is starting to engage in "worrisome habits." Olga works at a high-end retail store and dreams of attending college to become an accountant. Olga came to counseling complaining about excessive worrying, which leaves her exhausted, tense, and very irritable. She expressed she has been a "worry wart" since she was a teenager, but Carlos's recent developments are exacerbating her presentation. Olga feels she is starting to lose concentration at work

> as she tries to manage her son's whereabouts, which gives her many concerns about her job and financial security. Olga stated her boss does not seem concerned. Olga also feels her body cannot relax due to excessive rumination, which prevents her from sleeping well at night. Olga thinks she is going *loca* (a Spanish term meaning "crazy" and carries negative connotations) and is concerned about her health (because of sleep deprivation and excessive worry); she decided to come to counseling by heeding her primary care provider's advice. Olga came to counseling dressed well, and she is slightly overweight. She was fidgeting a little; her speech was coherent, and she denied hallucinations, obsessions, compulsions, delusions, or phobias. Olga does not experience panic attacks. Olga does not have much social support, as she spends her time working or caring for her son. She is a Catholic Christian but does not find community in her place of worship, which she attends sporadically. Olga's parents moved to another state.

Reflecting Feelings from a Multicultural and Social Justice Perspective

Olga is now your client, and this chapter will guide you in reflecting feelings with her in sessions. Now, let's discuss what reflecting feelings is, as a microskill of counseling. Reflecting feelings is based on a person-centered approach (Rogers, 1961) that assumes a person can verbally express emotion. This counseling technique is used to demonstrate the counselor's attunement to the client's emotional state. The assumption is that feelings can be experienced consciously and, thus, can be expressed through language. The education and training of counselors for the last 60 years has emphasized the importance of "talk therapy" and using the Rogerian approach in counseling sessions. The microskill of reflecting feelings is an effective strategy to support clinical movement, foster awareness, validation, and progress (Sommers-Flanagan, 2016). Reflecting feelings is a core intervention used in almost every counseling session and within all theoretical frameworks. It is a primary skill that all counselors must learn and implement through a culturally responsive manner. Before we dig any further, it is important to note that feelings reflect the emotions that encompass our entire being and are intricately linked to our bodily sense of experiencing the world around us. Feelings are vast, expansive, and ever-present, yet sometimes, they are feared and avoided, especially feelings those that make us uncomfortable. Counseling is effective when it creates a safe and courageous place for feelings to be noticed, normalized, and validated.

Thus, reflecting feelings involves mirroring the client's emotions, allowing them to feel heard, understood, and validated. Reflecting feelings effectively can foster rapport, trust, and emotional insight within the therapeutic relationship (Ivey et al., 2018):

1. Active Listening: Reflecting feelings begins with active listening or attending to verbal and non-verbal cues from clients. This includes the tone of voice, body language, facial expressions, and the words clients use to express their emotions. We will explore some of these aspects from a multicultural perspective later in the chapter.
2. Empathy and Understanding: As clients express their emotions, counselors respond with empathy and understanding. This involves demonstrating genuine care and concern for the client's emotional experience that is shaped by their worldview.
3. Using a sentence stem, like "You feel …" or "Sounds like you feel …" or "Could it be you feel … ?"

4. Add the feeling word that the client provided or one that may match the client's non-verbal or cognitive description of emotion.
5. The context may also be added. For example, "Looks like you feel happy about [insert situation (i.e., context)]."
6. In many cases, using a present tense reflection is more powerful than a past tense or future one.
7. Make sure your reflection of feeling is accurate. The counselor might respond with "Am I hearing you correctly?" or "Is that close?"
8. Encouraging Self-Exploration: Reflecting feelings encourages clients to explore their emotions further. When clients hear their emotions reflected back to them, it prompts them to dig deeper into their feelings and gain a better understanding of what's going on within themselves.
9. Non-Judgmental Approach: Reflecting feelings requires a non-judgmental stance. Counselors should avoid imposing their own values or opinions on the client's emotions. Instead, they create a safe and accepting space for clients to express themselves. This can only be done when counselors have self-awareness of their values and biases, which is a part of the MSJCC.
10. Assisting Emotional Regulation: Reflecting feelings can help clients regulate their emotions. When clients see their emotions reflected objectively, it can lead to a more controlled and balanced emotional response, allowing them to think more clearly and make healthier decisions. We will discuss this further in the context of neurology and trauma.
11. Enhancing Communication: Reflecting feelings improves communication between the counselor and client. It ensures that the counselor accurately understands the client's emotional state, reducing misunderstandings and miscommunications. This is especially vital when practicing culturally affirming counseling to ensure that clients are understood within their cultural context.
12. Supporting Goal Achievement: Ultimately, the goal of reflecting feelings is to support the client in their therapeutic journey. By addressing and exploring their emotions, clients can work toward personal growth, healing, and positive change.

Reflecting feelings also has its limitations. When overdone, clients can start to dismiss its benefit, leaving them confused at the counseling skill. Additionally, clients might feel it is unnecessary as it interrupts the story that they are focused on telling the counselor. With time and patience, most counselors learn the dance and rhythm of the counseling session. So be kind and patient with yourself. Finally, be cognizant of this caveat: A client may feel a sense of intrusiveness when you reflect emotions, which can contribute to a rupture in the therapeutic rapport. If a client tells you that the technique of reflecting feelings made them feel uncomfortable, misunderstood, or violated, stop immediately, apologize, and inquire more about this response with empathy and curiosity. This feedback should be honored and taken in consideration in how future reflection of feelings is handled. These limitations should be kept in mind. For this reason, the counselor should consistently work on their craft of reflecting feeling, which ultimately generates comfort and authenticity in implementing the skill. This should include having a grasp on when it is most appropriate and beneficial to the client (Ivey et al., 2018).

Carl Rogers is known to have penned the term "reflections of feelings" (Slack, 1985). Yet he addresses the caveat of turning this counseling intervention into a rote and wooden technique, inadvertently affecting the expected outcome, which is mainly to hold an accurate and undistorted mirror in front of clients so that they can see their inner experience and feel understood and validated. Rogers warns that worrying about having a correct feeling word reflection misses the whole point. As counselors, we must trust our intuition, relax, and rely on our authenticity, genuineness, intuition, intelligence, and empathy to be present and open with the person in front of us. Make it your goal to be real and be genuinely curious about the person in front of you without inputting your own judgment and misconceptions. Always challenge yourself by pondering and becoming self-aware of your attitude and beliefs by incorporating how your status, strengths, limitations, values, biases, power, and privilege colors the picture you are devising in your mind (Ratts et al., 2016).

In summary, reflecting feelings is a foundational counseling skill that involves active listening, empathy, and mirroring to help clients explore and process their emotions. Counselors develop this skill to create a therapeutic environment that promotes emotional understanding, trust, and progress in therapy from a multicultural and social-justice perspective. It was also a strategy designed from a particular cultural and temporal worldview that values the verbal expression of emotional states. Oftentimes, emotions and feelings are used interchangeably; thus, an explanation of the distinction between them is warranted.

Emotions vs. Feelings: The Distinction

When person-centered counseling evolved, the scientific knowledge of how emotion was processed by the brain was limited, and so was the awareness of how culture and social justice tenets play a role in therapy. In the last 40 years, the research on emotion and neurology has blossomed and provided us with knowledge on how feelings are encoded in the brain and in the body. Further, research has helped us understand the distinction between emotion and feeling as well as how culture and social justice play a role in their expression.

Research purports that emotions can be manifested unconsciously and through bodily reactions that result from neurological outcomes to emotional stimuli. Feelings are the conscious experience of these reactions (Adolphs, 2016). Common mainstream belief emphasizes six primary emotions, which are sad, mad, glad, scared, disgust, and surprise (Ivey et al., 2018). These emotions are interchangeable amongst cultures and a part of the human experience. However, the way these emotions are expressed as feelings, verbally or nonverbally (i.e. through body expressions, hand gestures, sounds, facial expressions, or somatic manifestations) differ across cultures (Ivey et al., 2018). In other words, feelings are expressions of emotions, and these expressions are shaped by beliefs, experiences, memories, thoughts, appraisals, and attribution of meaning (Phillips et al., 2003; van der Kolk, 2014). Thus, emotional perception and experiences vary tremendously within individuals, and various factors influence their awareness and ability to express them through language.

Yet most counselors emphasize "talk therapy" and the reflection of feelings as a microskill of this type of therapeutic framework. Current research on emotional neurology and trauma encourages us to rethink this emphasis and consider other ways to reflect feelings other than through "talk therapy." Talk therapy relies on the client's ability to articulate their emotions through words. Articulating emotions through words is a form of verbal language expression that utilizes the brain's prefrontal cortex. Yet emotions are stored in the limbic system, not in the prefrontal cortex (Phillips et al., 2003; Porges, 2007; van der Kolk, 2014).

To express an emotion through talking, the brain must transfer and interpret this emotion (that is stored in the limbic system) and attach a suitable word to it (such as, angry, sad, disappointed). Individuals with traumatic pasts have a limited ability to integrate and interpret input from their bodies, which then triggers fight/flight/freeze reactions. Van der Kolk states that this interplay does not require conscious effort or cognitive input, which affects people's ability to focus and know what they feel. Therefore, how can we, as counselors, reflect something our clients do not even know is going on inside their bodies due to trauma?

We need to help them feel safe within the therapeutic relationship and within their bodies by assisting them in curiously noticing and observing their embodied selves through a trauma-informed protocol (Shapiro, 2018; van der Kolk, 2014). This protocol involves counselors also noticing and observing their *own* reactions and bodily sensations to facilitate co-regulation in the shared therapeutic space. Our bodies are designed to react to reactivity, and as we notice this reactivity, it is paramount that we learn to calm and regulate ourselves. The multicultural humble counselor calmly guides clients to observe their emotions by creating a safe space to explore not only their conscious language expression of feelings but also to explore how these emotions are held in the body without hastening change. Pell and coresearchers (2009) point out that facial expressions and vocal intonation display distinct traits that outweigh language expression. Thus, as you embark in this counseling career, foster a presence free from anxiety. When your client seems dysregulated, soften your tone, calm your own body, take long nice breaths, and relax your own shoulders while attuning to your client. This attunement can transcend sociocultural dimensions, as our bodies can help support our client's regulation of their bodies. The effective counselor holds a non-judgmental space for co-regulation without relying solely on language, predominantly since emotions may not be expressed mainly through words. Now, let's apply this concept to Olga.

UNDERSTANDING OLGA'S FEELINGS AND SOMATIC RESPONSES TO TRAUMA AND STRESS FROM A CULTURAL PERSPECTIVE

From a counselor's perspective, one would be curious to explore Olga's history of trauma and how her body has stored that experience because we are not always consciously aware of triggers to bodily responses (Genstche et al., 2022; van der Kolk, 2020). Research on the Latiné population suggests that somatic responses to anxiety, trauma, and stress symptoms are not uncommon (Bucay-Harari et al., 2020). Besides cognitive symptoms, such as excessive worry, rumination and emotional symptoms like irritability, Olga reported feeling tense in her body and having difficulties relaxing, resulting in difficulties with sleep. Further, Olga also endorsed a tragic event in her life, the death of the father of her child, who passed away when she was a year old. It is worth exploring whether internalized beliefs about gender roles and learned ways of expressing feelings influenced by her upbringing may have made it difficult for her to relax her body and communicate her feelings effectively.

As her counselor, you could monitor Olga's bodily responses, gestures, and congruence with her narratives. When articulating my observations using reflection, you might say, "You appear tense and seem to have difficulty relaxing when discussing what happened. Am I getting that right?"

Process Question

If you were working with Olga, how would reflecting feelings help increase her awareness and facilitate the conversation about emotions she may have trouble naming? How would you engage in collaborative clarification to ensure you understand what she is communicating?

Now that we have a more thorough understanding of the origin of reflecting feelings, the distinction between emotion and feeling, and what neuroscience and trauma research has taught us about feelings, let's discuss how to reflect feelings in a multicultural and social just manner. According to the MSJCC, the first step in assessing when to reflect feelings and how to implement it appropriately is through counselor self-awareness.

Counselor Self-Awareness

Mastering self-awareness is an ever-evolving goal that warrants honest reflection throughout counseling career development. Self-awareness is an imperative goal for a professional counselor; as counselors, we must be aware of our intentions, emotions, feelings, vulnerabilities, attitudes, beliefs, thoughts, privilege, values, behaviors, power, limitations, assumptions, values, and motives as well as how our past experiences, memories, and personal cultural influence affect our counseling practice (Lee, 2007; Ratts et al., 2016). Self-awareness is hinged upon the immediacy of each counseling moment; each moment is new, which demands ongoing reflection. Accordingly, Collins and coauthors (2010) emphasize that cultural auditing may be an effective means through which counselors may reflect on the self, their clients, and on the therapeutic alliance, both in and in-between sessions.

Cultural Auditing Explained

Cultural auditing is a 13-step protocol that serves as a tool for counselors to reflect from initial client contact through termination and aftercare follow-up. Please refer to Collins et al. (2010), for specifics. Broadly, these steps encourage self-awareness, along with awareness of clients' cultures, alliance, presenting concerns, case conceptualizations, and goals. Through such intentional reflective practice, both the counselor and client experience a counseling atmosphere that is infused with respect, safety, and trust (Collins et al., 2010).

Counselors need to reflect and be aware of their reactions and comfortability with clients. In the case of reflecting feelings, counselors need to be aware of how their culture and family of origin reflect feelings as well as how feelings are reflected in their present interpersonal relationships. Counselors need to be conscious about their own attitudes, values, beliefs, and cognitions as well as how their own bodies react to clients' emotions and reactions. All these experiences illuminate how the counselor integrates what is happening within the session. Let's see how one of the authors, Dr. Sanchez, would handle this with Olga.

COUNSELOR'S SELF-AWARENESS AND ITS RELEVANCE ON THE APPLICATION OF REFLECTION OF FEELINGS TO OLGA: DR. AZILDE SANCHEZ'S PERSPECTIVE

As a counselor working with Olga, I must consider power dynamics and privilege. Although we are both women from a marginalized ethnic group, we have different backgrounds that must be acknowledged. The vignette reveals that Olga is a single mother, 34 years old, a high-school graduate, and struggling to balance work and personal life while caring for her 12-year-old son without much social support. In contrast, I am older, married, co-parent with my husband, hold a doctorate in psychology, and have more financial resources than the client. My profession also allows me to acquire a deeper meaning and understanding of human relationships and skills to cope with stress. Awareness of these differences is essential as they may impact our interactions. Ignoring them may lead to unintentional insensitivity or dismissiveness when reflecting Olga's feelings.

Process Questions
If you were working with Olga, what would you need to be self-aware? Would you have to monitor yourself from any biases? Are there any dynamics of power and privilege that may impact the application of the microskill of reflection of feelings?

Client Worldview

Once counselors have explored their own cultural worldviews and beliefs surrounding expressions of feelings and emotions, clients' worldviews need to be addressed, explored collaboratively, and understood. Clients' worldview informs their personal experiences of feelings and emotions, and their relationship with and expression of them are also essential data for the counselor and the therapeutic process. To serve as an undistorted mirror for your clients, you must assess and explore their worldview as it relates to feelings. For instance, I (Ana Berand) once had a male client, who kept apologizing for crying. Trying to resist the urge to cry kept activating him in ways he started to shut down. I gently inquired about the meaning he attributed to men who cry. He answered that, in his mind, it meant weakness, as his father had taught him so. We addressed this issue in therapy, and he started to feel in more genuine and authentic ways without imputing judgment on his emotions. This is our goal as counselors: to help clients feel the amazing freedom in feeling our feelings accurately, respectfully, and honorably!

As previously mentioned, the therapeutic skill of reflecting feelings is dependent on the client's verbal and nonverbal expressions of a feeling during a session. These expressions are influenced by the client's worldview, which is colored by their individual intersecting identities. Client worldview varies depending on many factors, such as cultural and racial identities, gender and sexual orientation, family of origin, and where the person grew up, amongst other variables. For example, gender socialization or conditioning dictates how men should and should not act, think, and feel (as previously exemplified). This conditioning inhibits men's development and full realization of their potential as relational partners; instead, they are rewarded for being "good providers" for the family. To be nurturing, share feelings, or express emotions is deemed "feminine" or vulnerable and weak and, thus, is suppressed, which may lead to depression (Flynn et al., 2010; McGodrick et al., 2005; Rice et al., 2020). So how do we, as counselors, reflect feelings for men—when they may not express feelings in sessions?

The first step is to examine our own lifetime experiences with men and how that shapes our views of masculinity. Next, we need to understand how men do express themselves, which usually is leaning on rationalization, intellectualization, and logical thinking. In other words, men discuss feelings in a detached, suppressed, and rational way (Flynn et al., 2010). Therefore, our role as a counselor is to invite the male client to explore how gender socialization has played a role in their emotional expressions of feelings. As counselors, we aim to guide our male clients to gain awareness of the source of fear of dependency, overwhelming focus on work, and the avoidance of being vulnerable. Men may feel stigmatized or judged if their emotional expression is open and genuine. As professional counselors, it is our job to normalize such ingrained role attributions and provide a safe space for feelings to be felt, explored, encouraged, and honored (Rogers, 1961; Sommers-Flanagan, 2016). In doing so, our clients may become comfortable with expressing feelings, and they may recognize their emotional needs as not only basic and valid but necessary for well-being (Rice et al., 2020).

Another important aspect that professional counselors must explore collaboratively with their clients is the internalized and implicit viewpoints and roles derived from one's ethnic and racial identity (as we will demonstrate with the case of Olga). No textbook can provide concrete information about how clients hold such beliefs and awareness. Thus, counselors must practice cultural humility and engage with clients curiously and respectfully. The next section will demonstrate how to apply the aspect of socialized gender differences, using the case of Olga.

OLGA'S WORLDVIEW AND GENDER DYNAMICS: DR. SANCHEZ'S PERSPECTIVE

In our case, Olga states that her parents neglected her emotionally. I would be curious to explore the relationship with her parents, how the expression of feelings was modeled in the household, and if cultural expectations of gender influenced any of these aspects and responsibilities. In traditional Latiné culture, the expectation is that a female's primary role in the family is to focus on childrearing practices and responsibilities at home. However, if a mother works, she still needs to capitulate to traditional gendered responsibilities, taking care of the children, the household, and the husband. It is the expectation that women sacrifice their personal goals for the common purpose of *la familia*, Spanish for "family" (Nuñez et al., 2016; Adames & Chavez-Dueñas, 2016). Could these standards have influenced the modeling of the expression of feelings by the mother? Could verbalizing feelings be repressed because the expectation is that a mother must fulfill the family's needs and not prioritize hers or self-care?

When working with Olga, exploring her relationship with the males in her life may be necessary, including her father. While the focus of this vignette is not on her relationship with men, it is still relevant to consider this aspect when building rapport and reflecting on her feelings. Olga's comfort level with a male counselor may be mediated by her cultural views and relationship with men. In Latino culture, *machismo* and *respeto* ("respect") influence the dynamics and relationships between sexes (Adames & Chavez-Dueñas, 2016). Machismo "describes beliefs and expectations regarding the role of men in society; it is a set of values, attitudes, and beliefs about masculinity, or what it is to be a man" (Nuñez et al., 2016, p. 204). Machismo influences the expectations for how men reflect and express feelings and expectations for women's behavior towards them. The counterpart of machismo is *marianismo*. Adames & Chavez-Dueñas defined marianismo "as socially constructed, learned, and reinforced behaviors comprising the content of the female gender role in traditional Latino/a society" (p. 90). Therefore, a male counselor must be sensitive to these dynamics to provide an environment

> in which Olga would be open to expressing feelings. If the counselor applies the microskill of reflection correctly, working with a counselor from the opposite sex may empower Olga to be more open about expressing her feelings to males and possibly resolve some of the conflict with gender expectations by sex from her cultural background. Another psychological aspect influencing the expression of feelings is acculturation.

Acculturation

Gibson (2001) as cited in Schwartz et al., (2010), define acculturation as "changes that take place as a result of contact with culturally dissimilar people, groups, and social influences" (p. 237). Among the various acculturation theories, Berry's acculturation model seems to have influenced the most updated research with multiculturally diverse populations. Berry studied the acculturation process with minority groups in North America, identifying the host culture as the dominant culture and the individual's culture of origin as the less-dominant culture (Leite et al., 2023; Schwartz et al., 2010). Berry proposed that acculturation occurred in three phases: contact, conflict, and adaptation (Adames & Chavez-Dueñas, 2016). *Contact* refers to the initial encounter of the individual with the dominant group, which may happen voluntarily or involuntarily. *Conflict* refers to the tension between the dominant and the less dominant culture. *Adaptation* is when individuals blend in to reduce the conflict between the dominant and less dominant groups. Berry (1997, 2003) proposed that two main issues stem from the acculturation process: the questioning regarding retaining values and attitudes of the culture of origin (cultural maintenance) and wanting to increase or decrease contact with the dominant group. Berry identified several acculturation strategies that individuals might employ to address these challenges. The first approach is *assimilation*, which involves embracing or adapting to the cultural values and practices of the dominant culture without any motivation to retain one's cultural heritage. The second is *separation* or *segregation*, wherein individuals show no interest in adopting the cultural values and practices of either the dominant culture or their culture of origin. The third approach is *integration*, which involves individuals maintaining their culture of origin while adopting elements from the dominant culture. Berry's acculturation model has been challenged in recent literature, and a multidimensional process is offered instead. Rather than focusing solely on one aspect of an individual's experience, it is proposed that different factors interact and influence each other and that acculturation is a dynamic process (Schwartz et al., 2010; van der Zee & van Oudehoven, 2022).

Considerations to the Counselor When Reflecting Feelings to Multiculturally Diverse Clients With Different Levels of Acculturation

When working with clients from diverse cultural backgrounds, counselors must consider a range of factors, including the client's legal status in the United States, their age at immigration, whether they were born in the United States, the number of generations they are removed from their culture of origin, and how intergenerational or transgenerational differences within their families may affect their relationships with others. These factors can significantly impact the client's experiences and perceptions, and counselors need to be aware of and sensitive to them.

Counselors must consider how their acculturation views and transgenerational gaps impact how they conceptualize the client's problems and monitor their worldviews when reflecting on feelings. Regardless of whether the counselor is part of the dominant culture, understanding where the client is within the process of acculturation or cultural identity is crucial to minimize situations in the session that may lead to abrupt termination of services by the client or that perpetuate the client's negative self-view as a minority (Sue et al., 2022). Counseling literature in multiculturalism discusses how cultural identity influences whether a client may prefer or reject a helper from the same culture or race. Counselors should monitor themselves and not take personal rejection from the client or avoid overly pleasing for fear of impacting the therapeutic relationship (Sue et al., 2022).

Counselors also should monitor their feelings about acculturation or cultural identity, as this may differ from the client's. The answer is not to avoid the conversation about culture as it relates to the client or push ideology about acculturation but to promote empathy, humility, and respect when discussing culturally sensitive topics. When counselors reflect feelings appropriately, with proper timing and kindness, clients may process and establish connections that help them challenge the negative views about themselves and further explore their cultural identity, likely leading to balance, decreased distress, and improved mental health.

THE IMPACT OF ACCULTURATION RELATIVE TO OLGA AND THE REFLECTION OF FEELINGS: DR. AZILDE SANCHEZ'S PERSPECTIVE

Let's continue to apply our knowledge of reflecting feelings from a culturally sensitive perspective to Olga's case. As Olga's counselor, I would use cultural auditing during the intake and counseling sessions to ensure that any reflection of feelings is respectful and sensitive to her cultural background (Boyer, 2020; Collins et al., 2010).

I would consider her position regarding the values of her culture and how these may influence the way she may respond to the microskill of reflecting feelings. For instance, cultural perspectives on values regarding dignity, respect, fatalism, and trust can influence Latiné clients' interpretations and responses to therapeutic interactions (Adames & Chavez-Dueñas, 2016). In addition to those previously discussed, *personalismo* and *familismo* are other two relevant values counselors must consider when providing multiculturally sensitive services to Latiné clients. Adames and Chavez-Dueñtas (2016) state that *personalismo*, also referred to as *simpatía*, is a "value that places considerable emphasis on the personal, smooth interactions of people while avoiding conflict or confrontation" (p. 180). *Familismo* is a value that revolves around the importance of family involvement, closeness with members of the nuclear and extended family, and those considered family prioritizing the collective well-being over that of the individual (Adames & Chavez-Dueñas, 2016; Ayón et al., 2010; Maercker et al., 2019).

How much importance is given to these values may be mediated by her level of acculturation. However, this aspect does not just pertain to her; my level of acculturation can also impact my internalization of these values. Although we both share the commonality of being first-generation American citizens, our backgrounds differ significantly. I was born and raised in Puerto Rico, a U.S. territory whose official languages are Spanish and English. However, most Puerto Ricans communicate primarily in Spanish and maintain their cultural traditions.

> On the other hand, Olga was born and raised in the mainland United States, possibly experiencing more direct exposure to the dominant culture's values. These disparities may result in differences in our acculturation levels. Consider that the level of acculturation of Latinés to the dominant culture, regardless of their country of origin, can affect how much weight specific cultural values and themes may hold. These differences can influence cognitions, feelings expression, content interpretation, and response to the microskill of reflecting feelings.

Now that we have explored how counselor self-awareness, client worldview, and acculturation influence reflecting feelings, let's discuss how language plays a role.

Language and Reflecting Feelings

Language and psychotherapy are deeply intertwined. The therapeutic craft is relational, and language plays a critical role in all human relationships (Espin, 2013). When the counselor and client meet for their first session, they embark on a journey that relies heavily on establishing open and trusting communication. As such, language plays a key role in establishing effective communication as it facilitates the development of a strong therapeutic bond. When working with nonnative English-speaking clients, communication barriers can pose challenges in conveying and decoding words and emotions. Studies have shown that individuals who are multilingual differ from monolinguals in how they cognitively and linguistically organize their perceptions, memory, comprehension, self-perception, and personal experiences (Cockcroft et al., 2017; Melo-Pfeifer, 2015). Therefore, understanding the interconnectedness between language, culture, and emotions when working with diverse clients, is critical for effective therapeutic work.

One of the challenges of counseling individuals in their nonnative language is the likelihood of misinterpreting terms, especially phrases that are culturally loaded (Georgiadou, 2014). Another complicating factor is that nonnative speakers may struggle with feelings of disingenuity, especially when expressing their affective experiences or emotions in a second language (Imberti, 2007). The combination of cognitive and emotional challenges which can adversely impact the production and processing of information can leave the client feeling tongue tied and misunderstood. MacIntyre and Gardner (1994) described this feeling of apprehension and tension experienced by nonnative speakers as foreign language anxiety. They observed that such individuals experience feelings of fear and self-consciousness, which can limit their ability to listen, speak, and learn effectively. To bridge this language divide, counselors should learn to attend to language-based issues that may negatively affect the therapeutic relationship and its outcomes.

Language and Emotional Expression

When working with nonnative English speakers, building rapport, and delving deep into sensitive and emotionally charged subjects can be a daunting task, especially for the novice counselor. Recent behavioral, developmental, and neurological studies have shown that language plays a significant role in both expression and interpretation of emotions (Lindquist et al., 2015; Brooks et al., 2017). These studies have demonstrated that language helps to store and access conceptual knowledge about emotions. In other words, the core meaning of specific emotion words can help the listener make sense of the speaker's affective feelings in a particular context. Lindquist et al. (2015b), observed that emotion words convey abstract concepts, which embody previous experiences combined with culturally acquired knowledge about bodily feelings, facial expressions, and situations associated with a specific emotion. To accurately capture the meaning behind a client's stated emotions, it is important for the counselor to appreciate the role that language plays in formulating the emotion word.

In their pioneering research on the development of linguistically and culturally sensitive training for clinicians, Dewaele and Costa (2013) established multiple familial, environmental, and sociocultural factors that affect language use in therapy. For instance, they found that individuals may only access emotions in a particular language, depending on how and when the words were learned. In other instances, clients may find it more therapeutic to speak in their second language, since it may provide opportunities for greater expression of emotions, especially for individuals who may have been discouraged from displaying emotions during their upbringing. These findings indicated that the decisions influencing the choice of appropriate language during counseling sessions can be quite complex. Clinicians should, therefore, not assume that nonnative speakers will always prefer to use their first language over the second (Costa & Dewaele, 2019). Given these complex issues, it is critical for the counselor to explore any constraining factors, including personal biases and assumptions that may undermine their clinical judgment.

Researchers have also shown that multilingual clients can vary their emotionality between languages based on a variety of factors, including how frequently they use a particular language (Degner et al., 2011; Simcox et al., 2012), the emotional contexts within which they learned and used specific feelings (Altarriba, 2008), the ease with which they can access their vocabulary (Segalowitz et al., 2008), and their proficiency level in a specific language (Eilola et al., 2011). Dewaele and Costa's (2013) study captured some of these differences among nonnative English-speaking clients. They showed that nearly 61% of the participants claimed that code switching from English to their first language enabled them to access more nuanced, rich, and emotionally charged vocabulary. Their research also demonstrated how some individuals felt liberated by the ability to express traumatic experiences in the language in which the trauma had occurred. Some participants claimed that switching between English and their native language during therapy felt like putting on different personas. One client, for instance, stated that this experience felt like a part of him did not attend therapy (Dewaele & Costa, 2013).

Language and Gestures With Nonnative Speakers

Another important component of language expression is the use of gestures. In his research on body-language communication, McNeil (2010) described hand gestures as windows to the brain and mind. Studies have shown that nonnative speakers are likely to use more gestures to make up for weaker communicative abilities when speaking in their nondominant language, especially individuals who acquired their second language later in life (Azar et al., 2019). Further, neuro-imaging studies, which showed that emotions can control specific action and motor related areas of the brain, have suggested that hand gestures play a vital role in communicating emotions (Catak et al., 2018; Guilbert et al., 2021). Incidentally, during our joint research meetings, the use of gestures in communicating visual and abstract concepts became apparent when one of the coauthors inadvertently used a representational gesture to help communicate a culture-specific concept to the team.

The bilingual coauthor unwittingly demonstrated a cognitive function of gestures between speakers (Macedonia et al., 2011) as she depicted lexical retrieval, language production, and communicative functions of gestures among bilingual speakers (Hostetter, 2011; Kita et al., 2017). During this interaction, another coauthor noticed this use of hand gestures and shared this observation with the speaker, which spurred a spirited discussion about the importance of acknowledging and validating such gestures with second language speakers. Given that counselors are in the business of helping individuals identify and explore difficult emotions, a better understanding of the use of gestures among clients can instantaneously yield useful therapeutic insights.

Process Questions

1. Considering the challenges in language, culture, and emotional expression, how can you ensure you are accurately interpreting and validating the emotions expressed by Olga?
2. In what ways can you explore Olga's preferences for using Spanish or English as well as code-switching during therapy sessions, while being sensitive to her upbringing, personal biases, and assumptions?
3. How can you recognize and attend to Olga's use of gestures to facilitate a deeper understanding of her emotions and experiences and overcome potential communication barriers?

OLGA'S LANGUAGE PREFERENCE AND ITS IMPACT ON REFLECTING FEELINGS: DR. AZILDE SANCHEZ'S PERSPECTIVE

To establish rapport with the client, one of the first things I would do is clarify the language preference. It is essential to ask about language preference before beginning a session and not make assumptions based on the client's appearance, name, or last name. Consider that just because a client was born in a particular country does not mean they exclusively communicate their feelings in the official language of that place of origin.

Our vignette mentions that Olga is a Latina born in the United States, and her parents are from El Salvador. I must consider what language she communicates in or expresses feelings. For example, in our vignette, the client fluctuates using English and Spanish to express feelings and share symptoms. She describes herself as a "worry wart" and then, in another moment, uses the word "*loca*" (a Spanish term for "crazy" in English) to suggest that she feels out of control or overwhelmed. Suppose clients fluctuate using words we do not understand. In that case, it is essential to clarify with the client the meaning and educate ourselves about the client's cultural use. Considering that I am Puerto Rican of Dominican descent and speak English and Spanish, and so does Olga, it would be simplistic to assume that there would not be communication issues. Notice that even if we speak similar languages, specific terms, colloquialisms, gestures, and idiomatic phrases may vary due to our cultural backgrounds, level of education, and socioeconomic status. Therefore, despite my similar background and language skills, communication issues may still arise due to cultural differences in terms, gestures, and phrases. It would be crucial to monitor my use of language and ask for clarification to ensure that I am reflecting feelings appropriately.

Process Questions

If Olga communicates in multiple languages, can we assume she will express, interpret content, and reflect feelings equally? What considerations should we have about language preference and use when working with Olga? As Olga's counselor, what aspects of verbal and nonverbal language would you consider when applying the microskill of reflection?

THE BENEFITS OF REFLECTING FEELINGS IN TREATMENT PLANNING AND ADVOCACY FOR OLGA: DR. AZILDE SANCHEZ'S PERSPECTIVE

Collaborating with the client and considering evidence-based practices are essential strategies when developing a treatment plan. However, it is crucial to remember that not all interventions are tailored or empirically validated for all groups, especially when working with minority populations. In such cases, culturally adapted models may be an option, but it is crucial to regularly check with the client to ensure their comfort with the intervention. The microskill of reflection of feelings is an excellent tool to bring awareness to clients about their level of comfort with the treatment. For instance, if I was working with Olga and we had developed a treatment plan she agreed to implement, I would periodically check her progress and obtain her feedback regarding her willingness to continue using the strategies. I always tell my clients that we work together, and if something does not work, we can always explore other interventions that may be a better fit.

Let us assume I engaged with Olga in a mindfulness exercise or a relaxation technique, and her gestures suggested discomfort. In that case, I could pause and use the microskill of reflection of feelings to help Olga bring awareness about affect, feelings, and emotions regarding her bodily responses. The technique could help clarify whether my impressions were consistent with my observations and whether I should continue or stop the intervention.

Throughout the treatment planning process, the microskill of reflection of feelings can help me navigate whether I understand Olga's affect and emotions as I apply interventions or give suggestions, particularly when she has difficulties expressing her feelings or disagreeing with my recommendations. It is also essential to recognize that Latiné patients may hold authority figures in high regard (Adames & Chavez-Dueñas, 2016; Boyer, 2020). As someone with a doctoral degree and older than Olga, she may hesitate to disagree with my recommendations openly. While she may verbally confirm the effectiveness of my interventions, her body language may convey a different message. Utilizing the microskill of reflection can prove valuable in addressing this potential discrepancy and empowering the client to self-advocate. Reflecting on her feelings and nonverbal cues, I can facilitate a conversation that allows Olga to feel at ease expressing any concerns or disagreements, ultimately reducing the likelihood of prematurely ending treatment due to fear of disagreeing or disappointing the provider. This can also be an opportunity to rehearse self-advocacy and increase assertive communication in other areas of her life.

Final Thoughts on the Case of Olga and the Reflection of Feelings

In my application of a culturally sensitive approach to the technique of reflection of feelings, frequently ask yourself the following questions: Am I aware of my own attitudes and beliefs that could interfere with reflecting feelings accurately? Do power and privilege dynamics, acculturation, or gender play a role in interpreting or reflecting feelings to my client? Am I knowledgeable about my client's culture and subculture, including verbal and nonverbal language? Have I consulted with experts or supervisors to enhance my cultural competence? Do I understand my client's worldview, their unique needs, and how my own worldview can interfere with our interactions? Am I using culturally appropriate interventions and collaborating with my client to meet their specific needs?

Self-reflection is essential for counselors to identify any biases, values, or attitudes that may negatively influence their application of the micro skill of reflection. Through reflection, counselors can recognize personal biases that may affect the therapeutic relationship. Self-reflection can also help counselors understand how their cultural background and worldview may influence their interpretation of a client's behavior or feelings, leading to more culturally sensitive practice. Engaging in self-reflection can help counselors avoid countertransference issues and effectively apply the microskill of reflection, fostering better outcomes for clients. If you were Olga's counselor, what questions would you develop for yourself?

CHAPTER SUMMARY

Reflecting feelings continues to be a core counseling skill that has withstood the test of time. Over time, the delivery of this technique has evolved to consider the diversity of emotional experiences, both in our lives as the counselor and in the lives of our clients. This chapter deconstructed the concept of reflecting feelings to be more than just stating back a verbally expressed feeling to the client and encouraged us to explore and examine it from a multicultural and social justice lens.

The Multicultural and Social Justice Counseling Competencies provided the praxis from which to complete this task of reimagining what reflecting feelings is and can be. Starting with counselor self-awareness, moving into client worldview and the counseling relationship, and including counseling and advocacy interventions, this chapter used the case of Olga to demonstrate how to reflect feelings in a culturally humble and socially just manner.

Cultural norms can affect how clients communicate, as some cultures may view the suppression of emotions as a sign of weakness, while others may value or disregard openness in therapy. Counselors must be multiculturally competent to avoid misinterpreting cultural differences and promote effective communication. They can use techniques like expressive therapy, encouraging clients to express their emotions through creative means, including bibliotherapy, cinematherapy, narrative therapy, and psychodrama (Henderson, 2012; Vernon, 2013). Additionally, advocacy intervention is another way counselors can support clients in expressing their needs and understanding how societal systems can impact their lives. Advocacy is a vital skill for counselors and can be applied in various domains at the micro, meso, and macro levels to promote trust and effective therapy outcomes.

To review, counselor self-awareness involves the counselor exploring their personal biases and beliefs about feelings and emotions. Self-awareness is complex because we are not aware of that which we are not aware. Thus, creating and providing space for us and our clients to explore the internal and external experiences within the immediacy warranted by the situation at hand, which may very well go beyond the therapy room, is very important. As a future counselor, you will learn to notice how and why you react to things. You will do well by reflecting on how your culture, family experience, values, biases, attitudes, and beliefs influence these reactions. Remember to always hold an atmosphere of humility, curiosity, and a nonjudgmental attitude to foster authenticity without fear. And always kindly check with your clients if you are grasping their experience correctly. Do not worry—this takes time and practice, but in time, you will learn that being authentic and curious is very powerful in reflecting feelings, as you will be modeling and empowering these traits in your clients.

CHAPTER REFLECTION AND DISCUSSION QUESTIONS

1. Reflecting feelings effectively can foster rapport, trust, and emotional insight within the therapeutic relationship (Ivey et al., 2018). Of the 12 aspects listed, choose one that would feel most comfortable achieving, and explain why. Also, choose one that brings you anxiety and explain why that one skill may be challenging for you.
2. Common mainstream belief emphasizes six primary emotions: sad, mad, glad, scared, disgust, and surprise (Ivey et al., 2018). These emotions are interchangeable amongst cultures and a part of the human experience. Share your thoughts on this information; do you agree or disagree?
3. How would you engage in collaborative clarification to ensure that you understand what your client is communicating? How does your counselor self-awareness influence your clinical engagement with the client?
4. The therapeutic skill of reflecting feelings is dependent on the client's verbal and nonverbal expressions of a feeling during a session. These expressions are influenced by the client's worldview, which is colored by their individual intersecting identities. So how do we, as counselors, reflect feelings for men—when they may not express feelings in sessions?
5. The answer is not to avoid the conversation about culture as it relates to the client or push ideology about acculturation but to promote empathy, humility, and respect when discussing culturally sensitive topics. What are your viewpoints on acculturation, and what has been your experience with it in your own life story?

ADDITIONAL RESOURCES

10 Best Self-Awareness Books for Increasing Reflection. https://positivepsychology.com/self-awareness-books/

Reiter, M. D. (2022). *Therapeutic Interviewing: Essential Skills and Contexts of Counseling* (2nd ed.). Routledge. https://doi.org/10.4324/9781003195832

Edmonds, C. L. (1998). *Reflections of feelings*. Winter Again Publications.

Geldard, K., & Geldard D. (2012). *Personal counseling skills: An integrative approach*. Charles C. Thomas.

Hill, C. E., & Norcross, J. C. (Eds.). (2023). *Psychotherapy skills and methods that work*. Oxford University Press. https://doi.org/10.1093/oso/9780197611012.001.0001

Schrantz, K. N., & McLean, A. L. L. (2020). Reflection (therapeutic behavior). In V. Zeigler-Hill & T. K. Shackelford, (Eds.), *Encyclopedia of personality and individual differences.* Springer, Cham. https://doi.org/10.1007/978-3-319-24612-3_841

Wilce, J. M. (2009). *Language and emotion.* Cambridge University Press.

REFERENCES

Adames, H. Y., Chavez-Dueñas, N. Y., Sharma, S., & La Roche, M. J. (2018). Intersectionality in psychotherapy: The experiences of an AfroLatinx queer immigrant. *Psychotherapy (Chicago, Ill.), 55*(1), 73–79. https://doi.org/10.1037/pst0000152

Adolphs, R. (2017). How should neuroscience study emotions? By distinguishing emotion states, concepts, and experiences. *Social Cognitive and Affective Neuroscience, 12*(1), 24–31. https://doi.org/10.1093/scan/nsw153

Altarriba, J. (2008). Expressions of emotion as mediated by context. *Bilingualism (Cambridge, England) 11*(2), 165–167. https://doi.org/10.1017/S1366728908003295

Ayón, C., Marsiglia, F. F., & Bermudez-Parsai, M. (2010). Latino family mental health: Exploring the role of discrimination and familismo. *Journal of Community Psychology, 38*(6), 742–756. https://doi.org/10.1002/jcop.20392

Azar, Z., Backus, A. M., & Özyürek, A. (2020). Language contact does not drive gesture transfer: Heritage speakers maintain language specific gesture patterns in each language. *Bilingualism (Cambridge, England), 23*(2), 414–428. https://doi.org/10.1017/S136672891900018X

Berg-Cross, L., Jennings, P., & Baruch, R. (1990). Cinematherapy: Theory and application. *Psychotherapy in private practice, 8*(1), 135–156.

Berry, J. W. (1997). Immigration, acculturation, and adaptation. *Applied Psychology, 46*(1), 5–34. https://doi.org/10.1111/j.1464-0597.1997.tb01087.x

Berry, J. W. (2003). *Conceptual approaches to acculturation.* American Psychological Association.

Boyer, W. (2022). Cultural auditing to enhance reflective counseling practices with indigenous families. *Journal of Multicultural Counseling and Development, 50*(3), 151–161. https://doi.org/10.1002/jmcd.12245

Brewster, L., & McNicol, S. (2021). Bibliotherapy in practice: A person-centred approach to using books for mental health and dementia in the community. *Medical Humanities, 47*(4), e12–e12. https://doi.org/10.1136/medhum-2020-011898

Brooks, J. A., Shablack, H., Gendron, M., Satpute, A. B., Parrish, M. H., & Lindquist, K. A. (2017). The role of language in the experience and perception of emotion: A neuroimaging meta-analysis. *Social Cognitive and Affective Neuroscience, 12*(2), 169–183. https://doi.org/10.1093/scan/nsw121

Bucay-Harari, L., Page, K. R., Krawczyk, N., Robles, Y. P., & Castillo-Salgado, C. (2020). Mental health needs of an emerging Latino community. *The Journal of Behavioral Health Services & Research, 47*(3), 388–398. https://doi.org/10.1007/s11414-020-09688-3

Casas, J. B., Benuto, L. T., & González, F. (2020). Latinos, anxiety, and cognitive behavioral therapy: A systematic review. *Revista Internacional De Psicología y Terapia Psicológica, 20*(1), 91–104. https://www.ijpsy.com/volumen20/num1/537/latinos-anxiety-and-cognitive-behavioral-EN.pdf

Çatak, E. N., Alper, A., & Tilbe, G. (2018). The relationship between handedness and valence: A gesture study. *Quarterly Journal of Experimental Psychology (2006), 71*(12), 2615–2626. https://doi.org/10.1177/1747021817750110

Chang, C. Y. (2012). *Professional advocacy: A professional responsibility*. Routledge.

Cockcroft, K., Wigdorowitz, M., & Liversage, L. (2019). A multilingual advantage in the components of working memory. *Bilingualism (Cambridge, England), 22*(1), 15–29. https://doi.org/10.1017/S1366728917000475

Collins, S., Arthur, N., & Wong-Wylie, G. (2010). Enhancing reflective practice in multicultural counseling through cultural auditing. *Journal of Counseling & Development, 88*(3), 340–347. https://doi.org/10.1002/j.1556-6678.2010.tb00031.x

Costa, B., & Dewaele, J. (2019). The talking cure: Building the core skills and the confidence of counsellors and psychotherapists to work effectively with multilingual patients through training and supervision. *Counselling and Psychotherapy Research, 19*(3), 231–240. https://doi.org/10.1002/capr.12187

Dana, D. (2020). *Polyvagal flip chart: Understanding the science of safety (Norton series on interpersonal neurobiology)*. W.W. Norton & Company.

Degner, J., Doycheva, C., & Wentura, D. (2012). It matters how much you talk: On the automaticity of affective connotations of first and second language words. *Bilingualism (Cambridge, England), 15*(1), 181–189. https://doi.org/10.1017/S1366728911000095

DeLee, F. R. (2014). *Group supervision of counselors-in-training implementing the awareness wheel* Texas. A&M University—Corpus Christi.

Dewaele, J., & Costa, B. (2013). Multilingual clients' experience of psychotherapy. *Language and Psychoanalysis, 2*(2), 31–50. https://doi.org/10.7565/landp.2013.005

Eilola, T. M., & Havelka, J. (2011). Behavioural and physiological responses to the emotional and taboo stroop tasks in native and non-native speakers of english. *The International Journal of Bilingualism: Cross-Disciplinary, Cross-Linguistic Studies of Language Behavior, 15*(3), 353–369. https://doi.org/10.1177/1367006910379263

Espin, O. M. (2013). "Making love in English": Language in psychotherapy with immigrant women. *Women & Therapy, 36*(3–4), 198–218. https://doi.org/10.1080/02703149.2013.797847

Etchison, M., & Kleist, D. M. (2000). *Review of narrative therapy: Research and utility*. SAGE. https://doi.org/10.1177/1066480700081009

Fickling, M. J. (2016). An exploration of career counselors' perspectives on advocacy. *The Professional Counselor, 6*(2), 174–188. https://doi.org/10.15241/mf.6.2.174

Flynn, J. J., Hollenstein, T., & Mackey, A. (2010). The effect of suppressing and not accepting emotions on depressive symptoms: Is suppression different for men and women? *Personality and Individual Differences, 49*(6), 582–586. https://doi.org/10.1016/j.paid.2010.05.022

Gentsch, A., & Kuehn, E. (2022). Clinical manifestations of body memories: The impact of past bodily experiences on mental health. *Brain Sciences, 12*(5), 594. https://doi.org/10.3390/brainsci12050594

Georgiadou, L. (2014). "My language thing ... is like a big shadow always behind me": International counselling trainees' challenges in beginning clinical practice. *Counselling and Psychotherapy Research, 14*(1), 10–18. https://doi.org/10.1080/14733145.2013.770896

Gibson, M. A. (2001). Immigrant adaptation and patterns of acculturation. *Human Development*, *44*(1), 19–23. https://doi.org/10.1159/000057037

Guilbert, D., Sweller, N., & Van Bergen, P. (2021). Emotion and gesture effects on narrative recall in young children and adults. *Applied Cognitive Psychology*, *35*(4), 873–889. https://doi.org/10.1002/acp.3815

Henderson, D. A. (2012). The creative arts in counseling. *Humanistic Perspectives on Contemporary Counseling Issues*, 63–83.

Hostetter, A. B. (2011). When do gestures communicate? A meta-analysis. *Psychological Bulletin*, *137*(2), 297–315. https://doi.org/10.1037/a0022128

Imberti, P. (2007). Who resides behind the words? Exploring and understanding the language experience of the non-English-speaking immigrant. *Families in Society*, *88*(1), 67–73. https://doi.org/10.1606/1044-3894.3593

Ivey, A. E., Ivey, M. B., & Zalaquett, C. P. (2018). *Intentional interviewing and counseling: Facilitating client development in a multicultural society.* (9th ed.). Cengage.

Johnson, S. M. (2019). *Attachment theory in practice: Emotionally focused therapy (EFT) with individuals, couples, and families.* The Guilford Press.

Kita, S., Alibali, M. W., & Chu, M. (2017). How do gestures influence thinking and speaking? the gesture-for-conceptualization hypothesis. *Psychological Review*, *124*(3), 245–266. https://doi.org/10.1037/rev0000059

Kring, A. M., & Gordon, A. H. (1998). Sex differences in emotion: Expression, experience, and physiology. *Journal of Personality and Social Psychology*, *74*(3), 686–703. https://doi.org/10.1037/0022-3514.74.3.686

Lai, N., & Tsai, H. (2014). Practicing psychodrama in Chinese culture. *The Arts in Psychotherapy*, *41*(4), 386–390. https://doi.org/10.1016/j.aip.2014.06.005

Lancaster, J., & Terepka, A. (2020). *Homework Assignments and Handouts for LGBTQ+ Clients.* Routledge.

Lee, C. C. (2007). *Social justice: A moral imperative for counselors.* American Counseling Association. https://www.counseling.org/resources/library/ACA%20Digests/ACAPCD-07.pdf

Leite, R. O., Pavia, V., Kobayashi, M. A., Lee, T. K., Prado, G., Messiah, S. E., & St. George, S. M. (2023). The effects of parent–adolescent acculturation gaps on adolescent lifestyle behaviors: Moderating role of family communication. *Journal of Latinx Psychology*, *11*(1), 21–39. https://doi.org/10.1037/lat0000215

Lindquist, K. A., MacCormack, J. K., & Shablack, H. (2015). The role of language in emotion: Predictions from psychological constructionism. *Frontiers in Psychology*, *6*, 444–444. https://doi.org/10.3389/fpsyg.2015.00444

Lindquist, K. A., Satpute, A. B., & Gendron, M. (2015). Does language do more than communicate emotion? *Current Directions in Psychological Science: A Journal of the American Psychological Society*, *24*(2), 99–108. https://doi.org/10.1177/0963721414553440

Lindquist, K. A. (2017). The role of language in emotion: Existing evidence and future directions. *Current Opinion in Psychology*, *17*, 135–139. https://doi.org/10.1016/j.copsyc.2017.07.006

Macedonia, M., Müller, K., & Friederici, A. D. (2011). The impact of iconic gestures on foreign language word learning and its neural substrate. *Human Brain Mapping*, *32*(6), 982–998. https://doi.org/10.1002/hbm.21084

MacIntyre, P. D., & Gardner, R. C. (1994). The subtle effects of language anxiety on cognitive processing in the second language. *Language Learning, 44*(2), 283–305. https://doi.org/10.1111/j.1467-1770.1994.tb01103.x

Maercker, A., Ben-Ezra, M., Esparza, O. A., & Augsburger, M. (2019). Fatalism as a traditional cultural belief potentially relevant to trauma sequelae: Measurement equivalence, extent and associations in six countries. *European Journal of Psychotraumatology, 10*(1), 1657371–1657371. https://doi.org/10.1080/20008198.2019.1657371

Marsick, E. (2010). Cinematherapy with preadolescents experiencing parental divorce: A collective case study. *The Arts in Psychotherapy, 37*(4), 311–318. https://doi.org/10.1016/j.aip.2010.05.006

McGoldrick, M., Giordano, J., & Garcia-Preto, N. (2005). *Ethnicity & family therapy* (3rd ed.). The Guilford Press.

McNeill, D. (2010). *Language and gesture*. Cambridge University Press.

Melo-Pfeifer, S. (2015). The role of the family in heritage language use and learning: Impact on heritage language policies. *International Journal of Bilingual Education and Bilingualism, 18*(1), 26–44. https://doi.org/10.1080/13670050.2013.868400

Neville, P. (2010). The reading cure? Bibliotherapy, healthy reading schemes and the treatment of mental illness in Ireland. *International Review of Modern Sociology, 36*(2), 221–244.

Nummenmaa, L., Glerean, E., Hari, R., & Hietanen, J. K. (2014). Bodily maps of emotions. *Proceedings of the National Academy of Sciences–PNAS, 111*(2), 646–651. https://doi.org/10.1073/pnas.1321664111

Nuñez, A., González, P., Talavera, G. A., Sanchez-Johnsen, L., Roesch, S. C., Davis, S. M., Arguelles, W., Womack, V. Y., Ostrovsky, N. W., Ojeda, L., Penedo, F. J., & Gallo, L. C. (2016). Machismo, marianismo, and negative cognitive-emotional factors: Findings from the Hispanic community health study/study of Latinos sociocultural ancillary study. *Journal of Latina/o Psychology, 4*(4), 202–217. https://doi.org/10.1037/lat0000050

Pell, M. D., Paulmann, S., Dara, C., Alasseri, A., & Kotz, S. A. (2009). Factors in the recognition of vocally expressed emotions: A comparison of four languages. *Journal of Phonetics, 37*(4), 417–435. https://doi.org/10.1016/j.wocn.2009.07.005

Peluso, P. R., & Freund, R. R. (2018). Therapist and client emotional expression and psychotherapy outcomes: A meta-analysis. *Psychotherapy, 55*(4), 461–472. https://doi.org/10.1037/pst0000165

Phillips, M. L., Drevets, W. C., Rauch, S. L., & Lane, R. (2003). *Neurobiology of emotion perception II: Implications for major psychiatric disorders*. Elsevier Inc. https://doi.org/10.1016/S0006-3223(03)00171-9

Pompeo, A. M., & Levitt, D. H. (2014). A path of counselor self-awareness. *Counseling and Values, 59*(1), 80–94. https://doi.org/10.1002/j.2161-007X.2014.00043.x

Porges, S. W. (2007). The polyvagal perspective. *Biological Psychology, 74*(2), 116–143. https://doi.org/10.1016/j.biopsycho.2006.06.009

Ratts, M. J., Singh, A. A., Nassar-McMillan, S., Butler, S. K., & McCullough, J. R. (2016). Multicultural and social justice counseling competencies: Guidelines for the counseling profession. *Journal of Multicultural Counseling and Development, 44*(1), 28–48. https://doi.org/10.1002/jmcd.12035

Rice, S. M., Kealy, D., Ogrodniczuk, J. S., Seidler, Z. E., Denehy, L., & Oliffe, J. L. (2020). The cost of bottling it up: Emotion suppression as a mediator in the relationship between anger and depression among men with prostate cancer. *Cancer Management and Research, 12*, 1039–1046. https://doi.org/10.2147/CMAR.S237770

Ricks, L., Kitchens, S., Goodrich, T., & Hancock, E. (2014). My story: The use of narrative therapy in individual and group counseling. *Journal of Creativity in Mental Health, 9*(1), 99–110. https://doi.org/10.1080/15401383.2013.870947

Rogers, C. R. (1961). *On becoming a person: A therapist's view of psychotherapy.* Constable.

Schaefer, C. E., & Drewes, A. A. (2015). Prescriptive play therapy. In K. J. O'Connor, C. E. Schaefer & L. D. Braverman (Eds.), *Handbook of play therapy* (pp. 227–240). John Wiley & Sons, Inc. https://doi.org/10.1002/9781119140467.ch10

Schmitt, D. P., Realo, A., Voracek, M., & Allik, J. (2009). "Why can't a man be more like a woman?" Sex differences in big five personality traits across 55 cultures: Correction to schmitt et al. (2008). *Journal of Personality and Social Psychology, 96*(1), 118–118. https://doi.org/10.1037/a0014651

Schwartz, S. J., Unger, J. B., Zamboanga, B. L., & Szapocznik, J. (2010). Rethinking the concept of acculturation: Implications for theory and research. *The American Psychologist, 65*(4), 237–251. https://doi.org/10.1037/a0019330

Schwartz, H. A., Eichstaedt, J. C., Kern, M. L., Dziurzynski, L., Ramones, S. M., Agrawal, M., Shah, A., Kosinski, M., Stillwell, D., Seligman, M. E. P., & Ungar, L. H. (2013). Personality, gender, and age in the language of social media: The open-vocabulary approach. *PloS One, 8*(9), e73791–e73791. https://doi.org/10.1371/journal.pone.0073791

Slack, S. (1985). Reflections on a workshop with carl rogers. *The Journal of Humanistic Psychology, 25*(2), 35–42. https://doi.org/10.1177/0022167885252004

Segalowitz, N., Trofimovich, P., Gatbonton, E., & Sokolovskaya, A. (2008). Feeling affect in a second language: The role of word recognition automaticity. *The Mental Lexicon, 3*(1), 47–71. https://doi.org/10.1075/ml.3.1.05seg

Shapiro, F. (2017). *Eye movement desensitization and reprocessing (EMDR) therapy: Basic principles, protocols, and procedures.* Guilford Publications.

Simcox, T., Pilotti, M., Mahamane, S., & Romero, E. (2012). Does the language in which aversive stimuli are presented affect their processing? *The International Journal of Bilingualism: Cross-Disciplinary, Cross-Linguistic Studies of Language Behavior, 16*(4), 419–427. https://doi.org/10.1177/1367006911425821

Sommers-Flanagan, J. (2016). Clinical interview. In J. C. Norcross, G. R. VandenBos, D. K. Freedheim, & R. Krishnamurthy (Eds.), *APA handbook of clinical psychology: Applications and methods* (pp. 3–16). American Psychological Association. https://doi.org/10.1037/14861-001

Sue, D. W., Sue, D., Neville, H. A., & Smith, L. (2019). *Counseling the culturally diverse: Theory and practice* (8th; ed.). John Wiley & Sons, Inc.

Toporek, R. L., Lewis, J. A., & Crethar, H. C. (2009). Promoting systemic change through the ACA advocacy competencies. *Journal of Counseling & Development, 87*(3), 260–268. https://doi.org/10.1002/j.1556-6678.2009.tb00105.x

Van der Kolk, B. (2014). *The body keeps the score: Brain, mind, and body in the healing of trauma.* Penguin Books.

Van der Zee, K., & van Oudenhoven, J. P. (2022). Towards a dynamic approach to acculturation. *International Journal of Intercultural Relations, 88*, 119–124. https://doi.org/10.1016/j.ijintrel.2022.04.004

Vaughn, L. (2019). *Psychology and culture: Thinking, feeling and behaving in a global context.* Routledge.

Vernon, A. (2013). Creative approaches to counseling. In D. Capuzzi & D. R. Gross (Eds.), *Introduction to the counselling profession* (6th ed., pp. 256–290). Routledge/Taylor & Francis Group

Reflection of Meaning

Dr. Amanda DiLorenzo-Garcia, Dr. Jessica Tinstman Jones, Dr. Gelawdiyos Haile, Dr. Everette Coffman, Dr. Amber S. Haley, and Brooke Alker

LEARNING OBJECTIVES

1. Readers will explore and learn personal factors of a client that impact their worldviews and contribute to their meaning making, such as cultural and identity factors.
2. Readers will learn about the skill of reflection of meaning including how and when to implement the skill in counseling sessions.
3. Readers will be provided with strategies and a case study to observe when to utilize and how to strengthen their reflections of meaning.

LEARNING OUTCOMES

1. Readers will explore the personal factors influencing a client's worldviews and contributing to their meaning making, including cultural and identity elements.
2. This chapter will impart knowledge to readers about the skill of reflecting on meaning, offering insights into when and how to implement this skill during counseling sessions.
3. Readers, following this chapter, will have gained strategies and a case study to guide them on when and how to employ and enhance their reflections on meaning.

> "Man's search for meaning is the primary motivation in his life and not a 'secondary rationalization' of instinctual drives."
>
> —Victor Frankl, *Man's Search for Meaning*

Understanding Reflection of Meaning

Diving into the heart of what a client is communicating is the essence of reflection of meaning. Reflection of meaning is moving through the content of a client's story to the underlying message a client is sharing. Young (2017, p. 123) describes "reflection of meaning" as "a significant step beyond reflection of content and emotion, because it helps us understand the client's unique background and perspective. It also allows clients to become aware of the lens through which they are seeing themselves and others."

When a counselor reflects meaning for a client, they are identifying and restating a core value, belief, or message that shapes the client's experiences and feelings. Oftentimes, the meaning is present throughout the client's narrative, yet this may be spoken or unspoken. Illuminating the underlying essence of an experience can be a powerful moment with a client. At times, this may be a meaning the client has expressed previously yet has not connected with their current situation or feelings. Other times, counselors can identify a value or message that the client has not vocalized:

> Reflections of meaning take the client to the deepest part of their psychological experience. As a helper, considering the client's experience, understanding, and inner reflections bring a deeper sense of meaning. This allows the client to have a "deep felt understanding" or a moment of relational depth. In moment of relational depth, clients may feel more understood, seen, and heard in the therapeutic context, bringing them back into a state of connectedness (Mearns & Cooper, 2018). The helper's presence and attunement can reduce a client's fight or flight response simply by being a safe and healthy collaboration. (Cozolino, 2014)

FIGURE 10.1 Nesting Dolls, Largest to Smallest. The largest doll represents the clients presenting concern, the next doll represents the content of the concern, the middle doll represents feelings associated with the concern, the second smallest doll demonstrates deeper feelings, and the smallest doll is the meaning within the client's narrative.

Reflection of meaning can feel abstract at times. As such, the following figures provide a visual aid that is intended to help CITs further understand the process of reaching a reflection of meaning with a client. The figurines in the images are known as nesting dolls, also known as Matryoshka Dolls, which are popular in Russia and other Eastern cultures. The nesting dolls in Figure 10.1 and Figure 10.2 are from Uzbekistan. As shown in Figure 10.1, the largest of the nesting dolls houses the smaller nesting dolls.

In this example, the largest nesting doll represents a client's presenting concern within the therapy process, such as a recent difficult situation. For example, the presenting concern could be a client stating that they were fired from work. In decreasing size order, the second doll represents the content of that presenting concern, which is commonly shared by the client in the initial conversation. Continuing with the example, this would include details about why and how the client was fired. The third nesting doll represents surface level feeling. Per the example, this level may sound like the counselor identifying the client's anger, frustration, and disappointment. The second smallest nesting doll represents deeper feelings such as resentment, insignificance, and purposelessness. The smallest of the nesting dolls represents meaning. In this example, the meaning may be, "You feel purposeless because this job was aligned to your ideals to work with communities in a sustainable way."

FIGURE 10.2 Nesting Dolls Representing Reflection of Meaning Within the Doll for Deeper Feeling.

The nesting dolls create a visual representation of how accessing the meaning of a client's story takes time to approach by first needing to acknowledge and understand the client's content and feelings. Meaning is often buried in the client's story, and we must take time to understand before asserting a reflection of meaning. The nesting dolls demonstrate the steps to reaching reflection of meaning, which are later shown through a case study.

Worldview Implications of Reflection of Meaning

> "We share a common interest, survival, and it cannot be pursued in isolation from others simply because their differences make us uncomfortable."
>
> —Audre Lorde, *Learning from the 60s*

Meaning making is part of an individual's worldview and consists of how they individually and collectively consider their view of self, view of others, and view of the world (Young, 2017). The way people make sense of the world is built through personal experiences, belief systems, culture, language, gender, spirituality, and values. It is vital to understand the client's worldview to understand their perspective and make sense of their internal world. Additionally, helpers should investigate their own worldview and values to give a better perspective to their internal world and how that may influence the therapeutic process.

Reflection of Meaning in Societal Context

In recent years, cultivating culturally competent counselors has received considerable attention. Counselors must be aware, curious, and optimally equipped to work with clientele who may bring an intricate dynamic to counseling. Understanding and honoring how clients assign meaning requires an awareness of the client's intersectionality, experiences, and worldview and requires counselors to be aware of their attitudes and beliefs and how they impact the meaning-making process. The framework that this textbook is anchored in (i.e., the multicultural and social justice counseling competencies [MSJCC]) can help CITs understand clients' meaning-making process. For helpers to efficiently facilitate the meaning-making process, one must first understand and be equipped with the awareness, knowledge, skills, and action to be a culturally competent counselor.

According to Ratts and colleagues (2016), to understand a client's worldview and meaning-making system, counselors' self-awareness plays a critical role. Counselors' self-knowledge can help them to recognize their (a) biases, (b) values (c) worldviews, and (d) social statuses (i.e., oppressed or privileged). Counselors' insight and understanding of their own and their clients' worldviews as well as their marginalized or privileged statuses assist the CIT to be curious, empathetic, and able to engage in unconditional positive regard. Most importantly, counselors' deeper understanding of themselves and their clients often enables them to view their clients' presenting concerns from a larger systemic and policy framework. These elements are the core of building strong therapeutic relationships and can enable the counselor to facilitate the therapeutic environment and meaning-making process efficiently. In short, Ratts and his colleagues (2016) accentuate counselor self-awareness, understanding clients' worldviews, therapeutic relationships, and advocacy as the four developmental domains of MSJCC.

These four developmental domains of MSJCC are paired with four aspirational competencies: attitudes and beliefs, knowledge, skills, and actions. Honoring how clients assign meaning requires an awareness of the client's intersectionality. Understanding clients' intersectionality requires counselors to be aware of their attitudes and beliefs and how they impact the meaning-making process. In addition to the counselor's awareness of their attitude and beliefs, honoring how clients assign meaning also asks for a level of knowledge that spells out the counselor's and their clients' stereotypes and worldviews. At the core of having the knowledge to work with clients who may be from privileged or oppressed societal status is one's ability to communicate. Once counselors increase their awareness about their attitudes and beliefs and have the knowledge to properly express, the next step in their case conceptualization is to utilize skills suitable for their client. Specifically, skills entail deploying culturally sensitive evaluations and interventions. Finally, counselors should take action by engaging in continuing education to illuminate their weaknesses in cross-cultural communication and join other change makers to develop their strengths beyond the counseling session. Counselors can have an impact in the communities and environments in which clients live and directly make a positive impact.

MULTICULTURAL CONSIDERATIONS FOR REFLECTION OF MEANING

To further counselors' understanding of a client's worldview, it's imperative for the helper to work to conceptualize the ways historical and present-day context may be directly or indirectly influencing the client's presenting concern(s) and sense of self. Clients may be aware of the impact of such influences or unconscious of the ways historical and societal factors may be impacting their sense of self and core beliefs. Clients develop their core sense of self across a significant amount of time, experiences, relationships, and contexts.

One's intersectional identities may significantly impact the ways they navigate the world and how the client may be viewed and treated by others. Beginning at birth, clients receive explicit and implicit messages about their sex; gender identity; religious or spiritual practices; race and ethnicity; socioeconomic position; ability or disability status; education; region and country of origin;

body size; and political affiliation. In the United States, messages of praise and acceptance may be reserved for those displaying dominant societal norms, such as being White, born male, heterosexual, Christian, able bodied, physically fit, a natural-born U.S. citizen, college educated, and with social and financial capital (middle to upper class). When offering a reflection of meaning, consider these individual and collective identities' influence on the client's sense of self and worldview. For instance, a Black, cis woman, who identifies as queer, working class, educated and gifted, Christian (Southern Baptist), democrat, temporarily able-bodied, and born in the Southern United States with a larger body frame may experience points of privilege and oppression across their lifetime and societal contexts. It's important for the counselor to work to understand the influence of these intersectional identities on the client's worldview and sense of self, including working to understand key experiences that may encapsulate the client's core beliefs and values. Historically, women, Black and Indigenous People of Color (BIPOC), and members of the LGBTQIA+ community living in the Southern United States have faced significant discrimination and systemic oppression. However, it is vital that the counselor acknowledges historical and present-day events alongside other significant factors shared by the client in conceptualization and treatment planning without imposing stereotypes, assumptions, or biases in their reflections of meaning. To do this, counselors must attentively listen to the client's narrative to comprehend the unique impact these cultural identities play in the client's paradigm rather than inserting their own interpretations of the client's lived experiences with potentially biased views. These cultural identity markers and associated messages help shape clients' worldview, core beliefs, values, and sense of self in relation to others that the counselor will need to identify and collaboratively uncover in the client's meaning-making process.

DIVERSE CLIENTS

Intersectionality is a term originally coined by professor, activist, and legal scholar Kimberlé Crenshaw (1989) to describe the ways individual cultural identities "intersect" with one another and, in some ways, compound marginalized identities and experiences of oppression. Through an intersectional, MSJCC lens, it is of vital importance that the counselor remains open and curious about the client as a whole person in their reflections of core beliefs and meanings. As society becomes increasingly more diverse (e.g., racial/ethnic backgrounds, ideologies, and immigration), so does the likelihood of cross-cultural counseling interactions. Counseling is a microcosm of life, and for many clients, cross-cultural communication in counseling may serve as an affirmative space of support or a reenactment of microaggressions and an additional source of distress (Lee et al., 2018). In working with diverse clients, counselors must be aware of their own identities, beliefs, and biases when posing reflections of meaning for clients as to not do harm or microaggress. *Microaggressions* are subtle, everyday verbal, behavioral, environmental slights, whether intentional or unintentional, that communicate hostile, derogatory, or negative messages to people from traditionally marginalized and oppressed communities (Sue et al., 2007).

Broaching perceived differences in cross-cultural counseling relationships may be warranted to deepen the therapeutic alliance, acknowledge the client's worldview, and strengthen reflections of meaning. It is the counselor's role and responsibility to broach cultural factors impacting the client or the client–counselor relationship, as it may be impacting the therapeutic alliance (one of the strongest predictors of positive therapeutic outcomes) or considering the client's presenting concerns. Use of open-ended, exploratory questions with clients, alongside a supportive tone, open body language, and unconditional positive regard, can gather precursory information for reflections of meaning. For example, a White, male therapist working with an Asian American male client struggling with depression and feelings of alienation, may broach with the client as follows: "I'm curious how identifying as the only Asian American family in your neighborhood might be impacting your feelings of loneliness and isolation." The client's response (confirmation or rejection) may provide critical information about the client's worldview, beliefs, and values to draw from in an appropriately timed reflection of meaning: "You feel alienated because you desire connection within your community which has yet to embrace and value your Asian-American cultural identity." This reflection of meaning takes into account important cultural information gleaned from the work and rapport built with the client and highlights the importance of beliefs and values driving the client's motivation and core sense of self in relation to others.

Meaning Making Through Attachment

Humans are relational, meaning-making, bonding beings. The influence of relationships helps to develop and form neural networks, internal working models (IWMs), and worldviews (Johnson, 2019). IWMs are mental representations or schemas that guide behavior, cognition, and emotions related to the view of self and others and are created through relationships (Gelso et al., 2013). They develop through relationships with others. IWMs, represented by secure attachment, include, "I am worthy, people are helpful, and I am lovable." Insecure attachment styles create IWMs that include, "I am unworthy, I am in danger, and people are not trustworthy."

From childhood to adulthood, individuals are taking in information through experience, which influences the way they view themselves, others, and the world. It is important for the helper to incorporate the MSJCC framework when exploring factors related to worldview. Using a MSJCC framework allows the helper to identify privileged and marginalized positions within their worldview and their clients by identifying assumptions; attitudes; beliefs; biases; social identities; social group statuses; and experiences with power, privilege, and oppression (Ratts et al., 2015). MSJCC provides structure for the helper to understand the narratives of their lives and their client's lives regarding the development of the self-view of others, view of the world, and their values (Table 10.1; Young, 2017).

TABLE 10.1 Examples of Worldview Statements

View of Self	View of Others	View of the World	Values
"I am adaptable."	"I can trust others."	"I am set up for success."	"An eye for an eye."
"I am smart."	"People tend to be helpful."	"The world is what you make it."	"Blood is thicker than water."
"I am not capable of succeeding."	"Nobody cares about me."	"Society is not for me."	"Treat others as you want to be treated."
"I am helpless."	"People are out to take from me."	"Social constructs are in place to limit me."	"Real men never cry."

It is important for helpers to gather information regarding MSJCC components to analyze their client's narratives and their worldview was developed. Some clients may have grown up in a difficult situation with a family that had mental health concerns, low socioeconomic status, or other adverse childhood experiences. Others may have experienced discrimination or racism; such events shape the client's worldview. Through personal experience and relationships with others, clients start to develop internal representation of their worldview.

Applying Reflection of Meaning in a Counseling Context

> There are stories in our lives that we carry with us and often need retelling and revisiting until the deeper meaning of them surfaces. When we sense or hear from a client that their story feels unfinished, this could be an invitation into exploring deeper meaning. As therapists, when we give ourselves permission to reflect on the deeper meaning of our life experiences, our own story, we develop a language of curiosity that we can then use with our clients. By entering this space with compassionate curiosity, we can find deeper knowing and meaning in who we are and what the events mean to us. As we learn to do this with ourselves, we can become more fluent in exploring meaning with our clients.
>
> —Alexandra, PhD, LMFT, Alachua County Crisis Center

When to Use Reflection of Meaning

Reflection of meaning is an advanced skill that takes time to develop. The first goal towards this skill is to have a holistic comprehension of a client's worldview and values. Counselors must get to know their client to understand the meaning behind the client's narrative content and expressions. The use of ROM helps to bring what is unconscious to the conscious level. Using this skill helps mirror the client's beliefs and viewpoints, providing moments of deep self-reflection and intrapersonal processing.

Throughout a session, a client may return to a piece of their narrative. At times, they may use the same language to describe their experience. Although validating this client is valuable, the return to the topic indicates a need to acknowledge a deeper meaning. Let's look at the following client narrative as an example:

> Client: I just don't know what to do with myself. I haven't known what to do with myself since the recession hit and we lost everything and I retired.
>
> Counselor: You're lost and paralyzed. (*reflection of feeling*)
>
> Client: Yeah. Me and my partner, we had everything we wanted, we took trips, we had a lot of friends, we had a lot of fun. But then overnight it was all over. I was in the construction

business for 20 years. We knew people who lost everything but since then were able to recover and get their lives back. But it just never happened for us. And now I just don't know what to do with myself. So if you have any ideas, I'm all ears.

Counselor: Well, as much as I wish I could, I can't provide any answers for you. But I've noticed you've circled around the idea that you don't know what to do with yourself now after the Recession while we are in session. Are you open to some feedback about that? (*closed question*)

Client: Sure.

Counselor: You've mentioned a lot of ideas for things to do in our sessions. In the past couple of months, you've mentioned getting back into fishing now that you have the time, finding a new meditation group to attend, volunteering with the local hospice, and launching a new part-time career as a copywriter. It seems like you know pretty well what you'd like to do with your life now. (*summary*)

Client: I guess hearing it all laid out like that at once, yeah, I've got some direction for my life to go in now.

Counselor: When I hear you say, "After the recession, I don't know what to do with my life," I hear, "I have some ideas of what to do with my life, but I'm terrified of putting them into motion because everything I gain and enjoy could get taken away again." (*reflection of meaning*)

Client: Yeah. Wow. Yeah, I didn't really think about that. I am terrified of that, and that's what keeps me from doing all this stuff I want to do. The idea that whatever life I build back up for myself could get pulled out from under me again. It made me absolutely terrified of success.

Disrupting this client's circling narrative with ROM aided them in accessing unconscious fears they had not engaged with previously in session and opened up space for them to explore a new avenue towards change. Feelings of disorientation and paralysis, while important to validate, were only part of the story for this client. The *meaning* of the paralyzing event—the recession—was that any positive change or progress could be snatched away from them again. This meaning had a freezing effect on any of the client's attempts to change their life; becoming aware of it and processing it in subsequent sessions liberated the client to pursue meaning-making more closely aligned with the life they desired.

Strategies for ROM

Reflection of meaning can be viewed as an advanced counseling skill. While it focuses on reflection, like the skills of paraphrasing and reflection of feelings, it requires the counselor to dig deeper with the client into what is driving their narrative. The following sections provide strategies to support counselors as they navigate learning and implementing this important skill.

SENTENCE STEMS AND FORMULAS

There are many approaches to phrasing a reflection of meaning. In the previous example, the counselor was able to reflect meaning through a restatement of the client's words and connecting them to the underlying concern the client is presenting. When first learning to reflect meaning, this approach may feel a bit challenging, but there are several helpful formulas and sentence stems that can be used to reflect meaning. Each of the following examples represents a possible approach to reflecting meaning, but it is important to note that this list is not exhaustive and should only be viewed as a guide.

Connecting Emotions to Meaning

The first formula to effectively implement a reflection of feeling is to reflect the client's feelings and connect the feeling to the client's underlying meaning. The structure of this reflection is similar to a reflection of feeling; however, it is essential to look at what is underneath rather than connecting to content alone. Focusing on meaning distinguishes this formula from a pure reflection of feeling.

> Formula: "You feel (emotion) because (underlying meaning)."
>
> Example: "You feel devastated because you saw this as your opportunity to make something of yourself."

Reflecting Values

Another approach to reflecting meaning can be to highlight the client's values based on what they have shared. Counselors can do this by highlighting what is important to a client, such as their identities, beliefs, and perspectives. Clients may share these messages directly or indirectly, and this formula encourages counselors to emphasize how a client's values are implicated in their narratives.

> Formula: "You value (client's value)."
>
> Example: "You value your role as a mother above all else."
>
> Formula: "It's important to you that (value)" or "(Value) is important to you."
>
> Example: "It's important to you that your partner treats you as an equal."
>
> Example: "Equality in your marriage is important to you."

MEANING MAKING THROUGH METAPHORS

Metaphors are powerful tools which humans as social and linguistic creatures use to communicate deeply emotional experiences that may otherwise be difficult for others to understand. They are also densely packed with meaning, cramming a great deal of information in just a few words. For example, it might take 5 minutes of a client sharing about their upcoming final exams, hectic work schedule, ailing parents, and ongoing breakup to pinpoint that balancing so many emergent events is nearly exhausting their capacity to cope. With careful attention, the same meaning could be inferred in 5 seconds by the client exclaiming, "My head is about to explode!"

In counseling, metaphors disclose not only narrative and content but also the emotional significance of an event or experience (Sims, 2003). Metaphors help us organize and communicate experiences quickly and effectively. They can give the counselor valuable insight into the client's worldview that might not otherwise be available, both in their content and in the fact that the client is using them at all. The use of metaphors by clients is associated with particularly intense emotional states, and their increased frequency of use is associated with states of emotional change (Wagener, 2017). When a client relies on metaphor, this tells the counselor that important meaning making is going on—meaning making that shouldn't be missed or overlooked in therapy. The counselor should maintain a posture of curiosity regarding client-generated metaphors and take opportunities to explore them further to reflect their meaning.

Returning to the client whose head is (metaphorically, we assume) exploding, the counselor can take this opportunity to go deeper by asking questions grounded in the world of the metaphor. What are some things that might occur to trigger an explosion or stave one off? If an explosion did occur, what would happen next? What does an explosion look like for this client? Simply asking these questions can signal to the client that the counselor has cared for the client's experience and, consequently, enhance the therapeutic relationship. This act of bringing attention to what could be considered a common enough figure of speech can also aid the client in entering more deeply into their own experience, their own process of constructing meaning (McMullen & Conway, 1996).

When exploring client metaphors, it's important to consider cultural differences between oneself and the client and how those differences affect construction of meaning. Words themselves are always individual and contextualized; their meaning is not essential from one context or even one person to the next (Anderson, 1997). Therefore, even if one shares cultural similarities with a client, one should never assume the meaning of a client metaphor without first exploring and entering the world of the metaphor. Ethical, equitable work with metaphor in the counseling space requires the counselor's awareness of how meaning making is influenced by one's own biases and prejudices as well as the counseling space itself (Levin, 2007). Particularly in Western intellectual traditions, the use of metaphor has historically been regarded as frivolous at best and dishonest at worst (Sims, 2003) and poetic and flowery rather than plainspoken. This history and the subjectivity of language make it essential that counselors reflect deeply on their own biases, processes of meaning making, and the ways they use metaphor in their own lives to communicate experience.

Challenges With Reflection of Meaning

Reflection of meaning may be difficult to practice and to uncover with a client. While the provided strategies can support counselors as they learn to use reflection of meaning effectively, it is helpful to consider some common challenges that can limit the usefulness of the skill. The next sections explore frequent shortcomings that may be faced in implementing reflections of meaning.

SURFACE-LEVEL REFLECTIONS OF MEANING

As counselors learn to reflect meaning, there are several helpful formulas that can be used to support intentional use of this skill, such as the sentence stems previously provided. However, it is important to recognize that use of a formula alone does not necessarily mean a counselor is providing an effective reflection of meaning. For example, if a client were to share in their session that they were feeling down and that they did not get a job they wanted, the counselor could respond, "You feel sad because you didn't get the job." While the counselor used the sentence stem, "You feel (emotion) because _____," which is appropriate for reflection of meaning. However, the statement "you didn't get the job" is a content reflection and fact that was expressed by the client, rather than a deeper meaning about what is underneath the stated feeling.

As such, this example would be more aligned with a reflection of feeling, where the feeling is linked to content. Having a strong understanding of clients' core values can assist the counselor to hear what is embedded within their narrative and to provide a more effective reflection of meaning. In this scenario, if the counselor knew more context—for instance, that the client places a deep value on family, has been living far from their family for some time, and that this job was located near their family home—the counselor could instead state, "You feel devastated because being close to your family again means everything to you." Through this revised statement, the counselor acknowledges greater depth in the feeling as well as connects the feeling to the reason underneath the client's desire to get the job.

TIMING REFLECTION OF MEANING

Oftentimes, it can be difficult to determine when it is appropriate to reflect meaning, and indeed, there is no exact time a reflection of meaning will be appropriate for all clients. While when to reflect meaning has already been discussed, it is important to consider when not to reflect meaning as well. In some cases, counselors may fall into the trap of choosing to reflect meaning too soon in the clinical relationship and process. For instance, well-intentioned counselors may seek to help clients to go deeper and navigate concerns more fully while not recognizing they have not heard enough about the client and their story to fully understand the client's worldview and accurately reflect meaning. Counselors may also fail to see that the rapport has not yet been established for the client to receive the reflection of meaning. In either situation, a reflection of meaning is likely to be ineffective.

On the other hand, counselors may wait too long to reflect meaning, due to concerns about being incorrect in their reflections or worries that going deeper might cause the client discomfort or distress. While it is an understandable concern and necessary principle to follow as a counselor to avoid doing harm, counselors must also recognize that a reflection of meaning may be the missing step that helps the client toward a significant breakthrough, change, or growth that they are looking for. Counselors that avoid reflecting meaning can prolong early stages of the clinical process and relationship rather than progressing, which may lead to dissatisfaction with clients and potential premature dropout.

SPACE TO PROCESS

Akin to issues that may arise with timing a reflection of meaning, the time spent after a reflection of meaning is of vital importance. Counselors seeking to keep the momentum of a session moving forward or that recognize signs of discomfort from the client may intentionally or unintentionally shift toward other skills, such as adding a question or door opener after the reflection of meaning before the client can respond. By doing this, counselors neglect to provide time for the client to process and contemplate the meaning reflected. Continuing without this space can lead to clients progressing and responding to a new prompt, which may lead the session back toward a more surface-level discussion, rather than getting the full effect of the reflection of meaning. Counselors can adjust for this concern by reminding themselves to pause after the reflection of meaning and practicing using therapeutic silence intentionally (Levitt & Morrill, 2023).

CASE EXAMPLE

Due to a recent family crisis, a Hispanic, middle-aged couple has decided to participate in counseling. On the intake paperwork, Fran self-identified as a 54-year-old, Dominican male with Spanish ancestry. Elly self-identified as a 48-year-old, Haitian and Dominican, Latina woman. Elly and Fran have two adult children. Their son Javier lives with them in the United States, while their daughter Ana stays with her tía (aunt) in the Dominican Republic.

The couple moved from the Dominican Republic to the United States several years ago. The couple has shared that they are grateful for the community they have built locally and the family that have supported them in immigrating. A goal of the couple was to find a sense of stability living in the United States. After relocating three times since moving to the United States, they are content with the city that they are living in. They feel secure and want to continue to develop their ties to the community in their area. Within their narrative, the couple discussed how protecting and providing for their children has been a priority within their relationship.

Recently, Javier was arrested for use and possession of illegal drugs, and the couple shared that he will likely be sentenced to a long-term rehabilitation center, in lieu of incarceration. Their son's arrest is the life event that brought the couple to counseling, as they are struggling to grapple with what has occurred. The counselor used the first and second sessions with the couple to establish rapport, hear the couples' presenting concerns, and understand their worldview and situation more thoroughly. During the couples' third session with their counselor, the counselor inquired about addiction in their family. Elly quickly established that their son is the only person with an addiction:

Counselor: Does addiction affect other family members?

Elly: No. No, just our son. He's the only one with a problem.

Fran: Well, Honey (referring to Elly), Ana has been acting out again. Your sister called concerned about her just the other day.

Counselor: (Noticing Elly move uncharacteristically in her seat, touch her neck and face, and stare sternly at her spouse.) Elly, you seem uncomfortable with this topic. (*reflection of feeling*)

Elly: Ana is a good person. She just ... loses her way sometimes.

Counselor: You feel protective of Ana and how she might be talked about. (*reflection of feeling*)

Elly: Yes. ... We've tried to help her, but she does not return our calls. We send money and check on her through our family. My sister says she needs her parents, but she will not move to the U.S. I don't know what she's doing, and I can't stop thinking about what she's getting into.

Counselor: You're feeling worried because being a mom is important to you but establishing your future in the U.S. has created distance between you and your daughter. (*reflection of meaning*)

Elly: Yes, the distance, not knowing how she *really* is awful. I feel like we left her too soon.

Counselor: A part of you regrets leaving her to move here. (*reflection of feeling*)

Fran: We just want her to know we love her and be alright. Be happy and safe. We don't know that what she is doing is safe. She could get hurt.

Counselor: It devastates you both that your kids are suffering and struggling in their own ways because protecting them has been your life's work. (*reflection of meaning*)

(Therapeutic silence)

Fran: (Tearing up) I failed. ... I was supposed to protect them.

Elly: We were supposed to, but we can't always. I just wish we could.

Counselor: You're heartbroken because this isn't the life you imagined for them. (*reflection of meaning*)

Elly: It's not. (crying) It's not at all.

(Therapeutic silence; Fran and Elly hold hands)

Elly: We want Javier to be sober and go back to school. He always wanted to be a doctor and we want that for him. Ana, well, I think she needs us to visit.

Fran: I think so too. We have to show her that we will be there for her.

Case Example Review

This case example demonstrates the narrative between a counselor and a couple in counseling. The values of the couple were present throughout their dialogue. The counselor attended to both people and acknowledged the individual and shared meaning in their statements. Being mindful, the counselor utilized therapeutic silence to offer the clients time to process. By doing so, the clients were able to feel their emotions and consider the meaning being reflected to them.

To further examine this case example, readers can refer to the example earlier in the chapter of the nesting dolls to visually understand the process of digging deeper to apply reflection of meaning. In this case example, the largest doll is the couples' children engaging with addiction. The second nesting doll is the context, such as Ana living with family in the Dominican Republic. Following the context are the initial feelings. An example of this scenario is when the counselor acknowledged that Elly was uncomfortable with Fran bringing up Ana's concerning behavior. The second smallest nesting doll represents the couples' deeper feelings, such as regret for not being present for Ana and devastation that their children are struggling with addiction. Importantly, the smallest nesting doll depicts reflection of meaning; in this case, one of the examples is that for Elly, being a mother and working toward a future in the United States are valued identities and meaningful goals but are at odds with one another in the present circumstance.

Although the counselor cannot fix the situations presented, the counselor supported the clients by pinpointing the meaning behind their concerns and emotions. By doing so, the clients are able to explore their distress and determine what is at its root. Moreover, they are able to process the emotions and become more attuned to themselves and one another.

CHAPTER SUMMARY

This chapter focused on the skill of reflection of meaning and provided strategies regarding implementation of the skill. Reflection of meaning can be a complex skill to learn and use effectively, as it requires counselors to have a strong understanding of who their clients are and what is important to them. Counselors seeking to go deeper in sessions with clients should be aware of their client's values, identities, beliefs, and worldviews and recognize how these differ substantially from one client to the next. This chapter discussed important considerations for understanding clients and their personal meaning, highlighting multicultural contexts to recognize with each client.

CHAPTER REFLECTION AND DISCUSSION QUESTIONS

1. How can you work toward removing your personal bias to better hear and understand the client's intended meaning in their narrative?
2. As explored in this chapter, clients' worldviews and personal meanings are diverse and multifaceted. What elements of a client's identity and narrative stand out as areas you find to be most important to you as a counselor or CIT?
3. Several challenges of reflection of meaning were discussed in this chapter. Which challenge do you believe is most likely to impact you as you develop this skill? What factors contribute to your answer?
4. After reviewing the case study, what did you notice about how the clients responded to reflections of meaning? How might the session have gone differently if the counselor had used questions or other skills instead of reflecting meaning?
5. Reflection of meaning encourages depth in the counseling process and can lead to clients feeling vulnerable. If you were a client, how might it feel to explore your personal values and meaning with your counselor?
6. Reflection of meaning requires counselors to recognize and understand the underlying motivations and perspectives of their clients. What strategies could you use to develop a deeper understanding of diverse beliefs, values, and identities?

ADDITIONAL RESOURCES

Collins, S., & Ko, G. (2023, May 16). *Counselling microskills: Reflecting meaning II* [Video]. YouTube. https://www.youtube.com/watch?v=u4ARW_YKfUQ

REFERENCES

Anderson, H. (1997). *Conversation, language, and possibilities: A postmodern approach to therapy.* Basic Books.
Cozolino, L. (2014). *The neuroscience of human relationships* (2nd ed.). Norton.
Crenshaw, K. (1989). Demarginalizing the intersection of race and sex: A Black feminist.

Critique of Antidiscrimination Doctrine, Feminist Theory, and Antiracist Politics. *University of Chicago Legal Forum*, 139–67.

Gelso, C. J., Palma, B., & Bhatia, A. (2013). Attachment theory as a guide to understanding and working with transference and the real relationship in psychotherapy. *Journal of Clinical Psychology*, *69*(11), 1160–1171. https://doi.org/10.1002/jclp.22043

Johnson, S. (2019). *Attachment theory in practice: Emotionally focused therapy (EFT) with individuals, couples, and families.* The Guildford Press.

Lee, E., Tsang, A. K. T., Bogo, M., Johnstone, M., & Herschman, J. (2018). Enactments of racial microaggression in everyday therapeutic encounters. *Smith College Studies in Social Work*, *88*(3), 211–236.

Levin, S. B. (2007). Hearing the unheard: Advice to professionals from women who have been battered. In H. Anderson & D. R. Gehart (Eds.), *Collaborative therapy: Relationships and conversations that make a difference* (pp. 109–128). Routledge.

Levitt, H. M., & Morrill, Z. (2023). Silences in psychotherapy: An integrative meta-analytic research review. *Psychotherapy.* https://dx.doi.org/10.1037/pst0000480

McMullen, L. M., & Conway, J. B. (1996). Conceptualizing the figurative expressions of psychotherapy clients. In A. N. Katz & J. S. Mio (Eds.), *Metaphor: Implications and applications* (pp. 59–71). Lawrence Erlbaum Associates, Inc.

Mearns, D., & Cooper, M. (2018). *Working at relational depth in counselling & psychotherapy* (2nd ed.). SAGE.

Sims, P. A. (2003). Working with metaphor. *American Journal of Psychotherapy*, *57*(4), 528–536. https://doi.org/10.1176/appi.psychotherapy.2003.57.4.528

Sue, D. W., Capodilupo, C. M., Torino, G. C., Bucceri, J. M., Holder, A., Nadal, K. L., & Esquilin, M. (2007). Racial microaggressions in everyday life: Implications for clinical practice. *American Psychologist*, *62*(4), 271.

Wagener, A. E. (2017). Metaphor in professional counseling. *The Professional Counselor*, *7*(2), 144–154. https://doi.org/10.15241/aew.7.2.144

Young, M. E. (2017). *Learning the art of helping: Building blocks and techniques* (6th ed.). Pearson.

Challenging Skills

Dr. Tristen Hyatt and Dr. Clay Rowell

LEARNING OBJECTIVES

1. Provide awareness of how challenging clients requires Multicultural and Social Justice Counseling Competencies (MSJCC) competencies and knowledge.
2. Enhance knowledge of techniques and types of challenges from an MSJCC framework.
3. Review skills related to challenging skills while discussing and reviewing MSJCC considerations.

LEARNING OUTCOMES

1. Students will learn common skills used to challenge clients.
2. Students will understand implications of MSJCC considerations when challenging clients.
3. Students will be able to apply appropriate challenging skills with cross-cultural clients.

Challenging

The therapeutic space should be a safe space in which an individual is free to explore their biases, beliefs, and feelings and how these beliefs came to be. Individuals, couples, and families seek counseling services for a variety of reasons; however, the decision to seek out counseling is not an easy one, and often, people many years before committing to counseling. However, one thing is certain: Individuals should work toward understanding their own beliefs, thoughts, and feelings—counseling is one way to begin this journey (Ratts et al., 2016). In counseling, an avenue for an individual to begin to explore and process their worldview is the challenge.

A *challenge*, in the counseling domain, is when the counselor will directly or discreetly challenge the client's beliefs, cognitions, feelings, or worldview on a situation, event(s), or long-standing set of feelings to move the client toward greater self-awareness, growth, and insight. Challenges should be client based and not a matter of value imposition for the counselor, which is why it is of the utmost importance for the counselor to be personally self-aware of their own values and worldview before working with clients on theirs (ACA, 2014). The ideal challenge should be done with immediacy, in the moment, to move a client toward growth and insight as well as done in a nonjudgmental and supportive manner to continue to move the client–counselor relationship forward, according the MSJCC competencies (Ratts et al., 2016; Wang et al., 2022). It is necessary for counselors to be able to provide a safe and supportive space while moving their clients toward greater awareness of themselves. Often, challenging clients requires them to examine their own beliefs and worldview, with the aim of clients reaching personal goals and having increased insight.

Challenging: A Microskill

There are numerous skills counselors must utilize to help facilitate growth and insight, within the therapeutic space; however, the *challenge* is one that can be difficult for counselors. There are numerous reasons for this, but often, this is because of perception around what a challenge is and how to deliver it. According to Hill et al. (2022), delivery of a challenge is a necessary part of counseling but must be provided to clients in such a way that clients are able to hear it, in a nondefensive manner, and then are able to do work with it. Furthermore, the challenge should be empathic, clear and move the client toward self-evaluation of their thoughts, feelings, or beliefs, thus allowing them to gain some greater insight into their lives. When delivering a challenge, counselors should be aware of its impact by utilizing a plethora of skills: attending to nonverbals, verbals (meta messages, body language, etc.), and redirections, to actively attend to readiness for change or openness to challenges (Hill et al., 2022). Furthermore, Johnson (2016) discusses the necessity of being able to be respectful when challenging clients' irrational beliefs. The author mentions the importance of understanding how beliefs shape actions and the value of being able to meet clients in a compassionate and empathetic manner when helping them move toward disputing long-held core beliefs.

Strong and Zenman (2010) expounded on the importance of being able to develop the skills of challenging clients in a dialogic manner that fits into the natural discussion taking place within the counseling conversation. They note the importance of a successful challenge being one that moves the client toward change behavior. According to their research, counselors must consider the issue of power; however, individuals are challenged frequently, in and out of the counseling realm, and delivery is important. Therefore, when challenging clients, counselors should focus on delivering the challenge in a natural way that fits into the ongoing dialogue taking place, thus making this a fundamental counseling skill (Hill et al., 2022). Furthermore, Trotter et al. (2015) compare challenging clients to motivational interviewing, and they stress the importance of being positive and encouraging when offering the confrontation (challenge) to the client.

As previously discussed, challenging a client is necessary for growth, but counselors must be able to evaluate whether the client is ready to face what comes with the challenge. A client must be ready to evaluate their irrational beliefs, previously held biases, worldview, or discrepancies in their thinking patterns. If a client is not ready, then the counselor should be able to process and address this, in a supportive and understanding manner. It is fear of harming the client–counselor relationship or pushing a client too fast that can move a counselor to avoid challenging a client; however, to do so can create nonmovement in the counseling process.

In the challenging process, counselors should note the responsibility of being able to move clients toward congruence within their lives and the role the challenge has in moving them toward that goal. In a study conducted by Trotter et al. (2015), it was found that positive, strengths-based challenges were reported to have positive impacts on clients, thus reinforcing the importance of counselors learning how to deliver challenges and being culturally sensitive to their clients' needs. Furthermore, Wang et al. (2022), in a study of 1,233 participants, found that distress was decreased when challenges were balanced with support, in the therapeutic process.

MSJCC and Challenging Clients

From an MSJCC perspective, it is first necessary that counselors have an ongoing self-reflective nature of their worldview to work with clients (Ratts et al., 2016). MSJCC (2016) competencies highlight that counselors should be able to evaluate and challenge their own thinking patterns before being in the room with clients. Counselor self-awareness and the ability to be personally self-evaluative are necessary components of challenging clients. When a counselor is personally self-aware and open to their own growth, they are better able to walk the path of assisting others in self-exploration, which requires utilizing challenging skills (Ratts et al., 2016).

Types of Challenges

In counseling, there are numerous ways a client's incongruent thinking patterns, beliefs, feelings, or discrepancies can be brought forth through challenges; however, as reviewed, there are several facets to delivering the challenge. Counselors have many options when deciding to challenge their clients, but as previously stated, a dialogic approach can have positive results. Also, counselors should be able to remain positive, encouraging, strengths-based, and empathetic while moving clients toward self-exploration and personal growth (Hill et al., 2022; Johnson, 2016).

The Gentle Nudge

The counselor might consider prompting the client to consider their thoughts, feelings, beliefs, or worldview through the *gentle nudge*. Take the following example:

> *Client: "I've always just done what was the easiest thing, and avoided conflict, and I am happy with living life that way."*

> *Counselor: "I hear you saying that you have always done what is easiest and you're happy. Let's think back to what brought you into counseling and what your goals were then."*

This can be viewed as gently nudging the client to reflect on what was just stated as well as their original goals. The client made a statement that they are happy; however, the gentle nudge is moving the client to think about what brought them into counseling. This technique leads the client toward evaluating their belief that they are happy with the status quo of living their life as is and to think back to what their goals were, which contradicted this statement.

Pointing Out Discrepancies

The counselor might consider prompting the client to consider their thoughts, feelings, beliefs, or worldview by *pointing out discrepancies*, as in the following example:

> *Client: "I've always just done what was the easiest thing, and avoided conflict, and I am happy with living life that way."*

> Counselor: "I hear you saying that you are happy living life as is, but last week, you stated that avoiding conflict in your current relationships have led you to a point where you feel like you have no voice and that you feel stuck and discontent."

First, it is important to note that the counseling relationship needs to be well developed and have a positive working alliance, and this statement should be delivered in a supportive and empathic manner. Pointing out discrepancies moves the client toward gaining awareness of incongruence within their lives, and this is one example of it. The client has made a statement that they do not want to face conflict and that they are happy with life as is; however, the discrepancy is brought forth that the client has made contradictory statements and is living life in incongruent manner causing psychological distress. Without pointing out this discrepancy, the counselor would be doing a disservice to the client by not allowing them the chance to begin processing the internal incongruence within their thinking patterns.

Wondering Out Loud

The counselor might consider prompting the client to consider their thoughts, feelings, beliefs, or worldview by *wondering out loud*. Take the following example:

> Client: "I've always just done what was the easiest thing, and avoided conflict, and I am happy with living life that way."
>
> Counselor: "I wonder if that's really accurate."

This could be a longer statement; however, sometimes concise wonderings followed by silence will move the client toward processing what they just stated. The goal is to allow the client to start the process of analyzing what they stated and begin the self-evaluative process. This challenge may have the client ask follow-up questions in which the counselor would need to do more wondering aloud to further guide the self-explorative process for the client.

Direct Confrontation

The counselor might consider prompting the client to consider their thoughts, feelings, beliefs, or worldview through *direct confrontation*, as in the following example:

> Client: "I've always just done what was the easiest thing, and avoided conflict, and I am happy with living life that way."
>
> Counselor: "I hear you saying that you are happy avoiding conflict, and I can definitely understand how difficult confrontations can be, but I feel I'd be doing you a disservice if I didn't remind you that your stated goals for counseling were to be able to face life in a more assertive manner, as you feel that you are constantly being taken advantage of and it makes you feel very sad."

This is a direct confrontation. The counselor is bringing the client's own words and goals back into the room to ask them to process the incongruence. Some counselors might find this the most difficult, as it is more confrontational, in nature; however, if the relationship is built and support is offered, direct challenges can be quite therapeutic in creating change for clients.

Barriers to Challenging Clients

Intrapersonal

As stated throughout this book, the 2016 Multicultural and Social Justice Counseling Competencies (MSJCC) (Ratts et al., 2016) provide a framework for counselors to develop awareness, knowledge, skills, and action. The MSJCC provides a roadmap for this by including developmental domains that reflect the different layers that lead to multicultural and social justice competence. There is a good reason why counselor self-awareness is listed first in those domains. Awareness of our own worldview, including biases and prejudices, must occur to approach our clients with humility and curiosity so that we may better understand our clients' worldviews (the second developmental domain of the MSJCC). Moreover, awareness has no outcome; it is an ongoing process. As counselors, we should continually examine ourselves to truly understand how we influence the counseling relationship (the third developmental domain of the MSJCC). Finally, without new awareness, counseling and advocacy interventions (the fourth developmental domain of the MSJCC) is rudderless. Simply stated, the more self-awareness we have, the more we can better understand our clients and the better we can attend to the relationship and develop strategies for change. With this in mind, let us then discuss our own personal barriers to challenging our clients.

What do you feel when you hear the word "challenge"? What about when you hear the word "confront"? Take a moment to really reflect on what you feel when you hear those words used in everyday communication. For many, the actions those words represent conjure automatic feelings of defensiveness. For others, they may spark some simple discomfort. Where does this come from? Why do we feel a certain way just from hearing a certain word? The truth is words have metamessages that have been ascribed to them through cultural socialization. Usually, those metamessages that we internalize are dualistic in nature. They are either good or bad, positive or negative. If someone says they want to support you, the metamessage is typically that supporting someone is good or positive. If someone says they want to confront you, the metamessage is typically bad or negative. If we take this discussing deeper into emotions, we can see that we will feel a certain way because of the metamessage we ascribe to the word.

If you have internalized that supporting someone is positive, then you will feel good when someone says they want to support you. If you have internalized that confronting someone is negative, then you will feel defensive when someone says they want to confront you. We could do this with almost any verb used to describe something done while communicating with others. Of course, some things are contextual, but in general, the metamessages (and accompanying automatic feelings) are consistent. Let us dig in for what this all means for counselors.

As noted, the words "challenge" and "confront" generally have what we label a negative meta message, and therefore, they spark emotional reactions we have also labeled as negative. It is commonplace for people to want to avoid emotions that have been labeled as negative. Taking it even further, we often feel vulnerable with these negatively labeled emotions. Vulnerability is one of the toughest states for people to sit in with themselves or others. Mix this with the tendency to want to help others, and it can be a struggle to do something that may cause another person to feel vulnerable. Do you see where this is going?

Something I often hear from counseling students goes something like this: "I am concerned about challenging this client because I don't want to harm the relationship." Or they say, "I didn't want to challenge this client too early while I was building rapport." This is a direct influence of the metamessage. The automatic assumption is that challenging or confronting is going to cause the client to feel uncomfortable and, therefore, damage the counseling relationship. Certainly, the manner in which a counselor goes about challenging or confronting clients plays a role in this, but it is the automatic assumption that is the barrier here.

What is most important about these statements is that it is the counselor's feelings that are getting in the way. Remember, the desire to help, coupled with the negatively labeled feelings, is what is driving the counselor to avoid challenging the client. My students would tell you that one thing I say a lot to them is that we must become comfortable with discomfort—our own and others'. If counselors are not comfortable with the discomfort that inevitably happens in counseling, then they will direct the process away from dialogue that causes them to feel uncomfortable. The irony is that not only is discomfort inevitable in counseling, but it is also often necessary.

Many clients will continue living the way they always have unless some discomfort causes them to reflect and develop new insight. Counselors often can attend to the discomfort simply by acknowledging it. "Hey, I know this might be uncomfortable, but is it OK if I challenge you a little because I think this is important for you?" Another example might be, "I know this is hard, and we can go at your pace, but let's talk about this more if you're ready." How would you feel if you counselor said something like this to you? Perhaps more importantly, how would you feel saying something like this to a client?

If you feel uncomfortable challenging clients right now, that is OK—it is fairly normal. Accept it, and make a plan to grow in your comfort with discomfort. Perhaps, the first step is to lean into your desire to help. Keep telling yourself that challenging a client is often a necessary step in helping them. Furthermore, if it is difficult for you to get past the wording, you could change the wording you use. Perhaps, instead of "challenging" a client, you are "nudging" a client toward their goals or "encouraging" them to see things differently. Practice these skills, and process what you are experiencing with a supervisor and your peers. Also, you may not be highly skilled at challenging clients right now, so allow yourself to be inadequate. You cannot become good at something new without starting somewhere, so be gentle with yourself as you are growing.

Systemic

Just as there are individual barriers to overcome when growing your challenging skills, so are there systemic barriers to consider with your clients. First, there is an inherent power differential within the counseling relationship. Counselors need to be aware of how this influences the process and must develop knowledge of their clients' cultural communication styles. This allows the counselor to make better decisions when applying skills. Furthermore, communication styles are developed within a cultural context. The way one learns to communicate is influenced by so many outside factors. For example, some are socialized in a family or cultural context that values direct communication. In other words, you say what you mean, and you mean what you say. Others, however, are raised to communicate more indirectly because being direct is considered rude or disrespectful. With different clients, we must shift our style of challenging so that it is received appropriately.

POWER AND INFLUENCE

It is widely accepted that counselors begin a counseling relationship with more power in the relational dynamics than clients. Clients typically seek help because they don't feel they can solve their problems themselves. This automatically gives the counselor power because the client will see the counselor as potentially having the answers that have eluded them. Therefore, the cultural status given to counselors by clients influences the legitimacy of the power dynamic. From this perspective, challenging clients might be seen as using that power to get clients to do what the counselor thinks they should do.

Because of this, it is widely taught to counseling students to try to even out the balance of power so that clients feel more ownership in the decision-making process. This makes adjusting our style and meeting the client where they are very important. We want to work within the client's frame of reference so that challenges can be worked out relationally to achieve the desired outcome (Strong & Zeman, 2010). What does that mean exactly? Using relational skills to challenge clients means it is not just what the counselor says that matters. It also matters how the counselor says it, the timing with which it is delivered, and the attention to processing the client's reaction to the challenge.

The processing of the challenge is often an important piece in the lasting effect it will have. If a counselor simply challenges a client's thought patterns, for example, and then moves on, there is potential for the client to be sitting with something profound yet unexamined. Therefore, the use of both silence and here-and-now dialogue is key. For example, if a counselor challenges a client by pointing out that their unforgiveness of a friend is influencing their daily life, the counselor may allow the client to reflect with silence. Then, the counselor may say, "What was it like for me to point that out to you?" or "How are you feeling in this moment given what I just said?" This is what it means to be relational with challenging clients. As counselors, we continually check in with our clients to both shift the power dynamic toward the client and to help guide the process. Through processing, the client may feel more valued and more empowered. We now deepen the focus of this topic by discussing the role that culture plays within the dynamics of the counseling relationship.

CULTURAL COMMUNICATION STYLES

The framework of the MSJCC shows us how important client worldview is in the counseling relationship. Worldview may be defined broadly as a comprehensive conception of the universe and humanity's place within it (Dictionary.com, n.d.). This conception is heavily influenced by the messages received throughout socialization. Those messages are often steeped in bias, stereotypes, prejudices. The metamessage of stereotypes follows a dualistic pattern of something or someone being either good or bad. People internalize these messages about groups of people and about themselves. Once internalized, these messages shape our biases and, therefore, our worldviews. Awareness of our own worldview helps us extend that awareness to understanding our clients' worldviews. In turn, this helps counselors develop knowledge about how culture, power, privilege, and oppression influence the counseling relationship (Ratts et al., 2016). Cultural and familial values also contribute to the shaping of worldview. While a full examination of this is beyond the scope of this chapter, we can examine how this influences communication styles. This is vital because most of the major theories of counseling rely on verbal communication to promote growth and change.

Verbal and Nonverbal Communication

Language differences between counselor and client can create difficulties. Most of the major counseling approaches require clients to tell the counselor what they want directly. This can be frustrating for a client if their native language is different than the counselor's (Hays & Erford, 2018). Clients may spend a lot of emotional energy trying to get the counselor to understand them. This makes it difficult to build a trusting therapeutic alliance between the counselor and client. Without that, the counselor may stumble when it comes time to challenge a client.

Furthermore, even if the client speaks the same language as the counselor, but not as their native language, nuances of communication may interfere with accurate understanding. As mentioned earlier in this chapter, words or phrases often have an underlying meaning beyond their technical definitions. Someone who has learned the counselor's language as a nonnative speaker may be proficient in the technical use of the words or phrases, but they may not have learned the metamessages of those words or phrases. The counselor then may misinterpret the true meaning and, therefore, not develop an accurate understanding of what the client is trying to express. When this happens, the counselor's empathy may be skewed, and their assessment of the client may miss the mark. Finally, the counselor might develop treatment plans and guide the process in a false direction.

Similarly, communication involves cues that often happen nonverbally. For example, in Western cultures, direct eye contact is often associated with confidence, and lack of direct eye contact is often associated with shame or insecurity. However, in Eastern cultures, lack of direct eye contact often indicates respect. It could be easy to misinterpret this if the counselor lacks awareness of their own and their client's worldview. It is important for counselors to interpret a client's nonverbals within the context of the client's cultural communication style (Hays & Erford, 2018). If the counselor is now aware of the differences in presentation, then they may unknowingly apply their own communication norms to the counseling relationship. Again, the counselor may then assess the client and guide the counseling process in directions that may be inappropriate and unhelpful for the client.

Expressing Oneself

As previously mentioned, most major counseling approaches require clients to be able to express themselves directly. Attending to thoughts and behaviors may be easier for some clients than focusing on emotions. While all people experience emotions, the skill with which to both recognize and express those emotions varies widely within cultural groups (Hays & Erford, 2018). I used the word "skill" here because most people can develop the capacity to recognize and express their emotions accurately. Depending on how they were socialized, however, this could be a difficult task to accomplish.

Some clients may have been raised in familial or cultural environments that valued and affirmed emotional expression, while others may have been socialized in environments that stifled or ignored emotions. This is a continuum, and counselors need to be aware of where their clients are on this continuum when challenging them. Furthermore, the beliefs about the causes of emotions may be different from client to client, depending on how they were socialized (Hays & Erford, 2018).

Some clients may come from cultures that believe emotions are indicative of mental health issues. Therefore, challenging clients emotionally may cause a reaction wherein they shut down during the session. On the opposite side of the continuum, some clients may be free in sharing emotions but may use them in manipulative ways in their relationships. With these clients, using direct confrontation may cause them to feel invalidated. These two brief examples highlight the importance of both knowing your clients' cultural and familial backgrounds and utilizing appropriate challenging skills to match them.

Acculturation

Sometimes, the mismatch between a counselor's challenging skill or style and a client's verbal or emotional expression style requires a shift in the counseling relationship. *Acculturation* typically refers to the way an immigrant identifies with or conforms to their new society (Hays & Erford, 2018). If we think about the counseling process as its own culture, we can explore how new clients may acculturate to being in counseling. We have discussed how counselors need to shift their styles and approaches to match clients' expressive skills. This is one way a counselor can help a client feel more confident within the counseling process.

Some upfront and ongoing education about the counseling process also may help a client be more relaxed. For example, a counselor may say, "Part of this process is for me to try to understand what it is like being you. I may ask you to tell me what you're feeling or thinking so that I can get a sense of what you're experiencing. That may be difficult at times, but I am patient. We can explore these things together at your own pace. How does that sound to you?"

This type of education may benefit the client's acculturation to the counseling process. The counselor should continually check in with the client and their comfort with the direction of the counseling process. Again, this handling of the process is key to helping the client feel empowered and trusting of the counselor. It helps in building and developing the relationship so that appropriate challenges can take place within the process.

CASE EXAMPLE

Taissa is a 29-year-old African American, middle-class, cisgendered, heterosexual woman who came to counseling because of her frustration with her husband of 3 years. The counselor is a 44-year-old White, middle-class, cisgendered, heterosexual male. Taissa has never been in counseling and stated that she does not know how to solve the tension that has arisen in her relationship. Background exploration uncovered that she and her husband have differing communication styles and domestic role expectations. The following transcript provides examples of the counselor utilizing various challenging skills while attempting to be culturally sensitive.

> Client (CL): An example of not being respected is around house cleaning. For years, I have asked my husband to help with cleaning, but he rarely does. So I end up doing it. It's become really frustrating because I don't think he cares about what I want.
>
> Counselor (CO): OK, so with this example, you say this has been going on for years.
>
> CL: Yes, as long as we've been married.
>
> CO: Right, so I'm assuming that you have tried different ways of getting him to listen to you. Is that correct?
>
> CL: I guess so. It's usually just an argument that happens because I just do all the cleaning and let my frustration build up. Then I try to talk to him about it, but we both end up raising our voices and saying things we don't mean.

CO: That sounds hard.

CL: Yes.

CO: Is that all you've tried? Talking to him?

CL: Well, I tried once to just not do the cleaning to see if he would step up, but he didn't. Then the house got trashed.

CO: I see. I imagine you were really frustrated then.

CL: Yeah. Then it was a whole extra week's worth of cleaning that I had to do.

CO: So you tried to step out of the role of cleaning and telling him that he needs to do this and this and this, and what happened was it got worse (*gentle nudge*).

CL: Right.

CO: It obviously did not trigger the same for him that it does for you.

CL: Right.

CO: It seems from your perspective that it's much more important to you.

CL: It is important to me and so we are at a standoff a little bit.

CO: So would you say it's fair to assume that the real issue isn't about the cleaning?

CL: Sure, it's about our communication, our respect, or lack of it. I feel like I'm mothering sometimes.

CO: Can you think of another way that you can step out of that role, that mothering as you call it. Is that the right word?

CL: It's mothering, it's nagging.

CO: And you don't want to do that.

CL: No.

CO: But you do (*direct confrontation*).

CL: Yeah, I feel like I have to in order to get things done.

CO: You have to put yourself in a role you don't want to be in so that you can get what you want (*pointing out discrepancy*).

CL: Yeah.

CO: (Silence)

CL: Seems totally at odds with each other, or otherwise, I just do it all myself. And then end up feeling resentful.

CO: (Silence)

CL: Which seems worse actually.

CO: So you say, well I'm not going to do that because I don't want to feel resentment, so I'll just put myself in this role, even though that's not the relationship that I want because I've got to have things done the way I want them done (*direct confrontation*).

CL: (Nods)

CO: Is that right?

CL: Yeah.

CO: (Silence)

CO: How does that sound to as I say it out loud (*gentle nudge*).

CL: Sounds frustrating, and like I'm settling to be something I don't want to be to achieve what I want. It's really conflicting.

CO: I hear that. This is the conflict within you, and it also adds to your part in the conflict with your husband (*direct confrontation*).

CL: (Silence)

CL: You're saying the conflict in me causes the conflict with him?

CO: Well, conflict between two people usually occurs because of both, but I'm wondering what the truth of that is? The part that you play (*wondering out loud*).

CL: I completely see it now, but I don't like it and I don't know how to change it.

CO: Which is why you came here, right?

CL: Right.

CO: One question I would have for you, so that I can really get to know you better, is maybe you could tell me your thoughts on how this inner conflict developed for you.

CL: What do you mean?

CO: Well you and I are obviously different genders and races, so I don't want to assume that I know how this role developed or how your desire to have a clean house developed. I just want to really know you in this context so that I can better help you.

CL: Oh OK, I see. Yes, I guess the mothering role that we've talked about probably stems from my family. The women in my family take care of everything and are strong.

CO: And the men?

> CL: The men are taken care of. I mean they work and all, but the women are like the head of the household.
>
> CO: So that's definitely part of your culture.
>
> CL: Absolutely.
>
> CO: Would you say that your husband's background is similar?
>
> CL: Yes, his family has a similar culture.
>
> CO: Then you married a man that was raised in a similar family environment?
>
> CL: Right.
>
> CO: So then I guess he unconsciously expects to be taken care of?
>
> CL: (Silence)
>
> CO: You see where this is going.
>
> CL: Uh, yeah.

CHAPTER SUMMARY

When evaluating the importance of developing the nuances of being able to challenge clients, it is necessary to highlight the numerous facets of the challenge. Challenging clients requires being able to be genuine, authentic, considerate of cultural considerations, aware of one's of worldview, empathetic, and supportive all while delivering the challenge in a manner that impacts the client and helps to foster inner-change and processing (Hill et al., 2022; Johnson, 2016; Strong & Zenman, 2010). Furthermore, counselors need to be aware of their clients' socialized ways of recognizing and expressing themselves and adjust their styles and interventions to better serve them.

CHAPTER REFLECTION AND DISCUSSION QUESTIONS

1. How do your values impact your behaviors when engaging in challenging techniques? Why is this?
2. Think about your beliefs about challenging others and if any of those beliefs have changed after reading this chapter. Why, or why not?
3. Reflect upon times when you have been challenged—once that left you feeling positive with your learning and once that left you feeling negative. What factors made the impacts of these experiences different (presentation of information, collaboration, buy-in, cultural respect, knowledge of presenter, etc.).
4. What, in your opinion, is the most important outcome from being challenged and challenging others?
5. What is the most important thing to keep in mind when utilizing challenging techniques?

ADDITIONAL RESOURCES

Al-Darmaki, F., & Kivlighan, D. M. (1993). Congruence in client–counselor expectations for relationship and the working alliance. *Journal of Counseling Psychology, 40*(4), 379–384. https://doi.org/10.1037/0022-0167.40.4.379

Arnkoff, D. B., Glass, C. R., & Shapiro, S. J. (2002). Expectations and preferences. In J. C. Norcross (Ed.), *Psychotherapy relationships that work: Therapist contributions and responsiveness to patients* (pp. 325–346). Oxford University Press.

Constantino, M. J., Vîslă, A., Coyne, A. E., & Boswell, J. F. (2018). A meta-analysis of the association between patients' early treatment outcome expectation and their posttreatment outcomes. *Psychotherapy, 55*(4), 473–485. https://doi.org/10.1037/pst0000169

Hook, J. N., Davis, D. E., Owen, J., Worthington, E. L., & Utsey, S. O. (2013). Cultural humility: Measuring openness to culturally diverse clients. *Journal of Counseling Psychology, 60*, 353–366. http://dx.doi.org/10.1037/a0032595

Johnson, W. B. (2016). Challenging clinically salient religion: The art of respectful confrontation. *Spirituality in Clinical Practice, 3*(1), 10–13. https://doi.org/10.1037/scp0000099

Mariani, L. (1997). Teacher support and teacher challenge in promoting learner autonomy. *Perspectives: A Journal of TESOL Italy, 23*(2), 1–10. https://www.learningpaths.org/papers/papersupport.htm

Moeseneder, L., Figlioloi, P., & Caspar, F. (2018). Confronting patients: Therapists' model of a responsiveness based approach. *Journal of Contemporary Psychotherapy, 48*(2), 61–67. https://doi.org/10.1007/s10879-017-9371-x

Ratts M. J., Singh A. A., Nassar-McMillan S., Butler S. K., McCullough J. R. (2016). Multicultural and social justice counseling competencies: Guidelines for the counseling profession. *Journal of Multicultural Counseling and Development, 44*, 28–48. https://www.doi.org/10.1002/jmcd.12035

Strong, T., & Zeman, D. (2010). Dialogic considerations of confrontation as a counseling activity: An examination of Allen Ivey's use of confronting as a microskill. *Journal of Counseling & Development, 88*(3), 332–339. https://doi.org/10.1002/j.1556-6678.2010.tb00030.x

Trotter, C., Evans, P., & Baidawi, S. (2016). The effectiveness of challenging skills in work with young offenders. *International Journal of Offender Therapy and Comparative Criminology, 61*(4), 397–412. https://doi.org/10.1177/0306624x15596728

Wampold, B. E., & Imel, Z. E. (2015). The great psychotherapy debate: The evidence for what makes psychotherapy work. *Routledge.* https://doi.org/10.4324/9780203582015

Wilson, K., & Devereux, L. (2014). Scaffolding theory: High challenge, high support in academic language and learning (ALL) contexts. *Journal of Academic Language & Learning, 8*(3), A91–A100. https://journal.aall.org.au/index.php/jall/article/view/353

REFERENCES

American Counseling Association. (2014). *2014 ACA code of ethics.* https://www.counseling.org/docs/default-source/default-document-library/2014-code-of-ethics-finaladdress.pdf

Borders, L. D., & Giordano, A. L. (2016b). Confronting confrontation in clinical supervision: An analytical autoethnography. *Journal of Counseling & Development, 94*(4), 454–463. https://doi.org/10.1002/jcad.12104

Corey, G. (2014). *Theory and practice of group counseling* (9th ed.). Cengage Learning.

Dictionary.com (n.d.). Worldview. In Dictionary.com. Retrieved December 16, 2022 from https://www.dictionary.com/browse/worldview

Hays, D. G., & Erford, B. T. (2018). *Developing multicultural competence: A systems approach.* Pearson.

Hill, C. E., Morales, K., Gerstenblith, J. A., Bansal, P., An, M., Rim, K., & Kivlighan, D. M., Jr. (2022). Therapist challenges and client responses in psychodynamic psychotherapy: An empirically supported case study. *Psychotherapy, 59*(1), 74–83. https://doi.org/10.1037/pst0000424

Johnson, W. B. (2016). Challenging clinically salient religion: The art of respectful confrontation. *Spirituality in Clinical Practice, 3*(1), 10–13. https://doi.org/10.1037/scp0000099

King, K. M. (2021). "I Want to, But How?" Defining counselor broaching in core tenets and debated components. *Journal of Multicultural Counseling & Development, 49*(2), 87–100. https://doi.org/10.1002/jmcd.12208

Levitt, D. H. (2002). Active listening and counselor self-efficacy: Emphasis on one microskill in beginning counselor training. *Clinical Supervisor, 20*(2), 101. https://doi.org/10.1300/J001v20n02_09

McCarthy, A. K. (2014). Relationship between rehabilitation counselor efficacy for counseling skills and client outcomes. *Journal of Rehabilitation 80*(2):4, 4–12.

Ratts M. J., Singh A. A., Nassar-McMillan S., Butler S. K., McCullough J. R. (2016). Multicultural and Social Justice Counseling Competencies: Guidelines for the counseling profession. *Journal of Multicultural Counseling and Development, 44*, 28–48. https://www.doi.org/10.1002/jmcd.12035

Strong, T., & Zeman, D. (2010). Dialogic considerations of confrontation as a counseling activity: An examination of Allen Ivey's use of confronting as a microskill. *Journal of Counseling & Development, 88*(3), 332–339.

Trotter, C., Evans, P., & Baidawi, S. (2016). The effectiveness of challenging skills in work with young offenders. *International Journal of Offender Therapy and Comparative Criminology, 61*(4), 397–412. https://doi.org/10.1177/0306624x15596728

Wang, K., Chung, H., Stuart-Maver, S. L., Schreier, B., Galligan, P., Davis, H., & Kivlighan, D. M., III. (2022). The relationship between clients' expectation of therapist support and challenge and treatment outcome: A response surface analysis. *Psychotherapy, 59*(3), 481–486. https://doi.org/10.1037/pst0000440.supp

Watson, J. C., & Spurgeon, S. L. (2009). Development of the managing client resistance self-efficacy scale (MCRSE). *Journal of Counseling Research & Practice, 1*(1), 64–73.

Goal Setting

Dr. Letitia Browne-James, Shannon Kratky, and Dr. Karla Sapp

LEARNING OBJECTIVES
1. Counseling students will identify and explain two ways their worldviews and lived experiences impact the counseling process.
2. Counseling students will describe and model three skills to include clients in the culturally responsive goal-setting process.
3. Counseling students will identify and practice three skills for creating culturally responsive treatment goals with clients.
4. Counseling students will summarize the importance of helping clients access resources in goal setting and treatment planning and create a list of at least five local resources.

LEARNING OUTCOMES
1. Discuss strategies for identifying and implementing culturally responsive treatment goals.
2. Explore how the development of culturally responsive goals strengthens therapeutic relationships, processes, and outcomes.
3. Explain how counseling students and practitioners can attend to culture as it relates to the content and process of culturally responsive goal setting.
4. Apply culturally responsive goal setting skills to case studies involving diverse clients.
5. Explore the Multicultural and Social Justice Counseling Competencies (MSJCC) perspective with regards to:
   - cultural responsiveness
   - cultural competence
   - cultural humility
   - acculturation
   - cultural self-awareness
   - intersectionality
   - anti-oppressive practice
   - goal setting and treatment planning
   - salient resources

Goal Setting

Counseling begins with the intake process, including goal setting. During the intake process, it is imperative for culturally responsive and ethical practices to be present to form the foundation for a trusting and successful therapeutic alliance. Researchers have found that building a trusting, culturally competent, ethical therapeutic relationship in the initial counseling phase with clients plays a vital role in successful therapeutic outcomes, across every cultural group (Solomon et al., 2017). For example, creating a trusting relationship with LGBTQiA2S+ youth may set the tone for a successful therapeutic relationship.

Feelings of trust, safety, and acceptance in the counseling relationship are necessary for multiple populations, as noted in the American Counseling Association (ACA) Code of Ethics (2014) and the Multicultural and Social Justice Counseling Competencies (MSJCC; Ratts et al., 2016). Each reiterates the importance of counselors' self-awareness, including the awareness of one's biases, worldviews, values, and perceptions. In the counseling relationship, the client's lived experiences and the counselor's level of self-awareness contribute to the client's success in reaching their therapeutic goals. Beyond counselor self-awareness, counselors must also consider and attend to clients' worldviews, build positive counseling relationships with clients, and use counseling and advocacy interventions throughout all phases of counseling.

Awareness, knowledge, and skills about the populations counselors work with through an intersectionality lens can lead to effective counseling outcomes. These may include counselors' knowledge of relevant resources, applicable terminology, social disparities, stressors, and more. Intersectionality is a theory focusing on interlocking systems of power and oppression that affect people in various ways based on their social locations or identities (Collins & Bilge, 2016). For example, when working with a client with an LGBTQiA2S+ identity, disability, minoritized racial or ethnic identity, or a combination of these intersecting identities (i.e., genderqueer, disabled, Black woman), there are important implications to consider throughout the counseling process. While the life challenges clients face may relate to their intersectional identities, they may or may not present to counseling for identity-related concerns (Solomon et al., 2017).

If a counselor is not knowledgeable about how to work with people from certain backgrounds, they must practice cultural humility by recognizing one's limitations and seeking to understand and learn more about it. Cultural humility is infused into the MSJCC (Ratts et al., 2016). When considering clients' worldviews, the MSJCC state, "Privileged and marginalized counselors are aware of clients' worldviews, assumptions, attitudes, values, beliefs, biases, social identities, social group statuses, and experiences with power, privilege, and oppression" (Ratts et al., 2016, p. 6). Cultural humility, like cultural competence, is an ongoing developmental process. According to Hermawan and Pransiska (2020),

> Counselors would be encouraged to continue growing in their cultural awareness and humility by actively seeking formalized training, webinars, and presentations at conferences. Counselors at this stage demonstrate a more comprehensive, nuanced understanding of how cultural humility is used within interventions and how this influences clients and their goals. Moreover, they are encouraged to continue their personal reflection and achieve congruence with their personal and professional personas. They have a marked understanding of how this positively impacts their clinical work. (p. 16)

Practicing cultural humility aids counselors' abilities to practice cultural competence in goal setting with the clients they serve. As counselors "acquire culturally responsive conceptualization skills to explain how clients' privileged and marginalized status influence their culture, worldview, experiences, and presenting problem," (Ratts et al., 2016, p. 8) they are better equipped to help clients move forward in the process of setting goals.

Treatment Planning and Goal-Setting Considerations

Treatment planning and goal setting in counseling do not occur in a one-size-fits-all approach. Culturally responsive treatment planning and goal setting have unique considerations, including, but not limited to, the following: familiarization of clients with goal setting and treatment planning processes; identification of clients' strengths and access to resources; client-centered collaboration; identification of clients' cultural strengths and challenges; integration of culturally responsive case management; integration of clients' beliefs, values, and preferences; empowerment of clients with voice and choice; and promotion of wellness and resilience (Attia et al., 2023; Substance Abuse Mental Health Services Administration [SAMHSA], 2016; Miller et al., 2018; Summers, & Nelson, 2022).

Goal setting is essential to the counseling process. Geurtzen et al. (2020) identified how goal clarity in mental health care has favorable effects on motivation and outcomes for clients. Goal setting reinforces collaboration between clients and counselors and provides clarity in the counseling process. If counseling is a journey, goal setting is the way to identify the destination(s) and the route(s) to get there.

While the terms "treatment planning" and "goal setting" appear to be interchangeable in counseling, there are distinct differences in how they are perceived from a cultural perspective. These differences in perception may influence the ability of counselors to provide culturally competent counseling interventions in which the clients they serve are willing to commit to.

Impact of Stigma

Among many cultures, negative stigmas regarding mental health, including the concept of treatment planning, are considered significant barriers for some culturally diverse people who seek mental health counseling. Research shows that members of racial and ethnic minority groups within the United States are less likely than White people to seek mental health services out of fear of shame, embarrassment, and rejection by their communities (Tucker et al., 2022).

For instance, historically, families of African American descent have been reluctant to seek mental health treatment, due to the continued discrimination, racism, and mistreatment the African Americans have experienced at the hands of an unjust mental health system within the United States. As a result, individuals and communities who identify as African American or Black often handle their adversities independently and rely more on faith-based resources for mental and emotional support (Tucker et al., 2022).

Studies have also shown that individuals and communities who identify as Latin American or Latinx are just as likely to lack trust in mental health providers when compared to those who identify with a more Eurocentric ethnic background (Tucker et al., 2022). It is common for persons of Latin American cultural or ethnic identities to rely more on the support of their extended families and community members for their mental, emotional, and social well-being (Tucker et al., 2022).

Additionally, when discussing challenging life experiences, individuals of Latinx cultural or ethnic identities often focus more on their physiological symptomology than their thoughts and feelings.

Among the Asian American, Asian and Middle Eastern American, and Middle Eastern communities, there is a widespread cultural belief that seeking mental health treatment will bring shame and dishonor to the family (Tucker et al., 2022). Some of these individuals then internalize their symptoms instead of seeking counseling. Individuals of Asian American or Asian identities are often described as feeling pressured to appear perfect and successful, which may force them to hide their potential struggles with mental health (Tucker et al., 2022). It is also noted that persons who identify as Middle Eastern often on their families and religious leaders much like those who identify as either African American, Black, Latin American, or Latinx.

Ultimately, while the beliefs held may be valid based on their lived experiences, the overly negative views of mental health treatment may be a barrier for those with minoritized identities to access specific mental health interventions and receive adequate mental health services necessary to reduce symptomology and increase their overall functioning and well-being (Attia et al., 2023; Tucker et al., 2022). Therefore, counselors should strive to approach treatment goals holistically and include objectives to improve physical health and spiritual strength (SAMHSA, 2014, p. 29).

Though the examples provided are broad in nature, they are illustrative of a few reasons why cultural, racial, and ethnic minorities are less likely to engage in mental health treatment when there is a need. Now, more than ever before, it is the responsibility of mental health counselors to deconstruct the stigma of mental health treatment and treatment planning by engaging in anti-oppressive counseling practices.

Shifting from Treatment Planning to Goal Setting

Though treatment planning has been synonymous with goal setting throughout the evolution of the counseling profession, it is imperative that culturally responsive counselors have an awareness of societal perceptions of treatment planning, from a historical context. The process of treatment planning dates back as far as the early 1800s when psychiatric hospitals first opened. Treatment planning has been considered a critical element in the delivery of mental health services to individuals diagnosed with severe mental illness who require the intervention of a multidisciplinary treatment team. The process of treatment planning has increasingly become an area of concern among counselors in recent years as more individuals with minoritized identities without severe mental illness seek counseling.

While treatment planning in counseling is often perceived as a blueprint that outlines the interventions used throughout the therapeutic relationship, the term "treatment planning" may characterize a process that is potentially dismissive and upholds an institution that continually perpetuates oppression for cultural and ethnic minorities. Therefore, from a culturally responsive perspective, a shift from treatment planning to goal setting is necessary to ensure that the counseling process is more inclusive of cultural and ethnic minorities.

Goal Setting and the Counseling Process

Goals are referred to as the object of an individual's effort and/or desired result, and *goal setting* is a "commonly used therapeutic process" that is now commonly used as "many studies have demonstrated the effectiveness of goal setting on behavior change" (Renger & Macaskill, 2021, p. 357). Geurtzen et al. (2020) found perceived goal clarity in psychological treatment to have "direct favorable effects on patients' distress and wellbeing, as well as on their motivation and treatment outcomes" (p. 915). Maintaining consistency with a person-centered, focused, goal-setting approach allows for processes to be tailored toward cultural and ethnic minority clients. Often, these clients are then more motivated to engage in the process as their "goals are individually defined rather than designed around broad measures of problematic symptoms" (Renger & Macaskill, 2021, p. 358).

According to Berking et al. (2005), the achievement of goals within the counseling process can signify success (Kiselnikova et al., 2019). Furthermore, studies have demonstrated the effectiveness of goal setting and benefits in the facilitation of the mental health treatment, including guiding the collaborative therapeutic process, maintaining focus, and evaluation of the overall treatment (Michalak & Holtforth, 2006; Tiemens et al., 2010).

As noted, extensive research highlights the necessity and effectiveness of goal setting within the counseling process (Locke & Latham, 1990, 2002; Seijts & Latham, 2001; Seijets et al., 2004). Clients of diverse cultural and ethnic backgrounds seek out mental health services for a wide array of interpersonal challenges and life circumstances. For these clients, goal setting is instrumental in the elimination of unhealthy behaviors, the development of healthy and adaptive behaviors, reframing negative thinking, cultivating a more optimistic view, alleviating feelings of hopelessness, and instilling feelings of hope (SAMHSA, 2014). Culturally responsive goal setting in counseling assists cultural and ethnic minority clients to evolve into the people they desire to become, boost their confidence, stretch them beyond their comfort zone, provide them with purpose and meaning, and encourage them to be more trusting of themselves and their decision-making.

Familiarize Clients with the Goal Setting Process

Due to systemic oppression, health inequities, and other factors, some people from historically and presently marginalized populations may have never experienced counseling before, much less culturally responsive counseling. According to SAMHSA (2014), it is essential for culturally responsive counseling professionals to "remember that clients are typically new to treatment language or jargon, program expectations, and schedules, and the intake and treatment process" (p. 22). Therefore, it is necessary for the culturally responsive counselor to familiarize clients with the process of goal setting, beginning with initial intake and interviews (SAMHSA, 2014, p. 22).

Additionally, it is the responsibility of culturally responsive counselors to provide diverse clients with psychoeducation about collaboration and prioritize the client at the center of goal setting in counseling. The following are some suggestions on how to orient clients to the goal-setting process:

- Ask clients if they have experienced counseling before and, if so, what that experience was like for them (Bray, 2019).
    - *When you were in counseling previously, what were the goals you worked towards?* (Note: Do not be surprised if clients report earlier counseling experiences that did not focus on their goals).
- Acknowledge the power differential between clients and counselors and emphasize the client as the expert on their own life (Pope & Vasquez, 2016, pp. 34–40).

- - *Often, clients see me as an expert. Although I am a professional counselor who is here to help you, I recognize and respect that you are the expert of your life.*
  - *I don't know what it's like to walk in your shoes or to have had all the unique experiences you have lived through.*
- Before goal setting, explain the process to clients (SAMHSA, 2014).
  - *First, we will talk about what brought you to counseling.*
  - *Then, we will talk about the goals you have for yourself and what you are hoping to gain from counseling.*
- Explain to clients their power and choice in receiving counseling services and how their strengths, preferences, and goals will be incorporated into the process (Protecting Access to Medicare Act [PAMA], 2022).
  - *I am here to support you in reaching the goals you have for yourself.*
  - *This relationship is not about me telling you what to do.*
- Avoid clinical jargon (Fernández-Garrido & Medina-Domenech, 2020; Bottema-Beutel et al., 2020; Howard et al., 2013).
  - *Together, we will identify what your goals are for yourself (and/or your family) and work toward accomplishing those goals.*
- Directly ask clients for their input, interpretations, and understanding throughout the process (SAMHSA, 2015).
  - *What is your understanding of goal setting?*
  - *How would you prefer to set goals together?*

Ultimately, the purpose of goal setting is twofold, according to Locke and Latham (1990). More specifically, goal setting motivates and directs client behavior (Locke & Latham, 1990). For goal setting to be effective within the counseling process, cultural and ethnic minority clients must accept and commit themselves to the goals collaboratively identified in session.

Empowering Clients With Voice and Choice

Culturally responsive goal setting centralizes clients' experiences, voices, and choices (Helling & Chandler, 2019). As stated previously, goal setting is not a one-size-fits-all process with clients, nor is it about the goals and plans counselors have for the clients they serve. It is imperative that culturally responsive counselors engage clients "in a process that involves implementing agreed-upon goals that are consistent with [clients'] life experiences and cultural values … and acknowledges multiple client identities" (Childs, 2020, pp. 40–41).

Throughout the goal-setting process, culturally responsive counselors must effectively engage in cross-cultural communication skills as explained in the MSJCC (Ratts et al., 2016). Although some counseling agencies may require the use of clinical jargon in treatment plans, it is always recommended for counselors to include the client's words for each goal and objective for many reasons.

First, including the client's words in these goals and objectives reminds both the counselor and the client of the client's power and choice, eliminating oppression, and promoting empowerment. Second, when counselors match their language to the client's language, they communicate that the client's experiences are seen, understood, and can be safely shared with the counselor (Borelli et al., 2019). Third, when revisiting and updating goals in the future, it is helpful to have the client's own words to refer to when helping them to define their progress towards their goals. The following are examples of integrating client language into goal-setting objectives:

- Damian (he/him/his): "I want to get more involved at my church."
    - *Goal: "I want to get more involved at my church."* Damian agrees to attend church services at his church at least three times per month and identifies at least one additional way he would like to be more involved with his church.
- Sky (they/them/theirs): "I want to stop drinking every night after work. I don't know why I do it."
    - *Goal: "I want to stop drinking every night after work. I don't know why I do it."* Skye agrees to identify at least two reasons why they drink after work and at least two alternatives to drinking that will work for them.

Identifying Client Strengths and (Lack of) Access to Resources

Another important task in culturally responsive goal setting is the identification of clients' strengths and access, or lack of access, to resources. Counselors must first believe clients have strengths that are available to resolve difficulties and then recognize and integrate clients' strengths into the counseling relationship and the goal-setting process (Sparks & Duncan, 2010). The identification of cultural and ethnic minority clients' strengths are foundational to goal setting and the ongoing counseling process. It is important for culturally responsive counselors to be comfortable with directly inquiring about how the clients they serve perceive their strengths. If clients struggle to identify their strengths, supplemental questions may include the following:

- What is unique about you?
- What would (your family) say that they love or appreciate most about you?
- What are you proud of?
- How have you overcome the challenges in your life?

Cultural and/or ethnic minority clients may express strengths including, but not limited to, the following: a sense of humor, familial support, commitment to their family or cultural community, spiritual or religious beliefs, unique hobbies or abilities, or personal qualities such as resilience, tenacity, empathy, or courage. Other counseling skills for identifying clients' strengths include listening for "heroic stories" and "punctuating" clients' strengths (Sparks & Duncan, 2010, p. 75). Listening for "heroic stories" entails keen listening skills when clients may report their successes, achievements, or moments of resilience, while "punctuating" clients' strengths involves the counselor directly commenting on these strengths when they hear them and inquiring about them further (Sparks & Duncan, 2010).

Sparks and Duncan (2010) noted that it is necessary for culturally responsive counselors to actively seek out cultural and ethnic minority clients' strengths, including personal, interpersonal, social, and cultural resources. Cultural and ethnic minority client strengths are forms of resources, both internal (i.e., qualities such as courage or empathy) and external (i.e., supportive relationships and sense of belonging). Additionally, the MSJCC requires counselors to identify both supportive and nonsupportive sources for clients in their relationships with family, friends, and peers and support clients in fostering these relationships (Ratts et al., 2016). Culturally responsive counselors "draw, when appropriate, upon the institutions and resources of clients' cultural communities" to assist with the identification of resources and needs in relation to diverse clients' goals (Ratts et al., 2016, p. 30).

Maslow's hierarchy of needs (1943) is useful in identifying resources cultural and ethnic minority clients have access to and those in which they are not afforded access to. Maslow identified lower-level basic needs as physiological needs (i.e., food, water, and shelter). When physiological needs are unmet, clients' bodies cannot function optimally, which makes physiological needs the most important (McLeod, 2018). Culturally responsive counselors can help connect clients with resources, such as food pantries, access to clean water, and housing support, when appropriate. Maslow (1943) also identified safety needs (i.e., security and safety); psychological needs, such as belongingness and love needs (i.e., intimate relationships, friendships); and esteem needs (i.e., appreciation, respect, and accomplishment). Finally, Maslow identified self-actualization needs as achievement of one's full potential as a human being. Culturally responsive counselors play a significant role in connecting clients with appropriate, culturally informed resources.

Maslow's hierarchy of needs (1943) is not free from criticism regarding its applicability to cultural and ethnic minorities. Maslow's hierarchy is a theory of individual needs that more closely reflects an individualistic and ethnocentric perspective. More specifically, Hofstede (1984) claimed Maslow's Hierarchy of Needs is based upon a highly individualistic society of the United States in the 1950s, unlike the collectivistic society he observed while living at the Blackfoot Reserve in Siksika in 1938. While living among the Blackfoot, Maslow observed the Blackfoot view their community responsibilities as working to meet their basic needs, ensuring their safety, and developing conditions that foster purpose.

The COVID-19 pandemic generated numerous widespread social, psychological, and economic consequences, which disproportionately impacted already marginalized populations, specifically racial or ethnic minority groups and sexual and gender minority populations, according to Ruprecht et al. (2020). Not only were already marginalized populations at greater risk of exposure and susceptibility to the COVID-19 virus, but they also experienced greater difficulties in accessing resources, such as food, supplies, work-from-home privileges, health care, and mental health care. The COVID-19 pandemic highlighted the vast disparities in health equity and access to resources between cultural and ethnic minority populations that have existed for centuries, due to systemic oppression.

Culturally responsive counselors must advocate for and connect cultural and ethnic minority clients to culturally responsive resources based on their needs to achieve their goals. According to Kozan and Blustein (2018), "connecting clients with resources [means] taking extra steps to increase … clients' access to mental health care" and helping them to navigate the complex, multiple systems that often interfere with their ability to obtain these resources on their own (p. 170). Ratts et al. (2016) stated that culturally sensitive counselors

> Explore with privileged and marginalized clients the extent to which social institutions are supportive. Connect privileged and marginalized clients with supportive individuals within social institutions (e.g., schools, businesses, church, etc.) who are able to help alter inequities influencing marginalized clients. (p. 12)

Far too often, those "who decline to use resources as offered or as mandated are labeled resistant [or] judged to be of poor character," when these "bureaucratically organized resource referral interventions … assume a prior acculturation into effective use of professionalized systems" (Helling & Chandler, 2019, pp. 153–154).

To connect clients with resources and help them navigate these complex systems, culturally responsive counselors must first be knowledgeable about the resources in their community (Ratts et al., 2016). This task goes beyond searching through a list of agencies (Lam, 2006). Lam (2006) states, "Expanding options and support for struggling families from diverse cultural backgrounds requires that counselors stretch their comfort zone, leave the confines of their offices, and reach their clients' communities" (p. 155). Culturally responsive counselors must "acknowledge that the counseling relationship may extend beyond the traditional office setting and into the community" by practicing culturally responsive case management (Ratts et al., 2016, p. 9). Here are some tips for identifying culturally responsive resources in your community:

- Focus on pragmatic problem-solving (Ravitz et al., 2019).
- Connect with other frontline community mental health and social service agencies, and learn about the services they provide and how they deliver these services (Ravitz et al., 2019).
- Connect with local, state, and national counseling organizations and associations that may direct counselors toward vetted resources.
- Arrange a meeting with mental health professionals, other health-care professionals, and leaders as well as members of diverse identities to learn about existing services in the community; provide mental health education, obtain suggestions from others, and establish personal relationships between professionals, leaders, and community members (Miller-Fellows et al., 2018).

Stop Calling Clients "Resistant": It's Oppressive!

Resistance is any form of pushback, stance, or an act to maintain or gain power mentally or behaviorally (Afuape, 2011). When thinking about clients who may behave in these ways, it is important to understand the etiology of their behaviors and ambivalence towards change. It does not always mean clients are resistant in the ways counselors historically consider "resistance" to change or progress as willful avoidance or escape. A client's actions that may seem "resistant" may be the result of many factors. Some of these factors may include (a) the direct effect of barriers to accessing and maintaining their counseling, (b) their mistrust of the counselor or counseling process, (c) their lack of feeling validated and supported, which causes them to stop coming to counseling, (d) fear of change, or (e) need for a different approach than the counselor is using. For example, a client with financial struggles may stop going to counseling because they must choose between working to pay their bills or coming to counseling during work hours, without having paid time off. This client may feel embarrassed to tell the counselor about their financial struggle and may just stop going to counseling. Another example is when a client experiences difficult emotional work in a previous session as too overwhelming or painful for the client to continue the work at present. Instead of recognizing the client's feelings of pain and being overwhelmed, the counselor may think the client "ghosted them" and label them "resistant."

Labeling the clients as "resistant" can be avoided if the counselor engages in broaching. *Broaching* involves a counselor intentionally taking steps to consider the sociopolitical, sociocultural, and cultural influences on a client's treatment (Attia et al., 2023; MacCutcheon, 2018; Summers & Nelson, 2022). Knowing the difference between "resistance" and other factors that may cause a client to behave differently can support counselors in taking appropriate actions based on what is occurring and adjust their goal setting accordingly.

Here are some questions to consider:

1. What is client "resistance"?
2. Is it possible that "resistance" is a lack of understanding, access to resources, and not feeling safe or validated in the counseling process?
3. Have you labeled clients "resistant" when they weren't responding to treatment the way you wanted or expected them to? Can you think of ways you may avoid inaccurately labeling a client as "resistant" when they may not be responding to treatment the way you intended?
4. Have you considered assessing potential barriers that may be blocking their engagement in the counseling process to help them focus on their current goals?

Individualized Goals on the Treatment Plan

The MSJCC states that counselors "assist privileged and marginalized clients with developing self-advocacy skills that promote multiculturalism and social justice" (Ratts et al., 2016, p. 11). Additionally, counselors "take action by using language to explain how clients' privileged and marginalized statuses influence their culture, worldview, experiences, and presenting problem" (Ratts et al., 2016, p. 9).

Goal setting and treatment planning require identifying the client's presenting concerns and how these concerns manifest in their actions, thoughts, or feelings. Culturally responsive counselors acknowledge there are "within-group differences, between group similarities, and differences among privileged and marginalized clients" (Ratts et al., 2016, p. 7).

Next, counselors must diagnose, when appropriate, using the DSM-5-TR criteria, in a client-centered and culturally competent way (Summers, & Nelson, 2022). Then, the counselor moves onto goal setting with measurable goals (O'Leary et al., 2014). Goal setting and treatment plans should have behavioral definitions of the clients' presenting concerns, long-term goals, short-term objectives, and diagnoses, when appropriate.

Case Examples

THE CASE OF MIKE (HE/HIM/HIS)

Mike came to a private practice for counseling for anxiety. He is a 50-year-old White, heterosexual, cisgender man who works as an accountant for a successful firm in Georgia. He is recently divorced and has two children, whom he sees weekly, per the custody agreement with his ex-wife. When Mike attended his first session, he appeared emotionally and physically anxious. He stuttered in his speech, physically shook, and sometimes rocked back and forth. His speech was fast and pressured, and his face and ears were red.

Mike explained to the counselor that he feels anxious most of the time and admitted that his anxiety worsens after he listens to "alternative media" podcasts and reads information from similar sources.

He did not state a political affiliation. He said that the media he consumes discusses conspiracy theories about climate change and renewable and alternative energy.

Mike said he lives alone in a rural area and spends time at his parents' house at least twice weekly, although they live one town over from him. He commutes one hour each way every day to work in a major city. Mike stated that his boss and co-workers are supportive of him during his mental health struggles. He said his boss suggested that he contact their company's employee assistance program (EAP) to get help managing his anxiety. Mike shared that it was through the EAP that he located the counselor, an African American woman in her 50s.

Mike said he "just wants to feel better" because he sometimes has a hard time getting out of bed in the morning. He reported feeling "stressed out" and he believes his neighbors have "turned against him and are doing things to [his] property to try to aggravate [him]." He senses his neighbors are watching him and his property constantly, and although he is not sure why, he believes his neighbors, or someone affiliated with them, will try to hurt him. He is thinking about putting up cameras around his house to confirm his theory, so he can get some sleep. Mike's fear of his neighbors hurting him or damaging his property is very intense and causes lapses in his judgment at work. This is concerning for Mike because his line of work requires precision.

After seeing his counselor weekly for three weeks, Mike canceled his last appointment and emailed his counselor through the electronic health record (EHR) to inform her he was in an inpatient facility and would be there for several weeks. He said he wanted her to know that he gave permission to the facility's counselor for them to share information about his treatment with each other.

Applying the MSJCC to Mike's Case

Applying the MSJCCs to this case begins with the counselor's self-awareness, including her attitudes and beliefs, knowledge, skills, and actions. At the intake session, Mike shared his reasons for coming to counseling, including feeling anxious; having difficulties performing work tasks, due to anxiety; and consuming alternative media, which makes him more anxious. While Mike shared, the counselor immediately noticed herself becoming more hypervigilant and suspicious of Mike's motives for specifically initiating counseling services with her, a Black, woman owner of a mental health counseling practice with all counselors of color and an emphasis on minority mental health. Her attitudes and beliefs caused her to ask herself, "Why did this person seek *me* out during this time in our country, when racial tensions are high, and everyone who is not rich, White, male, heterosexual, able-bodied, and Christian with American citizenship seems to be under attack?"

She reflected on her work as a social justice warrior, which can easily be found online and wondered if the client was honestly there to address his anxiety or if he had another motive that could cause her harm. Nevertheless, she owned her self-awareness while also validating her concerns about the client during the initial session. As a professional counselor, she also has knowledge of and a responsibility to the ACA (2014) Code of Ethics, which tells her to do no harm and treat every client with fairness, dignity, respect, and nonjudgment.

She was also aware of her privileged and marginalized identities (privileged/marginalized counselor) and the client's privileged and marginalized identities (privileged/marginalized client) and how they may impact the counseling relationship (Ratts et al., 2016). From a privileged perspective, Mike is a White, heterosexual, cisgender male, who is educated and from a high socioeconomic class. From a marginalized perspective, he is a divorced, single father with anxiety symptoms.

The counselor also has privileged and marginalized identities. From a privileged perspective, she is a doctoral-level licensed and board-certified counselor, from a high socioeconomic class and holds religious and nationality privilege. She also identifies as heterosexual and is in a heterosexual marriage. From a marginalized perspective, she is a Black woman who has experienced discrimination, marginalization, oppression, and microaggressions, which impact her perception of this client.

The counselor understood how those with marginalized identities, including herself, have lived experiences that influenced her suspicions about this client, which caused her to be hypervigilant. The counselor's awareness, knowledge, and skills inform her that she can be kind to herself and her experience, while still demonstrating unconditional positive regard, empathy, and care with Mike.

After the session, the counselor acted by taking time to self-reflect on her feelings and perceptions about Mike and sought consultation to ensure she could work with him objectively and professionally in a way that helped, not hindered him, while still tending to her own safety. She took the time over the next few sessions to learn about the client's worldview and paid careful attention to her suspicions, thoughts, feelings, and beliefs. She soon learned that Mike did not have any harmful intentions; he was experiencing psychosis that contributed to his paranoia and anxiety symptoms. Therefore, the counselor was able to continue counseling with Mike. The counselor reflected on how the therapeutic alliance strengthened after each session.

A few weeks into their work together, Mike contacted the counselor through the EHR, informing her that he was admitted into an inpatient facility for severe psychosis. She interpreted Mike's communication with her through the EHR to inform her of his admission into the inpatient facility as a sign of the strength of the therapeutic relationship. She plans to continue supporting him when he is discharged from inpatient care if he wants to continue outpatient counseling with her. They cocreated Mike's treatment plan and included goals to reduce anxiety and psychotic symptoms as well as increase coping skills.

The counselor used the following treatment plan model by O'Leary et al. (2014) to cocreate Mike's treatment plan with him. The treatment plan includes behavioral definitions of his problem, long-term goals, short-term objectives, therapeutic interventions, and diagnostic suggestions.

Behavioral Definitions

1. Recurrent experiences of perceived threats and worries impeding daily functioning.
2. Social isolation, due to debilitating anxiety symptoms.

Long-Term Goals

1. Learn to identify anxiety triggers and how to use cognitive and behavioral coping skills to combat them.
2. Use positive, healthy, and practical self-talk to eradicate anxious thoughts.

Short-Term Objectives

1. Verbally identify the triggers for symptoms of anxiety concerns.
    - *Therapeutic intervention:* Ask the client to explain the anxiety and triggers that provoke his anxiety response.
2. Verbally say how anxiety issues manifest over time.
    - *Therapeutic intervention:* Identify three settings and ways anxiety symptoms impact his daily functioning.

Diagnoses

300.02 F41.1 Generalized Anxiety Disorder
309.24 F43.22 Adjustment Disorder, With Anxiety

THE CASE OF ALEX (THEY/THEM/THEIRS)

Alex sought counseling services to "deal with [their] anxiety, anger, and drinking" at a private practice specializing in LGBTQiA2S+ needs. Alex is a 23-year-old Latinx individual, who identifies as genderqueer and queer. Their pronouns are "they/them/theirs." Alex is single and lives with two roommates, whom they consider their "chosen sisters." They report no relationship with their family of origin in two years: "They hate me for not being their little 'princess' anymore. I know it's weird, but I still love them and miss them."

Alex was born and raised in the Texas Rio Grande Valley (RGV) and relocated to Portland, Oregon, for college. They reported "dropping out" of college when their parents "cut them off" financially and emotionally 2 years ago. They currently work two jobs for 50 hours per week between two coffee shops "just to keep the lights on."

At their first session, Alex had difficulty making eye contact with the counselor. They sat on the couch in the counselor's office while holding their knees to their chest, biting their lips, and primarily looking at the area rug. Alex explained they are afraid of their own anger and anxiety. They stated they began drinking in high school on the weekends with friends, "like everyone else in the RGV." However, they shared that their drinking is getting worse. Now, they drink most days after work "just to fall asleep and make the noise stop."

Alex reported being close to their roommates, though they admitted their chosen sisters "hate it" when they drink because they get "loud, obnoxious, and flirty with everyone." One morning last week, Alex's chosen sisters woke them up in the morning and took them to breakfast: "It wasn't just breakfast, though. It was like an intervention or something that you see on TV. They both told me that I needed to talk to someone." Alex told the counselor that they don't want to wind up drinking like their mother.

They also told their counselor that they "can't really afford counseling right now" and don't have health insurance. They let you know that their sisters are helping them pay right now, but they can only come to counseling once a month because "it's so expensive."

Alex reported a previous counseling experience when they were in college. However, they stated that the experience was "awful," and that's how their parents found out they were genderqueer and queer: "My counselor there made me tell them. She promised me they would still love me, and I told her they wouldn't. Now, here I am." Alex shared that since then, they haven't trusted mental health professionals, "much less the ones who don't know anything about being queer."

Applying the MSJCC to Alex's Case

The first application of the MSJCC to Alex's case must begin with the counselor's own self-awareness. Even though the counselor identifies as queer themselves and has worked with LGBTQiA2S+ individuals for many years now, the counselor must be careful to recognize their own attitudes, beliefs, and assumptions about Alex's experiences and presenting concerns. When Alex shared about their parents' reaction to them being genderqueer and queer, the counselor was filled with indignation and felt protective of Alex. The counselor found themselves immediately wanting to tell Alex they were better off without their parents. However, the counselor noticed their internal response to Alex's story and decided to pause. The counselor also reminded themselves LGBTQiA2S+ individuals cannot be painted with a broad brush.

The counselor later consulted with their colleague, a Latina heterosexual, cisgender female who grew up in the RGV. The counselor wanted to get a better understanding of where Alex came from. The colleague shared the importance of family in Latin culture and adherence to the predominant conservative, anti-queer Catholic teachings. However, their colleague also reminded the counselor that although she is Latina and grew up in the RGV, too, only Alex had Alex's life experiences. The colleague suggested the counselor attend a virtual workshop with an RGV-based counseling agency about mental health stigmas in Latinx culture. The counselor agreed, as expanding their awareness, knowledge, and skills of marginalized clients is part of becoming a multicultural and social justice competent counselor.

In the next counseling session with Alex, the counselor noticed that Alex made eye contact a few times throughout the session. The counselor touched base with Alex about their life since the previous session and asked them how they felt following the first session. Alex reported, "Honestly, I wasn't sure how a White lady could help me or why I was coming back to counseling at all, to begin with ... but I've been looking forward to coming back, and here we are." The counselor smiled and self-disclosed their pronouns: "they/them/theirs." Alex laughed and said, "Well, it makes sense now!"

The counselor familiarized Alex with the treatment planning and goal-setting process, something Alex reported they never did with their previous counselor. The counselor highlighted Alex's power, voice, and choice in setting their goals for counseling. The counselor also informed Alex that treatment planning and goal setting is an ongoing process, not a one-time occurrence. The counselor then asked Alex what their goals for counseling were, and together, they collaborated and cocreated Alex's treatment plan.

Behavioral Definitions
- "I need to deal with my anxiety, anger, and drinking." Alex reports drinking four to five nights per week after work "just to fall asleep and make the noise stop."
- "I need to deal with my anxiety, anger, and drinking." Alex reports being "afraid of [their] own anger and anxiety."

Long-Term Goals
- "I want to be able to go to sleep without drinking, and I want to make all the 'noise' in my head stop. Sometimes I can't even hear myself think." Alex agrees to work with the counselor to identify and practice harm-reduction skills with their drinking habits.
- "I want to not be so angry and scared all the time. Sometimes, I don't even know why I'm mad or anxious—I just am." Alex agrees to work with the counselor to identify activators for their feelings of anger and anxiety as well as coping skills to manage these feelings.

Short-Term Objectives
- *Objective 1*: "I want to be able to go to sleep without drinking, and I want to make all the 'noise' in my head stop. Sometimes I can't even hear myself think." Alex agrees to learn and implement at least two harm-reduction skills to manage their drinking.
    - *Therapeutic Intervention*: Psychoeducation regarding substance use and harm-reduction skills, motivational interviewing (MI) to identify reasons Alex wants to manage their drinking; explore Alex's hobbies and interests to identify potential alternatives to alcohol use;

> provide additional referrals for medical care (i.e., detox, intensive outpatient, or inpatient substance use treatment), psychiatric evaluation and medication management, and/or other health care, if appropriate.
> - *Objective 2*: "I want to not be so angry and scared all the time. Sometimes, I don't even know why I'm mad or anxious—I just am." Alex agrees to work with the counselor to identify at least two activators for their feelings of anger and at least two coping skills to manage their feelings of anger.
>   - *Therapeutic Intervention:* Psychoeducation regarding trauma and anger, highlighting anger as an appropriate emotional response to trauma; psychoeducation regarding the differences between anger as an emotion and rage as a behavior; psychoeducation regarding coping skills for anger; explore Alex's hobbies and interests to identify potential existing coping skills; collaborate with Alex's sisters to support Alex in reducing their alcohol use, if Alex agrees.
> - *Objective 3*: "I want to not be so angry and scared all the time. Sometimes, I don't even know why I'm mad or anxious—I just am." Alex agrees to work with the counselor to identify at least two activators for their feelings of anxiety and at least two coping skills to manage their feelings of anger.
>   - *Therapeutic Intervention:* Psychoeducation regarding trauma and anxiety, highlighting anxiety as an appropriate emotional response to trauma; psychoeducation regarding the experience of anger in the mind, body, and emotions; psychoeducation regarding coping skills for anxiety; explore Alex's hobbies and interests to identify potential existing coping skills.
>
> *Diagnosis*
> The counselor elected to withhold a diagnosis for Alex, based on the direct connections between Alex's distress and presenting concerns with their lived experiences of oppression by systems of heterosexism, sexism, genderism, and racism.

CHAPTER SUMMARY

As we conclude this chapter, we want to stress the importance of cultural competence and ethical and anti-oppressive practices in goal setting with clients to strengthen their counseling outcomes. For this to occur, counselors must use a culturally competent lens to practice self-awareness, understand the clients' worldviews and the intersecting factors involved, and continue to build their culturally responsive skill sets (ACA, 2014; Collins & Bilge, 2016; Ratts et al., 2016).

Counselors must work collaboratively with clients to identify and accomplish these goals. The voices and choices of clients should be amplified throughout goal setting, and counselors should continuously expand their knowledge, abilities, and skills concerning the cultural and lived experiences of the clients they serve. Historically, counseling has been practiced through a monolithic and Eurocentric lens. Counselors who strive to be culturally responsive must be intentional in serving diverse clients.

CHAPTER REFLECTION AND DISCUSSION QUESTIONS

1. What are some of your takeaways from this chapter as they relate to your burgeoning counseling identity?
2. What are some ways you anticipate incorporating clients' intersections in the goal-setting process? What are some ways you can continue to do so in a culturally responsive way after reading this chapter?
3. How will you take an anti-oppressive stance in goal setting with clients going forward?
4. What are three important considerations for goal setting and treatment planning from a multicultural and social justice perspective?
5. What is the counselor's role in the goal setting?

ADDITIONAL RESOURCES

Berking, M., Holtforth, M. G., Jacobi, C., & Kruner-Herwig, B. (2005). Empirically based guidelines for goal-finding procedures in psychotherapy: Are some goals easier to attain than others? *Psychotherapy Research, 15*(3), 316–324. https://doi.org/10.1080/10503 300500091801

Branson, J. S., & Branson, A. (2023). *Core counseling courses.* Counseling Education.

Collins, S. (2018). Collaborative case conceptualization: Applying a contextualized, systemic lens. In S. Collins (Ed.), *Embracing cultural responsivity and social justice: Re-shaping professional identity in counselling psychology* (pp. 572–601). Counselling Concepts.

Gallardo, M. E. (2012). *Culturally adaptive counseling skills: Demonstrations of evidence-based practices.* Faculty Books. https://digitalcommons.pepperdine.edu/facultybooks/50

Gallardo, M. E., Yeh, C. J., Trimble, J. E., & Parham, T. A. (Eds.). (2012). *Culturally adaptive counseling skills: Demonstrations of evidence-based practices.* SAGE. https://doi.org/10.4135/9781483349329

Ibrahim, F. A., & Heuer, J. R. (2016). *Cultural and social justice counseling. International and cultural psychology.* https://doi.org/10.1007/978-3-319-18057-1

Jones, C. (2017). Review of Hill Collins, P., & Bilge, S. (2016), "Intersectionality." *Canadian Journal of Disability Studies, 6*(4), 210–215. https://doi.org/10.15353/cjds.v6i4.390

King, K. M. (2018). Setting the stage for culturally responsive counseling: An experimental investigation of White counselors broaching race and racism. *Dissertation Abstracts International: Section B: The Sciences and Engineering, 79*(11-B(E)).

LaFerriere, L., & Calsyn, R. (1978). Goal attainment scaling: An effective treatment technique in short-term therapy. *American Journal of Community Psychology, 6*(3), 271–282. https://doi.org/10.1007/bf00894357

Levounis, P., Arnaout, B., & Marienfeld, C. (Eds.). (2017). *Motivational interviewing for clinical practice.* American Psychiatric Pub.

Locke, E. A., & Latham, G. P. (1990). *A theory of goal-setting & task performance.* Prentice-Hall, Inc.

Locke, E. A., & Latham, G. P. (2002). Building a practically useful theory of goal-setting and task motivation. *American Psychologist, 57*(9), 705–717. https://doi.org/10.1037/0003-066x.57.9.705

Locke, E. A., & Latham, G. P. (2006). New directions in goal-setting theory. *Current Directions in Psychological Science, 15*(5), 265–268. https://doi.org/10.1111/j.1467-8721.2006.00449.x

Loh, D., Wrathall, J., & Schapper, J. (2000). *The Maslow revival: Maslow's hierarchy of needs as a motivational theory.* Monash University (Working Paper, 78/00). Caulfield, Vic., Monash University, Faculty of Business and Economics.

McNichols, C., Zinck, K., Witt, K. J., & Neel, J. (2016). Counselors as agents of change: Writing behaviorally stated goals and objectives. *Vistas Online, 36,* 1–12. https://www.counseling.org/docs/default-source/vistas/article_365efd25f161 16603abcacff0000bee5e7.pdf?sfvrsn=4

Maslow, A. H. (1943). A theory of human motivation. *Psychological Review, 50*(4), 370–396. https://doi.org/10.1037/h0054346

Maslow, A. H. (1987). *Motivation and personality* (3rd ed.). Harper & Row Publishers.

Mead, E. (2019, June). *45 goal setting exercises, tools, & games.* PositivePsychology.com. https://positivepsychology.com/goal-setting-exercises/

Naz, S., Gregory, R., & Bahu, M. (2019). Addressing issues of race, ethnicity and culture in CBT to support therapists and service managers to deliver culturally competent therapy and reduce inequalities in mental health provision for BAME service users. *The Cognitive Behaviour Therapist, 12,* E22. https://doi.org/10.1017/S1754470X19000060

Nelson-Jones, R. (2002). Diverse goals for multicultural counseling and therapy. *Counseling Psychology Quarterly, 15*(2), 133–143. https://10.1080/09515050110100965

Oh, H., & Lee, C. (2016). Culture and motivational interviewing. *Patient education and counseling, 99*(11), 1914–1919. https://doi.org/10.1016/j.pec.2016.06.010.

Ponterotto, J. G., Casas, J. M., Suzuki, L. A., & Alexander, C. M. (Eds.). (2010). *Handbook of multicultural counseling* (3rd ed.). SAGE.

Ratts, M. J., Singh, A. A., Nassar-McMillan, S., Butler, S. K., & McCullough, J. R. (2016). Multicultural and social justice counseling competencies: Guidelines for the counseling profession. *Journal of Multicultural Counseling and Development, 44*(1), 28–48. https://doi.org/10.1002/jmcd.12035

Ravits, P., Berhout, S., Lawson, A., Kay, T., & Meikle, S. (2019). Integrating evidence-supported psychotherapy principles in mental health case management: A capacity building pilot. *The Canadian Journal of Psychiatry, 64*(12), 588–862. https://doi.org/10.1177/0706743719877031

Sommers-Flanagan, J., Richardson, B. G., & Sommers-Flanagan, R. (2010). A multi-theoretical, evidence-based approach for understanding and managing adolescent resistance to psychotherapy. *Journal of Contemporary Psychotherapy, 41*(2), 69–80. https://doi.org/10.1007/s10879-010-9164-y

Substance Abuse Mental Health Services Administration. (2016). *Treatment improvement protocol 59: Improving cultural competence.* Substance Abuse and Mental Health Services Administration. https://store.samhsa.gov/product/TIP-59-Improving-Cultural-Competence/SMA15-4849

Summers, L. M., & Nelson, L. (2022). *Multicultural counseling: Responding with cultural humility, empathy, and advocacy.* Springer Publishing Company.

The Counseling Roundtable. (2023). *The counseling roundtable: A global collaborative community.* The Counseling Roundtable. https://www.thecounselingroundtable.com/

REFERENCES

Afuape, T. (2011). *Power, resistance, and liberation in therapy with survivors of trauma: To have our hearts broken.* Taylor & Francis Group. ProQuest Ebook Central. https://ebookcentral.proquest.com/lib/waldenu/detail.action?docID=735289

Attia, M., Das, B., Atiyeh, S., & Browne-James, L. (2023). Integrating multicultural competencies in ethical decision-making with immigrant populations. *Counseling and Values, 68*(1), 1–17. https://doi.org/10.1163/2161007X-68010005

American Counseling Association. (2014). *ACA code of ethics.* http://www.counseling.org/docs/ethics/2014-aca-code-of-ethics.pdf?sfvrsn=4

Borelli, J. L., Sohn, L., Wang, B. A., Hong, K., DeCoste, C., & Suchman, N. E. (2019). Therapist–client language matching: Initial promise as a measure of therapist–client relationship quality. *Psychoanalytic Psychology, 36*(1), 9–18. https://doi.org/10.1037/pap0000177

Bottema-Beutel, K., Kapp, S. K., Lester, J. N., Sasson, N. J., & Hand, B. N. (2020). Avoiding ableist language: Suggestions for autism researchers. *Autism in Adulthood, 3*(1), 18–29. https://doi.org/10.1089/aut.2020.0014

Bray, B. (2019, January 29). Counselor self-disclosure: Encouragement or impediment to client growth? *Counseling Today.* https://ct.counseling.org/2019/01/counselor-self-disclosure-encouragement-or-impediment-to-client-growth/

Childs, J. R. (2020). Proceeding with caution: Integrating cultural humility into multicultural supervision practices with master-level counseling students. *Reflections: Narratives of Professional Helping, 26*(2), 40–41. https://reflectionsnarrativesofprofessionalhelping.org/index.php/Reflections/article/view/1749

Fernández-Garrido, S., & Medina-Domenech, R. M. (2020). "Bridging the sexes": Feelings, professional communities, and emotional practices in the Spanish intersex clinic. *Science as Culture, 29*(4), 1–22. https://doi.org/10.1080/09505431.2020.1718088

Geurtzen, N., Keijsers, G. P. J., Karremans, J. C., Tiemens, B. G., & Hutschemaekers, G. J. M. (2020). Patients' perceived lack of goal clarity in psychological treatments: Scale development and negative correlates. *Clinical Psychology & Psychotherapy, 27*(6), 915–924. https://doi.org/10.1002/cpp.2479

Helling, J., & Chandler, G. E. (2019). Meeting the psychological health & growth needs of black college students: Culture, resonance, and resilience. *Journal of College Student Psychotherapy, 35*(2), 1–29. https://doi.org/10.1080/87568225.2019.1660291

Hofstede, G. (1984). The cultural relativity of the quality of life concept. *The Academy of Management Review, 9*(3), 389–398. https://doi.org/10.2307/258280

Howard, T., Jacobson, K. L., & Kripalani, S. (2013). Doctor talk: Physicians' use of clear verbal communication. *Journal of Health Communication, 18*(8), 991–1001. https://doi.org/10.1080/10810730.2012.757398

Kozan, S., & Blustein, D. L. (2018). Implementing social change: A qualitative analysis of counseling psychologists' engagement in advocacy. *The Counseling Psychologist, 46*(2), 154–189. https://doi.org/10.1177/0011000018756882

Lam, S. K.-Y. (2006). Preparing counseling students to use community resources for a diverse client population: Factors for counselor educators to consider. *VISTAS Online, 33*, 153–156.

https://www.counseling.org/docs/default-source/vistas/preparing-counseling-students-to-use-community-resources-for-a-diverse-client-population-factors-for-counselors-educators-to-consider.pdf?sfvrsn=31db7e2c_10#:~:text=After%20analyzing%20themes%20expressed%20in,confusion%20over%20what%20resources%20

MacCutcheon, M. (2018). *How broaching can help strengthen the therapeutic relationship.* https://www.goodtherapy.org/blog/how-broaching-can-help-strengthen-therapeutic-relationship-0116184

McLeod, S. (2018). *Maslow's hierarchy of needs.* Simply Psychology. https://canadacollege.edu/dreamers/docs/Maslows-Hierarchy-of-Needs.pdf

Michalak, J. and Holtforth, M.G. (2006). Where do we go from here? The goal perspective in psychotherapy. *Clinical Psychology: Science and Practice, 13,* 346–365. https://doi.org/10.1111/j.1468-2850.2006.00048.x

Miller, G., Johnson, G. S., Feral, T., Luckett, W., Fish, K., & Ericksen, M. (2018). The use of evidence-based practices with oppressed populations. *Counseling Today.* https://ct.counseling.org/2018/12/the-use-of-evidence-based-practices-with-oppressed-populations/

Miller-Fellows, S. C., Adams, J., Korbin, J. E., & Greska, L. P. (2018). Creating culturally competent and responsive mental health services: A case study among the Amish population of Geauga County, Ohio. *Journal of Behavioral Health Services and Research, 45*(4), 627–639. https://doi.org/10.1007/s11414-018-9612-0

O'Leary, K. D., Heyman, R. E., Jongsma, A. E., Jr. (2014). *The couples psychotherapy treatment planner* (2nd ed.). Wiley.

Pope, K. S., & Vasquez, M. J. T. (2016). *Ethics in psychotherapy and counseling: A practical guide* (4th ed., pp. 34–40). Wiley.

Protecting Access to Medicare Act, 223. (2022). https://www.samhsa.gov/section-223/about

Ratts, M. J., Singh, A. A., Nassar-McMillan, S., Butler, S. K., & McCullough, J. R. (2016). Multicultural and social justice counseling competencies: Guidelines for the counseling profession. *Journal of Multicultural Counseling and Development, 44*(1), 28–48. https://doi.org/10.1002/jmcd.12035

Renger, S., & Macaskill, A. (2021). Guided goal setting in therapy towards being fully functioning. *Journal of Contemporary Psychotherapy: On the Cutting Edge of Modern Developments in Psychotherapy, 51*(4), 357–364. https://doi.org/10.1007/s10879-021-09505-8

Ruprecht, M. M., Wang, X., Johnson, A. K., Xu, J., Felt, D., Ihenacho, S., Stonehouse, P., Curry, C. W., DeBroux, C., Costa, D., & Phillips II, G. (2020). Evidence of social and structural COVID-19 disparities by sexual orientation, gender identity, and race/ethnicity in an urban environment. *Journal of Urban Health, 98*(1). https://doi.org/10.1007/s11524-020-00497-9

Shahrawat, A., & Shahrawat, R. (2017). Application of Maslow's hierarchy of needs in a historical context: Case studies of four prominent figures. *Psychology, 8,* 939–954. https://doi.org/10.4236/psych.2017.87061

Solomon, D. T., Heck, N., Reed, O. M., & Smith, D. W. (2017). Conducting culturally competent intake interviews with LGBTQ youth. *Psychology of Sexual Orientation and Gender Diversity, 4*(4), 403–411. https://doi.org/10.1037/sgd0000255

Sparks, J., & Duncan, B. (2010). Client strengths and resources: Helping clients draw on what they already do best. In M. Cooper & W. Dryden (Eds.), *The Handbook of Pluralistic Counselling and Psychotherapy* (pp. 68–79). SAGE Publications Ltd. https://betteroutcomesnow.com/wp-content/uploads/2018/01/client-strengths-resources.pdf

Substance Abuse and Mental Health Services Administration. (2014). *A treatment improvement protocol: Improving cultural competence.* U.S. Department of Health and Human Services. https://store.samhsa.gov/sites/default/files/d7/priv/sma14-4849.pdf

Substance Abuse Mental Health Services Administration. (2016). *Based on TIP 59 improving cultural competence: Quick guide for clinicians.* U.S. Department of Health and Human Services. https://store.samhsa.gov/sites/default/files/d7/priv/sma16-4931.pdf

Sue, D. W., Sue, D., Neville, H. A., & Smith, L. (2019). *Counseling the culturally diverse* (8th ed.). Wiley. https://www.perlego.com/book/990651/counseling-the-culturally-diverse-theory-and-practice-pdf

Summers, L. M., & Nelson, L. (2022). *Multicultural counseling: Responding with cultural humility, empathy, and advocacy.* Springer Publishing.

Tucker, E. B., Schmidt, A., & Walker, V. P. (2022). Addressing bias and disparities in previable counseling and care. *Seminars in Perinatology, 46*(3), 151524. https://doi.org/10.1016/j.semperi.2021.151524

Reframing Termination Through a Culture-Centered Lens

Dr. Ebony E. White, Dr. Selma d. Yznaga, Dr. Deryl F. Bailey, Ashley D. Holmes Cosby, and Tabitha Rodriguez

LEARNING OBJECTIVES

1. Understand the factors related to early termination for people of color.
2. Increase awareness about the termination continuum for people of color.
3. Reframe termination by reconceptualizing commitment and readiness to change.
4. Provide tools for ethical and competent termination with clients of color.

LEARNING OUTCOMES

1. Students will identify their biases and beliefs around termination.
2. Students will increase their understanding of relational termination when working with clients of color.
3. Students will distinguish between session termination and termination of the counseling relationship.
4. Students will understand reasons termination or prolonged absence occurs in populations of color.

Chapter Highlights

The following are some of the important concepts, terms, and information we will explore in this chapter, from an MSJCC perspective.

1. Termination exists on a continuum.
2. Early termination is common, and reasons for early termination vary.
3. Self-awareness around biases and beliefs regarding termination is necessary to avoid mislabeling client behavior.

Introduction

Termination in counseling ideally occurs as a planned course of treatment (e.g., the achievement of goals or the client's perception of improvement; Lee et al., 2021). Early termination, defined as the client's unilateral decision to end treatment prior to the counselor's recommended treatment plan, is reported to occur at rates from 20% to 70% in outpatient settings (Anderson et al., 2019; Owen et al., 2012). Given the wide range of occurrence, it is important to understand and address the issues that lead to early termination. Premature termination is poorly understood and has been attributed to environmental factors such as transportation, language, and economic barriers; dissatisfaction with progress; a weak therapeutic alliance; and the counselor's lack of multicultural competence (Maramosh, 2022). Furthermore, unilateral termination is more frequently experienced by historically marginalized populations, including clients of color, the undereducated (formal), gender and sexual minorities, and women (Anderson et al., 2019).

Despite the American Counseling Association's (ACA) mandate for multicultural competence, the discrepancy between the prevalence of mental health symptoms and counseling utilization remains wide for those on the margins of dominant culture (Anderson et al., 2019). Thus, although many counseling programs offer courses focused on multicultural competence, that has not often translated into positive client experiences in counseling. To correct this, previous chapters have introduced innovative and inclusive strategies for psychotherapeutic healing intended to appeal to a broader range of clients than the discipline has been able to attract and retain. We understand that even when implementing these strategies, barriers still exist, especially with marginalized clients. Thus, in this chapter, we focus on termination at various points on a continuum.

We must also underscore the unique relationships clients of color develop with their therapists, which may result in short (one therapy session) or long-lasting interventions. Thus, termination with the same client may occur at multiple points over a span of time. Additionally, given the history of harm in the health-care system to communities of color, resulting in cultural mistrust (Terrell & Terrell, 1981), once a client finds a provider they trust, they often recommend family members and friends. This often leads to prolonged relationships with clients and meaningful integration into their lives. In this chapter, the authors posit that termination occurs on a continuum and propose the reconceptualization of termination as a cyclical rather than a linear event.

Historical Considerations

Expanding the definition of termination regarding counseling requires an expansion of our understanding of counseling as a whole. In the United States, we tend to have a constrained definition of counseling that disregards the ways counseling has occurred in communities of color for centuries (Gamby et al., 2021). Before colonization, Indigenous populations on this land engaged in wellness practices, such as talking circles and sweat lodges, to foster connection to community and land, restore balance, and promote healing (Moghaddam et al., 2015). Furthermore, current discussions around wellness involve practices derived from India, which have been occurring for thousands of years (Gamby et al., 2021). Additionally, Africans who were taken to the United States and enslaved continued to practice traditional healing methods, including seeking counsel from an elder or traditional healer to help restore stability to their lives, despite the stripping of language and culture that occurred through colonialism (Kpobi, & Swartsz, 2019). This was predicated on the belief that instability in an individual's physical, mental, spiritual, or social life led to physical illness. Even in the Western context, spirituality and religion continue to be the chosen method of counseling for African American, Latine, and Indigenous communities (Cervantes & Parham, 2005). Recognizing the history of counseling in communities of color is necessary for two reasons: (a) We must recognize that counseling occurs within community, and (b) we must acknowledge and validate the sources of support embedded in communities of color that have helped clients sustain and thrive.

As traditional counseling emerged and grew, there was an intentional exclusion of people of color at every level (i.e., client and clinician), giving access only to society's elite population. Given that wellness was not afforded to those who were not White and other factors, such as media misrepresentation, it is unsurprising that individuals may misconceive the scope of counseling services and its benefits (Fripp & Carlson, 2017). As the field continues to grow, it is our duty to be responsive to client needs. As such, conventional models of counseling must be expanded to effectively serve communities of color. This includes allowing flexibility around termination, particularly because many clients may not have the resources to start and commit to long-term therapy (Thomas, 2016).

Conventional Termination

Termination is typically the final stage of counseling signaling the end of the counselor–client relationship. However, if afforded the opportunity to engage in long-term counseling with clients, it is important to think about and discuss termination along the way, beginning with the informed consent. Clients have the right to know that the tentative number of sessions is negotiable, with consideration for the client's needs and desires and the counselor's expertise and recommendations. The treatment planning process in which goals are identified is another optimal time to consider termination since the criteria for meeting goals are clearly outlined. Progress toward attaining these goals could serve as a barometer for client's readiness for discharge or termination. Thus, as we ask clients, "How can we tell when you have achieved this goal?" we can also ask, "How will we know when you are ready to be discharged for therapy?" Asking clients these questions remind them that counseling does not have to last forever and helps them to monitor their own progress toward completion.

Counselors support clients through termination by allowing ample time to process the end of therapy. This could occur over multiple sessions, depending on client needs. Additionally, counselors ensure a clear aftercare plan has been developed to help support clients' continued success after termination. However, termination rarely means *the end* when working with clients of color. Therefore, culturally competent counselors ensure clients can return to therapy when or if they deem necessary. Interpersonal relationships are important to clients of color; therefore, the idea of never seeing their therapist again may be daunting. Relaying that the door is open and processing clients' emotions are essential in providing culturally competent care.

Reasons for Termination

Termination is a standard part of the counseling process, as previously explained. However, early termination often occurs with clients of color. We define early termination as the client discontinuing therapy prior to the completion of their identified goals or the suggested timeframe. Within recent years, there has been an increase of clients of color seeking and participating in counseling; however, early termination continues to be a barrier in treatment. Environmental constraints, such as transportation needs and employment demands, continue to impede utilization and consistency in counseling. Aside from limited access and unaffordable costs, the longevity of clients of color in counseling can also result from cultural, ethnic, or linguistic differences between counselors and clients (Presley & Day, 2018). This is exacerbated by the experiences of racism and discrimination clients suffer in their interactions with mental health providers, leading to prolonged absences or termination (Alegria et al., 2016). All these issues demonstrate the need for counselors to be well versed in the Multicultural and Social Justice Counseling Competencies (MJSCC), which were designed to support counselors' cultural competence by enhancing counselor self-awareness, amplifying clients' worldview, improving the counseling relationship, and providing counseling and advocacy interventions (2015).

Counselor Self-Awareness

Counseling in the Western world is often incongruent with the cultural values of people of color. For example, many theories taught in counseling programs encourage counselors to support their clients in identifying individual goals, often disregarding their cultural contexts, which may amplify the collective over the individual. Have you ever heard someone say, "Don't think what others may want for you, what do you want for you?" Although well meaning, this is antithetical to individuals from collectivistic cultures and could ultimately lead to problems in their familial relationships. Therefore, it is important to identify any preconceived notions about counseling and termination, especially when working with clients of color. For example, how is success measured in counseling? How many sessions must clients attend for counseling to be seen as successful? Counselors are taught to help their clients identify goals to work toward in therapy. Can these goals be achieved in one session? As you reflect on these questions, think about the restrictions your answers may put in place for clients of color.

Consider crisis counselors who know they may only have one encounter with a client who recently experienced a traumatic event. Although they may only meet with the client once, much can be accomplished in that single encounter. If we broaden our ideas around crisis, we might include clients of color contending with discrimination daily or clients living in under-resourced communities plagued by violence. There may not be housing instability or food insecurity; however, the effects of having to navigate a heightened environment daily could limit the opportunity to engage in prolonged counseling. Furthermore, counseling is often seen as a luxury in communities of color—thus prioritizing it over other necessities may be unrealistic. Despite these valid barriers, we are often taught to view clients who terminate therapy prematurely as lacking commitment, unready to change, or resistant to the process. We rarely indict the system that actively impedes the ability of our clients to enter, maintain, and complete the therapeutic process of counseling.

As counselors, an openness to reframing termination is warranted. Later in the chapter, we discuss the need for counselors to approach work with some clients as one-at-a-time sessions because each session could be the last. Alternatively, it is important to note that early termination can also be viewed as success. Some clients may believe they received what they needed after one or a few sessions and decide to discontinue counseling. Other clients may have prolonged absences from therapy but return intermittently when circumstances permit or as issues arise. This can also be viewed as a success, as it can be an indicator of the level of connection a client feels to a therapist, resulting in their continual return. Thus, although early termination can be an indicator of systemic issues, lack of resources, or lack of counselor competence, it can also be a sign of success.

Termination Continuum

In this chapter, we introduce the *Yzanga, Ebony, and Bailey (YEB) termination continuum*. The traditional definition of "termination" in counseling has espoused a model dependent on an agreed-upon number of sessions; a treatment plan with measurable short-, intermediate-, and long-term goals; and the achievement of these goals. Falling outside of these parameters inspired guilt: Failure to attend counseling consistently and comply with the treatment plan meant that either the client or the counselor had not succeeded. More contemporary models of counseling have expanded the notion of termination to occur at different points with varying reasons and levels of success, mitigating guilt and blame for not adhering to the long-established protocol for ending therapy. Figure 13.1 shows varied points in the counseling relationship during which termination can naturally occur with sound rationale.

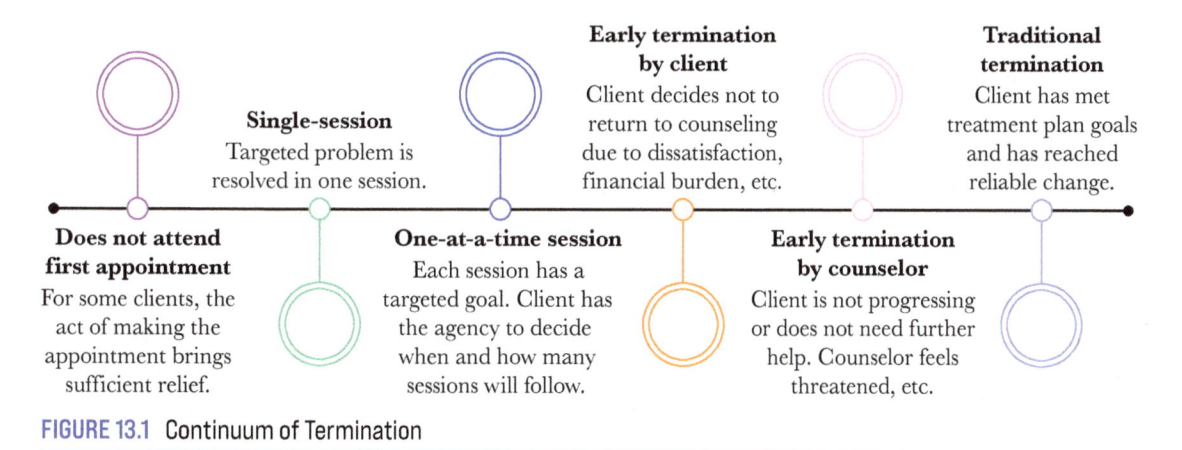

Does not attend first appointment
For some clients, the act of making the appointment brings sufficient relief.

Single-session
Targeted problem is resolved in one session.

One-at-a-time session
Each session has a targeted goal. Client has the agency to decide when and how many sessions will follow.

Early termination by client
Client decides not to return to counseling due to dissatisfaction, financial burden, etc.

Early termination by counselor
Client is not progressing or does not need further help. Counselor feels threatened, etc.

Traditional termination
Client has met treatment plan goals and has reached reliable change.

FIGURE 13.1 Continuum of Termination

As previously stated, termination does not occur on a linear path; instead, it exists on a continuum. Whether the client has 1 session or 30, we propose there are five points on the continuum of termination in any given session: (a) alliance building and understanding of the problem, (b) collaborative goal setting, (c) rehearsal, (d) evaluation, and (e) session termination. It is important to note that termination may refer to the end of one session or the temporary end of the counseling relationship with the client.

Mental health stigma is a stubborn barrier to treatment in traditional counseling for communities of color. In Latiné populations, for example, seeing a therapist can be perceived as an admission of weakness—an inability to tolerate psychological discomfort—or a mental illness or disorder so serious that the family has not been able to provide relief (Grieb et al., 2023; Torres et al., 2011).

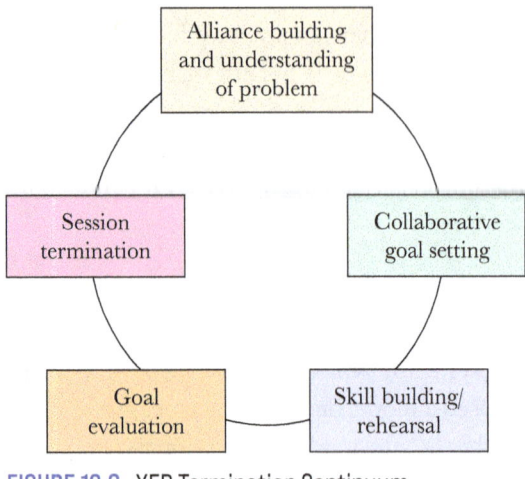

FIGURE 13.2 YEB Termination Continuum

Conceptualizing therapy as a problem-solving collaboration that identifies problems as external and commonplace could help reduce the shame associated with help-seeking. As White (2007) reminds us, "The problem is the problem. The person is not the problem." In the first step of the continuum, the therapist and client build a working alliance by efficiently naming the client's reason for seeking help without emphasizing the client's history that traditional therapy typically endorses.

Once the therapist knows what is most bothersome to the client, they can proceed to verbalizing what the client wants this issue to look like ideally. Humanistic therapists acknowledge that the client is the expert in their problem and assume the role of humble expert (Yao & Kabir, 2023). Exploring the client's attempts to ameliorate the problem as well as the obstacles they have experienced allows for the development of an action plan to which the client will most likely adhere. Skill building and role-playing/rehearsal of alternative behaviors, cognitions, and affect follows.

Before the client leaves each session, the counselor elicits the client's satisfaction with the action plan, and any necessary revisions can be made. The session terminates with the confidence that the client has a concrete plan to approach the problem. Session termination conceptualized as therapy termination appears in brief therapies (e.g., one-at-a-time [OAAT]). The rationale for treating each session as comprehensive respects the hierarchy of needs for clients of color in which self-reflection and enrichment trail far behind more salient basic needs. Additionally, it honors the agency of each client to decide how much therapy they need and when they need it. Ultimately, the client learns that life challenges are ubiquitous and can be addressed once the preceding model is learned.

For clients who have resources like time and insurance, the therapy process might proceed as provided in more conventional training. The YEB continuum of termination considers an alternative that allows clients to feel successful in each session and make choices about returning without feeling they have abandoned the process.

Termination as Cyclical

Considering the pretermination variables described above (e.g., economic, language, and cultural barriers), it is imperative that mental health professionals shift their paradigm to better serve clients living outside of the margins of the dominant culture. For Latinés, the concept of counseling is replete with ironies. The Spanish word for counselor is *consejera/o*, which directly translates to "advice giver." Yet counselors are professionally trained to refrain from giving advice. Evidence abounds that one of the most salient predictors of successful counseling is the therapeutic alliance, or the relationship (Martin et al., 2000). In fact, counselors devote significant time to developing this relationship to encourage deep disclosure from the client. Yet therapists begin this intimate and sensitive relationship with the end in mind. For people from collectivist cultures who value continuity in relationships (most Indigenous and Black communities), this makes no sense and would cause healthy skepticism and suspicion about the therapist's intentions.

As has been noted, economic and time variables frequently direct pretermination decisions. Clients who have the expectation that one attends counseling for problem-solving or advice may be disappointed by the current model of a more significant investment in time and money to gain insight into the underlying causes of the problem. Single-session therapy (SST) and OAAT may have advantages for populations traditional psychotherapy has not been able to reach. Both models have been used interchangeably and share commonalities. In these models, the client is respected as the expert in the problem with inherent ability to solve it themselves with brief guidance from a professional (Hoyt & Talmon, 2014; Dryden, 2019). The therapist ensures the client understands the process and has realistic expectations of the single session, including the generation of a specific session goal; works with the client to identify the problem and the client's previous attempts to solve it; and then focuses on the client's strengths to collaborate on a plan for resolution.

SST is offered as only one of the options in an agency's service delivery options; SST might be contraindicated for clients with more serious or persistent issues in mental health. In both SST and OAAT, clients are welcomed to schedule additional sessions as they see fit, making "single session" a misnomer. According to Young (2018), the label has persisted due to its descriptive clarity and appeal to clients who are not interested in or cannot afford longer-term counseling. Before making a subsequent appointment when using the OAAT model, the client works post-session to reflect on and digest what they learned in the session and to let time pass before making a subsequent appointment (Dryden, 2019).

These models have utility as a multiculturally competent approach for several reasons: They address the pretermination variables of economy, temporal commitment, and an expectation of more directive problem-solving. They are founded on the agency and respect of the client to be the expert in their own problems and exhume, emphasize, and reframe the client's strengths to achieve satisfactory resolution. Furthermore, the client is always welcomed to return—termination is reimagined as *session termination,* as opposed to the traditional ultimate termination most clinical therapists are trained in. In other words, the client has agency over when the relationship is terminated. An additional benefit of SST and OAAT is that they reduce the stigma of attending mental health counseling by reframing it as collaborative problem-solving without the implication that there is something inherent in the client causing the problem.

Using the preceding models, the authors propose that termination can be reconceptualized as cyclical, rather than linear. For each discrete session, the client and counselor agree on the session goal and work to achieve it. The client can return at any time other problems arise. Each session, then, is a termination of the problem, rather than of the relationship. This model is more aligned with the collectivist value of long-term relationships and an effort to improve the client's life as a communal, rather than individual, goal. Figure 13.1 offers a visual representation of the reconceptualization of termination as cyclical.

Case Studies

CASE STUDY 1

Ximena presented with concerns about her 8-year-old son Wilmer's misbehavior and her frustration of not being able to discipline him because of what she referred to as "American laws." The family immigrated to the U.S. in 2019 to escape their deficit circumstances (e.g., lack of access to education, health care, and upward mobility) in Guatemala. Ximena stated that she had never had trouble with her children, who were raised to be respectful and work hard to contribute to the well-being of the family as a whole.

We began by clarifying the process of OAAT therapy and establishing Ximena's goal for the session, which was to correct her son's behavior without getting in trouble with U.S. authorities, as their asylum claims were still pending. I asked Ximena how she had disciplined her children in Guatemala, and she said they all understood that everyone works together to cook, clean, and accomplish tasks like homework. In Guatemala, Wilmer had never talked back to her or questioned his chores. Now, he complained about it and said that his other friends did not have chores and were allowed to play video games. When Ximena tried to hold Wilmer accountable by spanking him, he threatened to call Child Protective Services, telling her it was illegal to spank children in the United States. Ximena's neighbors confirmed that this was a possibility.

I clarified the laws around corporal punishment for Ximena and gave her the link to the Texas Family Code for Protection of the Child. Ximena was surprised to learn that spanking was not illegal unless it met certain abusive criteria, which she was certain that her spanking did not. We discussed differences between Guatemalan and U.S. cultural values regarding child rearing and generated a plan for integrating her Guatemalan family values with Wilmer's developing American values to maintain the best of both cultures.

Ximena admitted that she had not been cooking Wilmer's favorite Guatemalan dishes and that they were no longer speaking their native K'iche' dialect, which was frustrating for Wilmer. She felt that she thought the best way to adjust to the United States was to leave all of that in the past and insisted the children speak English at home to practice. Ximena's affect brightened visibly when she spoke of Guatemala and the life her family had there. She also shared that they were eager to become Americans and prioritize educational and occupational opportunities.

Ximena and I rehearsed the conversation she would have with Wilmer to acknowledge how difficult it must have been for him to come to a new country where everyone, including his parents, were behaving differently. Together, we devised a plan to identify Guatemalan values that they wanted to retain (e.g., clear hierarchical parental roles) and American values they wanted to incorporate (e.g., more flexibility in free time for Wilmer). Ximena felt empowered to be her "Guatemalan" self with the authority to discipline her son as well as to reconnect with Wilmer by speaking K'iche and cooking his favorite dishes of *pepián* and *pupusas*. We created a chore chart that was less rigorous than it had been previously and included rewards for extra playing time with his new friends.

When I spoke with Ximena in a scheduled 15-minute check-in phone call the following month, Ximena said that Wilmer's behavior had improved significantly with the restoration of her authority and some of their traditional family customs. They were learning to negotiate the values of their home and host countries, retaining those that made sense and discarding those that didn't. Ximena stated that her return to the mother that Wilmer missed as well as her willingness to compromise and incorporate new values had allowed all of them to change for the better. I invited Ximena to return in the future with any additional concerns she might want to collaborate about, and she said that she was going to tell her friends and family members how helpful counseling is.

Reflection

Ximena represents many clients of color who prefer a more directive, brief, and collaborative problem-solving orientation to therapy. Acknowledging the client's agency and parental authority is critical to therapeutic alliance building in a host country where people of color are frequently, albeit insidiously, given the message that their values are wrong. Validating home country (even when they are generations removed) cultural values strengthens the therapeutic context by validating the client, helping them to feel seen and heard. Following up with a brief phone call reinforces the continuity of care and the open-ended offer for future sessions.

CASE STUDY 2

Winston and LaChelle have received couple's counseling on and off for the past 3 years to manage values conflict in their marriage. Less than 3 months into counseling, they inquired about counseling services for their 15-year-old daughter, Siobhan. Although they were given recommendations for therapists who could support their daughter, they were adamant that she sees *their* therapist. Potential ethical concerns, such as triangulation and the necessity of confidentiality, were discussed with Winston and LaChelle, and they conveyed their understanding. The following week, a family meeting was held with Winston, LaChelle, Siobhan, and the therapist. It was learned that Siobhan was the person who asked about receiving counseling. She expressed eagerness to begin sessions with the therapist. During this meeting, concerns were discussed again, and ground rules were set. All parties agreed there were no expectations for anyone to share information from their counseling sessions. The family understood the therapist was still bound by HIPAA and would not disclose session information either.

A few weeks after Siobhan began counseling, her older sister, Linnea, who is 22 contacted the office, asking if she could also be seen by the therapist. She explained that it has been difficult to find a Black, female therapist and heard from her family how helpful counseling has been. The therapist decided to begin counseling sessions with Linnea.

For a little over 2 years, the entire family has received counseling from the same therapist in multiple capacities (individual, couple, and family). Throughout this time, as progress has been made, sessions have been tapered off. For example, Winston and LaChelle began couple's counseling weekly. After a while, sessions decreased to biweekly and then monthly. Although they currently only have sessions as needed, periodically they asked to return to weekly sessions. At times, when they attended biweekly sessions, they would attend therapy individually as well.

Siobhan and Linnea have also progressed to as-needed sessions. However, given their mental health needs, it is common for them to seek more support if symptoms increase or when significant life events occur. For example, Siobhan experiences social anxiety and will seek support if she believes her coping skills are no longer effective. Prior to Siobhan returning to therapy recently, we had terminated our counseling relationship, and I had not heard from her in several months. In the past, she has experienced success employing her coping skills without therapeutic intervention. However, she reached out because of an incident with her friend group that resulted in increased anxiety impacting her academic performance and social relationships. During our first session, she discussed the event and was validated by the therapist. She identified some of her thinking errors, and a plan was developed to address her friends. In our second session, we discussed what occurred when she executed the plan with her friends and talked through her thoughts and emotions. During our third, and final, session (for now) we recapped and revisited her skills. We also added new skills to include in her toolbox.

Reflection

This case study provides an example of termination occurring at multiple points with multiple family members over an extended period of time. When counseling within communities of color, or with clients of color, termination rarely means *the end*. As stated early in the chapter, counselors are often integrated into their clients' lives, especially if they reside (e.g., work, play, and worship) within the community. Furthermore, clients returning after termination, even multiple times, is not an indicator of failure. In this example, it is an indicator of trust, connection, and success.

CHAPTER SUMMARY

Counselors are often trained to view termination as the final chapter of therapy, the signifier that goals have been met and the client has improved. A quick Google search of "termination in counseling session" offers countless results and videos, demonstrating termination with compassion. Although these resources may be accurate and helpful, the voices of people of color are neglected and largely absent. Furthermore, termination is largely seen as linear. In this chapter, we challenged this notion, understanding the macro- and micro-level issues and strengths that contribute to termination, including premature termination. Furthermore, we emphasized termination not signaling *the end*, especially in communities of color in which therapists become embedded—not only within the community but also in clients' lives. Thus, we emphasize the importance of cultural competence and becoming intimately familiar with the MSJCC to avoid making ethical or cultural errors. Termination is a significant part of the counseling process and, as highlighted, occurs on a continuum. Therefore, counselors must be skilled in competently supporting this process, seeking supervision that specifically focuses on termination.

With nurtured respect, both counselors-in-training and practicing counselors will recognize the need to approach therapy from a totally different world view that implements an empathetic and inclusive approach to the therapy process. With this type of open mindset, a therapist working with a person of color seeks to make their client feel safe, especially given the historical relationship between a predominantly White profession and communities of color. Explaining the possible utilization of either the SST or OAAT models could alleviate clients' concerns relative to time, transportation, or financial commitment while simultaneously demonstrating a pathway to viable solutions.

Additionally, clients often bring complex problems to therapy that likely require more than one session. An explicit understanding between therapist and client, that termination represents the attainment of a particular goal, or the end of a particular session, could promote more of an open-door policy. Thus, clients may be more likely to return to therapy, even intermittently, and may view the therapeutic space as respite from the everyday stressors of life (e.g., financial strain or racism). Ultimately, the model provided in this chapter encourages counselors to have a more open stance on their view of termination in counseling, and the case studies provide examples of implementation. Termination is cyclical—it's nice to know you can always return.

CHAPTER REFLECTION AND DISCUSSION QUESTIONS

1. Given the high percentage of people of color who choose not to use therapy as a way to address mental health issues, brainstorm specific strategies for each of the following communities to help them understand its benefits:
   a. African American
   b. Latin American
   c. Asian American
2. If a high percentage of POC potential clients terminate after the first session, how could this session be reconstructed to address this issue?
3. Discuss the barriers associated with early termination and under-resourced clients. What kinds of outside of the box solutions could be employed when income represents a barrier to therapy for clients of color?
4. Reflect on your own educational background. Discuss the strengths and weaknesses of your training relevant to your work with clients of color.
5. Examine the MSJCC, and review potential issues that might arise for each level of interaction resulting in early termination.
6. Through the lens of the MSJCC, analyze the effectiveness of culturally relevant practices you have employed when working with clients of color.

ADDITIONAL RESOURCES

Bein, A., Torres, S., & Kurilla Jr., V. (2000). Service delivery issues in early termination of Latino clients. *Journal of Human Behavior in the Social Environment, 3*(2), 43–59. https://www.doi.org/10.1300/J137v03n02_04

Natwick, J. (2017). On the ethics of ending: Terminations and referrals. *Counseling Today.* https://www.counseling.org/docs/default-source/ethics/ethics-columns/ethics_may_2017_terminations-and-referrals.pdf?sfvrsn=ea25522c_6

Moore III, J.L. & Ford, D. (2021). Culture must be up front and center-not an afterthought- in counseling Black and other minoritized clients. *Diverse Issues in Higher Education.*

https://www.diverseeducation.com/opinion/article/15281714/culture-must-be-up-front-and-center-not-an-afterthought-in-counseling-black-and-other-minoritized-clients

Owen, J., Imel, Z., Adelson, J., & Rodolfa, E. (2012). "No-show": Therapist racial/ethnic disparities in client unilateral termination. *Journal of Counseling Psychology, 59*(2), 314–320. https://doi.org/10.1037/a0027091

Terrell, F., & Terrell, S. (1984). Race of counselor, client sex, cultural mistrust level, and premature termination from counseling among Black clients. *Journal of Counseling Psychology, 31*(3), 371–375. https://doi.org/10.1037/0022-0167.31.3.371

REFERENCES

Acosta, F. X. (1980). Self-described reasons for premature termination of psychotherapy by Mexican American, Black American, and Anglo-American patients. *Psychological Reports, 47*(2), 435–443. https://doi.org/10.2466/pr0.1980.47.2.435

Anderson, K. N., Bautista, C. L., & Hope, D. A. (2019). Therapeutic alliance, cultural competence and minority status in premature termination of psychotherapy. *The American Journal of Orthopsychiatry, 89*(1), 104–114. https://doi-org.ezhost.utrgv.edu/10.1037/ort0000342

Bein, A., Torres, S., & Kurilla, V. (2000). Service delivery issues in early termination of Latino clients. *Journal of Human Behavior in the Social Environment, 3*(2), 43–59. https://doi.org/10.1300/j137v03n02_04

Cervantes, J. M., & Parham, T. A. (2005). Toward a meaningful spirituality for people of color: Lessons for the counseling practitioner. *Cultural Diversity and Ethnic Minority Psychology, 11*(1), 69–81. https://doi.org/10.1037/1099-9809.11.1.69

Dryden, W. (2019). *Single-session 'one-at-a-time' therapy: A rational emotive behavior therapy approach.* Routledge.

Fripp, J. A., & Carlson, R. G. (2017). Exploring the influence of attitude and stigma on participation of African American and Latino populations in mental health services. *Journal of Multicultural Counseling and Development, 45*(2), 80–94. https://doi.org/10.1002/jmcd.12066

Gamby, K., Burns, D., & Forristal, K. (2021). Wellness decolonized: The history of wellness and recommendations for the counseling field. *Journal of Mental Health Counseling, 43*(3), 228–245. https://www.doi.org/10.17744/mehc.43.3.05

Grieb, S. M., Platt, R., Vazquez, M. G., Alvarez, K., & Polk, S. (2023). Mental health stigma among Spanish-Speaking Latinos in Baltimore, Maryland. *Journal of Immigrant and Minority Health, 25*(5), 999–1007. https://doi.org/10.1007/s10903-023-01488-z

Hoyt, M. & Talmon, M. (Eds.). (2014). *Capturing the moment: Single-session therapy and walk-in services.* Crown House Publishing.

Komiya, N., Good, G. E., & Sherrod, N. B. (2000). Emotional openness as a predictor of college students' attitudes toward seeking psychological help. *Journal of Counseling Psychology, 47*(1), 138–143. https://doi.org/10.1037/0022-0167.47.1.138

Kpobi, L. & Swartz, L. (2019). Indigenous and faith healing for mental health in Ghana: An examination of the literature on reported beliefs, practices and use of alternative mental health care in Ghana. *African Journal of Primary Health Care & Family Medicine.* 2071–2928

Lampropoulos, G. K., Schneider, M. K., & Spengler, P. M. (2009). Predictors of early termination in a University Counseling Training Clinic. *Journal of Counseling & Development, 87*(1), 36–46. https://doi.org/10.1002/j.1556-6678.2009.tb00547.x

Lee, P., Wang, L., & Swift, J. K. (2021). Clients' and counselors' termination decisions and experiences in counseling. *Current Psychology*, 1–11. https://doi-org.ezhost.utrgv.edu/10.1007/s12144-021-01725-4

Marmarosh, C. (2022). *The other side of psychotherapy: Understanding clients' experiences and contributions in treatment* (pp. 351–378). American Psychological Association. https://doi-org.ezhost.utrgv.edu/10.1037/0000303-013

Martin, D. J., Garske, J. P., & Davis, M. K. (2000). Relation of the therapeutic alliance with outcome and other variables: a meta-analytic review. *Journal of Consulting and Clinical Psychology, 68*(3), 438–450.

Moghaddam, J., Momper, S.L., & W Fong, T. (2015). Crystalizing the role of traditional healing in an urban Native American health center. *Community Mental Health Journal, 51*(3), 305–314. https://www.doi.org/10.1007/s10597-014-9813-9

National Council of La Raza. (2005). *Critical disparities in Latino mental health: Transforming research into action*. (White Paper, 2005). Institute for Hispanic Health. https://www.unidosus.org/wp-content/uploads/2021/07/file_WP_Latino_Mental_Health_FNL.pdf

National Institute of Mental Health. (2020). *Substance Abuse and Mental Health Administration, 2020 national survey on drug use and mental health*. https://www.nimh.nih.gov/health/statistics/mental-illness

Owen, J., Imel, Z., Adelson, J., & Rodolfa, E. (2012). "No-show": Therapist racial/ethnic disparities in client unilateral termination. *Journal of Counseling Psychology, 59*(2), 314–320. https://doi-org.ezhost.utrgv.edu/10.1037/a0027091

Presley, S., & Day, S. X. (2019). Counseling dropout, retention, and ethnic/language match for Asian Americans. *Psychological Services, 16*(3), 491–497. https://doi.org/10.1037/ser0000223

Ratts, M. J., Singh, A. A., Nassar-McMillan, S., Butler, S. K., & McCullough, J. R. (2016). Multicultural and social justice counseling competencies: Guidelines for the counseling profession. *Journal of Multicultural Counseling and Development, 44*(1), 28–48. https://doi.org/10.1002/jmcd.12035

Terrell F., Terrell S. L. (1981). An inventory to measure cultural mistrust among Blacks. *Western Journal of Black Studies, 5*, 180–184.

Torres, L., Yznaga, S.D. and Moore, K.M. (2011). Discrimination and Latino psychological distress: The moderating role of ethnic identity exploration and commitment. *American Journal of Orthopsychiatry, 81*, 526–534. https://doi.org/10.1111/j.1939-0025.2011.01117.x

Vogel, D. L., & Wester, S. R. (2003). To seek help or not to seek help: The risks of self-disclosure. *Journal of Counseling Psychology, 50*(3), 351–361. https://doi.org/10.1037/0022-0167.50.3.351

Yao L, Kabir R. (2023). *Person-centered therapy (Rogerian therapy)*. StatPearls. https://www.ncbi.nlm.nih.gov/books/NBK589708/

Young, J. (2018). SST: The misunderstood gift that keeps on giving. In M. F. Hoyt, M. Bobele, A. Slive, J. Young, & M. Talmon (Eds.), *Single-session therapy by walk-in or appointment: Administrative, clinical, and supervisory aspects of one-at-a-time services*. Routledge.

Assessment and Diagnosis in Counseling

Jessi Budyka, LPC, NCC, and Dr. Marty Jencius, NCC

LEARNING OBJECTIVES

1. Students will know:
   - three types of assessment (i.e., qualitative, standardized, non-standardized),
   - what a diagnosis is,
   - the history of assessment and diagnosis in counseling, and
   - ethical and cultural considerations related to assessment and diagnosis in counseling.
2. Students will begin to be able to interpret assessments and diagnoses collaboratively with clients.
3. Students will begin to be able to collaboratively compare and contrast assessments and diagnoses with clients.
4. Students will begin to be able to have a cultural understanding of assessments and implement a strategy for choosing, administrating, and presenting assessments.
5. Students will begin to be able to integrate assessment and diagnoses into client treatment plans.

LEARNING OUTCOMES

1. The reader will be able to understand and articulate the historical and cultural context of assessment and diagnosis in mental health, applying ethical standards from the American Counseling Association and the Multicultural and Social Justice Counseling Competencies.
2. The reader will develop skills to interpret assessment results and diagnose collaboratively with clients, emphasizing cultural understanding, sensitivity, and the application of CACREP standards.
3. The reader will enhance self-awareness of their implicit biases in assessment processes and learn to integrate culturally sensitive practices into client treatment plans, aligning with ethical and legal standards.

4. The reader will be skilled in communicating assessment results to clients clearly and culturally sensitively, utilizing tools like the *DSM-5-TR*'s Cultural Formulation Interview and AARC Standards for multicultural assessments.
5. The reader will adopt a holistic and inclusive approach to mental health care, recognizing the importance of cultural factors in client well-being and integrating these considerations into comprehensive treatment planning.

Assessment and diagnosis have been facets of mental health services predating the counseling profession. The historical contexts of their development have been largely influenced by Western culture and colonialism through the fields of psychology and psychiatry. While counseling is a related field, our profession is unique in how we practice through our professional values and ethical principles. This chapter aims to provide a starting foundation in your development in becoming culturally competent in the skills behind assessment and diagnosis aligned with the American Counseling Association's (ACA) ethical standards (ACA, 2014) and the Multicultural and Social Justice Counseling Competencies (MSJCC; Ratts et al., 2016) toward counseling excellence. The goals driving the content of this chapter follow *Bloom's Taxonomy of Learning* (Armstrong, 2010) and are informed by the 2024 Council for Accreditation of Counseling and Related Educational Programs (CACREP; 2023) standards.

Bloom's Taxonomy

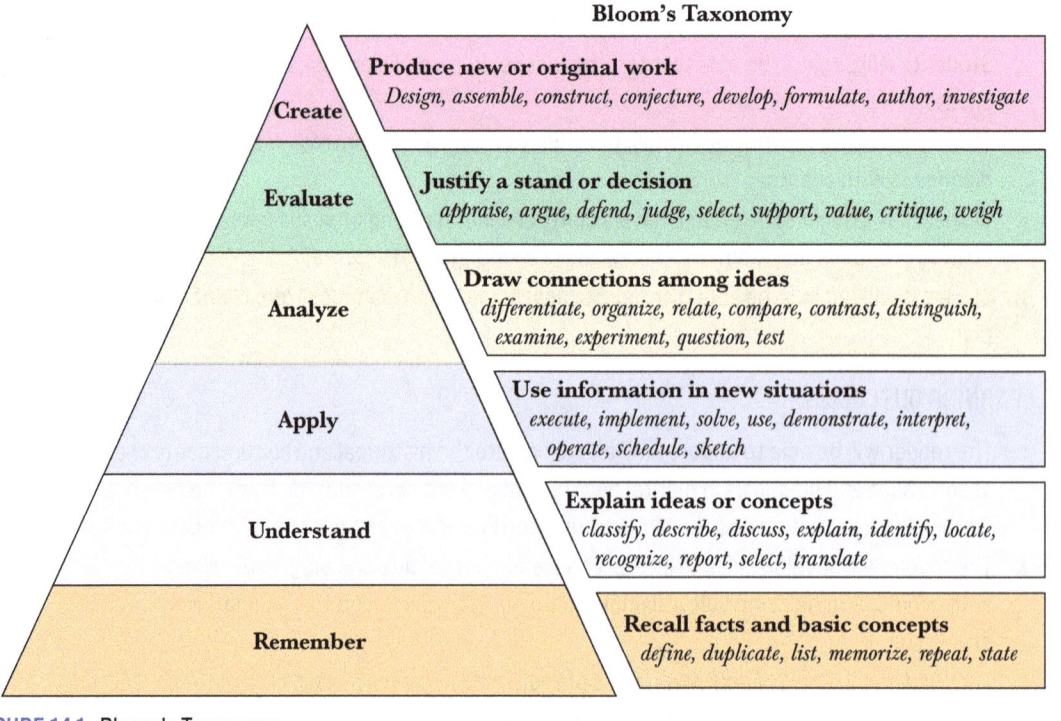

Level	Description	Keywords
Create	Produce new or original work	Design, assemble, construct, conjecture, develop, formulate, author, investigate
Evaluate	Justify a stand or decision	appraise, argue, defend, judge, select, support, value, critique, weigh
Analyze	Draw connections among ideas	differentiate, organize, relate, compare, contrast, distinguish, examine, experiment, question, test
Apply	Use information in new situations	execute, implement, solve, use, demonstrate, interpret, operate, schedule, sketch
Understand	Explain ideas or concepts	classify, describe, discuss, explain, identify, locate, recognize, report, select, translate
Remember	Recall facts and basic concepts	define, duplicate, list, memorize, repeat, state

FIGURE 14.1 Bloom's Taxonomy

2024 CACREP Standards Informing this Chapter

3.G Assessment and Diagnostic Processes

1. Historical perspectives concerning the nature and meaning of assessment and testing in counseling
2. Basic concepts of standardized and non-standardized testing, norm-referenced and criterion-referenced assessments, and group and individual assessments
3. Culturally sustaining and developmental considerations for selecting, administering, and interpreting assessments, including individual accommodations and environmental modifications
4. Ethical and legal considerations for selecting, administering, and interpreting assessments
5. Use of culturally sustaining and developmentally appropriate assessments for diagnostic and intervention planning purposes

What Is Assessment?

Assessment is the process through which counselors gain a holistic understanding with the use of evidence. As counselors, we engage in nearly constant qualitative assessment of our clients, ourselves, and the counseling relationship (Hays, 2017b). Think back to the earlier chapters of this text. How would you know if you delivered an accurate reflection of feeling? You would assess your client's verbal and nonverbal responses. The way a client responds is the evidence that informs the accuracy of the reflection; provides insight to their emotional state; as well as determines the counselor's level of understanding, competence in the skill, and the quality of the relationship between client and counselor. This single moment provides evidence to inform an assessment of the three levels of counseling (i.e., the counselor, the client, and the counseling relationship).

The qualitative nature of assessment requires the counselor to essentially be the researcher or the measure; therefore, any outcomes of the assessment are subject to be influenced by the counselor's beliefs, values, and implicit biases (Hays, 2017b). An *implicit bias* is an unconscious habit of the mind that has been formed through repeated personal experiences and socialization (Burgess et al., 2017).

Think about the brain as a giant game of association. If I were to say the word "apple," what are all the things that would come to mind in response? You might think of the fruit; the color red; apple juice; teachers; Apple products, such as an iPhone; or an apple orchard you have a memory of visiting. Perhaps, you are a person who does not enjoy eating apples, and when they are mentioned, there is a brief moment in which you are "turned off." Perhaps, you have never eaten an apple but you were raised in an environment where those around you have only responded poorly to apples. You likely will experience the same initial feeling of being "turned off," even if you have never tasted one yourself. This is because your brain has made unconscious associations about apples based on the way the people around you have continuously reacted to them. Your distaste for apples was not something that you consciously chose, it's just what your brain tacitly learned through unconscious observation of your world over time and thus created an implicit bias.

All of this to say that this same pattern of learning and association happens with everything all the time and is shown at varying degrees from "painfully obvious" to "extremely subtle." Consider how the greater society generally treats people with currently and historically marginalized cultural

> **Chicago Tribune** @chicagotribune · Follow
> ✓ Official
>
> Wife of a Bears' lineman wins a bronze medal today in Rio Olympics trib.in/2asmvvr

FIGURE 14.2 A Sexist Headline

identities. I bet you can think of some painfully obvious atrocities. Now, try to think of more subtle messages that might feed into culturally bigoted implicit biases. One example is shown in Figure 14.2.

The original caption for this news article reads "Wife of Bears' lineman wins a bronze medal today in Rio Olympics." The way it is written subconsciously reinforces a reader's sexist implicit bias that the value of a woman is relative to the men with whom she is associated. As you can imagine, the internet had a field day responding to this explicit microaggression, exposing the authors' internalized sexist implicit bias.

> **Copy McPasty, Writer** @KashannKilson · Follow
>
> You spelled "3-time Olympian Corey Cogdell-Unrein wins second bronze medal today in Rio Olympics" wrong.
>
> > **Chicago Tribune** @chicagotribune
> > ✓ Official
> >
> > Wife of a Bears' lineman wins a bronze medal today in Rio Olympics trib.in/2asmvvr

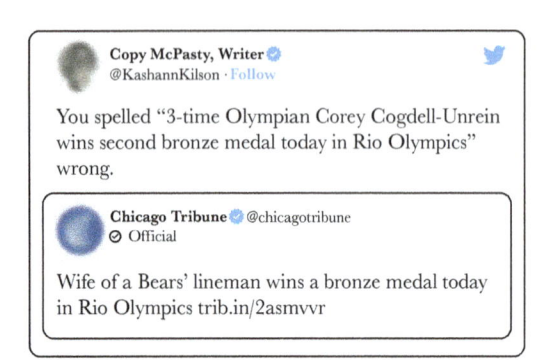

FIGURE 14.3 An Assertive Response

X user @KashannKilson took a generally neutral approach as they responded with "You spelled '3-time Olympian Corey Cogdell-Unrein wins second bronze medal today in Rio Olympics' wrong." The proposed title is suggested in a way that is assertive, removes the sexist undertones, and does not evoke feelings of shame. I implore you to take a similar stance with yourself and your clients as you assess the impact and existence of biases. Remember that you and your client likely did not choose a bias and that its existence is a reflection of the world around us. It is what is done with those biases that defines one's character.

As you can extend from this example, anything created by humans is subject to reflect the creators' and society's biases. This is true for standardized and nonstandardized assessments counselors use in practice. *Standardized assessments* are questionnaires that have a set of questions and purpose for evaluation and may be referred to as tests or inventories. They include intelligence tests, ability tests, personality inventories, interest inventories, and values inventories. *Nonstandardized assessments* are typically structured as rating scales, behavioral observations, and projective techniques (Hays, 2017b). Nonstandardized assessments are typically regarded as less reliable; however, one of the strengths of nonstandardized, and even qualitative, assessments is that they allow counselors to take environmental and cultural factors into consideration. Counselors use these three ways of assessing (i.e., qualitative, nonstandardized, and standardized) to inform practices, the creation of a treatment plan, and diagnosis.

What Is a Diagnosis?

A *diagnosis* is a classification of a "mental disorder" (Cooper, 2004; Shorter, 2013). In the United States, mental health professionals use the *Diagnostic and Statistical Manual of Mental Disorders* (DSM), published by the American Psychological Association (APA) as the primary source for diagnoses. The DSM is essentially the American version of the World Health Organization's (WHO) International Classification of Diseases (ICD), though the DSM has been gaining international popularity in the recent decades (Shorter, 2013). Diagnoses are used for many purposes, including informing practice, treatment planning, communicating with clients and other practitioners, and for insurance company approval for counseling services in relevant specialty areas.

Some scholars have argued that racist attitudes historically have been and still are embedded within diagnoses and the diagnostic process (Fernando, 2017). Diagnostic assessments are intended to be objective; however, as we discussed earlier, anything created by humans is subject to reflect the implicit biases of the greater society. Cultural and implicit biases are present in the content and assumptions of the assessments as well as through the lack of cultural diversity of groups on which assessments are normed (Council of National Psychological Associations for the Advancement of Ethnic Minority Interests [CNPAAEMI], 2016). This often leads to cultural disparities in diagnostic rates. One example is the racial disparity in schizophrenia diagnosis between Black and White individuals.

A recent meta-analysis analyzed 52 studies between the years 1983 and 2016 and found that Black individuals were diagnosed with schizophrenia about 2.4 times more often than White individuals in the United States (Olbert et al., 2018). The authors point out that it is possible that contextual factors, such as limited access to mental health services, cultural mistrust of medical institutions, and higher social stigma among Black individuals may contribute to delayed treatment and thus resulting in more intense symptoms when seeking services (Olbert et al., 2018; Schwartz & Blankenship, 2014). It is also possible that the way in which symptoms, such as paranoia, are described in the DSM may contribute to the overdiagnosis of Black individuals with schizophrenia. An example may be if a Black client states they feel as though they are constantly being watched in public. On the surface this statement could be interpreted as paranoia. It is imperative to gather more information to consider contextual social factors, such as stores sending employees to watch "suspicious" customers to prevent theft; suddenly, the feeling of being watched seems more reasonable.

While diagnoses may be helpful in some respects, it is imperative to consider the stigmas and biases associated with each diagnosis as well as how those stigmas and biases may cause harm to our clients. Assessment and diagnosis in counseling has evolved throughout the history of our profession. It is crucial to know our histories so that we can critically analyze and evaluate our present to make changes in support of equity and justice aligned with counseling values.

Historical Context of Testing and Culture

The evolution of psychosocial and intellectual assessment has not been a linear journey. Instead, it has been punctuated by transformative research and pioneering documents that have emphasized the fundamental role of culture in understanding human behavior and cognition. These groundbreaking endeavors have set the stage for a more holistic, nuanced, and inclusive approach to assessment. From Adrian Dove's satirical yet enlightening counterbalance intelligence test, which spotlighted the inherent cultural biases in standardized assessments to Geert Hofstede's intricate mapping of cultural dimensions that delineated societal influences on individual behaviors, our understanding of culture's omnipresence has expanded. Furthermore, the DSM's cultural formulation interview signaled a watershed moment in mental health assessment, emphasizing a structured exploration of a patient's cultural context. And underscoring the commitment to this inclusive approach, the AARC Standards for Multicultural Assessments provided a robust framework for professionals to incorporate cultural sensitivity into their practices.

Dove's Counterbalance Intelligence Test

The American education and testing system has long been criticized for biases that inadvertently disadvantage certain groups, particularly those of racial or ethnic minorities. One of the most iconic illustrations of this issue is Adrian Dove's counterbalance intelligence test, commonly known as the "chitlin test." Developed in the late 1960s, this test presented a set of questions that were culturally specific to African Americans, particularly those from inner-city areas (Dove, 1967).

The chitlin test was never meant to be a genuine intelligence test; rather, it was a satirical critique of the racial biases in standardized testing. Traditional intelligence tests of the time often contained content unfamiliar to Black Americans, especially those from lower socioeconomic backgrounds. This unfamiliarity could lead to lower scores, not due to a lack of intelligence but due to a lack of exposure to certain cultural knowledge or experiences (Sue, 2001). Adrian Dove created the chitlin test to highlight this discrepancy by reversing the roles, making the test's content deeply rooted in Black culture and unfamiliar to most White test takers.

For example, questions on the chitlin test quizzed the taker's knowledge of Black slang, music, and other cultural references. While many Black Americans would find these questions intuitive or based on common knowledge, most White Americans would find them puzzling or alien. Through this inversion, Dove emphasized the cultural biases inherent in many standardized tests of the time (Helms, 1992).

Today, the chitlin test serves as a historic reminder of the importance of cultural sensitivity and inclusiveness in educational assessment. While we have made strides in ensuring that tests are more culturally neutral, the lessons from the chitlin test are still relevant. It highlights the need to design assessments that accurately measure their intent without being swayed by the test taker's cultural background. As we continue to develop and refine educational assessments in our increasingly diverse society, we must remain vigilant in ensuring that they are fair, valid, and free of cultural bias (APA, 2014).

Geert Hofstede's Dimensions

Geert Hofstede's seminal work on cultural dimensions has played a pivotal role in understanding how culture influences behaviors, values, and perceptions. His framework, developed through extensive research at IBM in the 1960s and 1970s, proposed a set of dimensions to categorize various cultural norms and values across different countries and regions (Hofstede, 2003). These dimensions are instrumental in understanding the cultural nuances that can impact various spheres, including mental health assessment:

- **Power distance index (PDI):** This dimension pertains to the extent to which less powerful members of organizations and institutions accept and expect that power is distributed unequally. In mental health assessment, high power distance cultures might expect a more authoritative role from the therapist and may be less likely to question or challenge their perspective. Conversely, low power distance cultures may expect a more collaborative approach (Hofstede et al., 2010).
- **Individualism vs. collectivism (IDV):** Individualism denotes societies in which ties between individuals are loose and everyone looks out for themselves and their immediate family.

In contrast, collectivism characterizes societies with strong, cohesive groups. A mental health professional assessing someone from a collectivist culture should consider family dynamics and group norms as these could be crucial in understanding the individual's mental health (Triandis, 1995).

- **Masculinity vs. femininity (MAS):** This dimension looks at the distribution of roles between the genders. Masculine societies are driven by competition, achievement, and success, whereas feminine societies prioritize caring for others and quality of life. In mental health assessment, the expectations and pressures arising from these societal norms can shape an individual's mental well-being and expression of distress (Hofstede, 2003).
- **Uncertainty avoidance index (UAI):** Uncertainty avoidance deals with a society's tolerance for uncertainty and ambiguity. Societies with high UAI try to minimize uncertain situations through strict rules and rituals. This can influence how individuals from such cultures handle anxiety and ambiguity and react to therapy sessions, which sometimes delve into uncertain and ambiguous realms of the mind (Hofstede, 2003).
- **Long-term orientation vs. short-term normative orientation (LTO):** This dimension reflects how societies maintain links with their past while dealing with present and future challenges. An individual's perspective on time can influence their patience with therapeutic processes, expectations for change, and how they make sense of their distress in the context of past experiences and future aspirations (Hofstede et al., 2010).

The implications of Hofstede's dimensions for mental health assessment today are profound. They provide a lens through which clinicians can approach individuals as clients and as cultural beings. Recognizing these cultural differences helps ensure assessments and subsequent interventions are tailored, meaningful, and effective. As our world becomes increasingly interconnected, cultural competence in mental health assessment, guided by frameworks like Hofstede's, remains not just a recommendation but a necessity (Bhugra & Bhui, 2018).

The Cultural Formation Interview

The DSM, published by the American Psychiatric Association, is the primary reference for mental health professionals in diagnosing mental disorders. With each edition, there has been a growing recognition of the importance of cultural factors in understanding and diagnosing mental health conditions. This recognition culminated in the fifth edition of the DSM (*DSM-5-TR*), with the introduction of the Cultural Formulation Interview (CFI; American Psychiatric Association [APA], 2022).

The CFI is a structured tool designed to help clinicians obtain clinically relevant cultural information from patients, allowing for a more nuanced and culturally sensitive diagnostic process (Lewis-Fernández et al., 2016). Composed of 16 main questions (and supplementary ones), the CFI focuses on understanding the patient's cultural identity, cultural explanations of the illness, cultural factors related to the psychosocial environment and levels of functioning, and cultural elements of the clinician–patient relationship (APA, 2022). The primary goal is to understand how these factors may influence the presentation and experience of mental health symptoms.

Historically, mental health diagnostics and treatment often overlooked the profound impact of cultural context. Individuals from diverse backgrounds sometimes found that their experiences were misinterpreted or misunderstood due to cultural gaps between themselves and their health-care providers (Bhugra & Bhui, 2018). The CFI represents an attempt to bridge this divide, ensuring the diagnosis and subsequent treatment plans are aligned not just with the individual's symptoms but also with their cultural context and understanding of their own mental health.

As our global society becomes more interconnected and diverse, the implications of the CFI are more relevant than ever. The emphasis on cultural sensitivity in assessment underscores the importance of holistic, person-centered care. Mental health professionals are urged to move beyond mere symptom checking to truly understanding the individual's experience within their cultural context. This improves diagnostic accuracy and fosters trust and collaboration between the patient and clinician. As we advance in the mental health field, tools like the CFI are crucial reminders of the intertwined relationship between culture and mental well-being and the necessity for culturally informed care in our practice (Kirmayer, 2012).

The AARC Standards for Multicultural Assessments

The AARC Standards for Multicultural Assessments (2018) are designed to help professional counselors provide culturally competent assessments that are respectful, accurate, and effective for all clients. The standards emphasize the importance of recognizing and addressing personal characteristics and identities that may impact the assessment process for multicultural populations. This includes understanding clients' cultural backgrounds, language, communication styles, and unique experiences and perspectives.

Additionally, the standards highlight the need for counselors to recognize and address subtle biases that may impact the assessment process. This includes being aware of potential biases in assessment instruments and using procedures that comply with ethical guidelines when assessing diverse populations. Counselors are also encouraged to work collaboratively with community leaders to understand and address the needs of diverse clients while providing opportunities to access services if needed.

The standards provide examples of culturally responsive assessment practices that can be used with diverse clients. This includes selecting assessments and diagnostic techniques that are appropriate and effective for diverse client populations as well as using clear, unambiguous, jargon-free language when presenting assessment results to clients and other nonprofessional audiences.

The AARC Standards for Multicultural Assessments underscore the imperative of adhering to these benchmarks to guarantee that counselors deliver culturally competent evaluations characterized by accuracy, respect, and efficacy. In compliance with these directives, professional counselors are better positioned to provide unparalleled care to all clients, irrespective of their cultural heritage.

Some key works and ideas play a major role in testing how people think and behave. These include Adrian Dove's test, Geert Hofstede's ideas about culture, the CFI process in the DSM-5-TR, and rules by the AARC about understanding different cultures. All of these tell us the importance of considering where someone comes from and their cultural background when trying to understand them. As we learn more in this field, we must remember these big ideas and ensure we always include everyone's unique background and culture.

ACA Code of Ethics and Multicultural and Social Justice Counseling Competencies

The 2014 ACA Code of Ethics (ACA, 2014) provides guidance and standards for ethical practice in the field of counseling. The preamble of the Code of Ethics outlines counseling's core professional values and ethical principles. The core professional values are

1. Enhancing human development throughout the lifespan;
2. Honoring diversity and embracing a multicultural approach in support of the worth, dignity, potential, and uniqueness of people within their social and cultural contexts;
3. Promoting social justice;
4. Safeguarding the integrity of the counselor–client relationship; and
5. Practicing in a competent and ethical manner.

The five core professional values inform the basis for our six core ethical principles guiding practice, which are

1. **Autonomy:** fostering the right to control the direction of one's life;
2. **Nonmaleficence:** avoiding actions that cause harm;
3. **Beneficence:** working for the good of the individual and society by promoting mental health and wellbeing;
4. **Justice:** treating individuals equitably and fostering fairness and equality;
5. **Fidelity:** honoring commitments and keeping promises, including fulfilling one's responsibilities of trust in professional relationships; and
6. **Veracity:** dealing truthfully with individuals with whom counselors come into professional contact.

Section E: Evaluation, Assessment, and Interpretation of the ACA Code of Ethics (2014) describes how to apply the professional values and ethical principles to assessment and diagnosis. While the Code of Ethics is detailed, it is generally considered good practice to infuse the process of an "ethical decision-making model" into each and every professional decision counselors make. The ACA has published a recommended ethical decision-making model for counselors to follow in practice (Forester-Miller & Davis, 2016).

The ACA Code of Ethics (2014) frequently calls for ethical decisions to be made within the relevant cultural contexts. The MSJCCs

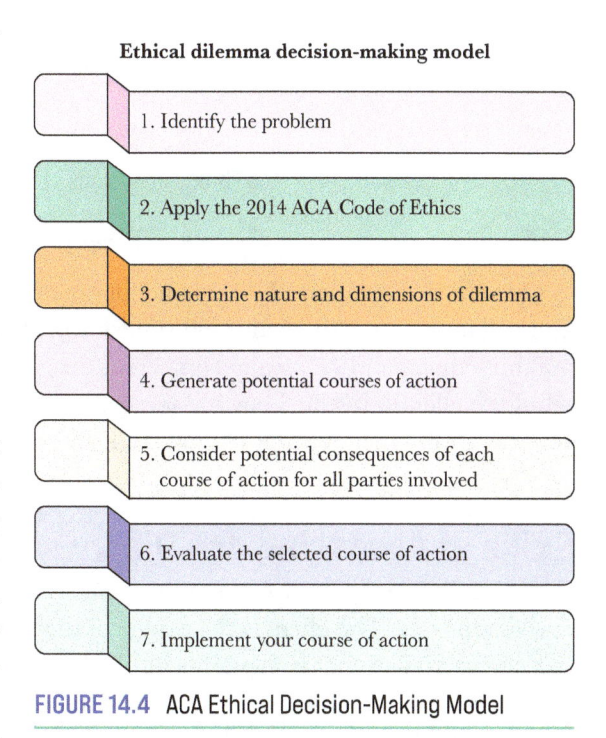

Ethical dilemma decision-making model

1. Identify the problem
2. Apply the 2014 ACA Code of Ethics
3. Determine nature and dimensions of dilemma
4. Generate potential courses of action
5. Consider potential consequences of each course of action for all parties involved
6. Evaluate the selected course of action
7. Implement your course of action

FIGURE 14.4 ACA Ethical Decision-Making Model

For more details, view the full model at https://www.counseling.org/docs/default-source/ethics/ethical-dilemma-posterv5.pdf?sfvrsn=2.

(Ratts et al., 2016) outline a process for counselors to develop overall cultural competency. The MSJCC framework posits that cultural competence is developed through four domains, first within the individual counselor and then moves through the external systems with regard to the cultural power dynamics between counselor and client: (a) counselor self-awareness, (b) client worldview, (c) counseling relationship, and (d) counseling and advocacy interventions. The MSJCCs are further specified by four aspirational and developmental competencies within the first three domains previously identified: (a) attitudes and beliefs, (b) knowledge, (c) skills, and (d) action, commonly referred to as AKSA.

Counselor self-awareness
Attitudes & beliefs
Knowledge
Skills
Action

Counseling relationship
Combined attitudes, beliefs, and knowledge
Skillful interactions
Action and advocacy based on client's narrative
Dynamic informed to model power-with, rather than power-over.

Client worldview
Attitudes & beliefs
Knowledge
Skills
Action

Intersection of cultural identities:
Privilege
Power
Cultural capital

Intersection of cultural identities:
Privilege
Power
Cultural capital

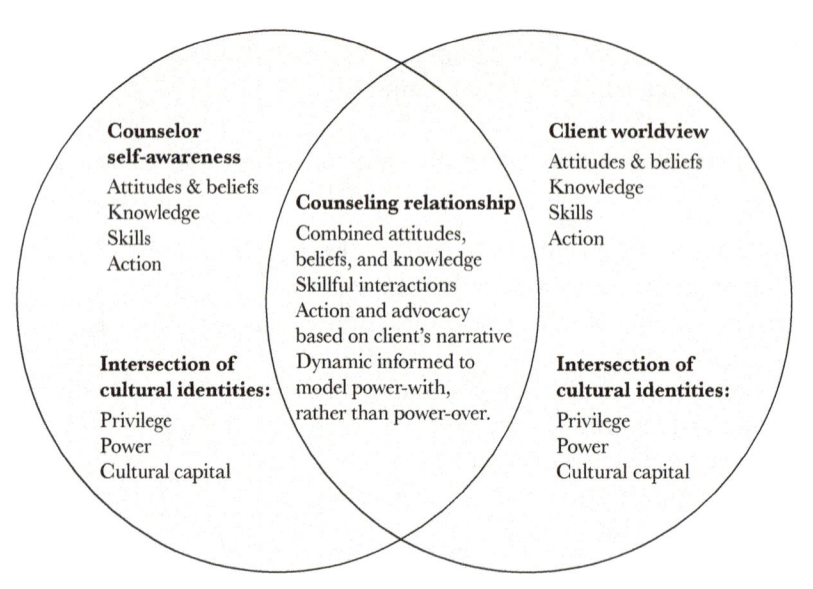

FIGURE 14.5 The Three Dimensions of Counseling: Client, Counselor, and Relationship

Qualitative assessment of the interactions of the domains and AKSA embedded should be ongoing and collaborative with clients and supervisors. Continuous reflection and intentional practice of making ethical and culturally competent decisions will support your development toward counseling excellence. In the following sections, we outline the skills of assessing and diagnosing with consideration to the ACA 2014 Code of Ethics and the MSJCCs.

Skills of Assessing and Diagnosing

First and foremost, counselors must be collaborative in everything we do, especially when assessing and diagnosing. The client is the expert of themselves, and no singular counselor is the expert of our clients and all that is mental health. When assessing and diagnosing our role as counselors is to learn all we can about our clients and filter that information through our professional lens to support our clients' wellness while upholding our professional values and principles.

Collaboration goes beyond the counseling relationship. Consultation with trusted colleagues, supervisors, treatment teams, and other relevant professionals is an integral part of being a professional counselor. Counselors often collaborate and consult with a variety of individuals related to the client's case when determining appropriate assessments and diagnoses; this may include doctors, social workers or case managers, teachers, or families, provided the necessary releases of information are signed. Counseling supervisors, psychologists, and psychiatrists may be helpful in selecting a culturally competent assessment or conducting a differential diagnosis. As we briefly discussed earlier, assessing and diagnosing is a necessary component of our jobs that may be both helpful and harmful to our clients. In the following section, we provide seven steps to assessment and diagnosis in counseling (Paniagua, 2016). Following the steps to assessment and diagnosis, there is a brief introduction on how to incorporate assessments and diagnoses into a treatment plan.

Steps to Assessing and Diagnosing

1. **Ongoing counselor self-assessment of MSJCCs:** Counselors are tasked with engaging in continuous self-assessment of their own (a) attitudes and beliefs, including implicit biases; (b) knowledge of cultures, intersectionality, and power dynamics; (c) skills, such as broaching and asking culturally appropriate questions; and (d) action through advocating for equity and social justice as outlined in the ACA Code of Ethics (2014) and the MSJCCs (Ratts et al., 2016). It may be helpful to engage in intentional reflection, particularly exploring feelings of discomfort or defensiveness, analyze tapes of your counseling sessions, and consult with your supervisor or other trusted colleagues. Developing cultural competence is a lifelong process. It is impossible to be "perfect," and it is always possible to grow (Ratts et al., 2016).

2. **Ongoing learning and understanding of the historical and current cultural contexts of assessments and diagnoses:** As mentioned earlier, assessments and diagnoses are a complex facet of our profession. Assessments and diagnoses have historically been developed from the perspective of the dominant western cultures as a way to pathologize anyone who is different, and there is still a kernel of truth in the existence of mental illness. Culturally competent counselors utilize all three kinds of assessment while maintaining our professional ethical values and principles to gather a holistic view of the client's experience so that we can support them in their wellness.

3. **Understanding legalities and ethics regarding assessment and diagnosis:** Understanding the legal limitations of counseling practice regarding assessment and diagnosis varies from state to state. Check in with your supervisor and state's revised code to best understand your role in assessment and diagnoses as a counselor. Section E of the ACA Code of Ethics (2014) outlines our standards of evaluation, assessment, interpretation, and diagnosis. If you are ever unsure of how to proceed, follow the ethical dilemma flow chart provided in Figure 14.4 and on the ACA website (Forester-Miller & Davis, 2016).

4. **Meeting with your client:** When initially meeting your client, engage your entire presence in your greeting; mind, body, attitude, and spirit (SAMHSA, 2016). Using small gestures, such as culturally appropriate handshakes, facial expressions, and small talk, may help you make a good first impression and begin building a therapeutic relationship. It is imperative to establish rapport before engaging in a series of questions. Your aim is to ensure your client leaves the first and every session feeling hopeful and understood. It is appropriate to draw attention to the presenting concerns; just be mindful of not probing too deeply. It is good practice to familiarize clients with the treatment and evaluation process. Ask clients about any previous experiences in counseling. Even if clients have seen a mental health practitioner before, it may be fruitful to learn their understanding of the process, their expectations, and

their rights. This can be an opportunity to establish collaborative norms and expectations for each other as well as an equitable power dynamic in the relationship.

5. **Selecting the least biased assessment strategy for diagnosis:**
    a. Standardized assessments have gone through multiple rounds of testing and the results, or "psychometric properties," should be available either through the publishing company or in the academic literature. When determining if an assessment is a good fit for your client, you may consider asking the following questions:
    b. What was the development process? Examine how the assessment was developed. Look for evidence of a diverse and representative sample during the development and validation phases. Assess whether individuals from different cultural backgrounds were included in the norming process to ensure the assessment's applicability to diverse populations.
    c. For which populations is the assessment suitable? Consider the original intended population for which the assessment was developed. Assess whether the assessment has been validated or adapted for use with individuals from different cultural backgrounds. Keep in mind that an assessment tool that was originally developed for one specific culture may not be equally applicable or valid for another cultural group.
    d. Is there a presence of cultural biases? Investigate whether the assessment tool contains any cultural biases or assumptions. Look for any content that may favor certain cultural groups over others. For example, questions that assume familiarity with specific cultural references, contexts, or experiences could disadvantage individuals from different cultural backgrounds.
    e. Is it reliable? Is it valid? And for whom? Examine the psychometric properties of the assessment, including its reliability and validity. Assess whether the assessment has been validated and found to be reliable with diverse cultural groups. Consider whether studies or research have been conducted to establish the assessment's reliability and validity across different cultural populations.
    f. Who made up the standardization sample? Evaluate the characteristics of the standardization sample used in developing the assessment. Look for information on the demographic composition of the sample, such as age, gender, ethnicity, and socioeconomic status. Assess whether the sample adequately represents the diversity of the population for which the assessment is intended.
    g. How is it scored and interpreted? Consider whether the scoring and interpretation guidelines account for cultural differences. Assess whether cultural factors have been considered in establishing cutoff scores or interpreting assessment results. Ensure the assessment's scoring and interpretation guidelines are sensitive to cultural diversity.
    h. Is the assessment available and valid in the client's preferred language? If not, is the language used appropriate for the client's level of English proficiency? You may need to consult with your client and supervisor on the use of an interpreter.
    i. Consult with your supervisor or other relevant professionals to gather holistic perspectives and ensure all considerations have been addressed.
6. **Administering the assessment:** Standardized assessments should be administered under the same conditions that were established in their standardization (ACA, 2014, E.7). The conditions of administration may need to be altered to accommodate clients with disabilities or when unusual circumstances arise during the administration. If so, it is necessary to document those conditions in the interpretation. It is possible the results may be designated as "invalid" or of "questionable validity."

7. **Presenting assessment results:**
   a. Prepare to present.
      i. *Review crucial documents regarding equity.* Before meeting with your client to present results, it would be helpful to review the Cultural Formation Interview questions and the AARC Guidelines for the use of assessments to help create a context for your conversation.
      ii. *Know your assessment/diagnostic tool.* Hopefully, you have fully investigated the instrument and looked to see that it has been normed on the demographic and ethnic group your client is a part of. Counselors should be well acquainted with the validity and reliability of any instrument they use.
      iii. *Look for cultural implications of the instrument/diagnostic tool.* Has your assessment been used with the demographic and ethnic group of your client? Has a particular diagnosis or assessment been shown to bias against particular ethnic or demographic groups?
      iv. *Prepare notes for your meeting that will help frame the results for your client.* Assessment and diagnostic results are often written with much professional jargon. Prepare notes before the meeting to make the results explainable within the context of the client's experience.
   b. Present the results.
      i. *Ask the client about their impressions of the assessment or diagnosis.* It is always a good idea to review the assessment process with your client and what thoughts or beliefs they had before you engage them in a discussion of the results. You may get a sense of how likely they are in agreement or disagreement with the results. Clients who perceived results as being tentative and not absolute were more helpful in the process (Jones and Gelso, 1988).
      ii. *Use client-first language when describing the results.* Use language that helps the client understand the results without the results becoming their identity. Use language like, "You have symptoms in common with people with depression" instead of, "You are depressed."
      iii. *Take time to review the assessment with your client.* Don't rush through the process. Pause often to get your client's impression of what you are relaying. Ask them to repeat what they heard you say so you can make adjustments and corrections. Monitor the client's reactions to the presented results.
      iv. *Use descriptive terms in presenting results rather than mathematical terms.* Try to minimize mathematical terms to describe client outcomes and use more impressionistic descriptive terms, such as "a majority of people fall into this response" or "one-third of people have similar experiences as you." Explaining results in terms of probabilities is better understood by clients (Lichtenberg & Hummel, 1998).
      v. *Once presenting the bulk of your results, ask for their impressions again.* Clients feel more connected to the results when they can be involved, ask questions, and contribute to the interpretation (Jones & Gelso, 1988). They are likely to integrate the results into creating useful life changes when they are involved.
      vi. *Discuss the implications of the diagnosis.* In discussing the implications of the diagnosis with the client, be thoughtful in finding ways that best fit the client and could be interpreted, by mutual agreement, as the least harmful. Be mindful of what needs to be included while at the same time respecting the client. You should develop a

mutual agreement of what needs to go into the official records. E.5.d of the ACA Code of Ethics (2014) states that counselors may refrain from reporting a diagnosis if they believe it would cause harm to the client. As always, consult and engage in an ethical decision-making model.

c. Follow up with the client.
   i. *Take an opportunity in a future session to get the client's reflection on the assessment.* Often, clients need time to reflect and integrate the new learning from an assessment. Good counseling practice should include following up and determining whether the client's impressions have changed.
   ii. *Consider using additional assessments with the engagement of the client.* An initial assessment experience may raise your client's interest in other measures. It is worth conversing with your client regarding other measures to help them with their treatment.
   iii. *Create an ongoing collaborative qualitative assessment of diagnosis and treatment plan.* Remember that diagnoses and treatment plans are not permanent. It is common for these elements to change and evolve as you learn more about your client and as they learn about themselves through the counseling process. It is good practice to periodically review diagnoses and treatment plans with your clients and collaboratively assess whether any changes need to be made.

A Culturally Integrative Framework for Crafting Comprehensive Treatment Plans

Understanding and addressing a client's mental health concerns requires more than a clinical diagnosis. It demands a multifaceted, inclusive approach (Kirmayer et al., 2003). Initiating this process begins with the psychiatric diagnosis or findings from the mental health assessment, serving as a direction for the treatment plan.

An integral component of this process lies in appreciating the cultural underpinning of the client. The DSM-5-TR offers counselors a structured path to grasp the nuances of cultural syndromes, variations, and idioms of distress (American Psychiatric Association [APA], 2022). For a better breakdown of what comes into play, the Cultural Formation Interview (CFI) is a guiding document aiming to uncover cultural influences on health, illness perceptions, and care-seeking behaviors (Lewis-Fernández et al., 2014).

Embracing an open therapeutic orientation perspective on therapeutic approaches, as emphasized by Kazdin (2017), can be beneficial. Such flexibility ensures treatment strategies remain adaptable, molding themselves to individualized client needs while retaining their roots in empirical evidence. Be willing to suspend your theoretical orientation for the client's benefit. An integrative stance ensures that clients receive a rounded, comprehensive care experience (Archer et al., 2012).

Regularly gauging therapeutic progress is pivotal. Quantitative metrics, particularly those focusing on symptom reduction, such as standardized assessments like the PHQ-9 or GAD-7, offer counselors tangible benchmarks for therapeutic adjustments (Kroenke et al., 2016; Spitzer et al., 2006). Clinical challenges, like therapy resistance or client noncompliance, often emerge. Foreseeing and preempting these challenges ensures therapeutic trajectories are maintained.

For a grounded perspective, consider Maria's following illustrative case. A blend of evidence-based and culturally attuned strategies supported by the work of Sue & Zane (1987) on the significance of culturally congruent care. Central to the therapeutic process is the active involvement of the client. The client's insights and participation anchor the therapeutic goals and pathways, ensuring alignment with their lived experiences. Ethical pillars like client confidentiality, informed consent, and respect for autonomy underline psychiatric practice, ensuring it stands robustly grounded in ethical integrity (Beauchamp & Childress, 2019).

The steps, derived from the previous discussion, for taking diagnostic/assessment information and crafting a collaborative treatment plan are as follows:

1. **Understanding the diagnosis:** Before delving into treatment options, ensure that you and your client clearly understand the psychiatric diagnosis or the findings of the mental health assessment. Familiarize yourself with and discuss the criteria and implications of the diagnosis.
2. **Cultural considerations:** Refer to the DSM-5-TR to understand the cultural aspects of specific diagnoses. Recognize the role of cultural syndromes, variations, and idioms of distress. It is considered good practice to also defer to the counseling literature to ensure your understanding of the diagnosis is aligned with our professional values and ethical principles.

    Utilize the CFI as a structured tool to gather culturally relevant information from the client. This should cover areas such as cultural identity, cultural explanations of the illness, cultural factors related to the psychosocial environment and levels of functioning, cultural elements of the counselor–client relationship, and overall cultural assessment.
3. **Therapeutic modalities:** While this guide remains therapy agnostic, it's crucial to consider the wide array of therapeutic interventions available. Evaluate evidence-based therapies suitable for the specific diagnosis while considering client preferences. Psychometric properties are also available for evidenced-based treatment modalities. Similarly to how you would critically assess an assessment, assessing the appropriateness of treatment modalities follows the same structure.
4. **Collaborative care integration:** Ensure that the treatment plan includes the potential to collaborate with other health-care professionals. This might include referrals to specialists, coordination with primary care physicians, seeking specific continuing education training, or consultation with supervisors or other therapists.
5. **Quantitative evaluation metrics:** Treatment goals that follow the SMARTER (Brown et al., 2016) acronym allow for ease of measurement.

    S: specific and significant

    M: measurable, manageable, and meaningful

    A: action-oriented, attainable, and agreed upon

    R: relevant, and realistic

    T: trackable and time-based

    E: engaging, ethical, excitable, engaging, and ecological

    R: rewarding, reassess, revisit, and recordable

Typically, treatment plans have multiple goals, with two to three objectives in each. Goals and objectives should be established and written from the assessment results and symptoms from the DSM-V-TR diagnosis. Objectives are the small steps that lead up to the main goal and should also follow the SMARTER model. Typically, each objective will be paired with the interventions you have chosen from the treatment modalities. It can be helpful to spread out goals to be short-, medium-, and long-term to support commitment to treatment and display evidence of growth.

Regularly measure symptom reduction to evaluate the effectiveness of the treatment.

While no specific scale is mandated, tools like the patient health questionnaire (PHQ-9) for depression or the generalized anxiety disorder seven-item (GAD-7) scale for anxiety can be utilized and adjusted as necessary. Depending on the symptom, goals, and objectives, you may also consider using client-tracking interventions such as diary cards.

6. **addressing potential challenges:** Recognize barriers like client noncompliance, medication side effects, or therapy resistance. Develop strategies to address these, such as enhanced client education, close monitoring, or therapy adjustments.
7. **client involvement:** Engage clients in the treatment planning process. Gather their feedback and preferences. Emphasize the importance of their collaboration in ensuring the effectiveness and success of the treatment.
8. **ethical considerations:** Prioritize client confidentiality and informed consent. Ensure the proposed treatments are in the client's best interest, avoiding potential harm. Respect client autonomy and choices, ensuring they understand the benefits and risks of suggested treatments. This guide provides a comprehensive blueprint for professionals to design a client-centered and culturally sensitive treatment plan, ensuring both clinical efficacy and personal relevance.

CLIENT CASE STUDY: MARIA AND THE "EVIL EYE"

Maria, a 35-year-old woman of Mexican descent, walked into the clinic looking visibly distressed. With drooping shoulders, an averted gaze, and a somber demeanor, she was the embodiment of someone who had been grappling with internal strife. Maria's symptoms included persistent feelings of sadness, a loss of interest in previously enjoyed activities, fatigue, changes in appetite, and sleep disturbances. These symptoms had been persisting for over 6 months. She mentioned she felt an overwhelming sense of guilt and shame but could not articulate a clear reason for these feelings.

Utilizing the Cultural Formulation Interview, the counselor probed deeper into Maria's understanding of her symptoms. It was crucial to discern how cultural factors played into her experience of depression. To the counselor's surprise, Maria didn't solely attribute her symptoms to a chemical imbalance or life events but to the influence of the "evil eye," or *mal de ojo*. In Mexican culture, the evil eye is believed to be a curse, usually caused by someone looking at you with envy or strong negative energy. The victim often doesn't know who cast the evil eye, intensifying feelings of vulnerability. It can lead to various physical and psychological disturbances.

To gather more context, with Maria's permission, her family was consulted. They shared their observations of Maria's withdrawn behavior and affirmed her belief in the evil eye. Some members mentioned they had seen neighbors giving Maria envious glances, particularly after she had received a promotion at her job. They believed Maria had been targeted due to her recent successes. Maria's community was tight-knit, and such beliefs were deeply rooted. Some community members suggested traditional remedies, including wearing amulets, consulting a local healer, or performing cleansing rituals.

Create a Treatment Plan for the Case of Maria

What are Maria's primary presenting concerns for seeking counseling? What questions might you ask? How would you employ the three types of assessment to get a holistic view of Maria's presenting concerns?

1. Qualitative:
2. Nonstandardized:
3. Standardized:

How would you collaboratively prioritize addressing each concern using the assessment strategies? How could each concern be worded as a SMARTER goal based on assessment and diagnosis results? What might be some SMARTER small steps (objectives) to reaching the larger goal? How might the *mal de ojo* factor into the goals, objectives, and interventions? How will you and Maria determine when she has achieved her goals?

CHAPTER SUMMARY

The chapter emphasizes the need for counselors to use evidence-based assessment tools and techniques to ensure their assessments are reliable, valid, and culturally sensitive. Also highlighted is the importance of using nonjudgmental language to document observations in clinical notes and treatment plans.

Moreover, the chapter provides examples of how assessments can inform the counseling relationship and treatment planning. Assessments can help counselors identify clients' strengths and challenges, monitor their progress, and evaluate the effectiveness of their interventions. The importance of using assessments ethically and responsibly to protect the client's confidentiality and privacy is emphasized. This chapter is a valuable resource for counselors, providing practical guidance on using assessments effectively and helping them gain a holistic understanding of their clients to provide the best possible care.

CASE EXAMPLE

Imagine you are a clinical mental health counselor working in a residential behavioral health agency, providing group, family, and individual counseling to adolescents aged 12–17. Your supervisor calls you to tell you to check your email for information about a new individual client you are receiving later that day. The supervisor tells you the client is 12 years old and is being transferred from a "militant residential" facility and says "you need to review his files prior to meeting with him to be ready."

Client: Jacoby "Coby" Smith

Age: 12

Sex Assigned at Birth: Male

Gender Identity: Male

Pronouns: He/Him

Sexual Orientation: N/A

Race/Ethnicity: Black

Custody: County Foster Care

Treatment Setting: Residential Behavioral Health

Type(s) of Counseling: Individual, group, and therapeutic behavioral support

Incoming Diagnoses: F91.3—Oppositional Defiant Disorder, F90.1 Attention-Deficit/Hyperactivity Disorder predominantly hyperactive/impulsive presentation, and F43.10 Post-Traumatic Stress Disorder

Relevant Notes from Intake Department and Previous Facility: Coby has spent a combined 5 years in and out of residential facilities since the age of 6. It has been noted that he is frequently disruptive in school, at home, and in treatment. The notes further state that he often engages in "oppositional," "defiant," and "impulsive" behaviors, such as not listening to adult instructions, pacing, making noise to annoy his peers, eloping from home, class, school, and counseling as well as becoming verbally and physically aggressive by means of screaming, threatening, hitting and punching himself and adults, and destroying property (e.g., breaking toys or pencils, tearing up his room, and ripping papers). Coby has historically struggled to make and maintain friendships with his peers and is "argumentative and disrespectful" with adults. You notice his file does not contain standardized assessments and that his diagnoses are primarily substantiated on qualitative and nonstandardized reports from his previous treatment team members.

Coby is the youngest of three siblings, all of whom are currently in county custody. His mother is imprisoned for drug charges, and it is noted that she has a long history of struggling with drug and alcohol abuse. It was noted that Coby's mother experiences symptoms of psychosis, and it cannot be determined if they are or are not a result of her substance abuse. It is unknown whether she was using substances during her pregnancy, and there are no reports of neurological or developmental testing. Coby's father lost custody following a Child Protective Services investigation revealing Coby's father being neglectful as well as physically and emotionally abusive to the children. Coby was placed in the most recent residential facility after eloping from a foster home where he struggled to get along with his foster siblings and parents.

Pause, Reflect, and Write:

1. What are your initial impressions of Coby?
2. How are you feeling about working with this client? Go with your gut instinct.
3. What do you imagine meeting Coby for the first time to be like?
4. What, if anything, is making you curious about this case?

First Meeting: You make your way from your office to the "cottages," where the clients live while in treatment, to meet Coby. When you get there you notice a group of staff gathered around his door all attempting to speak with him and get him to "calm down." You approach the group and ask them to give you a few minutes to speak with your client alone. They tell you they do not think that it is a good idea since he is "visibly distressed." You peer into the room and see a small-statured, thin boy pacing in circles on his toes, flap-clapping his hands, and looking at the ground wide-eyed. You tell the staff they can stay close if they want to and ask if they could at least give space and clear the doorway.

You introduce yourself as his new counselor and ask if you can come in to sit and get to know one another for a little bit. Coby responds with, "Yes, ma'am" (or another honorific that you prefer). You sit on the floor just inside the door and begin a lighthearted conversation. During your conversation, Coby consistently responds by addressing you with an honorific; however, he has not looked at you for longer than a second or two at a time. After a few minutes, you notice his pacing is slowing, the flap-claps stop, and his face and shoulders begin to relax. You learn that Coby loves superheroes and that Spiderman is his favorite. When you ask him why Spiderman, he stops pacing and tells you it's because "Spiderman is smaller and different from everyone else, even the other superheroes. I get how that feels because I am smaller and different from everyone." You ask Coby if we were in the Marvel Universe if he would be Spiderman? Coby says, "No, I think I would be a villain. Superheroes have friends, and villains don't." You help Coby get settled into his new room and share with him the typical schedule he will have while he is at the facility. As you prepare to leave you introduce him to a few specific staff and peers who you believe might be helpful in making him feel welcome on his first night.

Pause, Reflect, and Write:

1. What are your impressions of Coby after meeting him? How are they similar and different to your initial impressions based on his clinical file and diagnoses?
2. What, if any, biases were present in your initial impressions that may need to be checked after meeting him? Where did they come from?
3. What questions or curiosities do you have about the case after meeting Coby?
4. What are your impressions on the match of his diagnoses and what you experienced? What else would you like to learn about Coby's experiences?
5. How might you approach discussing diagnoses with Coby?

Individual Session #4 (About 1 Month Later): You have met with Coby for three individual sessions, and he has been in a number of your groups. He is mostly polite and respectful with peers and adults in individual and group counseling, and you are beginning to have a trusting counseling relationship. He continues to struggle with eye contact and engaging in the pacing and flap-clapping behaviors. He often fidgets in his chair or seems to need to be doing something with his hands at all times. You and fellow group leaders have consulted about his patterns of behavior in groups. It has been noted that his "aggressive outbursts" and eloping behaviors typically only happen when the groups are particularly loud or if he does not understand the instructions. Usually, he is able to regulate with some adult support, breaks, and by minimizing external stimuli like people and noise. Once regulated he happily gets back on task and has been improving asking for help before getting upset. The cottage staff report similar findings in all areas except in his nighttime routine. They say he has the most "outbursts" when going to bed, and complains he is afraid of the nightmares and being "trapped in residentials forever." They say he gets "stuck" in these thoughts and that it can last for hours. His principal at the agency's school encourages you to consider autism spectrum disorder, as they had previously worked in autism services for 10 years and suspects he may be on the spectrum. You decide to consult with your counseling supervisor and agency psychiatrist about his case. You learn your agency does not have the licensing to administer a standardized autism assessment (autism diagnostic observation schedule [ADOS]). They suspect you are on the right track, and you are instructed to do a full differential diagnosis and to be very detailed and use nonjudgmental language to document yours and other colleagues' observations in his treatment plan and clinical notes.

You decide to get Coby's opinion on his current diagnoses and the other diagnoses you are considering. In preparation, you create several cards using the DSM's descriptions of the diagnoses only translated into colloquial and developmentally appropriate language and omitting the names. You also include typical treatment interventions and supports in a similar fashion. During the session you explain that a diagnosis is a way counselors and other professionals communicate to let each other know about who he is and how to best support him. The two of you talk through the cards you prepared and ask him to rate how each one he feels fits him 0–10, with 0 being nothing like him and 10 being most like him. He reads the one describing oppositional defiant disorder and says, "This isn't me at all! I try really hard to be respectful and not annoy people, and I like adults a lot! I do get angry sometimes, but I'm usually scared or overwhelmed or confused! I don't like hurting people; that's why I usually just hit myself. This one is maybe one or two."

By the end of the session, Coby has scored the three that best describe him to be posttraumatic stress disorder (10), attention-deficit/hyperactivity disorder (6), and autism spectrum (9). He asks you the names of the diagnoses he has picked and has never heard of autism. You review the card with him again and add "for some people, autism can mean that their brain works differently than how others brains' work and that certain types of support like being in a quiet space, or being allowed to pace or fidget can help them more than it can others." Coby's face lights up with excitement, "That's definitely me! So other people have autism and think and feel different like me?" You tell him, "Yes there are many other people who think and feel different, like how you feel different, but I cannot 100% confirm you have autism because the test for it is not available here. There are other ways we can see if it fits, but it might take some time." He looks at the card again and says "okay let's do it because that's how I feel, and how I want others to see me and help me!" He asks which of the diagnoses are currently being used to describe him, and you answer honestly. He looks down and says, "So that's why people always treat me like I'm a bad kid. …"

Pause, Reflect, and Write:

1. How do you suspect Coby's current diagnoses to be impacting his life up to this point? How might they be impacting his relationships with others and his view of himself?
2. How do you suspect allowing Coby to engage in collaborative diagnosis might impact his treatment? How might it impact the counseling relationship and how he sees himself?
3. How might collaborative diagnosis uphold or contradict the ACA ethical principles and values?

4. What, if any, legal and ethical concerns do you have regarding assessment and diagnosis with this case?
5. What might have been contributing to Coby's initial diagnosis of oppositional defiant disorder?

Ongoing and Step-Down From Residential Treatment Over the Next Several Months: With the support of your supervisor as well as the principal, other group counselors, and cottage staff, you have implemented different support strategies that are typically used in autism services, such as cocreating visual schedules with Coby to represent a typical day and to display different events during the month that may disrupt his typical schedule, social stories to look through to support him during his "outbursts," and a new nighttime routine to help him relax as well as advocated for extra funds from his county worker to provide him with compression clothes and a weighted vest. The two of you have revisited the diagnostic cards and altered his treatment goals and plan together. You have thoroughly documented his responses and progress. He still has moments of struggles; however, he has improved in communication as well as experienced a decrease in number; intensity, as evidenced by verbal and physical aggressions; and length of "outbursts." You have been able to show this through a tracking spreadsheet. He is beginning to self-regulate in all areas of treatment by using his support strategies with minimal prompting or support from adults and peers. He has made a few friends among his peers, although still becomes very stuck in the idea that he "will be in residential forever" when one of them discharges before him and sometimes before bed.

All of your hard work engaging in and documenting continuous qualitative and nonstandardized assessment has paid off. Your counseling supervisor and agency psychiatrist feel comfortable signing off on replacing oppositional defiant disorder with autism spectrum based on your documentation. The principal and Coby's county worker updated his 504 and IEP. Additionally, Coby is set to be discharged into a foster home with foster parents, who have worked in autism services for many years. You have facilitated a few "family sessions" with the foster parents and were able to introduce him to his future out-patient counselor to support his transition. In your final session, Coby says, "I'm so excited to be going to a home where people will know how to see me and help me! Thank you for seeing me and helping me the way I needed it!"

Pause, Reflect, and Write:

1. What examples of qualitative assessment are present in this case study? How were they used?
2. What examples of nonstandardized assessment are present in this case study? How were they used?
3. How might you have approached assessment and diagnosis in this case differently?
4. What are a few key takeaways you learned through this activity?
5. What evidence of ethical practice, (i.e., values, principles, and decision-making) are present in the case study?

CHAPTER REFLECTION AND DISCUSSION QUESTIONS

1. How can counselors ensure they are not letting their implicit biases influence their assessments?
2. What is the purpose of the DSM's Cultural Formulation Interview?
3. What are the AARC Standards for Multicultural Assessments?
4. What is Dove's counterbalance intelligence test?

5. What is the purpose of assessing a client's cultural background in counseling?
6. What are some ethical considerations counselors should keep in mind when administering assessments?
7. How can counselors ensure their assessments are culturally sensitive?
8. What are some potential biases that can arise in assessments?
9. How can counselors use assessment results to inform treatment planning?
10. What is the difference between a diagnosis and an assessment?
11. What is the purpose of norming an assessment?
12. When administering assessments, what is the importance of considering a client's language proficiency?
13. What is the role of consultation in the assessment process?
14. Compare and contrast the three types of assessment? How might a counselor use all three to inform a diagnosis?

ADDITIONAL RESOURCES

YouTube

- Think Cultural Health: "Using the Cultural Formulation Interview" https://youtube/8SjBG9di8ss?si=1PDO38GddFZL2WI3

Podcasts (available on most platforms)

- Assessment Talks
- The Thoughtful Counselor

Counseling Organizations

- Association for Assessment and Research in Counseling: https://www.aarc-counseling.org
- Association for Multicultural Counseling and Development: https://www.multiculturalcounselingdevelopment.org/
- Counselors for Social Justice: https://www.counseling-csj.org/

REFERENCES

American Counseling Association. (2014). *ACA code of ethics.*

American Psychiatric Association. (2022). *Diagnostic and statistical manual of mental disorders* (5th ed., text rev.). https://doi.org/10.1176/appi.books.9780890425787

American Psychological Association. (2014). *Standards for educational and psychological testing.*

Archer, J., Bower, P., Gilbody, S., Lovell, K., Richards, D., Gask, L., Dickens, C., & Coventry, P. (2012). Collaborative care for depression and anxiety problems. *Cochrane Database of Systematic Reviews, 10,* CD006525. https://doi.org/10.1002/14651858.CD006525.pub2

Armstrong, P. (2010). *Bloom's taxonomy.* Vanderbilt University Center for Teaching. https://cft.vanderbilt.edu/guides-sub-pages/blooms-taxonomy/

Association for Assessment and Research in Counseling. (2018). *AARC Standards for Multicultural Assessments.* https://aarc-counseling.org/wp-content/uploads/2020/04/AARC-Standards-for-Multicultural-Assessments-2018.pdf

Ault, H. R., Gantt, H. S., & Barrio Minton, C. A. (2023). Anti-racist considerations for teaching CACREP assessment and diagnosis courses. *Teaching and Supervision in Counseling, 5*(1). https://doi.org/10.7290/tsc05dxpf

Beauchamp, T. L., & Childress, J. F. (2019). *Principles of biomedical ethics* (8th ed.). Oxford University Press.

Bhugra, D., & Bhui, K. (2018). *Practical cultural psychiatry.* Oxford University Press.

Brown, G., Leonard, C., & Arthur-Kelly, M. (2016). Writing smarter goals for professional learning and improving classroom practices. *Reflective Practice, 17*(5), 621–635. https://doi.org/10.1080/14623943.2016.1187120

Burgess, D. J., Beach, M. C., & Saha, S. (2017). Mindfulness practice: A promising approach to reducing the effects of clinician implicit bias on patients. *Patient Education and Counseling, 100*(2), 372–376. https://doi.org/10.1016/j.pec.2016.09.005

Council for Accreditation of Counseling and Related Educational Programs. (2023). *2024 CACREP standards.*

Cooper, R. (2004). What is wrong with the DSM? *History of Psychiatry, 15*(1), 5–25. https://doi.org/10.1177/0957154x04039343

Council of National Psychological Associations for the Advancement of Ethnic Minority Interests. (2016). *Testing and assessment with persons & communities of color.* American Psychological Association. from https://www.apa.org/pi/oema

Dove, A. (1967). The chitling test. *New Republic, 157,* 7.

Edwards, M., Saenz, S. R., Collins, R., & Bandstra, B. (2021). Social injustice and structural racism. In R. S. Shim & S. Y. Vinson (Eds.), *Social (in)justice and mental health* (pp. 53–55). American Psychiatric Association.

Fernando, S. (2017). *Institutional racism in psychiatry and clinical psychology: Race matters in mental health.* Springer International.

Forester-Miller, H., & Davis, T. (2016). *Practitioner's guide to ethical decision making.* American Counseling Association.

Hays, D. G. (2017). *Assessment in counseling: Procedures and practices* (6th ed.). American Counseling Association.

Hays, D. G. (2017b). *Assessment in counseling: Procedures and practices* (6th ed.). American Counseling Association.

Helms, J. E. (1992). Why is there no study of cultural equivalence in standardized cognitive ability testing? *American Psychologist, 47*(9), 1083–1101. https://doi-org.proxy.library.kent.edu/10.1037/0003-066X.47.9.1083

Hofstede, G. (2003). *Culture's consequences: Comparing values, behaviors, institutions, and organizations across nations* (2nd ed.). SAGE.

Hofstede, G., Hofstede, G. J., & Minkov, M. (2010). *Cultures and organizations: Software of the mind* (3rd ed.). McGraw-Hill.

Jones, A. S., & Gelso, C. J. (1988). Differential effects of style of interpretation: Another look. *Journal of Counseling Psychology, 35*(4), 363–369. https://doi.org/10.1037/0022-0167.35.4.363

Kazdin, A. E. (2017). Addressing the treatment gap: A key challenge for extending evidence-based psychosocial interventions. *Behaviour Research and Therapy, 88*, 7–18.

Kirmayer, L. J. (2012). Rethinking cultural competence. *Transcultural Psychiatry, 49*(2), 149–164.

Kirmayer L. J., Groleau, D., Guzder, J., Blake, C., & Jarvis, E. (2003). Cultural consultation: A model of mental health service for multicultural societies. *Canadian Journal of Psychiatry, 48*(3), 145–53. https://www.doi.org/10.1177/070674370304800302.

Kroenke, K., Wu, J., Yu, Z., Bair, M. J., Kean, J., Stump, T., & Monahan, P. O. (2016). Patient health questionnaire anxiety and depression scale: Initial validation in three clinical trials. *Psychosomatic Medicine, 78*(6), 716–27. https://www.doi.org/10.1097/PSY.0000000000000322

Lewis-Fernández, R., Aggarwal, N. K., Bäärnhielm, S., Rohlof, H., Kirmayer, L. J., Weiss, M. G., & Groen, S. (2016). Culture and psychiatric evaluation: Operationalizing cultural formulation for DSM-5. *Psychiatry, 77*(2), 130–154.

Lewis-Fernández, R., Aggarwal, N. K., Lam, P. C., Galfalvy, H., Weiss, M. G., Kirmayer, L. J., Paralikar, V., Deshpande, S. N., Díaz, E., Nicasio, A. V., Boiler, M., Alarcón, R. D., Rohlof, H., Groen, S., van Dijk, R. C., Jadhav, S., Sarmukaddam, S., Ndetei, D., Scalco, M. Z., Bassiri, K., … Vega-Dienstmaier, J. M. (2017). Feasibility, acceptability and clinical utility of the Cultural Formulation Interview: mixed-methods results from the DSM-5 international field trial. *The British Journal of Psychiatry: The Journal of Mental Science, 210*(4), 290–297. https://doi.org/10.1192/bjp.bp.116.193862

Lichtenberg, J. W., & Hummel, T. J. (1998). *Levels of therapist understanding and client feelings of being understood and the length of the therapy relationship* (ED420006). https://eric.ed.gov/?id=ED420006

Nashrulla, T. (2016, August 8). *People were pissed at this "sexist" tweet about an olympic winner.* BuzzFeed News. https://www.buzzfeednews.com/article/tasneemnashrulla/she-has-a-name

Olbert, C. M., Nagendra, A., & Buck, B. (2018). Meta-analysis of Black vs. White racial disparity in schizophrenia diagnosis in the United States: Do structured assessments attenuate racial disparities? *Journal of Abnormal Psychology, 127*(1), 104–115. https://doi.org/10.1037/abn0000309

Paniagua, F. A. (2016). Assessment and diagnosis in a cultural context. In M. M. Leach & J. D. Aten (Eds.), *Culture and the therapeutic process: A guide for mental health professionals* (pp. 65–98). Routledge.

Ratts, M. J., Singh, A. A., Nassar-McMillan, S., Butler, S. K., & McCullough, J. R. (2016). Multicultural and social justice counseling competencies: Guidelines for the counseling profession. *Journal of Multicultural Counseling and Development, 44*(1), 28–48. https://doi.org/10.1002/jmcd.12035

Schwartz, R. C., & Blankenship, D. M. (2014). Racial disparities in psychotic disorder diagnosis: A review of empirical literature. *World Journal of Psychiatry, 4*, 133–140. http://dx.doi.org/10.5498/wjp.v4.i4.133

Shorter, E. (2013). The history of DSM. *Making the DSM-5.* https://doi.org/10.1007/978-1-4614-6504-1_1

Spitzer, R. L., Kroenke, K., Williams, J. B., & Löwe, B. (2006). A brief measure for assessing generalized anxiety disorder: The GAD-7. *Archives of Internal Medicine, 166*(10), 1092–1097.

Substance Abuse and Mental Health Services Administration. (2016). *Improving cultural competence: Quick guide for clinicians*. U.S. Department of Health and Human Services. https://store.samhsa.gov/sites/default/files/d7/priv/sma16-4931.pdf

Sue, D. W. (2001). Multidimensional facets of cultural competence. *The Counseling Psychologist*, *29*(6), 790–821.

Sue, S., & Zane, N. (1987). The role of culture and cultural techniques in psychotherapy: A critique and reformulation. *American Psychologist*, *42*(1), 37.

Triandis, H. C. (1995). *Individualism and collectivism*. Westview Press.

Credits

Fig. 14.1: Copyright © by Vanderbilt University Center for Teaching (CC BY 2.0) at https://cft.vanderbilt.edu/guides-sub-pages/blooms-taxonomy/.

Fig. 14.2: *Chicago Tribune*, https://www.buzzfeednews.com/article/tasneemnashrulla/she-has-a-name. Copyright © 2016 by Chicago Tribune Company.

Fig. 14.3: KashannKilson, https://www.buzzfeednews.com/article/tasneemnashrulla/she-has-a-name. Copyright © 2016 by KashannKilson.

Fig. 14.4: Adapted from American Counseling Association, "So You Have an Ethical Dilemma?," https://www.counseling.org/docs/default-source/ethics/ethical-dilemma-posterv5.pdf?sfvrsn=2. Copyright © by American Counseling Association.

Fig. 14.5: Adapted from M.J. Ratts, A.A. Singh, S. Nassar-McMillan, S.K. Butler, and J.R. McCullough; adapted by Marty Jencius and Jessica Budyka, "Adapted from MSJCC," *Multicultural and Social Justice Counseling Competencies: Guidelines for the Counseling Profession. Journal of Multicultural Counseling and Development*, vol. 44, no. 1. Copyright © 2016 by John Wiley & Sons, Inc.

Creativity

Dr. Nivischi N. Edwards, Dr. Lynn Bohecker, Keyona Harper, and Monique Barber

LEARNING OBJECTIVES

1. Students will be provided with prompts and interventions to increase their knowledge and awareness of self and others related to values, beliefs, and worldviews.
2. Students will learn techniques for increasing their skills in broaching cultural identities and experiences with clients while actively engaging in multicultural and social justice praxis.

LEARNING OUTCOMES

1. Students will understand how to use creative expression in multicultural counseling.
2. Students will understand what interventions to use for personal growth or aid in client beliefs, growth, and development.
3. Students will understand the benefit of integrating case studies to increase social justice beliefs.
4. Students will understand how to adapt expressive arts for increased skill, knowledge, and enhanced awareness.

Counselor training consists of a combination of content and process. Counseling theories and concepts learned in books come alive in practical skills courses in counselor development, and experiential learning communities are formed through practice. Whether a program is entirely online, fully in-person, or a hybrid of the two, skills courses are where students gather in physical or virtual places to practice the counseling techniques they have been reading and hearing about in content courses, a theoretical-to-practical application. Both learning and counselor development theorists highlight that learning ideally comes from processes that help students explore their beliefs and ideas about a topic so they can be assessed, analyzed, and refined by existing ideas (Kolb & Kolb, 2005; Skovholt & Rønnestad, 2003). In addition, exploring creative expression in therapy enhances the client's psychological well-being (Shafir et al., 2020). Topics that require extensive exploration and student self-reflection are learning about the impact of the many overlapping or intersecting identities and contexts related to social constructs and diverse cultural factors.

Creativity in counseling helps develop cognitive restructuring in problem-solving skills, aiding students in the exploration and self-reflection needed to witness new relationships and new ideas and broaden insight for resolution (Lawrence et al., 2015). Discussions regarding creativity in counseling should occur early in counselor education programs, helping students navigate these developmental skills through creative approaches to obtaining self-efficacy (McCarthy, 2017). Low self-efficacy in counselors leads to elevated anxiety levels and decreased capacity to formulate a therapeutic alliance with the client (Greene et al., 2014). Exploring one's ideas, beliefs, and social constructs can become challenging and uncomfortable, prompting distress while expanding and questioning a student's cultural beliefs (Greene et al., 2014). Hence, a creative approach to these explorations helps individuals identify personal experiences while examining the thoughts that shape those experiences. Utilizing creative approaches helps individuals reach a course of action through imagery for alternative solutions to these experiences. Through self-discovery and resolution, counselors can establish a safe and accepting relationship with their clients, resulting in constructive creativity within the client (Lawrence et al., 2015).

Multicultural and Social Justice Counseling Competencies

Hilert and Tirado (2019) state that multicultural counseling courses evoke difficult emotions from the counselor educator and student. The self-examination of biases, values, and assumptions must be balanced in an environment of support, challenge, and reflection. At the same time, the counselor educator is simultaneously creating an atmosphere of safety and vulnerability. Elicited emotions from this experience are often feelings of shame, guilt, anger, and sadness. Creative, expressive art in multicultural-competent courses can aid in articulation, depth, and resolve of these emotions for a clearer understanding of how the student can create individual change by self-awareness, provoking change on a more significant measure for the client. A counselor's increased competency may result in an increased client's competency for greater accomplishment and fulfillment in an ever-changing, multifaceted society (Lawerence et al., 2015).

Key components of learning to become a competent professional counselor include (a) understanding the complexities of diversity and multiculturalism in the counseling relationship, (b) recognizing the negative influence of oppression on mental health and well-being, (c) understanding individuals in the context of their social environment, and (d) integrating social justice advocacy into individual, family, partners, and group counseling. These essential components encompass awareness, knowledge, skills, and actions and are identified as the Multicultural and Social Justice Counseling Competencies (MSJCC; Ratts et al., 2016). The purposeful integration of the MSJCC into counselor training helps students gain insight into the advantages afforded to clients from privileged groups and the discrimination and oppression experienced by clients from marginalized groups (Arredondo & Perez, 2003; Crethar et al., 2008; Ponterotto et al., 2010). The MSJCC has been endorsed by the American Counseling Association (ACA), the Association for Multicultural Counseling and Development (AMCD), and the Association for Spiritual, Ethical, and Religious Values in Counseling (ASERVIC), thus emphasizing its need for integration throughout counselor training.

Research indicates that some counseling students do not receive adequate training in the MSJCC, and many professors tend to focus on only a few cultures, both issues of which may have harmful implications for clients (Constantine & Sue, 2006; Day-Vines et al., 2013; Hemmings & Evans, 2018; Jones et al., 2016; Neville et al., 2006; Santos & Dallos, 2012). The inability of a counselor to understand their client's cultural perspective or their intersecting identities or to communicate with cultural sensitivity leads to unidimensional and surface-level counseling at best, but it is more likely that the client will experience harm (Chan et al., 2018; Constantine & Sue, 2006; Day-Vines et al., 2013; Hays, 2020). Therefore, counselor educators must seek more effective methods of incorporating activities that practice clinical interventions, strengthen skills, and foster confidence when working with clients who identify with a culture different from that of the counselor (Arredondo & Arciniega, 2001; Chan et al., 2018; Gonzalez & Cokley, 2021; Hays, 2020).

MSJCC Conceptual Framework

An infinite number of combinations of counselor and client identities intersect, interact, and influence the counselor–client relationship and therapeutic outcomes. Ratts et al. (2016) developed a conceptual framework with important terms to facilitate communication, knowledge, and awareness of multicultural and social justice constructs. The MSJCC conceptual framework contains quadrants, domains, and competencies. The MSJCC encourages counselors to be attentive to each of the racial, ethnic, gender, sexual orientation, economic, disability, and religious identities of themselves and their clients as well as how these identities are ever present in the counseling relationship (Ratts et al., 2016).

The overlapping, intersecting, and mixing of complex identities with the privileged and marginalized status of counselors and clients is a part of immediacy in the here and now of the counseling session and when counselor and client interact with each other (Chan et al., 2018). This chapter provides an introduction, or *intro*section, of specific interventions that facilitate student awareness of some of the ways power, privilege, and oppression are present in every counseling relationship. Professional counselors are charged with seeing client issues from culturally contextual perspectives, meaning interventions are used at the systems and individual levels. For some counseling students, this paradigm shift, or change in thinking, is an added layer of learning, increasing uncertainty, discomfort, and disequilibrium. Thus, counselor educators are challenged to assist students with managing their emotional responses to learning, especially within practical skills courses.

Experiential Learning

Experiential learning is a process that is ideal for many students and is valued in counselor education, encouraging self and other awareness by accessing cognitive and affective stages of learning through direct experience (Goodrich & Luke, 2010; Harrawood et al., 2011; Kolb & Kolb, 2005). Student learning through active experience facilitates personal growth and development and is essential to the felt significance moment when emotions and learning connect (Dewey, 1938; Gowin, 1981; McAuliffe & Eriksen, 2011). Counselor development models emphasize the importance of addressing the emotional aspects of learning (Loganbill et al., 1982; Stoltenberg et al., 1998; Rønnestad & Skovholt, 2003). Counseling students face the daunting task of navigating complex emotional states while simultaneously acquiring new skills (Bernard & Goodyear, 2019; Rønnestad & Skovholt, 2003; Stoltenberg et al., 1998). Students may be uncomfortable with not knowing when they are in the learning process, and some may experience disequilibrium.

Disequilibrium is essential for learning; however, students may not have the awareness or the tools to understand that their feelings are an ordinary and necessary component of educational attainment (Piaget, 1970; Rønnestad & Skovholt, 2003). Without this awareness, some students will minimize or abandon learning to reduce the risk of the intense feelings of not knowing when a cognitive task is perceived as too difficult (Zelan, 1991). Thus, teaching students' emotional regulation skills is a prerequisite to counseling students' professional growth and development (Bohecker et al., 2016; Oatley & Johnson-Laird, 1987; Prikhidko et al., 2020; Prikhidko & Swank, 2018). Therefore, counselor development is grounded in their ability to experience ambiguity and regulate the emotional discomfort and disequilibrium of learning. Successful navigation of the discomfort of learning new skills requires a tolerance for ambiguity and not knowing and may require counselor educators to develop creative learning plans and interventions (Bohecker et al., 2016; Hays, 2020; McGhee et al., 2019; Skovholt, 2001; Wasik et al., 2019; Zelan, 1991).

Expressive Arts in Counseling

Counseling requires divergent thinking and the ability to grasp things in a manner that is broad, flexible, curious, tentative, and exploratory of possibilities (Gladding, 2016). Expressive arts in counseling help clients create something tangible that can be reflected on during and after their treatment. Utilizing expressive arts in counseling may include art, poetry, music, and many others. For example, photography can be used as a metaphor to help CITs consider different viewpoints and perspectives of their opinion and bias (Schmidt et al., 2019).

The MSJCC and multicultural coursework is intended to develop divergent thinking and help CITs lean into working with diverse client populations. While training to become a counselor, expressive arts can be used. Parker et al. (2022) suggest activities that offer CITs a chance to explore their values and cultural identities to how they contribute to social justice and advocacy. You will likely be encouraged to keep a journal while learning the MSJCC, which will help you notice discomfort and manage ambiguity (Bohecker et al., 2016). Consider how you may use this assignment (with permission from your instructor) to be creative beyond written means. You may keep a digital journal with photos, videos, and artwork that convey your feelings as you progress through the course.

Sharing your experience with your peers as you learn the MSJCC and multicultural counseling bolsters your ability to tolerate discomfort. It is essential to share and learn from each other. Houin and Perryman (2021) found that CITs who participated in expressive art interventions in a multicultural counseling course found ways to connect with others, even when uncomfortable. Like group work, consider how confidentiality will be managed. Sacco and Amende (2021) highlight the importance of addressing confidentiality for the safety of students due to the self-reflection and sharing that go hand in hand with multicultural counseling courses. It is also essential to share in a way that does not push you into distress but challenges cognition and promotes more profound thought that elicits revelation. Once this technique is learned, CITs can utilize the approach with clients to identify how the client's intersectionality impacts the client's mental health. During multicultural counseling studies, CITs already experience anxiety and growth toward an increased sense of self and self-compassion (Houin & Perryman, 2021). Use Table 15.1 to gauge the content and depth of your shared experience. Intentionality in sharing will help you notice how your personal and professional identities are impacted (Houin & Perryman, 2021).

TABLE 15.1 Safety in What and How You Share, Based on Subjective Units of Distress Scale (Wolpe, 1969)

0–1	What you'd share with the person sitting next to you at a bus stop or a cashier
2–3	What you'd share with a co-worker
4–6	What you'd share with your classmates
7–8	What you'd share with family or close friends
9–10	What you'd share with your personal counselor

Another consideration is how you will provide feedback within your class. Sacco & Amende (2021) suggest that feedback given to students on creative expression assignments should focus on depth rather than the content itself. Consider how you would provide feedback to a classmate with a different perspective from you, as evidenced by how and what they shared about their creative assignment. How might you provide feedback that offers depth over content? Depth may be an examination of the feeling evoked from their work rather than the thoughts you notice. Feedback on feelings might sound like, "I notice how the colors you used are vibrant, and that makes me feel happy."

The experience you have learning and experiencing the MSJCC and multicultural counseling in a classroom setting will likely help when you begin work with a diverse clientele in a therapeutic setting. It is common for CITs to experience a broad range of emotions while balancing ethical decision-making with cultural considerations (Parker et al., 2022). Refer to the case studies and interventions in the resource section for creative ways you can continue to grow as a multiculturally competent counselor.

You may think, "This is all good, but how can I adapt this when working with a client?" This chapter intentionally begins with a focus on you, the counselor in training. Before working with clients, you must have a strong foundation on which you understand and have adopted the MSJCC competencies. The interventions Broaching With Case Studies and Exploring Multicultural View Through Expressive Poetry *can* be adapted in session with clients. Below each intervention is a section called Adapting to a Therapeutic Session, which will help you consider how to implement this in client sessions.

Intervention

Intervention: Broaching With Case Studies

Broaching behaviors in session provides a space for exploration while offering safety for the client and counselor (Day-Vines et al., 2007). As expressed in person-centered counseling, broaching race and culture requires openness and genuine care (Rogers, 1961). Although these conditions are necessary, the ambiguity of the outcome of a broaching experience (e.g., *I might say the wrong thing about their race, and it would make the client uncomfortable*) could be intimidating for those new to the technique. For example, using the following case studies to practice broaching in class may be a daunting experience that counselors-in-training (CITs) would prefer to escape, rather than risk misstepping in front of their peers. On the other hand, some CITs may feel an urgency to practice ethically and multiculturally competent treatment. Bohecker, et al. (2016) found that learning to tolerate ambiguity and moving from fear to integration can translate beyond clinical practice.

This intervention will help CITs practice using broaching in a session. CITs will consider how tolerating ambiguity can move them forward and create greater safety for themselves and their future clients.

Supplies needed

- Pen and paper/iPad/Tablet/Laptop
- Multiple locations where CITs can practice safely

Time required

45 to 60 minutes

Instructions

1. In your own words, write a definition for broaching.
2. Read the following case studies, and then answer these questions: When you consider broaching race, ethnicity, and culture in a session with clients A, B, C, or D, what feelings emerge for you? If fear is one of the emotions, in what ways are you afraid of broaching? What is the worst thing that could happen if your fears were realized? In what ways are you confident? Write your response using your device. You may decide to write it as a journal entry, poem, or drawing.
3. Act out a counseling session with a colleague, using the following case study. After the counseling session where you broach your client, debrief the experience with another colleague (supervisor Linda). Discuss three things: (a) how I feel about broaching, (b) why I fear broaching, and (c) how I will overcome my fear of broaching. Plan for each student to take 10 minutes to act out their play and 5 minutes to debrief.
4. Process the activity within your small group and then as a class. Start sentences with *When broaching,*

    I fear …

    I am learning …

    I am practicing …

    I am integrating …

CASE STUDIES

Linda (CIT) is a 55-year-old Arab American woman from the Southeast of the United States, who has been in practice for 25 years and is currently practicing in the Midwest. Linda is a social justice advocate for underprivileged communities. She is also a counselor educator and supervisor for master's level counseling students. Linda enjoys supervision as much as she enjoys the clinical atmosphere. Counselors have approached Linda in training during supervision with the following scenarios.

Scenario 1
Kimberly, a Black female (marginalized) counselor in training, engages in an intake session with Dallas, a 62-year-old Caucasian male (privileged client). While completing an intake session, the CIT reports that Dallas, the 72-year-old Caucasian male, has been watching and enjoying a show on a popular live streaming network, where a Black female therapist has been providing services to Caucasian clients. Kimberly reports asking Dallas if her skin color makes Dallas uncomfortable and if he would like another therapist. Dallas reports not being a racist and believing a Black counselor could help him with his issues. Kimberly reports, while in supervision, feeling uncomfortable by Dallas's statement but still being willing to engage with the client.

Scenario 2
Mark, a Latino male (marginalized) CIT, has been engaging in several sessions with Michael, a 44-year-old Caucasian male (privileged) client injured on the job and unable to return to work. Mark has been working with Michael to decrease symptoms of anxiety. Mark reports that while engaging in a therapeutic exercise, Michael explained how he was unsure of his financial future because of his injury, causing the client to experience anxiety. Mark then reported Michael's statement that "your people wouldn't understand hard work." Mark, the CIT, reports feeling discriminated against in supervision and refuses to continue sessions with the client.

Scenario 3
Kenneth, a Caucasian male (privileged) CIT, has completed an intake for Taylor, a 38-year-old female client who identifies as a divorced heterosexual biracial female (marginalized) with two male children. During the intake, Kenneth discovers that Taylor has experienced sexual, physical, and emotional abuse by her ex-husband. The latter has remarried, moved out of the country with his new family, and does not support her or their children. Kenneth reports feeling confused and unsettled about the client's presenting problems in supervision.

Scenario 4
Judith, a Caucasian female (privileged) CIT, has been counseling Patricia, a 25-year-old Caucasian female (privileged) client, for several months for major depressive disorder (MDD). Judith and Patricia have been working on coping skills to decrease symptoms of MDD. Judith shares in supervision that Patricia has experienced a recurrence of symptoms after interacting with a friend who identifies as a

minority. Patricia reports hearing about a racial injustice(s) shared by the friend's brother has Patricia feeling hopeless about the world's affairs.

With clients, CITs can begin to utilize the multidimensional model of broaching behavior (MMBB), asking the client to share experiences of race, ethnicity, and culture, communicating safety and acceptance of the client's exploration of their reality and the connection between the presenting problem. Giving the client permission to discuss these topics triggers cultural catharsis and resolve (Day-Vines et al., 2020).

Adapting to a Therapeutic Session

Suppose you are in session with a client that is experiencing distress related to their intersectional identity (e.g., race, gender, or social class). You may have them engage in poetry, art, or music to help them identify which parts of their identity are being activated. For example, you could invite the client to choose music related to their distressing symptom and then ask permission to play the song in session, perhaps printing a copy of the lyrics if that is important for the client. You may decide to follow this activity by processing sensations, feelings, and thoughts that have arisen for the client.

CHAPTER SUMMARY

The world is a collective of cultures, races, and ethnicities. CITs are learning that counseling sessions may imitate the world around them. A better understanding of the client's experiences will aid in developing the empathy and compassion needed to build the therapeutic alliance within the counselor–client relationship for a successful counseling outcome. The interventions in this chapter will open the eyes of the CIT's self-awareness and feelings about their own lived experiences, beliefs, biases, and privileges and how they may affect the clinical counseling setting.

In this chapter, we have introduced creative interventions that may address emotional regulation and cognitive complexity in students as they learn new counseling skills. When learning new counseling skills, CITs often feel anxious and overwhelmed by the magnitude of new information to learn. These creative skills aim to minimize feelings of anxiety and normalize the newness of counseling skills. Blending the social justice praxis will incorporate the multicultural lens needed to become a competent counselor. This experiential process will aid in helping the CIT articulate their feelings in a way that explains what their hearts or minds may be wrestling to say.

ADDENDUM

Intervention: Multicultural View Through Expressive Poetry Activity

Poetry in Motion (Poetry Society of America, 2022) is a public art initiative of the Metropolitan Transit Authority in New York City and the Poetry Society of America. This program features poetry overhead in subway cars and buses alongside billboard advertisements. The poems are short and vary in themes. Like poetry in general, they are intended to evoke a feeling and offer subway riders an opportunity to consider the lived experiences and perspectives of others.

This experiential activity is structured to recreate the subway Poetry in Motion experience in the classroom. Students will explore and reflect on their values, beliefs, and worldviews regarding power, privilege, and oppression. Each student will be invited to express their feelings and experiences by writing a short poem and creating a billboard, which will then be posted to develop a series for the course. Students will sit with another student in front of each poem as if seated on a subway. By seeing all the poems together, viewing their own and their peers, students will be exposed to the similarities and differences in the experiences and understanding of power, privilege, and oppression.

Supplies needed

- Timer
- Pen and paper/iPad/Tablet/Laptop
- Lined paper or journal/Electronic device
- Coloring supplies (watercolors, colored pencils, pastels, etc.)
- Mixed media paper (8.5 × 11 to 11 × 15)
- Ruler (optional)

Time required

60 to 90 minutes

Instructions

1. Review the definitions of power, privilege, and oppression provided by your instructor. Rewrite each definition in your own words.
2. Choose one or two prompts from the following options:
   - When I finally understood power, privilege, and oppression, I realized …
   - The painful thing about power, privilege, and oppression is … Healing from the pain is like …
   - How I was raised influenced my understanding of power, privilege, and oppression in the following ways …
   - What I want others to know about my power, privilege, and oppression (or lack thereof) is … What I choose to keep hidden is …
3. Set a timer for 10 minutes. Once you begin the timer, start writing responses to the chosen prompts, and do not let your pen or pencil lift from the page until the timer stops. You can write verses, journal, or arrange the words on the page like art. There are no rhythm or rhyme rules. Finally, try not to edit what you write, as you will be the only on who will see what you write. Just let it flow out of you. If you are unsure what to write, write about that experience.
4. Once the timer ends, take a 10-minute break. Perhaps, you'll engage in a self-care activity like a walk or meditative breathing during this time.
5. Return to the completed writing and highlight lines or words that stand out. Arrange the lines or words you highlighted into a poem. Give your poem a title.
6. Look at examples of Poetry-in-Motion billboards to derive inspiration (if needed): https://poetrysociety.org/poetry-in-motion.

7. Bring out your mixed media paper and draw a rectangle on the page (this will be your Poetry-in-Motion billboard).
8. Copy the poem on the billboard and use your art supplies to decorate it.
9. Hang each billboard around the class, a little above eye level if you're seated (like on a bus or a subway). Arrange a set of seats in front of each billboard. *Note to instructor*: Consider playing subway sounds (a YouTube search yields a variety of options) during this activity.
10. Sit silently in pairs, moving seats every minute, observing each billboard. You may choose to journal your experience with each billboard or with the activity.
11. Process the activity as a class.
12. *Optional*: Take one line from each poem and create a combined poetry-in-motion billboard. Decide on the title as a class.

Adapting to a Therapeutic Session

This intervention could be adapted to the client by considering the presenting issue that brings the client to treatment. For example, if clients have a major depressive disorder (MDD), they may begin by defining what MDD means to them. Then, you could follow the prompts that will help the client focus on the issue and the solution—for example, "Using all five of your senses, write a poem about how MDD impacts each sense." Another prompt may be, "Imagine MDD is a visitor to your home. Describe how you greet it and what you do with it. Write a satisfying resolution to the poem." Facilitate this intervention using steps 6–10, followed by processing.

CHAPTER REFLECTION AND DISCUSSION QUESTIONS

1. Give an example of a counselor in training using the four key components of being a multicultural social justice component counselor.
2. As a CIT, explain the importance of learning and implementing the art of creativity in a future counseling session.
3. How will you broach the idea to a client to gain buy-in when using one of the aforementioned interventions?
4. With a colleague, practice each intervention until you have mastered it and feel comfortable presenting it as a novice counselor.
5. Which intervention most resonates with you? Why?

ADDITIONAL RESOURCES

Degges-White, S., & Davis, N. L. (2018). *Integrating the expressive arts into counseling practice: Theory-based interventions* (2nd). Springer.

Gillam, T. A. R. (2018). *Creativity, wellbeing, and mental health practice.* Palgrave Macmillan.

Gladding, S. T. (2007). *Becoming creative as a counselor: the SCAMPER model.* Microtraining Associates.

Gladding, S. T. (2020). *The creative arts in counseling* (6th ed.). American Counseling Association.

McCarthy, J., Shannon, E., & Bruno, M. (2021). Creative Question-Framing: 12 Ideas for Counselors-in-Training. *Journal of Creativity in Mental Health, 16*(4), 499–510. https://doi.org/10.1080/15401383.2020.1800543

Rogers, N., Carlson, J., & Kjos, D. (1997). *Person-centered expressive arts therapy.* Psychotherapy.net. *The Journal of Creativity in Mental Health.* https://www.creativecounselor.org/journal

REFERENCES

Arredondo, P., & Arciniega, G. M. (2001). Strategies and techniques for counselor training based on the multicultural counseling competencies. *Journal of Multicultural Counseling and Development, 29*(4), 263–273. https://doi.org/10.1002/j.2161-1912.2001.tb00469.x

Arredondo, P., & Perez, P. (2003). Expanding multicultural competence through social justice leadership. *The Counseling Psychologist, 31*(3), 282–289. https://doi.org/10.1002/j.2161-1912.2001.tb00469.x

Bernard, J. M. & Goodyear, R. K. (2019). *Fundamentals of clinical supervision* (6th ed.). Pearson.

Bohecker, L., Vereen, L. G., Wells, P. C., & Wathen, C. C. (2016). A mindfulness experiential small group to help students tolerate ambiguity. *Counselor Education and Supervision, 55*(1), 16–30. https://doi.org/10.1002/ceas.12030

Chan, C. D., Cor, D. N., & Band, M. P. (2018). Privilege and oppression in counselor education: An intersectionality framework. *Journal of Multicultural Counseling and Development, 46*(1), 58–73. https://doi.org/10.1002/jmcd.12092

Constantine, M. G., & Sue, D. W. (2006). Factors contributing to optimal human functioning in people of color in the United States. *The Counseling Psychologist, 34*(2), 228–244. https://doi.org/10.1177/0011000005281318

Crethar, H. C., Rivera, E. T., & Nash, S. (2008). In search of common threads: Linking multicultural, feminist, and social justice counseling paradigms. *Journal of Counseling & Development, 86*(3), 269–278. https://doi.org/10.1002/j.1556-6678.2008.tb00509.x

Day-Vines, N. L., Bryan, J., & Griffin, D. (2013). The broaching attitudes and behavior survey (BABS): An exploratory assessment of its dimensionality. *Multicultural Counseling and Development, 41*(1), 210–223. https://doi.org/10.1002/j.2161-1912.2013.00037.x

Day-Vines, N. L., Wood, S. M., Grothaus, T., Craigen, L., Holman, A., Dotson-Blake, K., & Douglass, M. J. (2007). Broaching the subjects of race, ethnicity, and culture during the counseling process. *Journal of Counseling & Development, 85*(4), 401–409. https://doi.org/10.1002/j.1556-6678.2007.tb00608.x

Day-Vines, N. L., Cluxton-Keller, F., Agorsor, C., Gubara, S., & Otabil, N. A. A. (2020). The multidimensional model of broaching behavior. *Journal of Counseling & Development, 98*(1), 107–118. https://doi.org/10.1002/jcad.12304

Dewey, J. (1938). *Experience and education.* Collier.

Gonzalez, I. A., & Cokley, R. K. (2021). The case for a core anti-racist course for counselors in training. *Teaching and Supervision in Counseling, 3*(2), 4. https://doi.org/10.7290/tsc030204

Gowin, D. B. (1981). *Educating.* Cornell University Press.

Goodrich, K. M., & Luke, M. (2010). The experiences of school counselors-in-training in group work with LGBTQ adolescents. *The Journal for Specialists in Group Work, 35*(2), 143–159. https://doi.org/10.1080/01933921003705966

Greene, J. H., Barden, S. M., Richardson, E. D., & Hall, K. G. (2014). The influence of film and experiential pedagogy on multicultural counseling self-efficacy and multicultural counseling competence. *Journal of the Scholarship of Teaching and Learning, 14*(5), 62–78. https://doi.org/10.14434/josotl.v14i5.12656

Harrawood, L., McClure, C., & Nelson, J. (2011). Using experiential activities to prepare counselors-in-training to understand the power of cravings when addressing clients with addiction. *Journal of Creativity in Mental Health, 6*(2), 105–117. https://doi.org/10.1080/15401383.2011.579872

Hays, D. G. (2020). Multicultural and social justice counseling competency research: Opportunities for innovation. *Journal of Counseling & Development, 98*(3), 331–344. https://doi.org/10.1002/jcad.12327

Hemmings, C., & Evans, A. M. (2018). Identifying and treating race-based trauma in counseling. *Journal of Multicultural Counseling and Development, 46*(1), 20–39. https://doi.org/10.1002/jmcd.12090

Hilert, A. J., & Tirado, C. (2018). Teaching multicultural counseling with mindfulness: A contemplative pedagogy approach. *International Journal for the Advancement of Counselling, 41*(4), 469–480. https://doi.org/10.1007/s10447-018-9363-x

Jones, J. M., Kawena Begay, K., Nakagawa, Y., Cevasco, M., & Sit, J. (2016). Multicultural counseling competence training: Adding value with multicultural consultation. *Journal of Educational and Psychological Consultation, 26*(3), 241–265. https://doi.org/10.1080/10474412.2015.1012671

Kolb, A. Y., & Kolb, D. A. (2005). Learning styles and learning spaces: Enhancing experiential learning in higher education. *Academy of Management Learning & Education, 4*(2), 193–212. https://doi.org/10.5465/amle.2005.17268566

Lawrence, C., Foster, V. A., & Tieso, C. L. (2015). Creating creative clinicians: Incorporating creativity into Counselor Education. *Journal of Creativity in Mental Health, 10*(2), 166–180. https://doi.org/10.1080/15401383.2014.963188

Loganbill, C., Hardy, E., & Delworth, U. (1982). Supervision: A conceptual model. *The Counseling Psychologist, 10*(1), 3–42. https://doi.org/10.1177/0011000082101002

McAuliffe, G., & Eriksen, K. (2011). *Handbook of counselor preparation: Constructivist, developmental, and experiential approaches.* SAGE.

McCarthy, J. (2017). Teaching creativity: A look beyond counseling. *Journal of Asia Pacific Counseling, 7*(1), 37–45. https://doi.org/10.18401/2017.7.1.4

McGhee, C., Baltrinic, E. R., Laux, J., Clark, M., Liu, Y., & Harmening, D. (2019). A phenomenological investigation of creative teaching in counselor education. *Counselor Education and Supervision, 58*(2), 127–140. https://doi.org/10.1002/ceas.12136

Neville, H., Spanierman, L., & Doan, B. (2006). Exploring the association between color-blind racial ideology and multicultural counseling competencies. *Cultural Diversity & Ethnic Minority Psychology, 12*(2), 275–290. https://doi.org/10.1037/1099-9809.12.2.275

Oatley, K., & Johnson-Laird, P. N. (1987). Towards a cognitive theory of emotions. *Cognition and Emotion, 1*, 29–50. https://doi.org/10.1080/02699938708408362

Piaget, J. (1970). *Psychology and epistemology: Toward a theory of knowledge.* Viking Press.

Poetry Society of America. (n.d.). *Poetry in motion.* https://poetrysociety.org/poetry-in-motion

Ponterotto, J. G., Casas, J. M., Suzuki, L. A., & Alexander, C. M. (Eds.). (2010). *Handbook of multicultural counseling* (3rd ed.). SAGE.

Prikhidko, A., & Swank, J. M. (2018). Emotion regulation for counselors. *Journal of Counseling & Development, 96*(2), 206–212. https://doi-org.ezproxy.liberty.edu/10.1002/jcad.12193

Prikhidko, A., Su, Y. W., Houseknecht, A., & Swank, J. M. (2020). Emotion regulation for counselors-in-training: A grounded theory. *Counselor Education and Supervision, 59*(2), 96–111. https://doi.org/10.1002/ceas.12169

Ratts, M. J., Singh, A. A., Nassar-McMillan, S., Butler, S. K., & McCullough, J. R. (2016). Multicultural and social justice counseling competencies: Guidelines for the counseling profession. *Journal of Multicultural Counseling and Development, 44*(1), 28–48. https://doi.org/10.1002/jmcd.12035

Rogers, C. R. (1961). *On becoming a person: A therapist's view of psychotherapy.* Houghton Mifflin.

Rønnestad, M. H., & Skovholt, T. M. (2003). The journey of the counselor and therapist: Research findings and perspectives on professional development. *Journal of Career Development, 30*(1), 5–44. https://doi.org/10.1177/089484530303000102

Santos, O. D., & Dallos, R., (2012). The process of cross-cultural therapy between White therapists and clients of African-Caribbean descent. *Qualitative Research in Psychology, 9*(1), 62–74. https://doi.org/10.1080/14780887.2012.630827

Shafir, Orkibi, H., Baker, F. A., Gussak, D., & Kaimal, G. (2020). Editorial: The state of the art in creative arts therapies. *Frontiers in Psychology, 11.* https://doi.org/10.3389/fpsyg.2020.00068

Skovholt, T. M. (2001). *The resilient practitioner: Burnout prevention and self-care strategies for counselors, therapists, teachers, and health professionals.* Allyn & Bacon.

Skovholt, T. M., & Rønnestad, M. H. (2003). Struggles of the novice counselor and therapist. *Journal of Career Development, 30*(1), 45–58. https://doi.org/10.1177/089484530303000103

Stoltenberg, C. D., McNeill, B. W., & Delworth, U. (1998). *IDM supervision: An integrated developmental model for supervising counselors and therapists.* Jossey-Bass.

Wasik, S., Barrow, J., Royal, C., Brooks, R., Dames, L., Corry, L. & Bird, C. (2019). Online counselor education: Creative approaches and best practices in online learning environments. *Research on Education and Psychology, 3*(1), 43–52. https://dergipark.org.tr/en/pub/rep/issue/43787/524049

Wolpe, J. (1969). *Subjective Units of Distress Scale (SUDS)* [Database record]. APA PsycTests. https://doi.org/10.1037/t05183-000

Zelan, K. (1991). *The risks of knowing.* Springer Science & Business Media.

Sports Counseling Techniques

Dr. Taunya Marie Tinsley and Dr. Michelle D. Ellis

LEARNING OBJECTIVES

1. Understand that sports counseling has emerged as a specialization in the fields of counseling and psychology and understand the unique challenges and opportunities in providing counseling services within the context of sports that are accomplished through a proactive, growth-oriented approach that incorporates the principles of counseling, career development, movement science, psychology, and human development. The terms "sports counseling" and "athletic counseling" are used interchangeably within this chapter to describe the emerging field.
2. Develop awareness of personal biases and cultural assumptions that may influence counseling interactions with athletes from diverse backgrounds.
3. Explore models related to multicultural counseling and social justice, with a specific focus on their application in sports counseling.
4. Develop effective communication skills (e.g., attending, listening, and influencing skills) to engage with athletes from diverse cultural backgrounds, fostering trust and understanding.
5. Demonstrate ethical decision-making and cultural competence in counseling practices, ensuring the well-being of athletes while respecting their cultural backgrounds and identities.

LEARNING OUTCOMES

1. Demonstrate awareness of one's own emotions, triggers, and countertransference reactions, and employ self-reflection techniques to manage them effectively.
2. Demonstrate empathy and respect for diverse client experiences and perspectives, fostering a therapeutic environment that is inclusive and affirming.
3. Apply appropriate boundaries, ethical guidelines, and cultural competence in the counseling relationship, ensuring a safe and supportive environment for clients.
4. Employ evidence-based counseling interventions tailored to clients' unique needs, informed by counselor self-awareness and an understanding of the client's worldview.

Introduction

"Sport permeates all aspects of society; that is even a person with very little interest in sport will interact with it in some way" (Leslie-Toogood, 2008, p. 9). Additionally, sports are so ingrained in the social and cultural life of American society that they have become a reflection of American society and an inherent component of the national cultural identity (McDuff, 2012). Sport sociologists believe "sport is a microcosm of society," meaning every conceivable activity that occurs in society also occurs in sport (e.g., racism, sexism, commercialism, education, socialization, mental health challenges, and mental illness; Sailes & Harrison, 2008; Steinfeldt et al., 2010).

In July 2021, tennis star Naomi Osaka stated, "It's O.K. not to be O.K.!" after withdrawing from the French Open to take care of herself mentally (Osaka, 2021).

> Popular and social media quickly ignited, with Osaka facing both global admiration and admonishment. Other prominent athletes such as Serena Williams, Usain Bolt, and mental health advocate Michael Phelps, quickly voiced their support, and the mental health wellness app Calm went viral as the organization offered to cover Osaka's fines. (Meister & Lavanchy, 2021)

Soon after Osaka's withdrawal from the French Open, Simone Biles withdrew from the both the team final and all-around final at the Tokyo Olympics, citing her mental health struggles and her struggles to perform with the "twisties" (i.e., a mental block wherein competitors can lose track of where they are while in midair; Kallingall, 2021). Recent instances of these and other high-profile athletes prioritizing their mental health have triggered an important shift in the narrative of mental health in sports and the need for sports counseling services and multicultural sports counseling competent professionals that utilize sports counseling techniques (Cole & Tinsley, 2009; Meister & Lavanchy, 2021; Ward et al., 2005).

Literature Review

Multicultural and Social Justice Counseling Competencies (MSJCC) and Sports Counseling

For over 40 years, the developmental needs and concerns of athletes who require professional assistance have been highlighted in the literature on athletes and athletic counseling (Chartrand & Lent, 1987; Danish et al., 1993; Goldberg & Chandler, 1995; Heyman, 1986; Hinkle, 1994; Parham, 1993; Pearson & Petitpas, 1990; Stryer et al., 1998). However, the development of preparation programs for educating counselors for this specific population came long after the practice of counseling athletes had begun (Miller & Wooten, 1995). The competencies for athletic counseling were first outlined in 1995 as part of the Association for Counselor Education and Supervisors' project called "Counselors of Tomorrow" (Nejedlo et al., 1985). Nejedlo et al. (1985) wanted to ensure that counselor educators, supervisors, and practicing counselors "were not only maintaining pace with society's development, but also anticipating probable changing needs of our clientele in a society characterized by change" (p. iv). Extending the Nejedlo et al. project, Tinsley (2005) included high school and collegiate counselors and advisors, who provide effective support services to the athlete population. Furthermore, the multicultural sports counseling competencies have been extended to include athletes across the lifespan (i.e., youth sports programs, high-school athletes, collegiate athletes, professional athletes, elite athletes, and recreational and leisure athletes; Cole & Tinsley, 2009; Tinsley, 2008).

Athletic counseling (sports counseling) is defined as

> a process which attempts to assist individuals in maximizing their personal, academic, and athletic potential. This [athletic counseling] is accomplished through a proactive, growth-oriented approach that incorporates the principles of counseling, career development, movement science, psychology, and human development. (Nejedlo et al., 1985, p. 9)

Sports counseling as well as sports psychology are concerned with the athletic performance and the development needs of the athlete population. Whereas sports psychology focuses on "optimal performance and well-being of athletes, developmental and social aspects of sports participation, and systematic issues associated with sports settings and organizations" (Association for Applied Sport Psychology, 2023; American Psychological Association [APA], 2008), sports counseling specifically focuses on athletes' psycho-emotional needs and difficulties as well as their personal and psychosocial development, including personal and clinical issues (Hinkle, 1994; Pinkerton, 2009; Valentine & Taub, 1999).

Athletes face similar developmental challenges as those encountered by nonathletes (Cole & Tinsley, 2009; Fogaca, 2021; Loughran, 2019; Moreland et al., 2018). However, many athletes' difficulties are manifested by sport retirement; coping with injuries; role changes, public scrutiny; athletic achievement; identify formation and conflict; alcohol and substance abuse; interpersonal relationships; career development and decision-making; and intellectual, physical, or interpersonal competence (Tinsley, 2005; Etzel, 2009; Loughran, 2019). Additionally, athletic participating produces a patterned demand on athletes that results from long days; exhaustion; the pressure of competition; injury; pain; disappointment; and the requirement to balance sport with other important activities, such as school, relaxation, and socializing with family and friends (Fogaca, 2021; McDuff, 2012; Moreland et al., 2018). Furthermore, the demands of participating in sports may produce disruptions in sleep, energy, appetite, and an increase in daily stressors that could lead to mental illness if not well managed (Barnard, 2016; Etzel, 2009; Loughran, 2019; McDuff, 2012).

McDuff (2012, p. 8) identifies four stress reaction patterns that can interfere with performance [and life balance]:

- Anxiety (active thinking, worrying, arousal, tension, and poor sleep)
- Depression (disappointment, sadness, isolation, loneliness, negative thinking, loss of confidence, and crying spells)
- Anger (frustration, irritation, critical comments, impatience, acting out, and fights)
- Somatic symptoms (pain, gastrointestinal upset, rapid breathing and heart rate, chest pain, skin eruptions, and headaches)

Athletes can have one or several of these stress responses, which can impact emotional well-being and health behaviors, where higher levels of stress increase the likelihood of mental health issues and behaviors that are detrimental to health (Fogaca, 2021; Loughran, 2019; Moreland et al., 2018). Although these concerns vary from athlete to athlete, many experience the negative consequences of sports participation and competition on their overall development (thus the rationale for sports counseling, multicultural sports counseling competent professionals, and specific sports counseling techniques).

Multicultural Sports Counseling Competencies

The multicultural and social justice movements, the "fourth force in counseling" and the "fifth force in counseling," have transformed the thinking and practices of many helping practitioners and has contributed to the profession's greater and much needed understanding and appreciation of differences among racial, ethnic and cultural groups (D'Andrea & Heckman, 2008; Pedersen, 1991; Pope et al., 2004; Ratts et al., 2016). For more than 20 years, the training of professionals who can meet the needs of an increasingly diverse population has presented challenges (Holcomb-McCoy, 2001; Pope et al., 2004; Pope-Davis et al., 2003). By extending the principles of multicultural counseling to include the athlete population, counselors may be in a better position to receive formalized training beyond the basic counselor preparation, respond to the developmental needs of athletes, and enhance the quality of services they provide (Miller & Wooten, 1995; Pinkerton, 2009).

Athletes face myriad complex demands, stressors, and challenges due to their involvement with sports (Cole, 2006; Cole & Tinsley, 2009; Nejedlo et al., 1985; Tinsley, 2005). Thus, it is imperative that counselors who work with the athlete population acquire knowledge and skills beyond the basic counselor preparation as well as an awareness of self, perceptions, biases, or preconceived notions about this group (Cole, 2006; Cole & Tinsley, 2009; Nejedlo et al., 1985; Tinsley, 2005). "Training counselors who can address the unique needs of the athlete population, a group not always thought of as a specific and diverse culture, presents many challenges. Like many cultural groups, athletes may be underserved by counseling services" (Cole & Tinsley, 2009, p. 523). Care must be taken to provide effective counseling services (Etzel, 2009; Goldberg & Chandler, 1995; Valentine & Taub, 1999). Although the athletic environment may be alien to many professional counselors, one who is both open to learning and empathic, can grasp the meaning to the athlete client (Heyman, 1986).

Counselors who work with the athlete population should be culturally competent, including being multicultural sport counseling competent. Counselors should also have specialized knowledge and skills beyond their basic counselor preparation as well as an awareness of biases, misperceptions, and prejudices toward the athlete population (Cole, 2006; Nejedlo et al., 1985; Pinkerton, 2009; Tinsley, 2005). McDuff states that mental health clinicians who work with athletes

> need developmental and cultural competencies that address differences in gender, ethnicity, sexual orientation, geographic region, religion, values, philosophy, and politics. They can help athletes and coaches understand the potential strengths of these differences by discovering and revealing the common struggles and values within the detailed narrative of each athlete's life and unique family history. (2012, p. 228)

Tinsley (2005) developed the multicultural sports counseling competencies that utilize statements and language from the Multicultural Counseling Inventory (Sodowsky et al., 1994) and have been modified to be more inclusive of the athlete population.

By extending the principles of the multicultural and social justice competencies to include the athlete population, professional counselors as well as counselor educators and supervisors may be in a better position to receive formalized training, respond to the developmental and clinical needs of athletes, and enhance the quality of counseling services they provided to a specific and diverse culture. In 2005, Tinsley defined Multicultural Sports Counseling Competencies as the extent to which the counselor has developed and integrated the awareness, knowledge, and skills (and techniques), while maintaining a positive counseling relationship necessary to work with the athlete population (Sodowsky et al., 1994; Tinsley, 2005). These four dimensions are briefly outlined in the Table 16.1. While each of these dimensions are imperative to review and implement into clinical practice among athletes, the authors will further review multicultural techniques among the athlete population.

TABLE 16.1 Multicultural Sports Counseling Competencies

Multicultural Awareness	Multicultural Counseling Knowledge
The proactive multicultural sensitivity and responsiveness toward diverse athletes, extensive interactions and life experiences with sport and athletes, broad-based cultural understanding, advocacy within institutions.	The ability to conduct culturally relevant case conceptualization and treatment strategies, assess diverse cultural information, and conduct multicultural counseling research with athletes.
Multicultural Counseling Skills (and Techniques)	Multicultural Counseling Relationship
The retention of diverse athlete cases, recognition of and recovery from cultural mistakes, use of non-traditional methods of assessment, counselor self-monitoring, and tailoring structured versus unstructured counseling sessions to the needs of athletes.	The counselor's interaction process with diverse athletes, such as the counselor's trustworthiness, comfort level, stereotypes of athletes, and worldview.

Multicultural Techniques in Counseling

To better assist the athlete population as a culturally diverse population, it is imperative that counselors are trained to utilize techniques and skills that are most beneficial in establishing a therapeutic alliance within session and are proven to assist in addressing clients presenting concerns within clinical practice (Young, 2017). Foundational counseling techniques, such as the reflection of feelings (the recognition and identification of clients' emotional state), the reflection of meaning (the retelling of the significance of a client event), summarizing (a brief synopsis of a session), paraphrasing (reflecting story content and client thoughts), open- and closed-ended questions (questions requiring short, factual, yes/no responses and questions that allow for explanation and interpretation), immediacy (the ability to discuss what is occurring between counselor and client in the here and now), silence (an intentional pause in dialogue between counselor and client), and confrontation (the identification of discrepancies between a client's beliefs, behaviors, nonverbals and/or cognitions) are all vital skills for a counselor to develop and utilize with all clients (Ladany, 2004; Turock, 1980; Young, 2017). Building on these concepts, the techniques outlined within this chapter are targeted for use among the athlete population as a culturally diverse community in clinical practice. Thus, the skills of metacognitive strategies, broaching, and multicultural (cross-cultural) communication will be explored.

METACOGNITIVE STRATEGIES

Having the awareness required to identify one's own thinking and thought process is known as *metacognition* (Gredler, 2009). Metacognition requires the utilization of problem solving and goal development skills (Wilkinson, 2011). While clinical supervision is available for counselors, clinical practice is often performed independently, which emphasizes the necessity of metacognition skills (Mitchell & Brooks, 2022). Through a meta-analysis of metacognitive strategies, scholars have found a significant co-occurrence of the metacognitive strategies and cognitive functions, such as reasoning, critical thinking and problem-solving (Mitsea & Drigas, 2019). While standardized strategies for engaging in metacognition are debated in literature, metacognitive regulation is known to include aspects of (a) self-planning, (b) self-monitoring, and (c) self-evaluation (Mitsea & Drigas, 2019). Thus, engaging in the use of metacognition, a growth, not fixed, mindset is required (Claro et al., 2016).

More specifically, counselors are recommended to establish their own personal and professional goals designed to self-regulate when working with athletes. For this reason, the utilization of SMART goals may benefit counselors engaging with the athlete population and may be a way to assess the implementation, frequency, and degree to which the other counseling techniques are used in clinical practice. For goals to assist in the use of metacognition, SMART goals must be *specific* and narrow, to allow for achievability; *measurable*, to describe the proof necessary to evaluate progress or outcomes; *attainable*, to ensure one's current set of skills and abilities are present to achieve the goal; *relevant*, to ensure the goal relate and align with one's long-term goals; and *time-bound* (*time-based*), to establish a realistic task completion date (Kiresuk & Sherman, 1968).

SMART Goal Example

Counselor: Alex

Client: Jamie

Presenting Concern: High-school volleyball player struggling with body image

Background: Jamie is a 17-year-old high-school volleyball player, who has been experiencing body image issues, leading to a decline in her self-esteem and performance on the court. Alex, her counselor, has found herself becoming emotionally invested and relating too closely to Jamie's struggles. Alex understands the importance of maintaining professional boundaries and wants to set SMART goals to address this challenge.

SMART Goal

Alex will identify when she starts feeling overly empathetic in session with Jamie, will use a self-assessment tool after each session to track her emotional regulation and will demonstrate improved emotional regulation, as evidenced by lower self-assessment ratings of emotional involvement over the next four months.

Integrating metacognition with one's clinical practice not only encourages engagement in lifelong learning and continuing education, but it also requires clinicians to work toward skill expansion, like the way athletes are required to during performance training and practice. Furthermore, the binding of cognitive and metacognitive abilities will assist in the uncovering of one's true self (Mitsea & Drigas, 2019), a teachable, transferable skill that may be beneficial for the athlete population.

BROACHING

Broaching refers to the deliberate and intentional efforts to discuss racial, ethnic, and cultural (REC) concerns that may impact a client's presenting issue (Day-Vines et al., 2007). With this in mind, clinical concerns and issues may not only present differently depending upon one's cultural identities and values, but REC may also impact the language used by a client, meaning and purpose a client associates with counseling topics, and the acceptance and potential stigma associated with counseling subjects.

TABLE 16.2 Potential Impact of Broaching on the Counseling Process

Broaching Style	Description of Counselor Behavior
Avoidant	- Maintains a race-neutral perspective and argues that issues relating to representation and race require little attention - Tends to minimize REC differences, focuses on cultural unity based on their humanity, and contends racial oppression should not exist
Isolating	- Addresses issues of race and representation in a superficial manner - Assumes this activity can be removed from a prescribed list of counseling responsibilities
Continuing/Incongruent	- Invites clients to explore the relationship between their presenting problems and issues related to REC - May ask about race several times
Integrated/Congruent	- Can distinguish among and between culture-specific behaviors and unhealthy human functioning - Recognizes complexities associated with REC and acknowledge the vast heterogeneity that characterizes culturally diverse clients
Infusing	- Represents broaching through a way of being, not just integrated in the counseling process as a professional obligation - Considers broaching a lifestyle orientation

Note. Information within table was collected via broaching the subjects of race, ethnicity, and culture during the counseling process.

A failure to effectively broach REC concerns with clients is harmful considering actions or inactions may preserve the dominant culture's cultural standards and paradigms (Day-Vines et al., 2020). For this reason, the integration of active broaching behaviors is suggested for all clinicians. In fact, it is recommended that clinicians practice broaching similarly to other counseling techniques, in an effort to integrate the language required to explore one's REC concerns as well as to test out a counselor's style and timing (Day-Vines et al., 2018; King & Borders, 2019). At the core of broaching lies the act of bringing societal taboo topics into the counseling realm using accessible, deliberate, and significant methods (Cardemil & Battle, 2003; Day-Vines et al., 2020).

MULTICULTURAL CROSS-CULTURAL COMMUNICATION

The dynamics involved in the exchange of messages and information across cultures best describes what is known as "multicultural (cross-cultural) communication" (Mitchell & Brooks, 2022). Given the many types and forms of cultures that exist in society, it's important to acknowledge that multicultural communication does not just encompass communication efforts between languages, dialects, and colloquialisms. Multicultural communication also involves nonverbal facial cues, power distances, ethnolects, and sociolects (Mitchell & Brooks, 2022).

To uncover, unpack, and better understand the many dimensions and dynamics of communication present when engaging with athletes, counselors must become "data collectors." Counselors are called to actively seek out information about cultural groups they encounter in various clinical or consultative settings. This entails soliciting information about aspects of these cultural groups that may be unknown to them (McDuff, 2012), which means counselors who work with athletes face a critical clinical task. Their role involves being curious and outgoing, and they should have a specific intention to gain a deeper understanding of the various cultural groups present on a team or the specific cultural background of individual athletes (McDuff, 2012).

Given the increased use of technology for communication following the social isolation caused by the COVID-19 pandemic (Ogbogu et al., 2022), clinicians must remain attuned to the use and presence of multicultural communication through a variety of means. Thus, multicultural communication can occur in physical settings; however, it's crucial to recognize that communication can also occur through technology. Hence, it is imperative for clinicians to consider the use of the aforementioned skills through telehealth as well as via in-person service delivery.

THE CASE STUDY OF LARRY JONES

Overview of Case

Larry Jones was referred to counseling following the basketball season by one of the staff pastors at a local church. Larry is a member of the church and volunteers with numerous ministries. This is Larry's first time in counseling, and he is very skeptical about the process but is willing to try. Larry admits that the only reason he chose this counselor is because they are Black and utilize a culture-centered counseling, or multicultural and social justice counseling, process. Larry's presenting issues from the client's perspective is that he needs assistance with making good decisions, managing his anger, and becoming a better Christian. Larry admits to making spur-of-the-moment, unhealthy decisions and is feeling empty since the death of his father last year. In addition to losing his father, Larry's girlfriend of 2 years ended their relationship 3 months ago. Larry admits to being very angry lately, especially at his daughters' mother, who is seeking full parental custody of their daughters, due to Larry's financial situation. Larry is a 20-year-old Black male. He is currently single with a 3-year-old daughter, of whom he has parental custody. Larry is a junior student–athlete majoring in secondary education at a historically Black college and university (HBCU). He is a division II scholarship recipient basketball player. Larry admits that during his second year in college, he began feeling depressed but never sought counseling due to the stigmas of being a Black male seeking mental health counseling as well as the stigmas associated with athletes seeking mental health counseling. Larry stated the following within the first session:

> I really do not know what is going on with me. I just feel anxious and depressed. I just want some peace. I feel as if my soul is trapped at times. I want to be loved, but there are so few people that can handle my needs. I feel that all I have been doing is getting angry at people who try to tell me what I should do and when. I need to get back to working out and losing all this weight I have gained since the end of the season, but I just have so much on my plate with raising a daughter, school, and basketball. I feel my emptiness and frustration with food. Being raised in a Black family, you know what it's like to be taught to eat when you are happy, sad, angry, or whatever. It doesn't make a difference, but I still try to gorge myself with food as if I am trying to fill a hole inside of me.

Sports Counseling Techniques Guiding Questions

1. How can we incorporate metacognitive strategies into Larry's counseling process to help him become more aware of and reflect on his impulsive decision-making patterns and emotional responses?
2. In addressing Larry's cultural preferences for counseling, what are some effective broaching techniques we can use to explore his experiences as a Black male, considering the potential impact of race, ethnicity, and cultural concerns on his mental health?
3. What multicultural communication approaches can be employed to establish a strong therapeutic alliance with Larry and ensure he feels heard and understood as he discusses his feelings of emptiness, frustration, and the cultural aspects related to his eating habits?
4. How can we help Larry navigate the intersection of his roles as a student–athlete, single parent, and person seeking mental health support, all while addressing his concerns about stigma? What metacognitive strategies can we implement to assist him in managing these demands effectively?

Conclusion

Implications for Professional Development

There are several implications for professional development that should be considered. Athletes have a culture of their own with special issues and unique developmental needs (Cole & Tinsley, 2009; Harris et al., 2003; Jolly, 2008; Stambulova & Alfermann, 2009). As such, it is important for counseling professionals to not only be aware of their own cultural influences but also do their best to increase their awareness and knowledge of their athlete client's cultural background. International status, race, ethnicity, gender, and religion can all affect athletes' goals and objectives for participating and competing in sports (Cole, 2006; Cole & Tinsley, 2009; Steinfeldt et al., 2010; Tinsley, 2005). Athletes, like other minority groups, can also face oppression, prejudice, and discrimination (Baucom & Lantz, 2001; Simons et al., 2007; Steinfeldt et al., 2010).

By extending the principles of multicultural counseling and the cross-cultural psychology approach to include the athlete population, practitioners may be in a better position to respond to the developmental needs of athletes and enhance the quality of services they provide (Pinkerton, 2009; Stambulova & Alfermann, 2009; Tinsley, 2005; Ward et al., 2005). As with many cultural groups, athletes face a multitude of complex demands, stressors, and challenges that may extend outside the issues normally addressed by traditional counseling and psychological services (Etzel, 2009; Tinsley, 2005; Ward et al., 2005). To this point, the American Counseling Association recognized a need for specialized training more than 25 years ago and published a set of sports counseling competencies (Nejedlo et al., 1985). More recently, Tinsley (2005) developed multicultural sports counseling competencies, consisting of four dimensions for professional counselors, and Ward et al. (2005) identified 17 essential competencies for psychologists working with athletes.

Tinsley (2005) and Ward and colleagues' (2005) competencies both are categorized within the domains of attitudes/beliefs, knowledge, and skills, and they promote counseling awareness and sensitivity within the sport culture. More specifically, Ward and colleagues' competencies were designed to assist counseling professionals not trained in sport psychology to identify areas where further education, training, and experiences are needed to ensure effective and ethical service delivery. They believed developing and having

> competencies will (a) help psychologists and students not trained in sport psychology identify areas in which they need further education, training, or experiences in order to competently work with athlete clients; (b) further define the specialty of athlete-counseling; and (c) assist athlete clients, as well as non-athlete clients, to distinguish among available psychological services. (Ward et al., p. 321)

Additionally, counselors who are accustomed to working with clients in clinical settings, often find that clinical work with athletes is quite different from their traditional practice (Danish et al., 1993). The athletic system can be so narrowly focused that it becomes a closed system, where non-participants are seen as outsiders. Many athletes and coaches have reservations about working with clinicians whose lack of understanding of the sports environment can result in behaviors that are intrusive and potentially harmful to performance (Orlick & Partington, 1987; Petitpas & Tinsley, 2014; Van Raalte et al., 1992).

To gain access to the sports system, counselors and other helping professionals must demonstrate a general understanding of the sport environment and an appreciation for what athletes go through during practices and competitions (Danish et al., 1993). Counselors trained with a basic understanding of the sports sciences and who have experience as an athlete have clear advantages over their non-sports-oriented colleagues in gaining entry to the sports world. Counselors can enhance their knowledge and expertise related to sports by reading relevant literature, attending professional meetings related to sports counseling and sports psychology, talking to athletes and coaches, assisting with sports teams, becoming involved in sport and exercise themselves as participants, and observing the athletes and teams with whom they would like to work. It is critical to become familiar with the culture, rules, and language of sports to be effective.

Ethical issues may arise from counselors' lack of multicultural sports counseling competence, which may impact service delivery to the unique cultural group of athletes (Constantine & Ladany, 2001; Tinsley, 2005). It may behoove counselors to familiarize themselves with their appropriate professional organization's ethical codes and principles. Professional organizations have developed ethical codes to serve as guides for helping professionals' practice with clients and to increase the probability that counselors will not harm their clients and provide quality service (Kocet, 2006). For example, those who provide counseling services to athletes can use the ACA's Code of Ethics

(2014), the APA's Ethical Principles of Psychologists and Code of Conduct (2017), the Association for Applied Sport Psychology Ethical Principles and Standards (2011), and the MSJCC (Ratts et al., 2016).

Future Directions of Sports Counseling and Sports Counseling Techniques

The recent national attention given to the challenges athletes face has generated much-needed discussions regarding athlete mental health, the developmental needs of athletes, and the athlete culture. The information within this chapter in context with past research has significant implications to the provision of multicultural sports counseling training to counselors who work with athletes. Taken as a whole, the results of previous studies indicated a need for counselors and other helping professionals to be skilled and appropriately trained in sports counseling.

Future directions for counseling athletes should include strengthened training programs and professionals' awareness of multicultural sports-counseling competencies. Those designing curriculum in counselor education programs; student affairs; and student development in higher education, among others, may want to consider implementing strategies to address multicultural sports counseling training among counselor trainees. Those heading counselor education programs may want to incorporate the athlete population as part of the multicultural counseling course curriculum. Masters- and doctoral-level counselors could also be invited to sign up for these courses. The course developers may want to develop a complete course devoted to the mental health developmental needs of the athlete population that includes counseling during crisis situations. For example, Springfield College, California University of Pennsylvania, and Duquesne University have offered a three-credit course, Issues and Techniques in Counseling Athletes, based on the competencies and model developed by Nejedlo et al. (1985). The courses examined current counseling strategies, including counseling techniques, used with members of sports teams at the youth, high school, college, and professional levels.

A degree or certificate program in sports counseling may be useful to the increasingly diverse counseling profession as well as to other helping professionals interested in working with the athlete population. The many subscribers to the ACA's Sports Counseling Interest Network, the National Association of Academic and Student–Athlete Development Professionals, and the Association for Applied Sport Psychology may be interested in programs to prepare them for work with the athlete population. Currently, California University of Pennsylvania offers an online nine-credit sports counseling certificate that began in 2009. The certificate program is open to bachelor's-, master's-, and doctoral-level students and professionals. Furthermore, the first author of this chapter is working with a national, interactive platform of behavioral health professionals to develop a sports counseling certification program with advanced continuing education opportunities.

Recommendations for Counselors and Other Helping Professionals

There are several recommendations for helping professionals desiring to provide mental health services to athletes. For instance, given the insurgence of mental health awareness among professional athletes, it may be helpful for counselors to consider integrating pop culture influences within their clinical practice and sports counseling research. Knowing that six of the biggest U.S. sports unions (e.g., NFL Players Association, National Basketball Players Association, National Hockey League Players Association, MLB Players Association, MLS

Players Association, and Women's National Basketball Players Association) have been united to promote mental health awareness on both global and national levels (Golden, 2023), it may serve the athletic community to utilize the stories of professional athletes within clinical practice to normalize mental health.

Furthermore, as the world becomes more interconnected and with the use of social media having become prevalent, understanding the role the internet and media platforms play in athletes' perception of self and others is imperative. For instance, literature outlines how the presence of enhancement and filter-free photos is known to result in lower facial dissatisfaction compared to standard Instagram photos of the same women (Tiggmann & Zinoviev, 2019). This is merely one example of the impact that social media has had on self-concept, which has implications for clinical work with athletes. Social media has the potential to amplify the comparison of physique, performance, and popularity among athletes.

CHAPTER SUMMARY

Like many cultural groups, athletes are confronted with a multitude of complex demands, stressors, and challenges, for which they may be underserved by professional counseling services. Professional counselors who work with the athlete population should be competent in multicultural sports counseling and should have specialized knowledge and skills beyond their basic counselor preparation. Professional counselors must also be aware of the developmental and mental health challenges facing athletes as well as be appropriately trained to utilize multicultural techniques to the athlete population.

In this chapter, we highlighted some of the key foundational counseling techniques, including metacognition strategies and broaching, that can be utilized with the athlete population. In addition, a review of the literature that connected the athlete population as a unique cultural group, the role of helping professionals who work with athletes, and the multicultural sports counseling competencies were provided. Multicultural techniques in sports counseling, including multicultural cross-cultural communication, were also explained and applied to a case study with guiding questions and suggestions for working with athletes. Finally, we discussed recommendations and ethical issues for counselors and other helping professionals who work with the athlete population as well as implications for professional development.

CHAPTER REFLECTION AND DISCUSSION QUESTIONS

The following reflection questions are based on the multicultural sports-counseling competencies (Sodowsky et al., 1994; Tinsley, 2005):

1. Are counselors multiculturally aware or proactive in their sensitivity and responsiveness toward athletes? Do counselors have extensive interactions and life experiences with sports and athletes? Do they have a broad-based understanding of the athlete culture? Enjoy the athlete population? Have an increased athlete caseload?

2. Are counselors multiculturally knowledgeable or able to conduct culturally relevant case conceptualization and treatment strategies?
3. Are counselors multiculturally skilled or successful with the retention of athlete cases by utilizing nontraditional methods of assessment?
4. Are counselors able to develop a multicultural therapeutic relationship or interaction process with athletes?
5. What challenges may you encounter while implementing metacognitive strategies, and how did you address them? Consider both individual athlete differences and the context of the sports environment.
6. In what ways may you adapt your communication style to effectively connect with athletes from diverse cultural backgrounds? Reflect on any cultural nuances you considered and how you tailor your approach to build rapport.
7. Reflect on your own comfort level with broaching challenging subjects. Have there been situations in which you hesitated to address an issue, and if so, what were the reasons? How can you enhance your confidence in broaching difficult topics in the future?

ADDITIONAL RESOURCES

Books

Loughran, M. (2019). *Counseling and psychological services for college student athletes.* FiT Publishing.

McCarthy, P., & Moffat, Z. (Eds.). (2023). *Counselling skills in applied sport psychology: Learning how to counsel.* Routledge.

Nathanson, B., & Kimmel, A. (2008). *The college athlete's guide to academic success: Tips from peers and profs.* Pearson/Prentice Hall.

Petitpas, A., Champagne, D., Chartrand, J., Danish, S., & Murphy, S. (1997). *Athlete's guide to career planning: Keys to success from the playing field to professional life.* Human Kinetics.

Stull, T., Kamis, D., & Glick, I. D. (2018). *The International Society for Sports Psychiatry manual of sports psychiatry.* Routledge.

Journals

Journal of Applied Sport Psychology—https://appliedsportpsych.org/
Sport, Exercise, and Performance Psychology—https://www.apa.org/pubs/journals/spy

Professional Organizations and Websites

Academics in Motion (AIM)—http://www.academicsinmotion.org/
The AthLife Foundation—https://athlifefoundation.org/
American Counseling Association's Sports Counseling Interest Network—https://www.counseling.org/aca-community/aca-connect/interest-networks
Association for Applied Sport Psychology (AASP)—https://appliedsportpsych.org/
International Society of Sport Psychology (ISSP)—https://issponline.org/
The National Association of Academic and Student-Athlete Development Professionals—http://nfoura.nacda.com/home

Online Media

The Sport Psychology Show—https://podcasts.apple.com/us/podcast/the-sport-psych-show/id1434313037

The Mental Side Podcast—https://www.youtube.com/@MentalGamePods

Psychology Today Sports Section—https://www.psychologytoday.com/us/basics/sport-and-competition

REFERENCES

American Counseling Association. (2014). *2014 ACA code of ethics*. https://www.counseling.org/resources/aca-code-of-ethics.pdf

American Psychological Association. (2008). *APA sport psychology proficiency*. https://www.apadivisions.org/division-47/about/sport-proficiency

American Psychological Association. (2017). *Ethical principles of psychologists and code of conduct*. https://www.apa.org/ethics/code

Association for Applied Sport Psychology. (2023). *About sport & performance psychology*. https://appliedsportpsych.org/about-the-association-for-applied-sport-psychology/about-sport-and-performance-psychology/

Association for Applied Sport Psychology. (2011). *Ethics code: AASP ethical principles and standards*. https://appliedsportpsych.org/about-the-association-for-applied-sport-psychology/ethics/ethics-code/

Barnard, J. D. (2016). Student-athletes' perceptions of mental illness and attitudes toward help-seeking. *Journal of College Student Psychotherapy*, *30*(3), 161–175. https://www.doi.org/10.1080/87568225.2016.1177421

Cardemil, E. V., & Battle, C. L. (2003). Guess who's coming to therapy? Getting comfortable with conversations about race and ethnicity in psychotherapy. *Professional Psychology: Research and Practice*, *34*(3), 278.

Chartrand, J. M., & Lent, R. W. (1987). Sports counseling: Enhancing the development of the student-athlete. *Journal of Counseling & Development*, *66*(4), 164–167.

Claro, S., Paunesku, D., & Dweck, C. S. (2016). Growth mindset tempers the effects of poverty on academic achievement. *Proceedings of the National Academy of Sciences*, *113*(31), 8664–8668.

Cole, K. W. (2006). *An examination of school counselors' knowledge and perceptions of recruited student-athletes* (Unpublished doctoral dissertation). University of Iowa. Dissertation Abstracts International, 67, 2891.

Cole, K. W., & Tinsley, T. M. (2009). Sports counseling. In American Counseling Association (Ed.), *The ACA encyclopedia of counseling* (pp. 522–524). American Counseling Association.

Day-Vines, N. L., Wood, S. M., Grothaus, T., Craigen, L., Holman, A., Dotson-Blake, K., & Douglass, M. J. (2007). Broaching the subjects of race, ethnicity, and culture during the counseling process. *Journal of Counseling & Development*, *85*(4), 401–409.

Day-Vines, N. L., Cluxton-Keller, F., Agorsor, C., Gubara, S., & Otabil, N. A. A. (2020). The multidimensional model of broaching behavior. *Journal of Counseling & Development*, *98*(1), 107–118.

Day-Vines, N. L., Booker Ammah, B., Steen, S., & Arnold, K. M. (2018). Getting comfortable with discomfort: Preparing counselor trainees to broach racial, ethnic, and cultural factors with clients during counseling. *International Journal for the Advancement of Counselling, 40*, 89–104.

Danish, S. J., Petitpas, A. J., & Hale, B. D. (1993). Life development intervention for athletes: Life skills through sports. *The Counseling Psychologist, 21*(3), 352–385.

D'Andrea, M., & Heckman, E. F. (2008). Contributing to the ongoing evolution of the multicultural counseling movement: An introduction to the special issue. *Journal of Counseling & Development, 86*(3), 259–261.

Etzel, E. F. (2009). *Counseling and psychological services for college student-athletes.* Fitness Information Technology.

Fogaca, J. L. (2021). Combining mental health and performance interventions: Coping and social support for student-athletes. *Journal of Applied Sport Psychology, 33*(1), 4–19.

Golden, J. (2023, May 2). *Pro sports unions unite to discuss importance of mental health.* CNBC. https://www.cnbc.com/2023/05/01/pro-sports-unions-unite-to-discuss-importance-of-mental-health.html#:~:text=Six%20of%20the%20major%20professional,up%20about%20their%20own%20struggles.

Goldberg, A. D., & Chandler, T. (1995). Sports counseling: Enhancing the development of the high school Student-Athlete. *Journal of Counseling & Development, 74*(1), 39–44.

Gredler, M. E. (2009). *Learning and instruction: Theory into practice.* Merrill Pearson.

Heyman, S. R. (1986). Psychological problem patterns found with athletes. *The Clinical Psychologist, 29*, 68–71.

Hinkle, J. (1994). Integrating sport psychology and sports counseling: Developmental programming, education, and research. *Journal of Sport Behavior, 17*(1), 52–49.

Holcomb-McCoy, C. C. (2001). Multicultural training, self-construals and multicultural competence of school counselors. *Professional School Counseling, 4*, 202–208.

Kallingall, M. (2021, October 22). *Simone Biles opens up about her mental health post-Olympics: "I'm still scared to do gymnastics."* CNN. https://www.cnn.com/2021/10/22/sport/simone-biles-gymnastics-spt/index.html

King, K. M., & Borders, L. D. (2019). An experimental investigation of White counselors broaching race and racism. *Journal of Counseling & Development, 97*(4), 341–351.

Kiresuk, T. J., & Sherman, R. E. (1968). Goal attainment scaling: A general method for evaluating comprehensive community mental health programs. *Community Mental Health Journal, 4*, 443–453.

Ladany, N., Hill, C. E., Thompson, B. J., & O'Brien, K. M. (2004). Therapist perspectives on using silence in therapy: A qualitative study. *Counselling and Psychotherapy Research, 4*(1), 80–89.

Leslie-Toogood, L., & Gill, E. (2008). *Advising student-athletes: A collaborative approach to success* (MonographySeries Number 18). National Academic Advising Association.

Loughran, M. (2019). *Counseling and psychological services for college student athletes.* FiT Publishing.

McDuff, D. R. (2012). *Sports psychiatry: strategies for life balance and peak performance.* American Psychiatric Pub.

Meister, A., & Lavanchy, M. (2021). *Athletes are shifting the narrative around mental health at work.* Harvard Business Review.

Miller, G. M., & Wooten Jr, H. R. (1995). Sports counseling: A new counseling specialty area. *Journal of Counseling & Development*, *74*(2), 172–173.

Mitchell, M. D. & Brooks, M. (2022). Multicultural techniques in counseling. In S. K. Butler, A. F. Locke, & J. M. Filmore (Eds.), *Introduction to 21st century counseling: A multicultural and social justice approach*. (pp. 170–178). Cognella Academic Publishing.

Mitsea, E., & Drigas, A. (2019). A Journey into the metacognitive learning strategies. *International Journal of Online & Biomedical Engineering*, *15*(14).

Moreland, J. J., Coxe, K. A., & Yang, J. (2018). Collegiate athletes' mental health services utilization: A systematic review of conceptualizations, operationalizations, facilitators, and barriers. *Journal of Sport and Health Science*, *7*(1), 58–69. https://doi.org/10.1016/j.jshs.2017.04.009

Nejedlo, R. J. (1985). Counselors: Helping us live with change. *Wisconsin Vocational Educator*, *9*(3), 2–18.

Ogbogu, P. U., Noroski, L. M., Arcoleo, K., Reese Jr, B. D., & Apter, A. J. (2022). Methods for cross-cultural communication in clinic encounters. *The Journal of Allergy and Clinical Immunology: In Practice*, *10*(4), 893–900.

Osaka, N. (2021, July 8). Naomi Osaka: "it's O.K. not to be O.K." *Time*. https://time.com/6077128/naomi-osaka-essay-tokyo-olympics/

Ogbogu, P. U., Noroski, L. M., Arcoleo, K., Reese Jr, B. D., & Apter, A. J. (2022). Methods for cross-cultural communication in clinic encounters. *The Journal of Allergy and Clinical Immunology: In Practice*, *10*(4), 893–900.

Parham, W. D. (1993). The intercollegiate athlete: A 1990s profile. *The Counseling Psychologist*, *21*(3), 411–429.

Pinkerton, R. (2009). Forward. In E. F. Etzel (Ed.), *Counseling and psychological services for college student-athletes* (pp. viiii–xi). Fitness Information Technology.

Pearson, R. E., & Petitpas, A. J. (1990). Transitions of athletes: Developmental and preventive perspectives. *Journal of Counseling & Development*, *69*(1), 7–10.

Pedersen, P. B. (1991). Multiculturalism as a generic approach to counseling. *Journal of Counseling & Development*, *70*(1), 6–12.

Petitpas, A. J., & Tinsley, T. M. (2014). Counseling interventions in applied sport psychology. In J. L. Van Raalte & B. W. Brewer (Eds.), *Exploring sport and exercise psychology* (pp. 241–259). American Psychological Association. https://doi.org/10.1037/14251-011

Pope, R. L., Reynolds, A. L., & Mueller, J. A. (2004). *Multicultural competence in student affairs*. Jossey-Bass.

Pope-Davis, D. B., Coleman, H. L. K., Liu, W. M., & Toporek, R. L. (Eds.). (2003). *Handbook of multicultural competence for counseling and psychology*. SAGE.

Pope, R. L., Reynolds, A. L., & Mueller, J. A. (2014). *Creating multicultural change on campus*. John Wiley & Sons.

Ratts, M. J., Singh, A. A., Nassar-McMillan, S., Butler, S. K., & McCullough, J. R. (2016). Multicultural and social justice counseling competencies: Guidelines for the counseling profession. *Journal of Multicultural Counseling and Development*, *44*(1), 28–48. https://doi.org/10.1002/jmcd.12035

Sailes, G., & Harrison, L. (2008). Social issues of sport. In A. Leslie-Toogood & E. Gill (Eds.), *Advising student-athletes: A collaborative approach to success* (pp. 13–21). National Academic Advising Association.

Sodowsky, G. R., Taffe, R. C., Gutkin, T. B., & Wise, S. L. (1994). Development of the multicultural counseling inventory: A self-report measure of multicultural competencies. *Journal of Counseling Psychology, 41*, 137–148.

Steinfeldt, J., Reed, C., & Steinfeldt, M. C. (2010). Racial and athletic identity of African American football players at historically Black colleges and universities and predominantly White institutions. *Journal of Black Psychology, 36*(3), 3–24.

Stryer, B. K., Tofler, I. R., & Lapchick, R. (1998). A developmental overview of child and youth sports in society. *Child and Adolescent Psychiatric Clinics, 7*(4), 697–724.

Tiggemann, M., & Zinoviev, K. (2019). The effect of enhancement-free Instagram images and hashtags on women's body image. *Body Image, 31*, 131–138.

Tinsley, T. (2005). The self-reported multicultural sports counseling competencies among professional school counselors and Play It Smart academic coaches (UMI No. 3199518) [Doctoral dissertation, Duquesne University]. *Dissertation Abstracts International, 66* (11), 3942.

Tinsley, T. M. (2008). Advising and counseling high school student-athletes. In A. Leslie-Toogood & E. Gill (Eds.) *Advising student-athletes: A collaborative approach to success* (pp. 139–147). National Academic Advising Association.

Turock, A. (1980). Immediacy in counseling: Recognizing clients' unspoken messages. *Personnel & Guidance Journal, 59*(3).

Valentine, J. J., & Taub, D. J. (1999). Responding to the developmental needs of student athletes. *Journal of College Counseling, 2*(2), 164–179.

Wilkinson, R. T. (2011). Increasing counselor self-awareness: The role of cognitive complexity and metacognition in counselor training programs. *Alabama Counseling Association Journal, 37*(1), 24–32.

Young, M. E. (2017). *Learning the art of helping: Building blocks and techniques.* Pearson.

Appendix

Wellness as a Critical Clinical Technique

Dr. Kellie N. Kirksey, LPCC-S, CRC

You are about to read the shortest and, in my estimation, perhaps the most important section of this textbook. The technique discussed in this appendix is likely to challenge you and incessantly beg for your attention. Wellness is the technique and dedicated path to keep you functioning in an optimal manner, even when you are doubting your ability to complete your courses, questioning your internship hours, or sitting in front of a client feeling like an imposter because you have no idea what to do. A personal wellness practice will support you in those times when you want to cry and give up the idea of becoming a counselor. There will be days when you stay in the bed, avoid friends, and eat too much dark chocolate because life feels far too difficult to handle. What will help you in those moments are your wellness practices and tools you have "tried on" and know from experience can improve the way you feel. If a particular wellness modality helps you feel, perhaps, 5% better, it is, indeed, a worthy pursuit. My personal wellness practice involves an entire suitcase of strategies, including yoga, breathwork, journaling, tree hugging, beating the drum, dancing, personal therapy, and the list of techniques and tools continues (keep reading for a more extensive list). Stop right now, and ask yourself: What are my wellness go-to behaviors? Do I phone a friend? Do I balance my bank account, take a bath, or compose a gratitude journal page?

WELLNESS TOOLS AND STRATEGIES: A SELF-EVALUATION

Write down 3 tools that you are currently using to support your emotional and mental wellness.

1.
2.
3.

> What practice are you willing to engage in weekly for the rest of this semester?
>
> Who is or can be your accountability partner in this wellness journey?
>
> How have you responded in the past when doubt, fear and anxiety was present in your mind and body?
>
> How do you want to respond in the future when doubt and fear arise (and they will)?

A solid dedication to wellness as a personal therapeutic lifestyle is the first technique a helping professional must utilize. Wellness is about making a conscious commitment to continuous and proactive well-being. We cannot serve from a place of emotional and physical emptiness. We cannot perform the duties of our profession if we are not tuned into the needs of our mind, body, and spirit. If I am broken, depressed, and tired and my bank account is overdrawn, how can I show up for my client or myself? This is not to say we must be perfectly balanced humans; it is to emphasize the dire ethical imperative of being dedicated to doing our own personal work. I am offering the framework of wellness as an intentional lifestyle for helping professionals. Replenishing ourselves and being models for our clients is important. Congruent behavior on our behalf encourages our clients and supervisees to practice wellness skills. We become living reminders of these important tools and can share from the point of view of our lived experiences.

How did you take care of yourself today? This is not a rhetorical question. I want to know. Email me your response. Yes, I am checking in on you because you are at the threshold of a profession I love. I am a gatekeeper, and I want you to survive and thrive on this wild journey of life as a clinician. When you are sitting face to face with a client and sharing a technique yet feeling the weight of your own insecurity and fear, give yourself a break. Remind yourself that you are learning and growing, and this is a lifelong process. Being kind to yourself is a wellness practice. You are not an imposter. You are a human on a growth journey, moving through life while learning and expanding. Positive self-talk is a wellness practice. Yelling into a pillow is a wellness practice. There are so many wellness practices, and you get to decide what you will explore and practice. We can't just be the holder of the knowledge of these techniques. We must engage in wellness practices and feel them in our bones. I will share a list of wellness practices I have used over the years, and I invite you to list your own practices and even brainstorms ways you want to explore and expand.

My favorite wellness practices are journaling, drumming, dancing, tea with friends, meditation, yoga, chanting, walks in nature, quiet time alone, listening to music, circle time with close friends, long baths, affirmations, writing, singing, traveling, silence, gazing at flowers, shaking, walking the labyrinth. ... I could continue, but I will stop here. The idea is to cultivate activities that are nourishing and restorative for our nervous systems.

What wellness practice did you engage in today? Again, this is not a rhetorical question. Write down your response, and create a layer of self-accountability. I am checking in on you, to see if you are checking in on yourself, and you must check in on someone else. We must check in on each other as clinicians and as human beings. Counselors are in constant danger of burnout, over-caregiving, codependency, and simply an inability to say "No" to someone in need. Caring too much without a healthy mechanism to restore balance leads to the depletion of one's wellness meter. I have been there.

If I say that wellness must be a priority, then we must first define the term itself. Only then can we explore practical applications, potential roadblocks, and ways various wellness practices can be incorporated into our daily lives.

According to the World Health Organization (WHO), "wellness" is defined as a state of complete physical, mental, and social well-being, not merely the absence of disease or infirmity. Wellness is a process of committing to holistic health on a variety of dimensions that contribute to an overall state of optimal health, or at least close to it. Wellness is an action. We, as clinicians, must get down to action and remain proactive in pursuit of our holistic well-being. I am the first to admit that this is not a consistently challenge-free path. I could be engaged in a great routine of walking, gym, and meditation, and then one thing may happen that throws a wrench in my routine, and before I know it, I am sidelined, and my wellness practice lands in a heap on the side of the road. I can have the best intentions in the world but when confronted with a warm chocolate chip cookie on a cold afternoon, I might dive into that cookie and forget about the inflammation-producing sugar that will leave me lethargic and temporarily off my wellness path. In my humble opinion, as a counselor educator, who has taught counseling for health and wellness and presented globally on self-care and well-being, I firmly believe self-compassion must be an integral ingredient of one's life for the practice of wellness to be a fundamental part of one's daily life. Paying attention to our needs and being engaged in the holistic preservation of our whole self requires personal commitment at the highest level. Self-kindness and self-compassion are one hundred percent required on the wellness journey. Roadblocks to wellness are overflowing. Perfection and self-judgment must be thrown out of the equation of our life. Being rigid with ourselves will lead to self-criticism and a lifestyle devoid of flexibility and self-compassion. When we overdraw our bank account, have donuts for dinner, or skimp on movement, we must give ourselves a large dose of compassion to begin again. We are human beings on a journey, and beginning again is a natural part of that journey. Wellness is not about perfection. Wellness is about holding an inner compass directed at holistic health and wellness and course correcting when necessary; it will always be necessary to call ourselves back to wellness again and again.

We must be practical with our own wellness expectations. As we sit with clients, students, and supervisees, we must encourage self-kindness on this wellness journey. As noted, there will be roadblocks on your path that take the shape of milkshakes, late nights, overscheduling, substances, and a host of human doings that don't support our holistic wellness. Canceling the image of the perfect clinician and offering ourselves deep compassion as we are engaging in the triumphs and challenges of life. Wellness is like a highway destination. Sometimes, we hop off at the wrong exit, and sometimes, we get derailed by a tire blowout. Sometimes, we are simply distracted by the sparkly scenery and run ourselves off the road. We will need to invite wellness back into our lives on countless occasions. Wellness is, indeed, a journey—a continuum of calling ourselves back in a most compassionate way.

As students and future clinicians, now is the perfect time to make a commitment to self-care and wellness. Wellness is really the act of loving your future self enough to make choices that are in your best interest. Scheduling time now to prioritize your holistic wellness during your time as a student is about firming up your foundation for your future career as counselors and counselor educators. Let yourself explore the pillars of wellness, and ask yourself which areas need more attention and support.

The 8 Pillars of Wellness Simple Self Rating & Reflection

On a scale from 1 to 10 (1 = needs immediate attention, 10 = excellent functioning in this area), please rate how well you are doing in the following areas of wellness functioning:

Emotional/Mental (Effective management of self, having a sense of positive self-regard and creating satisfying relationships)

Rating _____ What action can I take to improve this area? _____

_____

Financial (Satisfaction with current and future financial situations)

Rating _____ What action can I take to improve this area? _____

_____

Environmental (Spending time in pleasant, stimulating environments that support well-being)

Rating _____ What action can I take to improve this area? _____

_____

Intellectual (Awareness of ways to expand knowledge and skills through intellectually stimulating activities)

Rating _____ What action can I take to improve this area? _____

_____

Social (Experiencing connection, belonging and a well-developed support system)

Rating _____ What action can I take to improve this area? _____

_____

Occupational (Experiencing satisfaction and enrichment from one's work)

Rating _____ What action can I take to improve this area? _____

_____

Physical (Prioritizing sleep, healthy nourishment, and movement)

Rating _____ What action can I take to improve this area? _____

_____

Spiritual (Attending to one's sense of purpose and meaning in life)

Rating _____ What action can I take to improve this area? _____

_____

Now, create a treatment plan for your own health and wellness. Just as you are learning skills and techniques to facilitate and enhance the lives of others, use these same practices on yourself. Imagine a simple intake process for yourself, in which you take an honest look at yourself and ask, *How am I functioning in the areas of lifestyle wellness, and what can I do to support and improve these areas?* In addition to reflecting on these aspects of your life, also ask yourself who could be a true accountability partnership for change. This wellness support person can be as close as a supervisor, practicum, or internship colleague. We stay healthy in our careers in the field of counseling by creating healthy action plans and healthy alliances with supportive community in our lives.

The wellness action steps you take during your academic career will transfer into your world of work and your ability to avoid burnout and to stay vibrant and healthy as you engage is this very noble profession of counseling and counselor education. You are on a great path. Your deep creativity, self-love, and curiosity toward your wellness needs will guide your journey. Thank you for your commitment to yourself and to the field of counseling.

Index

A

acculturation, 126–128, 163
adaptation, 126
adapting to a therapeutic session, 238
addiction counseling, 5
addictions counselor, 57–58
advocacy, 78, 118
African American Vernacular English (AAVE), 5, 71–72
All Lives Matter, 86
American Counseling Association's (ACA) Code of Ethics, 14, 16
    assessments, 211–212
    confidentiality and privacy, 67
    core professional values, 211
    definition of counseling, 26
    ethical mandates, 20, 190, 204
    self-care, 31
art and expressive therapies, 78
aspirational ethics, 16
assessment and diagnosis, 8, 19
    AARC Standards for Multicultural Assessments, 210
    ACA Code of Ethics, 211–212
    assessment, definition, 205–206
    case study, 218–223
    Cultural Formulation Interview (CFI), 209–210, 216
    diagnosis, definition, 206–207
    diagnostic assessments, 207
    Dove's counterbalance intelligence test, 208
    for collaborative treatment plan, 217–218
    Geert Hofstede's cultural dimensions, 208–209
    skills of, 212–218
    SMARTER, 217–218
    standardized and nonstandardized assessments, 206
    steps, 213–216
    testing and culture, 207
assimilation, 126
Association for Multicultural Counseling and Development (AMCD), 14, 39
Association for Specialists in Group Work, 56
Association of Black Psychologists (ABPSI), 39
autonomy, 4, 16, 19
avoidant counselors, 92–93

B

beneficence, 4, 16
biases, 111
    implicit bias, 205

biases of counselors, 19
Black feminist thought and liberation theory, 2
Black Lives Matter, 86, 94
Bloom's taxonomy, 204
broaching, 30–31, 91, 143, 249
    continuum of broaching behavior, 92–95
    inter-REC dimension, 96
    intra-counseling dimension, 95
    intra-individual dimension, 95
    intra-REC dimension, 96
    multidimensional model of broaching behavior, 95–97
    strategies and techniques, 84
    with case studies, 233–234

C

career counseling, 5, 59
challenging a client, 7, 19–20, 155–156
    as microskill, 156–157
    case study, 163–166
    cultural communication styles and, 161–163
    direct confrontation, 158
    gentle nudge, 157
    intrapersonal barriers to, 159–160
    MSJCC perspective, 157
    pointing out discrepancies, 157–158
    power dynamics and, 160–161
    systemic barriers to, 160–163
    wondering out loud, 158
clinical rehabilitation counselors, 58–59
cognitive-behavioral therapy (CBT), 77
collectivism, 69–70, 208–209
conflict, 126
connectedness to the community, 17
contact, 126
continuing/incongruent counselors, 93–94
continuum of broaching behavior, 92–95
Council for Accreditation of Counseling and Related Educational Programs (CACREP), 38–39, 204–205
counseling fieldwork courses, 3–9
counseling relationship, 112, 118
counseling skills
    as magnifier, 29
    as mirrors, 30
    as social justice advocate, 31
    consideration of client's community, 32–33
    ethics, 18–20
    strengths finder, 29

268 Intersectional Counseling Skills

counselor self-awareness, 57, 111–112, 118, 123–124
   in termination of therapeutic relationship, 192–193
counselor self-care and wellness, 9
counselors-in-training (CITs), 2–3, 5, 9, 29, 31, 33, 67–68, 70, 232–233
countertransference, 30
couples counseling, 27
creativity in counseling, 8–9, 229–230
   case studies, 235–236
   experiential learning, 231–232
   expressive arts in counseling, 232–233
critical race theory (CRT), 40–41
critical thinking, 6
cultural auditing, 123–124
Cultural Formulation Interview (CFI), 209–210, 216
cultural humility, 2, 5–6, 72–73
cultural identity, 56, 59, 73, 78, 127, 143–144, 209, 217, 244
culturally oriented techniques, 66
   African American Vernacular English (AAVE), 71–72
   case studies, 73–76
   confidentiality and privacy, 67
   critical consciousness, 68–69
   cultural humility and responsiveness, 72–73
   examples of counseling and advocacy interventions, 77–78
   individualism or collectivism, 69–70
   linguistics and multilingual abilities, 71
   mindfulness, 67
culturally responsive communication, 5
culture, 4–6, 8

D

diagnoses. *See* assessment and diagnosis
dialectical behavior therapy (DBT), 78
direct confrontation, 158
direct content summary, 105
discernment, 17
domains of counselor skills, 4
Dove's counterbalance intelligence test, 208

E

emotional expression, 162
empathy balance, 20
ethical decision-making, 4
ethics
   American Counseling Association's (ACA) Code of Ethics, 14
   aspirational, 16
   definition, 15–16
   in counseling skills, 18–20
   mandatory, 16
   multicultural competence and, 14
   principle, 16–17
   relational, 17
experiential learning, 231–232
expressing oneself, 162
expressive arts in counseling, 232–233
eye movement desensitization and reprocessing (EMDR) therapy, 27

F

facilitator
   as magnifier, 29
   as mirrors, 30
   facilitating a healing process, 30–31
   strengths finder, 29
familismo, 127
family systems therapy, 77
femininity, 209
fidelity, 4, 16
focusing summary, 105

G

Gaining Cultural Competence in Career Counseling (Evans), 59
gentle nudge, 157
goal setting, 7, 19, 170–171
   case studies, 178–183
   counseling process and, 172–177
   empowering clients with voice and choice, 174–175
   familiarizing clients with, 173–174
   identification of clients' strengths and access, 175–177
   impact of stigma, 171–172
   resistance to change and, 177–178
   treatment planning and, 171–172, 178
group counseling, 5, 27, 56–57, 78
   counselor's role in, 56
   diversity in, 57
group dynamics, 56–57
group leadership, 56

H

Hardy, Dr. Kenneth, 39
healthy paranoia, 89
humanistic aspects of counseling, 4

I

Implicit Association Tests (IAT), 111
implicit bias, 205
indirect content summary, 105
individualism, 69–70, 208–209
infusing counselor, 94–95
inpatient counseling, 26–27
integrated/congruent counselors, 94
integration, 126
integrity, 17
internal working models (IWMs), 144
intersectionality, 2–3, 67–68, 143
   context of racism and sexism, 2
   of cultural responsivity and ethical concepts, 4
intra-person barrier, 7
introspection, 6
invitational skills, 6, 85
   nonverbal, 85–91
   verbal, 91–92
invitational theory, 86–87
isolating counselors, 93

J
justice, 2–4, 8, 16

L
language
    differences between counselor and client, 161–162
    emotional expression and, 128–129
    gestures and, 129
    reflecting feelings and, 128–129
laws, 15
loan of the self, 20
long-term normative orientation, 209

M
mandatory ethics, 16
marriage and family counseling, 5, 59–61
    culture in, 60–61
masculinity, 209
metacognitive strategies, 247–248
microaggression, 70, 88, 143
mindfulness and meditation practices, 78
misinterpretation, 70
morals, 15
Multicultural Social Justice Counseling Competencies (MSJCCs), 3, 5, 7–10, 14, 32, 38, 91–92, 189, 230–231
    challenging clients, 157, 159
    conceptual framework, 231
    culturally contextual lens, 67
    developmental domains, 57
    distinction between emotion and feeling, 121–123
    factors related to worldview, 144
    of career counselors, 59
    paraphrasing, 111
    reflecting feelings from, 119–121
    reflection of meaning, 142
    summarizing, 111–112
multidimensional model of broaching behavior, 95–97

N
narrative therapy, 77
nonmaleficence, 4, 16, 18
nonstandardized assessments, 206
nonverbal communication, 18
nonverbal invitational skills, 85–91
    second layer of, 87–91

O
one-on-one counseling, 27
outpatient counseling, 26

P
paraphrasing, 6, 104
    case study, 112–113
    examples, 108–109
    procedure for, 107–108
    therapeutic reasons for, 106–107
    timing for, 110
parroting, 104
personalismo, 127
person-of-the-therapist, 31
planning summary, 106
play therapy, 27
Poetry in Motion, 236–238
pointing out discrepancies, 157–158
power distance index (PDI), 208
principle ethics, 4, 16–17
process summary, 105
professional communities, 33–34
professional roles of counselors, 5, 55
    addictions counselor, 57–58
    career counselor, 59
    case studies, 61–62
    group counselor, 56–57
    marriage and family counselor, 59–61
    rehabilitation counselors, 58–59
psychoeducation, 26
psychotherapy, 70

R
race, ethnicity, and culture (REC) dimension, 84, 87, 91, 93–96
    inter-REC dimension, 96
    intra-REC dimension, 96
reflecting feelings, 6–7, 119–121, 123–124, 126–128
    acculturation views and, 127–128
    benefits of, 131–132
    language and, 128–129, 130
reflection of meaning
    abstractness of, 140
    case study, 150–151
    challenges with, 148–149
    essence of, 140
    in a counseling context, 145–149
    in societal context, 141–144
    multicultural considerations, 142–143
    nesting dolls example, 140–141
    space for, 149
    strategies for, 146–148
    surface-level, 148–149
    through attachment, 144–145
    timing, 149
    worldview implications, 141–144
reflections of meaning, 7
rehabilitation counseling, 5, 58–59
relational ethics, 4, 17, 19

S
self-awareness, 17, 111–112
self-care, 31
self-of-the-therapist, 31
separation or segregation, 126–127
short-term normative orientation, 209
signaling summary, 105
SMART goals, 248–250
social determinants of health and mental health (SDHM), 2
sociocultural and political climate in United States, 2

SOLER, 69
sports counseling, 9, 244
   case study, 250–251
   future directions, 253
   implications for professional development, 251–254
   literature review, 244–248
   metacognitive strategies, 247–248
   multicultural cross-cultural communication skills, 249–250
   multicultural sports counseling competencies, 246–247
   recommendations, 253–254
   SMART goals, 248–250
standardized assessments, 206
summarizing, 6, 104–106
   case study, 112–113
   examples, 109–110
   procedure for, 107–108
   therapeutic reasons for, 107
   timing for, 110–111

T

talking cure, 70
talk therapy, 26
termination of therapeutic relationship, 8, 190
   as cyclical, 194–195
   case studies, 196–197
   conventional, 191
   counselor self-awareness in, 192–193
   historical considerations, 190–191
   reasons, 191–192
   Yzanga, Ebony, and Bailey (YEB) termination continuum, 193–194
thematic summary, 106
therapeutic relationship, 4–5
   appreciation for values, traditions, and culture, 42
   building, 28–29
   case studies, 43–48
   clinician-client relationships with African Americans, 41–42
   collaborative cultural techniques in, 68–70

contextual frameworks of individualism or collectivism, 69–70
counselor education training, 41
cultural interaction and relationship, 27–28
in historical and cultural context, 42
invitational skills, 85
race and ethnicity, role of, 38–39, 41–42
safety in, 42
silencing in, 42
skills of critical consciousness, 68–69
with underrepresented clients, 43
transference, 30
trauma-informed care with cultural competency, 78
treatment planning, 131–132

U

uncertainty avoidance index (UAI), 209

V

values, 15
veracity, 16
verbal invitational skills, 91–92
vocational counselors, 2
vocational guidance, 2

W

wellness, 2, 9, 261–264
   8 pillars of, 264–265
   tools and strategies, 261
Whiteness, 39–40
White racial frame, 89–90
wondering out loud, 158
worldview, 111–112
   gender dynamics and, 125–126
   of client, 69, 112, 118, 124–129, 144–145, 147, 149, 162
   of counselor, 68–69
   statements, 144

About the Editors

Dr. S. Kent Butler, Jr., NCC, NCSC is a professor of counselor education at the University of Central Florida. Dr. Butler is a past president of the American Counseling Association (2021–2022), is an ACA Fellow, and hosted an ACA weekly vodcast, "The Voice of Counseling." He has served the Association for Multicultural Counseling and Development as president, ACA governing council representative, and is a proud member of AMCD's Multicultural Counseling Competencies Revisions Committee, which produced the Multicultural Social Justice Counseling Competencies (MSJCC). Dr. Butler formerly served the University of Central Florida as the chief equity, inclusion, and diversity officer and is a National Association of Chief Diversity Officers in Higher Education Fellow (2020–2021). He has also served as a faculty fellow for inclusive excellence within the university's Office of the Provost. Dr. Butler is faculty advisor to Chi Sigma Iota; Counselor Education Doctoral Student Organization; Project for Haiti Knights; and the National Association for the Advancement of Colored People.

Dr. M. Ann Shillingford is an associate professor of counselor education at the University of Central Florida in Orlando, Florida. Dr. S, as she is fondly known by her students, has taught various core counseling courses and understands how to communicate with individuals from diverse populations. Dr. Shillingford's co-edited book, *The Journey Unraveled: College and Career Readiness of African American Students*, was published in fall of 2015. Her co-edited book, *Demystifying the DSM for School Counselors*, was published in September 2020.

About the Contributors

Dr. Adkison-Johnson believes all human beings have a purpose for their lives, and those who have suffered during life's journey have much to offer the world. It is the wisdom that is gained from trials and tribulations that builds strength and character.

Brooke Alker finds power in the experience of meaning-making, both individually and in relationship with others. Healing, meaning, and liberation are found through encounters with the other in which we hold compassionate space for each others' deepest identities. They believe justice is not the absence of tension but an honoring of the creative tension where our intersectionalities meet.

Dr. Deryl F. Bailey is a professor at the University of Georgia, the 2012 William Allen Boeing endowed chair and distinguished professor of education at Seattle University (2012). Past president of both SACES and ACES, he recently received the 2022 SACES Outstanding Tenured Counselor Educator Award.

Bosede Balogun is a Nigerian married woman, who is a doctoral student in Counselor Education and Supervision. She is also a resident counselor working toward becoming a licensed professional counselor.

Monique Barber is a Licensed Professional Counselor in Idaho, a National Board-Certified Counselor, and a Board Certified TeleMental Health Provider. Monique is pursuing her PhD in Counselor Education and Supervision at Liberty University. Her research interests include supervision and creativity in addiction and multicultural considerations in counseling.

Ana Barend identifies as a Brazilian married woman, who values spirituality and the dignity and worth of every human being. She is a licensed counselor and doctoral student at a CACREP accredited institution.

Dr. Lynn Bohecker earned a PhD in counselor education and is a licensed marriage and family therapist and an AAMFT-approved supervisor. Dr. Bohecker is a core faculty member at Liberty University and the marriage and family therapy program director. Dr. Bohecker's research interests include professional identity, spirituality, religion in counseling, group work, and advocacy.

Robtrice Brawner (University of Wisconsin—Parkside) believes in the importance of all people having a quality counseling experience. As we become a more diverse community, traditional ways of serving people may not always be equitable. As we begin to recognize the social justice needs of our communities, we must also be willing to rethink our counseling approaches.

Jessi Budyka is a licensed professional and nationally certified counselor, who has worked in myriad clinical settings and has gained most of her experience working with adolescents and families in a residential facility. She is completing the Counselor Education and Supervision doctoral program at Kent State University. Jessi serves as the Ohio Association of Specialists in Group Work Emerging Leader. Her research interests are centered on multiculturalism and social justice, specifically the integration of social justice into one's counselor identity, advancing leadership and advocacy within master's-level counselors, and utilizing Q methodology as a means of student evaluation, counseling intervention, and client-outcome research.

Dr. A'tasha M. Christian is teaching faculty at the University of Southern California. Dr. Christian has experience working with children, adolescents, and adults with myriad diagnoses. Her research interests include intersectionality and diversity, intergenerational trauma, and treating and advocating for communities of color and other marginalized communities. A national and international speaker, Dr. Christian served as a member of the American Counseling Association's Cultural Encounters Task Force and is the founder of a group practice and consulting agency.

Dr. Kristy Christopher-Holloway is an adjunct professor as well as the founder of a group private practice located in Georgia. She works with racial and ethnic minoritized women experiencing infertility trauma, birth trauma, reproductive loss, and issues related to perinatal mental health. Dr. Christopher-Holloway is a national and international speaker with a focus on topics such as African American mental health, the psycho-emotional impact of infertility in African American women, perinatal mood disorders, the strong Black woman syndrome, generational trauma, and cultural competence/humility.

Dr. Everette Coffman wholeheartedly believes in the power of connection and attachment. Experiences in this world impact not only our belief system but the way we view ourselves and the world. He believes the pathway to healing comes from a deep sense of feeling seen and understood through all parts of a person's intersectionality.

Erin Coleman is a PhD Student in the Counselor Education and Supervision program at Regent University. Her research interests include cultural competence within counselor education, increasing counselor readiness amongst counsclors-in-training of color and culturally responsive grief education in counseling. Erin Coleman is also a licensed marriage and family therapist and the owner of a private practice in North Carolina.

Norma L. Day-Vines (Johns Hopkins University) is committed to supporting counselors in their efforts to broach or explore the contextual dimensions of race, ethnicity, and culture with clients. Her life's work has involved the development of frameworks and assessment tools that help counselors engage in meaningful conversations with clients about the extent to which clients' sociocultural and sociopolitical realities are related to their presenting concerns.

Dr. Amanda DiLorenzo-Garcia is a counselor educator, therapist, advocate, and clinical supervisor, who regards meaningful collaboration and empowerment with fellow social-justice-minded colleagues as ways to encourage growth and change in the counseling field and the world. Dr. DiLorenzo-Garcia believes in supporting change through micro and macro levels of dedication and support, while never undervaluing the immense honor it is to witness change for an individual client.

Madelyn Duffey, MS, doctoral candidate, is passionate about working with counseling students to help them develop cultural humility and skills in critical thinking, clinical practice, and ethical decision-making. She is excited to see counselor educators integrate ethics, skills, and cultural competencies into counseling classrooms and into their scholarship.

Dr. Nivischi N. Edwards, LMHC, LPC, NCC, BC-TMH, received her Doctorate in Counselor Education from the University of Central Florida. Dr. Nivischi has been a practicing clinician for over 20 years. Her research areas include social justice, mentorship, marriage and family relations, and female faculty success. She has presented nationally and internationally on these topics. Learn more about Dr. Nivischi here: https://drnivischi.com.

Dr. Michelle D. Ellis has over 10 years of experience working with a diversity of clients across the lifespan. Dr. Ellis holds licenses as a licensed mental health counselor (FL), licensed professional counselor (PA), and qualified supervisor and is also an NBCC board-certified counselor (NCC). Her professional journey encompasses counseling experiences across residential, outpatient, school-based, and in-home settings. This breadth of experience has fueled her passion for working with a wide range of clientele. Dr. Ellis is currently a mental health columnist for Duval Sports, an online website that provides game day coverage of youth, middle, and high school sports within Northeast Florida. Dr. Ellis produces monthly articles that address mental health topics that arise among student athletes.

Timothy Eng is a doctoral student in the Counselor Education and Supervision program at the University of Central Florida in Orlando, Florida. He is a former community mental health and student affairs professional, who specialized in working with first-generation college students accepted into TRiO programs. Timothy's research interests include social justice and multicultural issues in BIPOC communities. Timothy co-authored a chapter, "Challenges Mostly Unique to African Americans," in *African Americans and Mental Health: Practical and Strategic Solutions to Barriers, Needs, and Challenges*, published in fall 2021.

Andrew Erway is a Spanish teacher in the Bronx, New York. He was born and raised in rural Pennsylvania but quickly learned of his passion for Latin culture. Upon completing his undergraduate degree, he moved to Colombia to solidify his language skills and experience the richness of Latin American culture. Andrew found his way back to the New York and has become passionate about serving the Bronx community. He is currently in his second year of counselor education at Lehman College.

Dr. Anna Flores Locke is a past president of counselors for social justice, an international award-winning author, Latina twin mom, and infertility warrior. She has been a mental health counselor for more than 18 years, owns Charlandra Counseling Services, and is an assistant professor at Lehman College in the Bronx. Her passion lies in destigmatizing reproductive and mental health challenges and mentoring graduate students to be social change agents.

Dr. Seneka Gainer's approach to the mental health field and counseling profession is grounded in a systemic lens and a lifelong commitment to equity and social justice. Driven by a vision of inclusive and equitable mental health care, her work emphasizes and advocates for equity in mental health care, highlighting the importance of empathy in counselor–client relationships, fostering cultural humility to ensure cultural sensitivity, and instilling hope as a powerful force for change. Dr. Gainer's systemic lens recognizes the need to address more significant systemic issues to tackle disparities in mental health access, working to transform the field and develop counselors who are not only culturally competent but also committed to making the mental health system more inclusive and accessible.

Sravya Gummaluri (she/her) is a licensed associate counselor (LAC) in New Jersey and a nationally certified counselor (NCC). She is a counseling PhD candidate at The George Washington University. Sravya is a 2022 NBCC doctoral minority fellow and has utilized this opportunity to serve diverse and historically marginalized communities through leadership, advocacy, and research. She is also a 2022 NARACES emerging leader, 2023–2024 Chi Sigma Iota (CSI) Leadership and Internship Program fellow, and current chair of the Association for Multicultural Counseling and Development (AMCD) Writers' Consortium. Additionally, she serves on CSI's Counselor Community Engagement Committee and Counselors for Social Justice's Advocacy Committee. Her professional interests center on anti-oppressive counselor education, supervision, leadership, and advocacy for BIPOC and migrant communities in navigating socio-political and socio-cultural stressors to promote overall wellness and liberation.

Dr. Gelawdiyos Haile is a counselor educator, researcher, and clinician. Dr. Haile's research and clinical work focuses on marginalized communities and performance anxiety.

Dr. Amber S. Haley identifies as a Black woman, scholar, counselor educator, and clinician of color, whose work and research is centered on diversifying the field of counseling and academia with healthy representations of traditionally underserved and marginalized communities. Dr. Haley values working collaboratively with diverse, social-justice-minded beings to collectively combat systems of oppression, educate and train current and future generations of change makers, and strengthen the transformative power of counseling.

Keyona Harper is a licensed professional counselor in Ohio, a national board-certified counselor, who operates a private practice. Keyona is pursuing her PhD in Counselor Education and Supervision at Liberty University. Her research interests include education, spirituality, and Black women and children.

Dr. Barbara Herlihy, NCC, has long believed cultural diversity and social justice competency are inseparable from ethics and that one cannot exist without the other. She welcomes this opportunity to integrate skill building into that frame of reference. After serving for decades as a counselor educator, she is optimistic about the future of our profession, which belongs to the skilled, ethical, culturally competent social justice advocates, who are being trained to meet the challenges that lie ahead of us.

Dr. Mary Hinson is a clinical faculty member at Southern New Hampshire University supporting graduate counseling students. Dr. Hinson has taught numerous diversity courses and trains practicing clinicians on multicultural considerations and missteps when communicating with diverse clients. Adding to her clinical work, Dr. Hinson is certified in diversity and inclusion in the workplace, serves as a diversity subject matter expert for military counseling programs, and has cocreated a training program, entitled Multicultural Faux Pas in the Clinical Setting for practicing counselors.

Ashley D. Holmes Cosby is currently a doctoral student in the Counselor Education and Supervision Program at The University of Georgia, a 2022 SACES Emerging Leader and an inaugural member of the Professional School Counseling Journal Emerging Scholars Cohort. She is also a nationally certified counselor.

Dr. Tristen Hyatt is a fully licensed counselor, counselor educator and CPCS, who believes that for lasting change to occur, one must be able to reflect on and challenge their strongly held beliefs, cognitions, and feelings. Furthermore, when working with clients, in a therapeutic setting, it is necessary for counselors to be able to challenge clients to create a space of growth and insight. Individuals should explore their biases and knowledge to develop insight into their personal beliefs and gain deeper personal awareness. Furthermore, counselors have an ethical responsibility to do the same to challenge and work with diverse (BIPOC) populations, with multicultural competency.

Dr. Jung (June) H. Hyun, LMHC, NCC is an associate professor in the mental health counseling program at Nova Southeastern University. Dr. Hyun teaches core counseling courses, such as basic counseling skills, counseling theory, multicultural counseling, group counseling, and systems theories and supervises practicum and internship students. Her scholarly pursuits center on multicultural counseling and social justice issues, promoting the school, family, and community (SFC) partnership, and fostering the resiliency of Asian American and Native Hawaiian/Pacific Islanders (AANHPI). Actively engaged in the professional community, she has assumed leadership roles and delivered presentations at conferences hosted by the American Counseling Association (ACA), Association for Multicultural Counseling and Development (AMCD), Association for Counselor Education and Supervision (ACES), Association for Assessment and Research in Counseling (AARC), and Association for Child and Adolescent Counseling (ACAC). She is a licensed mental health counselor in Washington and has provided play therapy for children and adolescents as well as parenting workshops for Asian American populations.

Dr. Marty Jencius has 26 years of experience in counselor education and 16 years in clinical practice, working in addictions, at-risk youth, schools, and family counseling. His work in technology includes integrating listservs, online journals, podcasts, and virtual reality with counseling. He has published over 120 works and produced 200 podcasts on counseling, counselor education, and faculty life. Dr. Jencius has taught internationally in Turkey, the Bahamas, Malaysia, Scotland,

and Singapore. He currently serves as the Treasurer of the American Counseling Association for 2023–2024 and was inducted as an ACA Fellow in 2023.

Dr. Aishwarya Joshi approaches the field of mental health counseling and counselor education from a global perspective. Her engagement in scholarly activities is around mental health challenges of international students and faculty in the United States, Black women's experience in STEM fields, and integrative practices of mental health inclusion in public policies. As a licensed counselor in India and the United States, Dr. Joshi shares a decade of experience providing multilingual mental health services both nationally and internationally. She believes it is imperative for mental health awareness, accessibility, and affordability to be seen as a worldwide issue and that counselors and counselor educators must collectively and interdependently work together to make this helping profession equitable for everyone.

Daniel Kimonyi is of African descent, male, Black, and Kenya born. He is a resident in counseling (2 years) and a doctoral student in counselor education and supervision.

Dr. Kellie Kirksey is a graduate of The Ohio State University with a doctorate in psychology and counselor education. She is a wellness consultant, poet, holistic psychotherapist, tea drinker, drummer, yoga instructor, dancer, expressive arts therapist, social justice activist, and nature lover. Dr. Kellie has been a psychotherapist for more than 30 years. As CEO of Creative Wellness Solutions, and the creator of the TMR (transformational movement and reflection) healing modality, which utilizes mindfulness, movement, and meditation, her main goal is to teach sustainable wellness strategies to corporations, organizations and individuals. Dr. Kellie N. Kirksey is the author of two poetry books, *Word Medicine* and *Poetry, Prose and Miscellaneous Musings*, and is a member of the faculty of the Northwest Creative and Expressive Arts Institute in Seattle, Washington. Dr. Kellie is married to dental activist, Dr. Cesar Augustin, and they are the super proud parents of Kelsie, Dominic, and Gabrielle.

Shannon Kratky (she/her/they/them) believes all humans deserve love, freedom, joy, and peace of mind, body, and spirit as well as that humans have all the answers inside of them. Shannon's mission in life is to simply love and be loved. They believe in the healing power of authentic human connection in the counseling relationship and culturally responsive techniques that prioritize the client as a whole person. They have been passionate about social justice and advocacy since they read a poster outside their elementary school's library at the age of 8 that read, "Stand up for what you believe in, even if you are standing alone." Shannon recognizes and celebrates that the road to cultural humility is a lifelong journey, and none of us have arrived yet.

Dr. Letitia Browne-James (she/her) is a firm believer in truly meeting clients where they are, from a multicultural and social justice perspective while attending to their spiritual, mental, social, and emotional needs in counseling. She believes that treating the whole person in a collaborative manner leads to lasting change, and goal setting/treatment planning is instrumental to that process. One of her frequently used quotes is, "Your provider may be an expert in their craft, but you are an expert on you." So together, you can achieve your goals through counseling.

Dr. Amirah Nelson is a licensed professional counselor with over 10 years of experience in the mental health field, serving populations from all backgrounds. Her research consists of social justice, diversity, equity, and inclusion practices; Black women; and international, especially race-based trauma, on which she has presented at the state, regional, national and internal levels. Dr. Nelson currently teaches at her alma mater, *thee* Jackson State University, as an assistant professor, where she consistently utilizes her social identities to address, model, and facilitate conversations related to advocacy and systemic issues in our world. Her passion, commitment, and experiences continue to inspire herself to link theory and practice, as she cultivates and maintains meaningful life-long relationships in the professional field of counseling and counselor education and supervision to educate and learn from others to promote healing.

Dr. Ngadjui strongly believes forming connections requires intention and empathetic care to receive the cherished life stories that many clients and people around us may dare to share. This is the start of facilitating an inclusive therapeutic relationship, the place of curiosity where we are able to affirm to a person that their story was worthy and held with honor, as opposed to invalidating their story through assumed knowing or harmful ethnocentrism. Therefore, the Black client's voice belongs, and the expansion and inclusion of Black client narratives persist as a precedent for more racially minoritized narratives.

Samantha Perez is a school counseling graduate of Lehman College in New York City. Samantha was born in the United States, is the middle child of three sisters, and grew up in a Dominican household. Her early educational years were heavily influenced by being an ELL student and adjusting to American culture. Currently, Samantha is working in the nonprofit field with an emphasis on improving youth development. Her passion is helping youth realize how they can be better and bigger than their communities and be successful leaders.

For **Dr. Gemarco Peterson**, connecting with others is an active choice and a vulnerable one. There is immense value in creating and fostering meaningful and appropriate relationships with others. We learn, we grow, and we increase our ability to empathize in spaces where relationships have been developed in respect to each other's values, beliefs, and culture.

Dr. Ashlei R. Petion, LPC, NCC is a licensed professional counselor and assistant professor of clinical mental health counseling at Nova Southeastern University in the College of Psychology. Dr. Petion's clinical experiences span generational trauma and healing, suicide prevention and intervention, crisis response, culture-centered and trauma-informed care, as well as LGBTQ+ concerns. Dr. Petion's research interests include generational trauma and healing, culture-centered group work, and participatory action-based research through qualitative and mixed methodologies. In addition to clinical and research work, Dr. Petion is also an active member of several professional counseling organizations, including ACA, CSI, and AMCD, all within which she has served in various leadership roles.

DeJaunté Marquel Reynolds-Villarreal is a master's-level clinical mental health counseling student at Texas A&M University—San Antonio. He is also the first student from the university to be selected for the master's level NBCC Minority Fellowship program. Throughout his graduate studies, DeJaunté has spoken at several universities as well as presented as a panelist at the NBCC Foundation's 2023 Bridging the Gap Symposium. His professional interests include LGBTQ+ relationship and family studies, substance and process addictions, and minority advocacy.

Tabitha Rodriguez is an alumna of The University of Texas Rio Grande Valley with a special interest in advocacy for body positivity. She graduated with a Bachelor of Science in Psychology and a Master of Education in Clinical Counseling. She contributed to pilot research in memory and recognition in her undergrad years, earning a scholarship to advance her education. Through her graduate studies, she expanded her knowledge in social justice, multicultural counseling, expressive arts therapy, dreamwork, and primary care behavioral health.

Marshaya Rountree is the senior staff clinician at Agnes Scott College and a doctoral student at the University of Georgia's Counselor Education and Supervision program. She completed a Master of Science in Clinical Mental Health Counseling from Georgia State University. She developed a focus on trauma work and completed the Virtual Trauma Competency Training facilitated by Dr. Melinda Paige. While completing her baccalaureate in psychology at the University of Arkansas—Little Rock, Marshaya participated in the Ronald E. McNair Post-Baccalaureate Achievement Program, researching the barriers that impact African American men from seeking mental health help. She is a current member of Chi Sigma Iota, the Association for Multicultural Counseling and Development, and the Southern Association for Counselor Education and Supervision.

Dr. Clay Rowell strongly believes clients must develop new insight for lasting change to occur. This often requires the counselor to utilize certain interpersonal skills that nudge, challenge, or even confront the client. There are various styles with which to implement these skills, and Dr. Rowell knows that counselor style sometimes needs to adjust to clients' cultural contexts. While some clients prefer a direct communication style, for example, others prefer a more indirect style. This is a continuum, and counselors need to continually develop their cultural competence for them to be more successful with a wider number of populations.

Dr. Azilde Sanchez is a Latina, married mother of three children, born and raised in Puerto Rico and currently residing in New Jersey. Dr. Sanchez is a licensed professional counselor, clinical addictions counselor, and clinical psychologist in New Jersey. She has over 20 years of experience in the mental health field. Dr. Sanchez is passionate about culturally sensitive practices and social justice. She is cofounder and owner of M&S Psychotherapy and Counseling in the state of New Jersey. Dr. Sanchez is also an adjunct professor at Southern New Hampshire University and Alliance University.

Dr. Karla Sapp (she/her) subscribes to the belief that words impact how we perceive individuals and the process of counseling from a multicultural perspective. As such, when working with a diverse array of individuals within the clinical setting, Dr. Karla is mindful that the language used sets the tone for therapeutic relationships and response to interventions used. Dr. Karla believes the process of goal setting is not a one-size-fits-all model but must be specifically tailored to the needs of the individual in a way that encourages their active participation and empowers them to take control of their own lives in a meaningful and fulfilling way.

Dr. LoriAnn Stretch is a full professor of counselor education and the director of scholarly engagement at the University of the Cumberlands in Williamsburg, Kentucky. Her students call her Dr. LA, and she loves teaching skills and fieldwork courses. Dr. LA strives to pass on her passion for social justice and "good trouble." She is the president and conference cochair for the Association for Creativity in Counseling, the cochair of the ACES Teaching Committee, and a member of AMCD's International Concerns Group. She is also a CACREP Team lead and consultant. Dr. Stretch recently coedited the *National Counselor Exam (NCE) and Counselor Preparation Comprehensive Exam (CPCE) Review: Your Study Guide for Success, Book and Online Exam Prep*, published by Springer. She also edited *Technology in Mental Health: Applications in Practice, Supervision, and Training*, published by C. C. Thomas.

Dr. Taunya Marie Tinsley has over 30 years working with culturally diverse educators, pastoral leaders, students, athletes, and congregants in the secondary and university-level, sporting, and faith-based environments. Dr. Tinsley has worked with the National Football Foundation, the National Football League (NFL), and the Pittsburgh Steelers to provide services to high school student athletes as part of the Play It Smart program and the Academics in Motion program. Additionally, her work continued in 2011 with the NFL Players Association (NFLPA), providing consulting and counseling services as part of "The Business of Football: Rookie Edition." Previously, Dr. Tinsley assisted NFL Player Engagement with their Transition Coaches Certification Training Program. Most recently, she assisted NFL Player Engagement with the mental health presentations at the NFL Rookie Symposium, the enhancement of the NFL Rookie Success Program, and the NFL Clinician Summit.

Dr. Jessica Tinstman Jones is a counselor educator, clinician, scholar, and advocate seeking to bring about and support meaningful change and growth in the counseling field through culturally aware, strengths-based, and empowering approaches. Dr. Tinstman Jones finds particular value in collaborating with social justice-oriented colleagues and supporting students and clients to find deeper meaning in their personal and learning experiences.

Dr. Ebony E. White is a clinician, counselor educator, researcher, and advocate. She has worked in community mental health for 20 years, supporting predominately Black, at-promise youth and their families through counseling support. She has seen the impact of maintaining long-lasting relationships with clients and understands that genuine connection can lead to growth and change. She is a past president of ACA's Counselors for Social Justice division and a past chair of the North Atlantic Region of ACA.

Dr. Selma D. Yznaga is a professor at The University of Texas Rio Grande Valley. She is the founder of Texas Counselors for Social Justice, a past president of ACA's Counselors for Social Justice division, and the coordinator of clinical services: Texas/Mexico projects for Counselors Without

Borders. Dr. Yznaga's teaching, service, and scholarship are informed by the provision of mental health and psychosocial support services to immigrants, refugees, and asylum seekers.

www.ingramcontent.com/pod-product-compliance
Lightning Source LLC
Chambersburg PA
CBHW080045250825
31610CB00015B/1026